FONDATION HARDT

POUR L'ÉTUDE DE L'ANTIQUITÉ CLASSIQUE

ENTRETIENS

Tome XXIX

SOPHOCLE

ENTRETIENS SUR L'ANTIQUITÉ CLASSIQUE
Publiés par Olivier Reverdin et Bernard Grange
TOME XXIX

SOPHOCLE

SEPT EXPOSÉS SUIVIS DE DISCUSSIONS

PAR

BERNARD KNOX, JEAN IRIGOIN,
GEORGE STEINER, BERND SEIDENSTICKER,
OLIVER TAPLIN, STEFAN RADT,
R.P. WINNINGTÓN-INGRAM

Entretiens préparés et présidés
par Jacqueline de Romilly

VANDŒUVRES-GENÈVE
23-28 AOÛT 1982

PRÉFACE

Sophocle est le cinquième poète grec auquel la Fondation Hardt consacre un de ses entretiens. Euripide, Hésiode, Archiloque, Ménandre l'ont précédé; Pindare le suivra en 1984. L'épigramme, en tant que genre littéraire, a aussi eu son tour. Cela fera donc sept entretiens consacrés à la poésie grecque sur les trente et un premiers!

Pourquoi Sophocle? On a beaucoup publié sur lui au cours des dernières décennies. Il a fait un retour en force sur la scène tragique, soit en plein air, dans les théâtres antiques, soit dans les salles de spectacle. Les interprétations que l'on donne de ses tragédies divergent souvent. Le moment était donc venu de faire de lui et de son œuvre l'objet d'entretiens au cours desquels quelques-uns des savants qui les étudient actuellement confronteraient leurs vues.

L'initiative de ces entretiens revient à Mme Jacqueline de Romilly, professeur au Collège de France, qui les a préparés et présidés. Elle a chargé le professeur Bernard M. W. Knox (directeur du Center for Hellenic Studies, à Washington) de les ouvrir par un exposé consacré aux rapports du poète avec la cité qui fut la sienne, Athènes, et avec la cité grecque en général.

Analysant les structures numériques des tragédies, le professeur Jean Irigoin (Paris) constate qu'on y trouve des symétries, des équilibres plus stricts, plus rigoureux qu'on ne l'a cru jusqu'ici.

Qu'il se suicide ou renonce à se donner à lui-même la mort, le héros sophocléen est confronté à un choix dont les termes ont été analysés, à la lumière des théories de la psychologie moderne, par le professeur Bernd Seidensticker (Hambourg).

Editeur de la nouvelle collection des fragments de Sophocle (TrGF 4, Sophocles), *le professeur Stefan Radt (Groningue) a montré que leur étude attentive aide à envisager l'œuvre du poète dans une perspective plus large que ne le permettent les sept tragédies conservées, lesquelles n'en représentent qu'une infime partie.*

De toutes les tragédies grecques, c'est Antigone *qui a le plus impressionné la postérité. Le thème en a été repris plus de six cents fois, au cours des âges, dans les littératures du monde entier. Le professeur George Steiner (Genève et Cambridge), qui prépare sur cette exceptionnelle survie un important ouvrage, a traité des versions diverses et souvent contradictoires qu'on a données du personnage de Créon.*

La reconquête, de nos jours, par Sophocle, de la scène tragique a permis de mieux étudier le parti qu'il tirait des ressources de son théâtre. «Sophocles in his Theatre» est le titre du sixième exposé, dont l'auteur est Oliver Taplin (Magdalen College, Oxford).

Plus de soixante ans de familiarité avec le poète, son œuvre, son temps, ont permis au professeur R. P. Winnington-Ingram (Londres) de parler avec maîtrise et sensibilité de «Sophocles and Women».

Ces sept exposés, les discussions auxquelles ils ont donné lieu et les index établis par M. Bernard Grange forment la matière de ce tome XXIX des Entretiens sur l'Antiquité classique. *Sans l'aide généreuse de deux entreprises genevoises, Montres Rolex S.A. et Sodeco-Saia S.A., la Fondation Hardt n'aurait pu le faire imprimer avec autant de soin et de goût que les vingt-huit volumes qui l'ont précédé, en respectant le modèle établi en 1953 par la prestigieuse Stamperia Valdonega de Vérone. Que ces deux mécènes veuillent bien trouver ici l'expression de sa gratitude.*

TABLE DES MATIÈRES

		Page
I.	BERNARD KNOX	
	Sophocles and the Polis	1
	Discussion	28
II.	JEAN IRIGOIN	
	Structure et composition des tragédies de Sophocle	39
	Discussion	66
III.	GEORGE STEINER	
	Variations sur Créon	77
	Discussion	97
IV.	BERND SEIDENSTICKER	
	Die Wahl des Todes bei Sophokles	105
	Discussion	145
V.	OLIVER TAPLIN	
	Sophocles in his Theatre	155
	Discussion	175

VI. STEFAN RADT

Sophokles in seinen Fragmenten 185

Discussion 223

VII. R. P. WINNINGTON-INGRAM

Sophocles and Women 233

Discussion 250

INDICES 259

I

Bernard Knox

SOPHOCLES AND THE *POLIS*

Towards the end of his long analysis of the religious and legal foundations of the ancient *polis*, Fustel de Coulanges speaks of "the omnipotence and the absolute empire it exercised over its members... The citizen was subordinate, in everything and without any reserve, to the city; he belonged to it body and soul... It is a singular error, therefore... to believe that in the ancient cities men enjoyed liberty. They had not even the idea of it. They did not believe that there could exist any right as against the city and its gods." [1]

This is of course an exaggeration, but it contains more than a kernel of truth: the ancient Greek *polis* (by which of course we mean Athens, the only one on which we are relatively well informed) made demands on its male citizens which today would be considered unreasonable [2]. It expected and obtained military service (combat service, not chair-borne) for its all too frequent wars on land and sea (from the battle of Plataea in 479 to Chaeronea in 338 Athens had not

[1] *La cité antique* (Paris 1864). Quoted from the English translation, Doubleday (New York 1956), 219-20; 223.

[2] Goethe had expressed similar sentiments in 1806. See H. Lloyd-Jones, *Blood for the Ghosts* (London 1982), 57 and references there.

one interval of peace longer than ten years and most of them were shorter); men were liable for campaigns beyond the frontiers up to the age of 50 and might be called on to defend the city walls until the age of 60. By its jealous restriction of citizenship the *polis* in effect limited its citizens' choice of wives; its wealthy citizens were liable to special income taxes as well as 'liturgies'—public service which could range from the organization and financial responsibility for a dramatic performance to equipment (and command) of a warship. Participation in the meetings of the assembly and the jury sessions of the law courts was not, as far as we know, enforced but it was certainly expected: "we alone", says Pericles, "regard the man who holds aloof from the city's affairs (τὰ πολιτικά) not as 'quiet' but as 'useless' "— ἀχρεῖον, a harsh word. It is Hesiod's term (*Op.* 297) for the man who can neither think for himself nor take advice from others and Herodotus' advocate for oligarchy in the Persian debate applies it to the common herd— "nothing more stupid or violent than a useless mob" (ὁμίλου . . . ἀχρηΐου III 81) [3]. The force of such public opinion (for this is clearly what Pericles expresses) should not be underestimated; in the modern megalopolis it is possible to live a completely private and anonymous life but in the ancient Mediterranean city, crowded, walled and built for outdoor living, public disapproval, concentrated and oppressive, could not be ignored. There was no escape from daily contact with one's fellow citizens [4]. Even in peace time communal cult and

[3] In the hopelessly corrupt text of Sophocles F 667 (Radt) it is nevertheless clear that ἀχρεῖοι are contrasted with εὐγενεῖς and that you would expect ἀχρεῖοι to produce children who become κακοί. At Eur. *Med.* 299 ἀχρεῖος is contrasted with σοφός; *OC* 627 ἀχρεῖον οἰκητῆρα is a forceful litotes.

[4] The one Athenian we hear of who tried to withdraw completely from society, Timon, became proverbial. A fragment of the 5th century comic poet Phrynichus sums up the Athenian idea of the unsocial man: "I live the life of Timon: no wife, no slaves, a quick temper; no visitors, no smile, no conversation—and my private point of view" (ἰδιογνώμονα), for which see Arist. *EN* VII 10, 1151 b 13.

sacrifice could not be dispensed with and in war the Athenian, side by side on the rowing bench of the galley or shield by shield in the hoplite phalanx, was an integral member of the body politic. The bonds which held the individual to the community were so strong that exile was considered a penalty on a level with death; the exile never ceased to intrigue, cajole and plot for the day of his return to the *polis* and his greatest fear was that his bones might not be buried in the soil where his ancestors lay. Themistocles, the hero of Salamis, was forbidden burial in Attic soil; he told his family to bring his body home, so Thucydides reports the tradition, and they did so secretly (I 138).

The city demanded a loyalty which overrode all others. Plato's Socrates puts its claims in the mouth of the city's laws, as they call on him to stand his ground and refuse to escape by leaving Athens. "Is this your wisdom—to fail to see that your fatherland deserves your respect, awe and reverence more than your mother, father, or all your ancestors? That it is considered more important both by the gods and by men of good sense? That when it is angry you ought to respect, obey and humor it more than you would an angry father; that you must either win its agreement or obey its orders, suffer in silence whatever suffering it assigns you—if it orders you to be beaten, if it orders you to be bound, if it leads you to war to be wounded or killed—its will be done. . . You must not give way, fall back or leave the ranks but in war and in the courts of law and everywhere you must do what the city commands. . ." (*Crito* 51 b-c).

But the city demanded more than obedience and conformity. In the great panegyric of Athenian imperial democracy which Thucydides attributes to Pericles, it demands a fanatical, irrational devotion, the devotion of a lover: the Athenians are to "fix their gaze daily on the power of the *polis* and become its lovers" (ἐραστὰς γιγνομένους αὐτῆς II 43). This is an extraordinary phrase and its significance has been generally undervalued; it is not to be compared, as most translations suggest, with such bland phrases as 'love of country.' The word ἐραστάς suggests an overwhelming romantic passion, an emotion usually associated in Athenian society of this period with homosexual love, one which takes exclusive possession of the soul of its victim, driving him to extreme demonstrations of devotion [5]. Such love is characterized in Plato's *Symposium*, the *locus classicus* for the subject, as "voluntary slavery" (ἐθελοδουλεία); the lover is "willing to serve in slavish ways no real slave would put up with" (δουλείας δουλεύειν οἵας οὐδ' ἂν δοῦλος οὐδείς *Smp.* 183 a). Pericles' phrase (and in view of the clear parody of it in Aristophanes' *Knights* 731 ff. and 1341 there can be little doubt that it is a genuine reminiscence of Pericles and not a Thucydidean invention) calls for a total dedication to the *polis*, a devotion inspired by contemplation of its power. That the call was answered is plain from the extraordinary record of Athenian activity in the years between 490 and 404 and the recognition on the part of Athens' enemies that they were facing no ordinary adversary. "They use their bodies in the city's service", say the Corinthians, "as if they were not their own and their minds as very much their own, for action in the city's interest"(I 70).

Sophocles' long life spanned almost the whole of the century which saw the creation, rise and fall of the Athenian empire. As a youth he took part in the victory celebration for Salamis [6]; as a grown man he served the *polis* at the height of

[5] The parodic scene in Ar. *Eq.* 731 ff., where the two demagogues compete for the favors of *Demos*, calling themselves ἐραστής and ἀντεραστής, evokes the familiar homosexual atmosphere (παισὶ τοῖς ἐρωμένοις 737).

[6] *Vita* 3. This tradition is dismissed as one of those stories "meant as representations of the poet's heroic stature, not as statements of literal fact" by Mary R. Lefkowitz, *The Lives of the Greek Poets* (London 1981), 77. It is not easy to see what such an anecdote about the poet's youth would have to do with 'heroic stature' and, in view of Sophocles' birth date, good family and early musical training, there is nothing improbable in the choice of such a man for such an occasion.

its power in military as well as civil offices; his last years were spent in the Athens of the Peloponnesian War, the protracted death agony of the *polis tyrannos*, but he died in 406, just before the ignominious end. Though he was by our standards a remarkably productive playwright (and we must not forget that he was also director of his own plays) his record of public service is impressive: he served as στρατηγός at least once (in the campaign against Samos, a dangerous crisis for the empire); he was treasurer of the Delian League (he may have been chairman of the board of ten [7], for his name appears first on the Tribute List inscription for the year 443-2), and it seems certain [8] (though it has been doubted) that he was one of the πρόβουλοι, the committee of public safety appointed to emergency rule in Athens after the disaster in Sicily. This public career, combined with what must have been prodigious creation as a playwright-director (a hundred and twenty-three plays in sixty-two years) exemplifies Pericles' proud claim for the Athenian citizen: "Our citizens attend both to public and private duties and do not allow absorption in their own various affairs to interfere with their knowledge of the city's" (II 40,2).

As a poet Sophocles inherited from his predecessor Aeschylus a dramatic medium which after some experiments with near-contemporary themes had narrowed its focus to stories of the heroes, kings and dynasties of the splendid but violent age which ended with the first generation after the Trojan War. These stories reflected the rudimentary social organization of an unsettled age—hereditary kingship, dynastic feuds—and the violence, uninhibited by communal restraints, of the god-descended heroes. One of the achieve-

[7] For a critical view of the whole concept of 'chairmanships' on collegiate boards see K. J. Dover, in *JHS* 80 (1960), 61 ff.

[8] Arist. *Rh.* III 18, 1419 a 26, cf. A. Lesky, *Die tragische Dichtung der Hellenen* (Göttingen [3]1972), 173. For a thorough review of the question see M. H. Jameson, "Sophocles and the Four Hundred", in *Historia* 20 (1971), 541 ff.

ments of Aeschylus was to impose on this primitive material the contemporary framework of the *polis*—still ruled by kings as in the saga but reminiscent in many suggestive details of the *polis* in which the audience lived. The king of Argos in *Suppliants* must consult his citizens before making a decision which will endanger the city and in the *Oresteia* the murder of Agamemnon by his wife is the first act in a drama which culminates in the foundation of the Areopagos and a hymn of blessing for Athenian democracy and empire. The *Seven* opens with an eloquent plea from Eteocles, defender of a city under assault; he summons the Thebans to the walls. "Now is the time for all of you—you that fall short of maturity, you that are past the time of youth, fostering the full growth of your limbs, and you that are in manhood's prime—as is your duty, every one of you must protect the city and the altars of our native gods—let not their worship be abolished—protect, too, the children and the land, your mother and most tender nurse—she, who, welcoming all the travail of their upbringing, has reared them, young shoots on the kindly plain, to be makers of homes and bearers of shields" (Aeschyl. *Th.* 10-19 Page)[9]. This is a mythic hero speaking but his voice is that of the man who fought at Marathon. Tragedy, as Sophocles inherited it from his rival, was a dramatic medium which could invest with broad contemporary significance the actions and sufferings of ancestral heroes, whose mythical remoteness, sustained by the dignity of the tragic style, ruled out facile identification with particular partisan issues or controversial figures of the day. It was only to be expected that Sophocles, given his record of participation in the highest offices of the *polis*, would follow the lead of his great predecessor.

[9] The emphasis on the city's role as nurse and mother of the citizen (μητρί, τροφῷ 16; παιδείας ὄτλον 18; ἐθρέψατ' 19) recurs in the Laws' address to Socrates (Plat. *Crito*: ἐγεννήσαμεν 50 d; γεννήσαντες, ἐκθρέψαντες, παιδεύσαντες 51 c; γεννηταῖς . . .τροφεῦσι. . . 51 e).

When we speak of Sophoclean tragedy we often tend to forget something which the presence of Professor Radt in this gathering forcibly reminds us of—that we have only a small fragment of a vast œuvre, seven complete plays out of 123. We can only hope that the seven are reasonably representative of the whole; in any case, it is on these seven that we must base our interpretation. And they do, in fact, show us a Sophocles who, like Aeschylus, poses the heroic figures of the ancient saga against the background of a half-mythical, half-contemporary *polis*, or, in the case of the Trojan War plays *Ajax* and *Philoctetes*, of the *polis* in arms, the στρατός. There is only one exception: *Trachiniae.* This play deliberately emphasizes the primitive, even monstrous, features of the Heracles saga—the fight with the river in his bull-shape, the centaur Nessos and his poisoned blood, the strident agony of Heracles' last hours and his bizarre end, whether it be death or apotheosis. The scene of the action is not a *polis* at all; the family of Heracles are guests of a 'foreigner' who is not even named and the *agora*, the meeting place of the people of Trachis, is a cow-pasture (cf. 188 with 372 and 424). The only *polis* of any importance in the action is Oechalia, a city which Heracles has sacked and razed (ἀνάστατον 240) [10] . The characters of this play seem to be untrammelled by any sense that they are part of a community and the young women of the chorus are given no words which will identify them, justify their presence or attach them to a locality.

Electra, on the other hand, opens with the most precise location of the action in a city landscape to be found in extant Greek tragedy: Orestes' old tutor points out to him, from the vantage point of the Atridae's palace at Mycenae, the salient features of the city of Argos—the *agora* of Lycean Apollo and

[10] Cf. Charles SEGAL, *Tragedy and Civilization: An Interpretation of Sophocles* (Cambridge, Mass. 1981), 62.

"on the left, the famous temple of Hera." Such a prologue seems the appropriate opening note for a drama which will emphasize the political aspect of Orestes' action: the overthrow of a tyranny, the restoration of freedom. But, in fact, nothing could be farther from the truth; Sophocles concentrates our attention almost exclusively on the violent hatreds and internecine violence of a doomed and cursed family. The dominant words in this text are not *polis* and πολίτης (they occur only rarely)[11] but πατήρ, μήτηρ, ἀδελφή, κασίγνητος, δόμος, δῶμα, and οἶκος; they recur with obsessive frequency from beginning to end of the play. And the word 'free' ἐλεύθερος is used always of personal freedom: Chrysothemis' freedom to marry once Aegisthus is dead (970); Electra's freedom to speak now Orestes has come (1256); of freedom to rejoice and smile once success has been achieved (1300). There is one passage, in fact, where the non-political nature of this 'freedom' is emphasized by a startling phrase, which Sophocles puts in the mouth of Chrysothemis, the conformist and self-confessed coward. She admits that Electra has right τὸ... δίκαιον (338) on her side. "But if I am to live free," she says, "I must obey every word of those in power" (εἰ δ' ἐλευθέραν με δεῖ/ ζῆν, τῶν κρατούντων ἐστὶ πάντ' ἀκουστέα 339-40).

Even in the one passage where the language suggests a political theme, Electra's vision of the glory she and her sister will win if they murder Aegisthus—its striking use of the dual a reminiscence of the battle-hymn of Athenian democracy, the Harmodios song—even here the achievement for which they will be celebrated is not the liberation of Argos but the salvation of the house of Atreus; to ἰσονόμους τ' Ἀθήνας ἐποιησάτην corresponds ὣ τὸν πατρῷον οἶκον ἐξεσωσάτην (978). And this restriction of the action to the domestic sphere is clearest of all in the final lines of the play, where

[11] πόλις 982; 1413; πολίτιδες 1227.

'freedom' is mentioned again: "Seed of Atreus, after much suffering, you have through struggle won freedom at last" . . .ὦ σπέρμ' 'Ατρέως . . .δι' ἐλευθερίας μόλις ἐξῆλθες. . .; it is the family, not the city, which has been freed. To appreciate the singularity of this treatment of the legend one has only to glance at Sophocles' model, the *Choephoroe* of Aeschylus. One of the motives which Orestes says would have urged him to action even if Apollo's oracle had not, is the thought that "fellow citizens, most renowned among mortals, the men who sacked Troy with blazing courage, should be thus subject to a pair of women" (302 ff.). And when the chorus of Trojan captives who see in the vengeance 'good for the city' (πόλει τάδ' εὖ 824) try to comfort Orestes and restrain him from going as a suppliant to Delphi, they tell him: "You have brought freedom to the whole city of the Argives" (ἠλευθέρωσας πᾶσαν 'Αργείων πόλιν 1046).

The other Electra play, that of Euripides, reinforces the contrast, for it is just as political, though in a markedly different way, as that of Aeschylus. Though the setting is a remote country farm, the characters live and move and have their being in the charged atmosphere of the late fifth-century *polis*. Orestes is all too easily recognizable as a political exile with a price on his head (33) who has come home secretly, staying close to the frontier so that he can escape if recognized (96-97); he has returned to sound out the possibility of support for a coup (101; 601). The vengeance itself—the treacherous assassination of Aegisthus, Electra's ghastly indictment of the tyrant's severed head—recalls, as has often been pointed out, Thucydides' account of στάσις on Corcyra—"the ingenuity of their enterprises and the ferocity of their reprisals" (III 82). And at the end of the play the Dioskouroi reset the action in its mythic frame: as in the *Eumenides*, Orestes is to be tried and acquitted in Athens. But Euripides takes the story farther still: he is to found a new *polis* in the West, one which will bear his name.

In his *Electra* Sophocles rejected the political element in the story of the Atridae, an element which, whether it was Aeschylean invention or traditional lore, was brilliantly exploited by Euripides in characteristically iconoclastic style. But in the remaining five of the extant Sophoclean plays we are securely placed in the world of the *polis*; in each play the *polis* or its wartime equivalent, the στρατός, provides the context for the heroic action; it has its own voice, the chorus, and its own spokesmen among the actors. In four of these plays the tragic tension stems from the incompatibility between the demands of the *polis* and the imperatives of the heroic will. In the fifth, the *Oedipus Tyrannos*, a ruler who embodies the supreme virtues of the devoted citizen ends, through his own heroic persistence, as an outcast from the *polis*, like the heroes of the other four plays.

In two of them, the hero's defiance of the *polis* leads to death: both Ajax and Antigone die by their own hand. Death, but not total defeat: Creon gives way and admits that he was wrong; Ajax will have his hero's funeral in spite of the vindictive order of the generals. But though there are resemblances between Ajax and Antigone, (since both share that stubborn heroic irreconcilability Sophocles saw as the core of heroic character) there are some basic differences between the plays in which they appear. Antigone's action, for example, can be defended and is in the end vindicated, whereas Ajax's murderous intentions far outrun any justification his injuries might have afforded. But the most striking difference lies in the terms used to express the demand of the community, στρατός or *polis*, for loyalty and obedience.

In the first part of the *Ajax* there is little discussion of the duty owed to the army, for attention is centered on the hero, his grievances, his failed revenge and his resolve to die; not only does Ajax feel no loyalty to the army, he includes it in the curse he levels at the Atridae as he prepares to fall on his sword: "Go to it, swift and vengeful Erinyes, show no mercy, take your fill of the whole army, every last man" (πανδήμου στρατοῦ 844). He had intended to kill the commanders only but this all-inclusive curse gives some ground for the rhetorical exaggeration of the accusation leveled against him: that "his plot (βούλευμ') was against the Argives" (Odysseus, 44); that he was a "plotter against the army" κἀπιβουλευτοῦ στρατῷ (the Argives, 726); and finally that he "plotted the death of the entire army" στρατῷ ξύμπαντι βουλεύσας φόνον (Menelaus, 1055). It is in the second half of the play, as the gigantic corpse of Ajax lies spitted on the sword of Hector, that the *polis* announces its claims. In the mouth of Menelaus, it does so in uncompromising terms. Ajax would never listen to Menelaus, Teucer is told: "there's a worthless man for you—a man of low degree (ἄνδρα δημότην) who takes it upon himself to ignore those set in authority over him" (τῶν ἐφεστώτων 1071-72). The words, as well as the situation they denote, are utterly un-Homeric; this is not the camp on the beachhead where rival chieftains grudgingly accept (or violently throw off) the loose and temporary authority of a pre-eminent king. The lines which follow make this even clearer. "You cannot have laws working smoothly in a city where fear does not have its established place, nor can you have discipline in an army without the protective shield of terror and respect." *Polis* and στρατός are different sides of the same coin; what goes for one goes for the other. When Menelaus returns to the theme of discipline (1081 ff.) he speaks of the *polis* alone. "Where there is no curb on licence—all do what they like—that's a city which may run now before a fair wind but will one day go down to the bottom. No, let me have fear installed, in due proportion. . ." (δέος τι καίριον 1084). These sentiments are echoed by Agamemnon. "Where such attitudes prevail" (he means Ajax's refusal to accept the award of the arms to Odysseus), "there can be no establishment of law of any kind. . ." (1246-47). And Teucer's offense, his insistence on Ajax's right to be buried, is characterized not only as ὕβρις, intolerable insolence, but also as "speaking freely" (κἀξελευθεροστομεῖς 1258).

These demands for discipline and submission, especially the elaborate formulas put in the mouth of Menelaus, are sometimes described as 'Spartan' [12]; they are supposed to represent, for the Athenian audience, a point of view alien to the tolerant spirit of Athenian democracy. But there is actually little in those lines which would not have seemed acceptable, if perhaps harshly expressed, to most Athenian citizens. Aeschylus' chorus in the *Eumenides* had stressed that fear had its place in the *polis*: "there are times when terror is a blessing; it must have its permanent seat as watcher over the mind" (ἔσθ' ὅπου τὸ δεινὸν εὖ 517 ff.) and Athena herself echoes their claim: "Do not utterly expel terror from your city...". Even the Funeral Speech, which so eloquently posed Athenian freedom of manners against the harsh Spartan discipline, reiterates the theme: "in our public life it is mainly through fear that we refrain from illegal action; we listen to those who are in office and to the laws..." (διὰ δέος μάλιστα οὐ παρανομοῦμεν... II 37, 3).

Familiar as these pronouncements of Menelaus and Agamemnon may have sounded to the average Athenian in the audience, their dramatic content must have given him pause. They are being advanced in favor of a decision to expose the corpse—"throw it out on the sand as food for the shore birds" (1064-5)—of a man whom even his enemy Odysseus celebrates as the best man, after Achilles, of all those who came to Troy (1340-41). The two kings who could not impose their will on Ajax living, as Menelaus admits

[12] R. C. Jebb (ed.), *Sophocles. The Plays and Fragments. Part VII. The Ajax* (Cambridge 1907), p. xliii; W. B. Stanford (ed.), *Sophocles. Ajax* (London 1963), on 1102 (cf. however, on 1073); J. C. Kamerbeek, *The Plays of Sophocles. Commentaries. Part. I. The Ajax* (Leiden 1953), on 1074. But contrast L. Radermacher (ed.), *Sophokles. Aias* (Berlin 1913), on 1079.

(1067), will have their way with him now that he is dead; Agamemnon even goes so far as to deny his pre-eminence in battle—"Where did he go or stand that I did not?" 1237—a question which anyone familiar with the *Iliad* could answer at once. The two kings do not even claim that the horrifying penalty is meant to be exemplary; they simply exult vindictively in their power over the lifeless corpse of the hero whom they feared to cross when he was alive. The claims of the *polis* are advanced by unworthy spokesmen whose low and spiteful ranting enhances the dignity of that heroic corpse they wish to defile.

In the *Ajax* the voice of the *polis* is heard late in the play and it strikes a sour note. In the *Antigone* on the other hand, it is given full and eloquent expression right at the start, in that speech of Creon which, as we know from the way Demosthenes later used it in the court room [13], became a classic text of the Athenian patriotic spirit. And in this play, although the setting is the moment of victory in war and the ruler Creon is a στρατηγός (8) who issues commands by proclamations (8; 27; 32; 34; 203), the background is not the armed camp on the Trojan shore but a *polis* , one with pillared temples (285-6), battlemented walls (131) and towers (122), gates (141), altars (1016), hearths (1083) and a council of elders (160). The *polis* is to be the scene of the execution by stoning (36) fixed as a penalty for disobedience to Creon's decree, which forbids the *polis* (ἀπόρρητον πόλει 44) to bury Polynices. Ismene, who will reluctantly obey those in authority, identifies the will of Creon with that of the *polis* as a whole, for she professes herself unable to act "in defiance of the citizens" (βίᾳ πολιτῶν 79). This judgement is confirmed by the conduct of the chorus, representatives of the *polis* summoned by Creon, who stand behind him and against Antigone until the last moment, when Tiresias makes it clear that Creon is wrong and also marked for punishment.

[13] *Or.* XIX (*Amb.*) 247.

The emotional background for their support of Creon's harsh sentence is vividly presented in their opening song, which recalls the terrors of the enemy assault on the walls, the miracle by which the city has escaped collapse in a welter of blood and fire. The invaders were recruited and led by a πολίτης, the man whose corpse Creon has now consigned to the birds and dogs.

This lyric evocation of the dangers and terrors of the siege, the city's hairs-breadth escape from destruction at the hands of one of its own citizens, prepares the audience for Creon's inaugural speech. ἄνδρες, τὰ μὲν δὴ πόλεος . . . "Gentlemen, as for the city. . . the gods who tossed our ship on a heavy swell have righted it again, it rides safely" (162-3). The declaration of principles which follows, full of reminiscences (or anticipations) of Periclean rhetoric, states firmly the precedence of loyalty to the *polis* over all other loyalties, whether to friend or relative (both included in the one word φίλος). This is the same large demand which the laws of Athens make on Socrates in Plato's *Crito* and it is given some validity by Creon's implied claim that only in the framework of civilization made possible by the *polis* can friendship or any personal relationship exist. ἥδ' ἐστὶν ἡ σῴζουσα. . . "This is the ship that brings us safe to harbor and we make our friends as we sail her and keep her upright" (189-90). These, says Creon, are the laws through which he plans to make the city great. His first official act makes a distinction between patriot and traitor and asserts the right of the *polis* to honor the one and punish the other in life and in death (209-10).

Creon began by mentioning the gods and he sincerely believes that the gods of the city approve of his decree. When the chorus tentatively suggests that the symbolic burial reported by the guard may be divine intervention he turns on them in what is obviously sincere anger. "Intolerable", he calls their suggestion: how could the gods take any thought for one who came to burn their pillared temples and the treasures inside them? To an audience which probably believed, with Herodotus, that the gods had punished at Salamis and Plataea the Persians who burned and sacked the temples on the Acropolis, Creon's religious beliefs, like his political principles, would have occasioned no surprise, still less objection [14]. In this play the case for the *polis* is made early and in impressive form but, as in the *Ajax*, it is also a case for denial of burial to a corpse. And as the action develops, Creon, under the pressure of events, will abandon both his political and religious principles, will insist, in speeches which betray a temper both tyrannical and blasphemous, on his own will, no matter what the consequences. He no longer speaks for the *polis*; that role is assumed first by his son Haemon, who tells Creon that the people praise Antigone's action (though the chorus gives no sign that they share that opinion) and lastly by the spokesman for the gods, Tiresias, who tells Creon that communication with the gods has been cut off. The hearths and altars are polluted by dogs and birds who fed on the corpse. "And it is because of your will that

[14] This aspect of Creon's position is sympathetically explored and discussed in the context of Athenian religious beliefs in Borimir JORDAN, *Servants of the Gods*, Hypomnemata 55 (Göttingen 1979), 85-102. Giovanni CERRI, "Ideologia funeraria nell'Antigone di Sofocle", in *La mort, les morts dans les sociétés anciennes*, ed. G. GNOLI and J.-P. VERNANT (Cambridge 1982), 121-131 puts an interesting case for the existence of exposure as penalty for treason in 5th century Athens. He sees it in every case as an emergency measure, sparked usually by political faction fights, and he suggests that there was in fact no established law defining public conduct in this matter. His thesis is based on the Themistocles story in Thucydides (which does not help it much), on the speech of Euryptolemos in Xenophon's *Hellenica* (I 7, 25 ff.) with its reference to the *psephisma* of Cannon (he follows the mss. reading ἀποθανόντα . . . ἐμβληθῆναι) and on Thucydides II 67, 4, the Athenian execution of the Spartan ambassadors to Persia, ἀπέκτειναν καὶ ἐς φάραγγα ἐσέβαλον (which, however, was a measure against foreigners not citizens and was in retaliation for similar treatment of captured Athenian crews by the Spartans). The thesis seems to me not fully proved but Cerri's article (and he promises a more extended treatment) does reopen the whole question of what he calls the "obiettivo rapporto semantico fra discorso mitico e realtà", which seems to have been largely ignored since H. J. METTE raised it in 1956 (in *Hermes* 84, 129 ff.).

this plague has come on the city" (καὶ ταῦτα τῆς σῆς ἐκ φρενὸς νοσεῖ πόλις 1015).

Antigone never claims to speak for the *polis*; her loyalties lie elsewhere, to the ties of blood-relationship, to the gods who, as she rightly insists, will disavow Creon's action. She acts and speaks for the most part as if the *polis* did not exist. In her farewell lament she mentions it only to turn away to other, more favorable, presences. "I am mocked," she replies to the chorus which has reproved her for comparing herself to Niobe. "By the gods of our fathers, why do you not wait for my death to insult me, but do it to my face? O *polis*, and its wealthy men!" (ὦ πόλις, ὦ πόλεως πολυκτήμονες ἄνδρες 843). This must be a phrase of indignant repudiation [15] for she goes on: "Hail, (ἰὼ) waters of Dirce, and grove of Thebes, city of chariots, you, at any rate (ἔμπας 846) I have as witnesses to my sorrow, as I go unwept by friends. . . to the rock bound prison of an uncanny tomb." And in her defence of her action she makes a clear admission that the *polis* did not enter into the reckoning when she made up her mind: if it had been someone else than my brother, she says, a husband or a child, "I would not have taken up this burden, defying my fellow citizens" (βίᾳ πολιτῶν—it is the phrase Ismene used to excuse her inaction in the prologue).

Yet it was Antigone who knew what was best for the *polis*, knew that there were everlasting laws more valid than those made by man, for all his ingenuity and daring. And it was Creon, devoted champion of the *polis*, whose action aroused the anger of the gods and sowed the seed of future disaster for Thebes (1080 ff.).

In both *Ajax* and *Antigone* the case for the *polis* was proclaimed by unworthy advocates and urged in defence of inhuman action; in the *Oedipus Tyrannos* the central figure is a

[15] So, with most commentators, G. Müller, *Sophokles Antigone* (Heidelberg 1967), 187, who suggests putting the question mark after ἄνδρες.

model statesman, the savior of the *polis* in its hour of danger, a king whose every thought and action is dedicated to the welfare of his plague-stricken people. The protagonist this time is not a rebel against the authority of the *polis* but an embodiment of that authority itself and in its noblest form. The voice of the *polis*, as we have heard it so far, expresses itself as a demand made on the citizens by the ruler; here the pressure is exerted on the ruler himself as the priests and citizens implore Oedipus to save them and as he suffers under his own sense of his obligation to the community. Nevertheless, this faithful servant of the *polis* will end, like Ajax and Antigone as an outcast ἐκβεβλημένος [16]. The fault lies not in his attitude or conduct but in a dreadful pollution of which he is ignorant; the force which drives him on to discover it is, in the opening scenes, his devotion to the welfare of his fellow citizens.

Oedipus is not only the savior of the city to whom all men now turn for help; he is a compassionate and responsible ruler, tormented by his inability to save the citizens who have put their trust in him. "Your sorrow," he tells them "comes on each one of you, each for himself, but my soul grieves for the city as well as for myself and you" (62-64). He has already sent Creon to Delphi and, after dismissing Creon's suggestion that the oracle's response be heard in private—it concerns the *polis* and so he proclaims: "Speak before all" (93)—he accepts the god's command and begins the search for the murderer of Laius. The solemn curse which makes the murderer an outcast from the *polis* is pronounced and Tiresias arrives, sent for by Oedipus. His stubborn refusal to speak is rebuked as "unfriendly to the city" (οὔτε προσφιλῆ πόλει 322) and his even more categorical refusal after phrases which hint that he knows something vital is interpreted as treason:

[16] A key word in the Sophoclean tragic vocabulary: cf. *Aj.* 1064; 1392; *OT* 386; 399; *El.* 590; *Ph.* 257; 600; 1390; 1391; *OC* 770; 1257.

"...you intend to betray me and destroy the city?" (καταφθεῖραι πόλιν 331). His veiled accusations of Oedipus are an "insult to the city" (ἀτιμάζεις πόλιν 340). But when he hints darkly that Oedipus' successful encounter with the Sphinx was his destruction, the answer is a proud defiance: "But if I saved this city, I don't care" (εἰ πόλιν τήνδ' ἐξέσωσ'. . . 443). Later when Creon, at the height of their altercation, returns Oedipus' epithet κακός (627) with a charge that he is a bad ruler (κακῶς γ' ἄρχοντος 629) he appeals indignantly to that *polis* which it has been his life's work to protect and preserve (ὦ πόλις πόλις. . .).

In the next scene Jocasta's attempt to comfort him plunges him into an agony of fear that he may have been the man who killed Laius where the three roads meet. And from this point on, though his unrelenting search for the truth is still the action of a ruler intent on the rescue of his people from the plague, it is also the convulsive effort of a frightened man to establish his own identity. At its end he stands revealed as the source of the pollution which afflicts the city and as an outcast doomed to death or exile by the terms of his own solemn curse. As he explains and defends his self-blinding he counts among the sights he could no longer bear to look on the physical features—town, tower, holy statues of the gods (1378-79)—of that *polis* from which he has expelled himself. He had accused Creon of conspiracy to expel him (ἐκβαλεῖν 386; 399) but his future as a blind beggar in exile is the product of his own strange destiny and the zeal with which he fulfilled his function as protector and preserver of the *polis*.

In all three of these plays, *Ajax*, *Antigone* and *Oedipus Tyrannos*, the action of the protagonist brings about exclusion from the society of the *polis*, in two cases through defiance of its representatives, in the other through devotion to its welfare. But in the remaining two plays, this motion is reversed: the hero begins as an outcast and ends reestablished, Oedipus in a *polis*, and Philoctetes in the στρατός which cannot take Troy without him [17].

Philoctetes is the most abused of all the heroes: he has been left to fend for himself for ten years, a sick man on a desert island, not because of any misconduct on his part but simply because he has been afflicted with a painful and offensive disease. The army has learned that it cannot win without him; the man it despised and rejected must now be courted and brought back into the ranks. It will not be an easy task; in fact, since the army has given the assignment to Odysseus, whom Philoctetes is ready to shoot on sight, it can only succeed through elaborate deception. Odysseus' chosen instrument for this is the young son of Achilles, Neoptolemos.

As in the *Ajax*, the spokesman for the *polis* does it no credit. When he urges Neoptolemos to play the liar in his plot (σόφισμα 14) to capture Philoctetes, the argument we expect to hear, that without Philoctetes' cooperation the army cannot return home victorious, appears only as a veiled suggestion: "If you don't do this, you will inflict pain on all the Argives" (66-67). The main thrust of Odysseus' argument is the advantage Neoptolemos will win for himself (κέρδος 111; 112)—his share in the glory of Troy's fall (119); to this he adds the prospect that if successful, Neoptolemos will be called clever σοφός (like Odysseus) as well as brave ἀγαθός (like his father Achilles). It is only when Neoptolemos decides to make amends for his deceit by giving back the bow that Odysseus invokes the army's name; he does so in a series of threats which begin as a challenge to arms (1243 ff.) but end ignominiously in a hurried exit: "I will go and tell this to the whole army—*they* will punish you" (1258). At the climactic moment, as Neoptolemos hands the bow back to its

[17] On these two plays see K. Matthiessen, "Philoktet oder die Resozialisierung", in *Würzburger Jahrbücher* N.F. 7 (1981), 11 ff.

owner, Odysseus, in a surprise entrance which is perhaps the most abrupt in extant tragedy [18], forbids the action "on behalf of the sons of Atreus and the army as a whole" (ὑπέρ τ' Ἀτρειδῶν τοῦ τε σύμπαντος στρατοῦ 1294). If it had not been for Neoptolemos' intervention, he would have paid for this gesture with his life; Philoctetes is in no mood to listen to the commands of the army. And when Neoptolemos now tries to persuade him to come to Troy he does not mention the common good of the army at all; his arguments are based on what would be best for Philoctetes. Whatever right there may have been in the community's case has been thoroughly compromised by Odyssean deceit; Philoctetes cannot be expected to trust appeals to his generosity and sense of duty after what has happened. Neoptolemos bears down hard on the fact that Philoctetes' only hope of cure from his painful sickness is to come to Troy where the sons of Asklepios will restore him to health, so that, together, the two of them can take Troy. All this, he tells him, is fated to happen and furthermore, it is to happen this very summer. So Philoctetes should comply willingly with what must happen anyway (δεῖ γενέσθαι 1339); he will regain his health and also, by taking Troy, win the highest glory. This plea moves the outcast at first but the memory of his wrongs comes flooding back in and he rejects it bitterly. Furthermore, he demands passage home, as promised, and Neoptolemos is in honor bound, now, to fulfil that promise, lie though it was. And Troy will not fall this summer, after all.

It does, of course; this time Philoctetes' patron and exemplar, the divine Heracles, appears to bring him into line. But not even now do we hear the argument from duty to the *polis*. Heracles makes known the will of Zeus (1415); it is that Philoctetes, using the bow and arrows of Heracles, shall take Troy, killing Paris, the cause of all the suffering. Philoctetes

[18] See O. Taplin, *Greek Tragedy in Action* (Berkeley and Los Angeles 1978), 32.

is to dedicate part of the spoils at the place where he lit Heracles' funeral pyre, near his home in Oeta. And Philoctetes will be healed; Neoptolemos had promised a cure by the sons of Asklepios but Heracles will send Asklepios himself. To these divine commands Philoctetes makes no resistance (οὐκ ἀπιθήσω τοῖς σοῖς μύθοις 1447), but there is no enthusiasm in his acquiescence. There is more than a hint of regret in his farewell to the island and his closing words are mere acceptance, no more. "Send me off with a fair wind and no complaints to where great Destiny conveys me, the wisdom of friends and the all-victorious divinity who made this decree" (1465-1468). What he accepts is the will of Zeus, not the right of the community, in war as in peace, to demand compliance.

The Oedipus of the last play is just as much an outcast as Philoctetes; he is not a sick man, but he is old, blind, ragged and filthy, a wandering beggar—and he has no such resource as the unerring bow and arrows of Heracles. The Greeks remembered Philoctetes only when the Trojan seer Helenos told them Troy could not be taken without him; the Thebans, on both sides, seek possession of Oedipus only when the Delphic oracle tells them his burial site will bring victory in battle to the land in which it lies. As against Philoctetes, lies, force and persuasion are all deployed, but to no effect. But in this plays no god appears to bring about the reintegration of Oedipus in the *polis*. He does become a citizen (ἔμπολιν 637) [19] but a citizen of Athens, not Thebes; and his citizenship begins and ends with his mysterious death, a death which, we learn from the messenger's account (1626-8), is the will of the gods.

[19] ἔμπολιν, Musgrave's conjecture for Mss. ἔμπαλιν seems solid (in spite of Campbell's objection). Both Jebb and Campbell assert that the word occurs only here (if it does) and at 1156 but it also occurs in the 5th century comic poet Eupolis (Fr. 137 Kock): τὸν ἀστὸν Εὔπολις ἐν τῇ Διάδι (?) ἔμπολιν εἴρηκεν, οἷον ἐγχώριον.

When Oedipus is challenged by the chorus to name his fatherland (πατρίδ' 206) he calls himself ἀπόπτολις—a word which can mean simply 'absent from the city' (*Tr.* 647) but also, as it must mean here, 'exile' [20]. Exiles, in Greece, had little thought for anything but their return; "the true lover of his city", says Alcibiades at Sparta, "is not the man who, unjustly deprived of her, fails to take the offensive, but the one who because of his desire for her, will go to any length to regain her" (Thuc. VI 92,4) [21]. This is of course exactly the program of Polynices (*OC* 379 ff.). But Oedipus is no ordinary exile; he has no wish to return to Thebes. As soon as he heard that the grove which sheltered him was sacred to the Eumenides, he announced his immoveable decision to stay (45); the gift of victory which his body brings with it is to be offered not to Thebes but to Athens.

Towards his own *polis* Oedipus is bitterly hostile; the hatred of Philoctetes for the Atridae and Odysseus was nothing compared to his for Thebes and everyone in it. His destructive hatred for his native *polis* is implicit in his recognition of the holy ground on which he stands as the place prescribed in the prophecy where he was to find rest and bring profit to those who received him and "destruction to those who drove me out and sent me here" (92-3). For this 'destruction', as we learn later, will not be confined to the individuals he blames for his present condition but will fall on a Theban army fighting on the ground where he lies buried. For his expulsion from Thebes he blames not only Creon (770) and his own sons (428) but the *polis* (432); he can even speak of the *polis* driving him out with violence (βίᾳ 440). His rage against the *polis* of Thebes has even deeper (and darker) sources: he lays on the *polis* the responsibility for

[20] *OT* 1000 (voluntary exile). Cf. ἀπόπολις : Aeschyl. *Ag.* 1410; ἄπολιν: Soph. *OC* 1357; *Ph.* 1018.

[21] Cf. Isocr. *Or.* XVI (*De bigis*) 14, 349 b-d.

the marriage which has made his name a byword. "The city", he tells the chorus, "bound me, all unsuspecting, in a marriage with destruction, a bed of evil" (525-26). It was a gift, he says later (539-41), a return for services rendered, which he wishes he had never received from Thebes. The Thebans will repay him with their blood. "This is the place", he tells Theseus, "in which I shall have victory over those who threw me out" (644, 646). Creon is speaking truth, for once, when he tells the old man: "You want victory over your own fatherland and your friends" (849-50).

The city's claim on Oedipus' loyalty is put in the mouth of Creon, who comes, he says, "not sent by one man, but under orders from the whole citizen body" (ἀστῶν ὕπο/πάντων κελευσθείς 737-38). This spokesman for the *polis* is even more suspect than the younger Creon of *Antigone* or the Atridae of *Ajax*, for, like Odysseus, he deals in lies. His invitation to come home pulls out all the stops of duty and affection: "Come of your own free will to the town and the home of your fathers, bidding a kind farewell to this city (Athens), for she deserves it. But your home city, as is only just, has a stronger claim on your devotion for it was she who nursed you long ago" (757-60) [22]. Not only does he intend, as Ismene has already told her father, to deny Oedipus burial in Theban soil; he has already seized Ismene as a hostage. He fully deserves the fury of Oedipus' rejection; the case for the *polis* could hardly have had a more contemptible spokesman.

There is another, of course, later in the play. Polynices implores Oedipus to come with him to Thebes and invokes "the springs and the gods of our people" (1333); he promises to settle the old man in his house and settle himself there too (1342-43). But he is calling for his father's help in an assault on his native city to be launched by foreign troops under his

[22] This customary appeal for loyalty (cf. p. 6, n. 9) happens to be falsely based: Oedipus did not grow up in Thebes—his τροφός was Corinth.

command. And his appeal is rejected with even more terrible imprecations than that of Creon.

Oedipus has a new *polis*, Athens; Theseus declares him a citizen (ἔμπολιν 637) as he announces that he will settle him in the land. But that status has not been easy to win. Though he knows, as soon as the name of the Eumenides is pronounced (42), that Athens is the land foretold in the prophecy as the recipient of his gift, he still has to convince the inhabitants and the king that his unsightly body and polluted name should be received into the Athenian community. He concludes his prayer to the goddesses of the grove with an appeal to Athens—"most honored city of all" (108)— for pity: "pity this wretched ghost of Oedipus the man—this is not the body he possessed once long ago."

Pity is not what he gets from the outraged chorus of old men from Colonos. He is ordered off holy ground with a promise of protection that is broken when they know his name; they want to be rid of him. "Out! Be off! Leave this land!" (226). Only his eloquent appeal to the reputation of Athens, protector of the weak and suppliant, saves him from expulsion; they will await the decision of the king. He has proclaimed himself to the chorus as a 'savior' for Athens (460; 463); with Theseus he explains the meaning of this large claim. Theseus, when he learns that the Thebans want him back, reproaches him for refusing (590; 592); it is the natural reaction of any Greek. But he is admonished in his turn and accepts not only Oedipus' explanation of his gift of himself to Athenian soil but also his sermon on the instability of all things human—Thebes may be friendly now but "the same wind does not blow forever between man and man, city and city" (612-13).

Oedipus is a citizen of Athens now and when, under Creon's assault he calls for help (ἰὼ πόλις 833), it is Athens he is calling on for help against Thebes. The help comes in time and Oedipus, his daughters restored to him, prepares to make good his promise. Once he hears the thunder he knows the time is short; he wants, he says to Theseus, "to die without failing to keep the promises I made to you and the city" (1508-9). With Theseus alone present he makes his way to where the gods impatiently summon him (1626-28) and the promise is fulfilled: Theseus will hand on to his son and he to his the secret of Oedipus' last resting place and "thus", as he told the king, "the city you live in will never be sacked by the men born of the dragon's teeth" (1533-34). Someday, he had prophesied to Theseus (619 ff.), the Thebans will invade Attica; "on some small pretext they will shatter with the spear the pledged agreements which now hold. And then my sleeping, hidden corpse, cold though it be, will drink their warm blood. . .".

These two final plays, as has often been pointed out, deal with the same situation: a community's attempt to reassert, by lies and force, control over a man it has rejected utterly and now finds essential to its welfare. This formulation is, as far as I can see, an exact description of what has been referred to in recent criticism as "an outcast's reintegration into society" or 'Resozialisierung'. It is of course true that Philoctetes returns to take his place in the army for the final assault on Troy and that Oedipus becomes a citizen of no mean city—welcomed by a Theseus who is the living embodiment of that Athenian civilization praised by the chorus in its famous ode. But the solution of the dilemma posed by Philoctetes' stubborn insistance in going home leaves, as Matthiessen rightly says, a "bitter aftertaste"; Heracles' warning against offending the gods when Troy falls could not fail to remind the audience that Neoptolemos would kill Priam on the altar of Zeus. Oedipus, on the other hand, turns against his own *polis* with malevolent hatred; there is a fierce exultation in his language as he dwells on the Theban blood which will be shed over his grave. Ajax prayed for destruction to fall not just on the Achaean princes who had injured him but on the whole host of the army; Oedipus knows that in his grave he will have his revenge not just on Creon and his sons but on the whole Theban host. The joyful theme of his adoption by Athens is of course dominant in the play but the dark side of his action, the injury to his mother city, should not be forgotten [23]. It is hard to think of a mythical parallel, but a historical parallel springs immediately to mind. It is of course Alcibiades, who cold-bloodedly gave the Spartans advice which, followed with alacrity, led to the defeat of his native city.

Matthiessen sees, in the ambivalent attitude to the *polis* which characterizes the last two plays, Sophocles' reaction to the sordid, desperate politics of the last phase of the war. There is some warrant for this claim but it does not take into account the fact that the early plays, *Ajax* and *Antigone* also raise questions about the right of the *polis* to demand obedience in all things—"in matters small and just, and their opposites", to quote Creon's cynical euphemism (*Ant.* 671). And in the *Oedipus Tyrannos* the hero's devotion to the welfare of the *polis* is the instrument of his downfall. In fact all five of the plays which explore the relation of the tragic hero to his *polis* end by suggesting that the *polis* is not the be-all and end-all of human life, that there are powers and laws which transcend its authority. The *polis*, as Sophocles had his chorus sing in *Antigone*, is a human invention, perhaps man's greatest creation, but it is no more than that. Such an attitude would not be out of place in a poet who was "the last great exponent of the archaic world view" but it is a little unexpected in a man whose life was such an exemplary record of full participation in the highest councils of the city's feverish activity. And yet that very fact may explain the

[23] It is given what may be deliberate emphasis by the contrast with the attitude of Theseus, who specifically exempts Thebes from blame for Creon's conduct (919 ff.).

paradox. Without that involvement in the politics and wars of the *polis* which in its brief imperial career justified the Corinthians' claim that it "was born never to rest itself and to prevent the rest of the world from doing so", he might not have become so keenly aware of the dangers inherent in the Periclean ideal. The word *theos* does not appear in the Funeral Speech (nor, for that matter, in any of the speeches Thucydides puts in the mouth of Athens' leading statesmen) [24]; there is more than a hint that this *dynamis* of Athens, which its citizens are to contemplate till they become its lovers, is the real object of Periclean religious feeling.

Jean-Pierre Vernant in the introduction to his *Mythe et tragédie en Grèce ancienne*, summed up, in a characteristically stimulating formula, the new vision which tragedy, with its chorus representing the community, imposed on the epic heroes it put on stage. ". . . ils sont en quelque sorte mis en question devant le public. . . Dans le cadre nouveau du jeu tragique, le héros a donc cessé d'être un modèle: il est devenu, pour lui-même et pour les autres, un problème." For Sophocles, one is tempted to add, the *polis* also, has become a problem.

[24] In the summary of Pericles' financial report to the Athenians (Thuc. II 13) the word occurs, but Pericles is talking about using the gold on the statue of Athena in case of emergency.

DISCUSSION

M. Winnington-Ingram: I am in general agreement with Knox's statement about the paramount authority of the *polis*. One should perhaps, however, recognize

1) that Socrates' attitude in *Crito* represents an extreme position which not all Athenians would accept in its full implications.

2) the passage in Pericles/Thucydides has the character of a persuasive manifesto (cf. the emotional appeal of the ἐραστής metaphor). Is the ἀπράγμων/ἀχρεῖος contrast intended to counter the notion of ἀπραγμοσύνη as a virtue (in private life)?

M. Knox: Certainly the case of Socrates is an extreme example; nevertheless the essence of his argument, that loyalty to the *polis* overrides all other loyalties, is so constant a theme in the literature—it is implied in the Funeral Speech and specifically stated by Creon in the *Antigone*, a passage cited by Demosthenes as a model—that I feel sure it was a sentiment shared by the Athenians as a whole. I am happy to be able to say that Mme de Romilly, in her book *La loi dans la pensée grecque*, cites the Platonic passage to the same affect. As for the ἐραστής metaphor, it is of course highly emotional, but the fact that it was used (and I think the Aristophanic parodies prove that it was) by a great statesman on a solemn public occasion suggests that it expressed a real and widespread feeling. I agree that the contrast ἀπράγμων/ἀχρεῖος is to some extent on assault on the idea of ἀπραγμοσύνη as a private virtue, but given the political context it must also function as a condemnation of those Athenians who called for a less active policy on the part of the δῆμος.

M. Seidensticker: Sie haben im Anschluss an Matthiessen für die beiden letzten Stücke des Sophokles von Re-Integration eines *outcast* in die Gesellschaft gesprochen. Gilt dasselbe nicht in gewissem Sinne auch für die dritte der späten Tragödien des Dichters? Die Problematik des Muttermords und seine Folgen sind am Ende der *Elektra* gewiss nicht völlig ausgeblendet, aber doch stark in den Hintergrund gedrängt. Die Ermordung der Mörder, mit der das Stück schliesst, re-integriert den Flüchtling Orestes in Heimat, Palast und Familie, und auch für Elektra bringt die Tat Befreiung und Re-Integration aus einer unerträglichen *outcast*-Situation.

M. Knox: Since in this particular play there is no attempt to present the action of Orestes in political terms and practically no mention of 'society' or *polis*, the most that can be said along the lines of Matthiessen's formula *Resozialisierung* is that Electra and Orestes are restored not so much to society as to the palace, as you rightly put it, and to the family. But since the family, with the death of Clytemnestra, no longer exists for them to be reintegrated into, this does not seem too meaningfull. I would say, too, that your view of the play's ending seems to me too comforting; I have been convinced by Winnington-Ingram's discussion of the play in his recent book that the *Muttermord ist n i c h t stark in den Hintergrund gedrängt* and that the Erinyes are very much present and throw a shadow over the future, so that whatever reintegration takes place has no stable foundation.

Mme de Romilly: J'aimerais faire deux remarques. La première ne vise pas spécialement Sophocle, mais la façon dont peut être présentée cette toute-puissance de la cité: si elle limite la liberté de chaque citoyen, c'est pour assurer sa liberté par rapport aux menaces extérieures et pour éviter la vraie servitude, qui suit la défaite. Ceci donne du prix à cette soumission d'ordre intérieur, et du rayonnement. L'autre remarque est que ceux qui prêchent cette soumission, chez Sophocle, sont des personnages qui ont tort, comme Créon; mais il n'est pas sûr qu'ils aient tort en tout: les principes peuvent être bons et l'application erronée. Et il est conforme au sens tragique même d'avoir pu combiner ces deux aspects.

M. Knox: Je suis entièrement d'accord avec Mme de Romilly en ce qui concerne sa première remarque: la restriction de la liberté personnelle était une conséquence nécessaire des menaces extérieures; pour citer Périclès «un individu peut avoir du succès dans ses affaires personnelles, mais, si la cité est détruite, il périt avec elle» (Thuc. II 60, 3).

Que les principes puissent être bons et l'application erronée, j'en conviens; pourtant, à la seule exception d'Œdipe dans *Œdipe Roi*, ceux qui parlent pour la cité sont, pour le moins, suspects. C'est troublant!

M. Steiner: Line 370 in the *Antigone* seems to concentrate problematically many of the issues raised by Bernard Knox. Its parataxic structure emphasizes the tension of the relevant concepts and polarities. The city in which man holds the divine law in honour and usage is a "lofty city", ὑψίπολις. He who fails to observe such usage and law is ἄπολις. But the haunted humanism of Sophocles's critique goes much deeper. He asks, notably in *Antigone*: "is it possible for man to construct, to inhabit a πόλις, in which he can both accomplish his own full humanity, the deployment of his moral being, *and* in which the civic and religious ideals of judicial piety are enacted?" There are suggestions throughout the extant plays—so few in number and only putatively representative—that Sophocles knows no unambiguous answer to this question.

The Fifth stasimon in *Antigone* further complicates and enriches the topic. The chorus, in what is existentially and technically a condition of ecstasy, calls upon Dionysus. His arrival in Thebes is as ambiguously fatal as it will be in the *Bacchae*. The gods literally swarm into the πόλις. We now encounter not only the 'Zeus of the hearth' at whose altar Eurydice kills herself, but Hephaistos of the 'denying' sacrificial flame, Hecate of the fatal cross-roads, Pluto. A city which the gods have thus entered is as doomed as a city from which the gods are absent. What, then, are the true distances between 'political' man and the transcendent dimension?

M. Knox: Line 370, and indeed the whole of the strophe in which that line occurs, does indeed concentrate many of the problematical issues raised by the play: I would accept the formulation of George Steiner—"is it possible for man to construct a πόλις etc." as valid for the issue I raised in my paper—the πόλις as *problème* for Sophocles. I can agree that the invocation of Dionysus in the stasimon which precedes the catastrophe is an ironic prelude and also, with Winnington-Ingram, an evocation of those forces which Creon has slighted in his rigid interpretation of the city's interest but do not recognize the phenomenon Mr Steiner describes in the words "the gods literally swarm into the πόλις". Hecate and Pluton are both invoked *outside* the city at the place where Polynices' body was been exposed (1199-1200) and the altar of Ζεὺς Ἑρκεῖος has been mentioned before. That Creon has offended the gods there can be no doubt, but I do not find sufficient evidence to justify the metaphors employed.

The relation of the city to the gods is of course a main theme of the play and is indeed the problem posed in the closing strophe of the great ode πολλὰ τὰ δεινά. That begins as a celebration of the triumphs of man, the conqueror of his environment: the culmination of his achievement is the creation of the city, the "social temper" ἀστυνόμους ὀργάς, which he has taught himself, ἐδιδάξατο. But if he neglects the other νόμοι, those of the earth (χθονός, which surely suggests the rights of the dead, their right to burial) and divine justice he will no longer be ὑψίπολις, "a citizen of no mean city" but ἄπολις, man thrown back to the primitive stage of human existence which preceded the creation of the πόλις.

M. Taplin: Perhaps we should see the play as showing, in the eventual fate of Creon, something worse than becoming ἄπολις? He will stay on as ruler of the city, but life no longer has any joy for him. He must stay in Thebes with the debris of his folly. This is, in effect, the view put by the Messenger in lines 1155-71.

M. Irigoin: Il ne faut pas, me semble-t-il, entreprendre une discussion sur ὑψίπολις/ἄπολις, au v. 370 de l'antistrophe 2, sans tenir compte des adjectifs du v. 360: παντοπόρος/ἄπορος, qui ont le même nombre de syllabes et occupent la même place dans la strophe 2, avec le même rejet du premier adjectif, la même ponctuation forte entre les deux, la même asyndète après le second adjectif, la même syllabe – πο – suivie d'une liquide en 3e et 6e positions.

La formation de ὑψίπολις, un *hapax* tout comme παντοπόρος, est claire. C'est un composé de possession qui entre, avec les autres adjectifs composés en ὑψι-, dans la série des composés à premier élément adverbial à laquelle appartient aussi l'adjectif ἄπολις. Il ne peut que signifier, mot à mot, «qui 'possède' une cité élevée», désignant donc le citoyen d'une cité élevée, à l'élévation de laquelle il participe par sa conduite, et non pas le degré d'élévation du citoyen à l'intérieur de sa cité.

M. Radt: Für diese Interpretation wäre es natürlich schöner wenn ὑψίπολις sich als Kompositum vom Typus τερψίμβροτος auffassen liesse. Aber das einzige Verbum, von dem man ὑψίπολις dann ableiten könnte, wäre ὑψόω, so dass man eine sehr ungewöhnliche Analogiebildung annehmen müsste.

M. Winnington-Ingram: ὑψίπολις/ἄπολις : what is the subject? In the first half of the antithesis (like παντοπόρος/ἄπορος above), it is a generalized ἄνθρωπος: if the laws of the gods are respected, man lives in a πόλις that rides high. The second half moves towards the individual offender (ὃς τάδ' ἔρδοι), as a result of whose τόλμα the πόλις ceases to deserve the name.

Mme *de Romilly:* La solution au problème qu'ont soulevé M. Steiner et l'exposé lui-même, ne serait-elle pas qu'une πόλις n'est digne de ce nom que si elle sait faire régner le juste, dans ses lois, écrites et non écrites, et si elle n'entre pas en conflit avec les dieux. La cité ne pourrait être mise en question que dans ce cas. Ce serait là le sens de l'avertissement de Sophocle.

M. Steiner: It is important to observe that the word αὐτόνομος, which appears nowhere else in Sophocles' vocabulary such as we know it, carries a heavy load of fear and reproach. The πόλις can contain neither Creon *nor* Antigone. The one has arrogated law unto himself; the second is a law unto herself. But what kind of πόλις would it be if it can house neither the civic authority of a ruler nor the self-fulfilment of a great human conscience?

M. Knox: M. Irigoin is right to suggest caution in the interpretation of the word ὑψίπολις and to stress the extraordinarily exact correspondence with παντοπόρος/ἄπορος. As for Creon becoming ἄπολις there is perhaps a sense in which that can still be applied to him at the end of the play—he still has a city in the sense that he will, as Oliver Taplin says, go on living there in the ruin of his life but he has lost all claim to respect as the ruler and possessor of a great city—the chorus treat him at the end of the play with something like contempt.

J'accepte la formulation de Mme de Romilly: elle présente très clairement ce que je crois être le sens essentiel de la strophe finale.

And George Steiner quite rightly draws our attention to the designation of Antigone as αὐτόνομος and the fact that the word carries a load of reproach. The two parts of the compound in fact contradict each other when the word is applied to an individual rather than a community.

M. Taplin: May I open up the question of the relationship of the politics of the created world of tragedy to those of Sophocles' Athens? In three plays the hero-figure condemns the whole πόλις: in *Ajax*, *Philoctetes* (note in both the recurrence of the phrase σύμπας στρατός: *Aj.* 407; 1055; *Ph.* 387; 1226; 1243; 1294)—and, as Mr Knox pointed out, Thebes in *OC*. In each case the στρατός is condemned for, in effect, ratifying the evils done by their leaders. Only, I think, in the Haemon Scene in *Antigone* (683 ff.) is the voice of the people, ὑπὸ σκότου, set in explicit contradiction to its leaders; but the possibility is implicit in these three plays under discussion. The whole πόλις is dragged down by its rulers. Would you see this as a consequence of the 'epic' distancing of the world of tragedy, or as a commentary on Sophocles' own world?

M. Winnington-Ingram: Oedipus' violent condemnation of his own *polis* is a characteristic product of the irrational workings of his θυμός, which increases as he approaches the status of a ἥρως (cf. the wildly exaggerated language of *OC* 1360 ff.).

M. Knox: The question of the relationship of the world of tragedy and that of Sophoclean Athens is a perennial puzzle: I tried to formulate some sort of working formula for the problem in my paper. I don't see very much evidence that Sophocles tries to exonerate the πόλις by playing the good sense of the people against the folly and crimes of the rulers: as you say, the only place where such a suggestion is made is Haemon's speech in *Antigone* and even there the representatives of the people on stage, the chorus, show no such disagreement with Creon, in fact they back him up all the way until Tiresias gives them pause. So I don't think the Sophoclean picture is that of a whole πόλις dragged down by its rulers.

There certainly is an irrational element in the wrath of Oedipus. He blames the Thebans as a whole for his exile but he goes further than that and even blames them for his marriage with Jocasta—κακᾷ μ' εὐνᾷ πόλις οὐδὲν ἴδριν/γάμων ἐνέδησεν ἄτᾳ (*OC* 525-6; cf. 539 ff. where the word πόλις recurs).

*M*me *de Romilly:* Il me semble que l'accusation portée par Œdipe est ici simplement un élément de sa propre justification. Cette justification est hardie, complète. Même si la justice conserve la culpabilité involontaire, ici elle est rejetée, et non sans de bonnes raisons. Ce procédé du rejet de responsabilité se rencontre souvent chez Thucydide, et montre un Sophocle qui n'est pas étranger aux discussions du temps et qui sait en utiliser les raisonnements et les arguments pour les causes défendues par ses personnages. Ce n'est pas soumission à une mode ou à la rhétorique, mais utilisation de tout au service du tragique.

M. Reverdin: A mon avis, ce n'est pas la question de la responsabilité qui est posée, mais bien celle de la culpabilité. Œdipe a commis un double crime (parricide et inceste); il en accepte la responsabilité, et, à la fin d'*Œdipe Roi*, il en tire les conséquences. Il est un être impur; mais il n'est pas moralement coupable.

M. Knox: Sans doute Sophocle est parfaitement capable d'utiliser les procédés rhétoriques qu'il a dû connaître dans l'assemblée et dans les tribunaux. Mais je ne crois pas qu'on ait le droit d'affaiblir la force d'une déclaration aussi outrée que celle d'Œdipe sur la responsabilité de son sort en se référant aux exigences de la rhétorique. Chez Euripide, en revanche, on trouve des arguments qui n'ont d'autre justification que l'effet rhétorique, et qui peuvent même sembler, quand on y réfléchit, mal accommodés au caractère du personnage; mais pas chez Sophocle.

M. Radt: Ich möchte mich Mme de Romilly anschliessen. Schon Goethe hat in dem bekannten Gespräch über die *Antigone* (28. März 1827) Eckermann, der fand dass Kreon doch «einiges Recht habe», davor gewarnt, sich nicht täuschen zu lassen von der rhetorischen Meisterschaft, mit der Sophokles seine Personen so überzeugend reden lässt, «dass der

Zuhörer fast immer auf der Seite dessen ist, der zuletzt gesprochen hat». Sophokles lässt, genau wie Thukydides, seine Personen τὰ δέοντα εἰπεῖν, und wir dürfen das bei der Interpretation seiner Stücke nie aus dem Auge verlieren. Auch der starke Ausdruck ἐρασταί des thukydideischen Perikles ist, wie mir scheint, rein *pour les besoins de la cause* gebraucht und erlaubt keine Schlüsse über das normale Verhältnis des Atheners zu seiner πόλις.

M. Knox: Je regrette de me trouver dans la situation de contredire Johann Wolfgang von Goethe, mais encore une fois, sa remarque sur l'effet des discours sophocléens me semble s'appliquer mieux à ceux d'Euripide. Prenez le discours de Créon dans *Œdipe à Colone*, par exemple — ou la tirade de Clytemnestre contre Electre — on ne se trouve pas, à la fin, «auf der Seite dessen..., der zuletzt gesprochen hat». Quant à la phrase de Périclès, devenue célèbre à Athènes, il ne me semble pas, toute frappante qu'elle est, et prononcée par le πρῶτος ἀνήρ d'Athènes, dans un moment dramatique, qu'elle puisse être qualifiée par les mots «rein *pour les besoins de la cause* gebraucht»; c'est un état d'âme idéal que Périclès propose à ses concitoyens.

M. Steiner: A supreme dramatic poet such as Sophocles is neither the servant nor the mechanical exploiter of the arts of rhetoric. When Creon, for example, proclaims the great and 'future' truth, i.e. "no man can bring pollution to the gods", he is neither being hypocritical nor mechanistically rhetorical. He is uttering a formidable insight in a context which *partially* negates that insight. He is, as Erasmus suggests, "speaking piously out of impiety". Only some such approach to the polysemic nature of poetry, and of dramatic poetry in particular, can do justice to the quality of the arguments which Creon puts forward on behalf of an absolute concept of πόλις and πολιτεία. In this respect, comparison with the overwhelming truths voiced by Macbeth towards the close of the drama is illuminating.

M. Seidensticker: Ich würde gern noch einmal zurückkommen auf die durch Herrn Steiner und Herrn Taplin angesprochene Frage der Bedeutung der von Ihnen so eindrucksvoll analysierten, in der Tat unüberhörbaren Kritik an der πόλις. Handelt es sich Ihrer Meinung nach um eine kritische Reaktion auf aktuelle politische Phänomene und Entwicklungen oder um eine viel weiter und tiefer reichende allgemeine Kritik, die man dann eigentlich gar nicht mehr Kritik nennen dürfte: ich meine — im Anschluss an Herrn Steiners Bemerkungen zum 1. Stasimon der *Antigone* — die tiefe Einsicht in die tragische Dialektik der menschlichen Situation als soziales Wesen: er kann nicht leben ausserhalb der πόλις und innerhalb der πόλις kann er in gewissem Sinne auch nicht 'leben', d.h. er kann sich nur verwirklichen als Teil eines sozialen Ganzen, zugleich aber kann er sich auch nicht voll in allen seinen Möglichkeiten und Träumen, verwirklichen als Teil des Ganzen, das ständig Einschränkungen auferlegt und Kompromisse verlangt.

M. Knox: It seems to me the critique of the πόλις goes much deeper than any reference to the contemporary situation, in fact I would accept Bernd Seidensticker's admirable formulation of tragic dilemma posed by the existence of the individual in a social context which he cannot live without but which restrains his freedom.

Kjeld Matthiessen, in the article I referred to in my paper, sees the dark mood of the last two plays as a reflection of Sophocles' rejection of the leaders and policies of imperial Athens in the final years of the war; I tried to show that the critical attitude to the πόλις is a constant in Sophoclean tragedy and goes much deeper than contemporary allusion.

M. Taplin: Phrynichus' error was that he dramatised οἰκήια κακά (Hdt. VI 21), suffering too particular to his audience. I would agree with the sentiment that the politics within tragedy transcend those of their immediate historical world, or, rather, that these are subsumed into a broader political setting.

M. Seidensticker: Haben Sie eine Erklärung für die Zurückdrängung des politischen Aspekts in der *Elektra*? Handelt es sich um eine Antwort oder doch Reaktion auf die aischyleische (oder vielleicht auch die euripideische) Version des Stoffs?

M. Knox: No, I have no ready explanation for the absence of the political element in *Electra*. It may be simply that Sophocles felt it necessary to write a play that was clearly not a remake of the *Choephoroe*—remember the scholion which explains that Ajax in Sophocles kills himself on stage because Aeschylus had already described the suicide in a messenger speech. It may be, too, that he wished to concentrate attention on the hatreds of the family so as to suggest the menacing future Winnigton-Ingram has so eloquently presented: the political theme of liberation of the city would have undercut that effect.

II

Jean Irigoin

STRUCTURE ET COMPOSITION DES TRAGÉDIES DE SOPHOCLE

Le titre de cet exposé réclame quelques explications pour que les limites en soient déterminées d'entrée de jeu. Il y sera question des tragédies — et non pas de la tragédie — de Sophocle, l'emploi du pluriel visant à éviter toute généralisation abusive. En effet, à la différence de la comédie ancienne, dont les éléments ont été analysés et décrits par T. Zielinski dès 1885 dans sa *Gliederung der altattischen Komödie* — titre où le mot comédie est au singulier — la tragédie attique présente une structure beaucoup plus souple. De plus, chacune des sept tragédies de Sophocle offre des particularités structurelles qui ne permettent pas de les ramener à un patron unique.

D'autre part, en opposant structure et composition, je cherche à distinguer un cadre formel et la manière dont le poète le remplit quand il compose son œuvre, l'ensemble aboutissant à la composition que nous avons aujourd'hui sous les yeux comme un texte à lire alors qu'il était fait pour être représenté. J'écarte donc délibérément tout ce qui concerne le déroulement de l'action, avec ses péripéties et les relations dialectiques des épisodes ou des scènes, et renvoie pour cela aux ouvrages spécialisés dont le plus récent est la thèse estimable d'Albert Machin [1].

La première contrainte structurelle qui s'impose au poète tragique est la durée de la représentation: le temps dont il disposera au théâtre détermine les limites extrêmes de son œuvre. Il est notable, à cet égard, que les tragédies d'Eschyle, à l'exception d'une, aient un nombre de vers presque fixe: quatre se situent entre 1073 et 1078 vers (*Perses*: 1077; *Sept*: 1078; *Suppliantes*: 1073; *Choéphores*: 1076), soit un écart moyen de 3 vers (1075 ± 3); deux autres s'éloignent un peu, les *Euménides* avec 1047 vers et, s'il est d'Eschyle, *Prométhée* avec 1093 vers, soit, pour les six tragédies, un écart moyen de 23 vers (1070 ± 23); avec 1673 vers, l'*Agamemnon* est d'une longueur exceptionnelle par rapport à ce que nous connaissons de la production d'Eschyle. Certes, ces nombres, si frappants à première vue, peuvent être quelque peu trompeurs: le début du prologue des *Choéphores* comporte des lacunes, le dénouement des *Sept* passe pour être le résultat d'un remaniement, enfin les *côla* lyriques sont décomptés au même titre que les vers du dialogue. Il reste que la durée de la représentation s'impose au poète même si ce n'est pas la clepsydre qui la règle comme pour les plaidoyers. Sophocle semble avoir été moins rigide ou moins strict qu'Eschyle, puisque sa production varie de 1278 vers *(Trachiniennes)* à 1779 vers *(Œdipe à Colone)*. Si l'on met à part cette pièce dont la représentation fut posthume, le total maximum est de 1530 vers avec *Œdipe Roi*, d'où un écart moyen de 126 vers (1404 ± 126) pour les six tragédies: la marge de variation est donc cinq fois plus grande que pour Eschyle, alors que le total moyen des vers n'est supérieur que d'un cinquième (exactement 22%). En composant des tragédies qui comptent un nombre de vers plus grand et plus varié, Sophocle semble

[1] A. Machin, *Cohérence et continuité dans le théâtre de Sophocle* (Haute-Ville [Canada] 1981).

être moins asservi que son devancier à une durée fixe de représentation. La place tenue respectivement par les chants et par le dialogue — le débit de ce dernier étant plus rapide — pourrait justifier l'augmentation du nombre moyen des vers chez Sophocle par rapport à Eschyle. Certes, dans la production même de Sophocle, le pourcentage des vers parlés varie entre 65,5% (*Antigone*: 1353 vers) et 77% (*Œdipe Roi*: 1530 vers), ce qui paraît en accord avec cette hypothèse; mais la pièce la plus courte, les *Trachiniennes*, contient 74,5% de vers parlés sur un total de 1278, alors que la plus longue, *Œdipe à Colone*, n'en a que 70% pour un total de 1779 vers. Il vaut donc mieux renoncer à l'essai d'explication proposé à l'instant.

Une fois déterminées les limites, et donc l'extension de la pièce, la structure interne de la tragédie a pour fondement l'alternance de parties où seul le chœur chante et de parties où les acteurs dialoguent, que ce soit entre eux ou avec le chœur, et même si la déclamation fait place au chant. Ce principe capital admet quelques aménagements; il arrive que des chants dialogués soient substitués à des chants du chœur, par exemple en fonction de *parodos*, comme c'est le cas dans *Électre* et dans *Œdipe à Colone*. Éléments de suture entre le prologue et le premier épisode *(parodos)* ou entre les épisodes successifs *(stasima)*, les chants du chœur ont une structure à la fois fixe (responsion antistrophique ou triadique) et libre (forme et nombre des éléments strophiques). La liberté du poète croît dans les chants alternés lyriques ou semi-lyriques, mais, à de rares exceptions près, la responsion est de règle, avec des finesses remarquables aussi bien dans le jeu d'échange des parties que dans la répartition des éléments de vers non chantés [2]. Enfin, les systèmes anapestiques, avec

[2] Je me contenterai de mentionner, pour la répartition régulière des trimètres insérés dans le chant, le passage d'*Œdipe à Colone* (v. 1447-1499) où chacune des strophes du chœur, à l'exception de la dernière, est suivie de cinq trimètres iambiques dits les

leur débit particulier — la *parakatalogè* — et leur accompagnement musical, paraissent laissés à la discrétion du poète, qui les emploie librement mais s'astreint à y introduire une responsion s'il les traite comme un morceau lyrique, ce qui arrive à Sophocle dans les anapestes de la *parodos* d'*Électre*, chantés par l'héroïne et non confiés au chœur [3].

Le rôle fondamental de la responsion dans les ensembles lyriques ou semi-lyriques, son caractère secondaire dans les systèmes anapestiques, où la liberté du poète va croissant, semblent impliquer que cette liberté culminera dans les parties de la tragédie qui sont parlées — prologue et épisodes — et que les vers du dialogue dramatique — trimètre iambique et, fort rare chez Sophocle, tétramètre trochaïque — avec leur répétition stichique et leur absence de variation, ne sont pas soumis à un type de composition proprement

deux premiers et les deux derniers par Œdipe, celui du centre par Antigone; pour l'alternance des personnages qui échangent leurs parties, le troisième couple antistrophique du second *commos* d'*Ajax* (v. 394-429), où, dans l'antistrophe, le coryphée prend la partie tenue par Tecmesse dans la strophe, alors que dans le second couple (v. 364-393), ils échangent leurs parties; pour la répartition des éléments de vers, le chant alterné final d'*Électre* (v. 1398-1441), où l'extrême précision des reprises permet de déceler plusieurs lacunes dans l'antistrophe telle que les manuscrits médiévaux nous l'ont transmise.

[3] Dans les v. 86-120, l'attaque par un monomètre, la suite de deux dimètres catalectiques en troisième et quatrième positions, faits exclus des systèmes anapestiques habituels, avertissent le lecteur du caractère lyrique de ces vers (A. Dain et P. Mazon, dans leur édition de Sophocle [t. II, p. 141, n. 1], sont d'un avis contraire), caractère confirmé par la composition antistrophique du passage (bien vue par les mêmes auteurs), qui se divise en deux strophes égales (à un monomètre près, suppléé *in lacuna* par R. D. Dawe au v. 115 de son édition), dont la seconde offre aux quatre premiers vers (v. 103-106) les particularités signalées au début du morceau. On peut rapprocher, dans les *Trachiniennes*, le système anapestique qui introduit le chant alterné entre Héraclès, Hyllos et le vieillard (v. 971-1003): la structure et la répartition des vers 974-982 répond à celle des vers 984-992, y compris la coupe exceptionnelle avant la longue de l'anapeste second aux vers 981 et 991; les trois premiers vers (v. 971-973), qui servent d'introduction, ont exactement la même composition que les vers 1 et 3-4 des deux strophes du chant d'Électre (v. 86 et 88-89 = 103 et 105-106) mentionné ci-dessus, soit un monomètre anapestique et une suite de deux dimètres catalectiques.

lyrique, hormis le cas où ils font partie d'un ensemble partiellement chanté. Il est d'ailleurs exceptionnel, chez Sophocle, qu'une correspondance s'établisse entre le nombre des vers de deux tirades où s'affrontent deux personnages soutenant des thèses opposées, comme le font Créon et Hémon dans *Antigone*: aux 42 vers de Créon (v. 639-680) répondent, après une brève intervention du coryphée, 41 vers d'Hémon (v. 683-723). Le procédé est bien attesté chez Euripide (Médée et Jason: 54 vers chacun; Polymestor et Hécube: 51 vers chacun; Clytemnestre et Électre: 40 vers chacune), mais Sophocle n'en offre qu'un exemple [3 bis] et encore avec une égalité seulement approchée dans laquelle on pourrait voir un effet du hasard. Toutefois, si l'on considère non pas seulement deux tirades, mais tout l'ensemble auquel elles appartiennent, des parallélismes apparaissent, plus significatifs qu'une simple égalité qui pourrait être aléatoire. En voici deux exemples.

Les tirades de Créon et d'Hémon font partie d'un ensemble plus vaste qui constitue la première des deux scènes du troisième épisode d'*Antigone*, de l'entrée d'Hémon à sa sortie brutale (v. 631-765). Le tableau ci-dessous (à lire de gauche à droite et de haut en bas) permet de mesurer la précision du parallélisme:

Créon	coryphée	Hémon	
4		4	
42	2	41	
	2		
2		2	
14 × 1		14 × 1	(stichomythie)
4		4	
66	4	65	

[3 bis] Pour les tirades égales placées à distance, voir p. 45 ma remarque sur cinq tirades d'*Ajax*.

Le parallélisme est évident et on serait tenté, avec Dindorf que suit Dawe, de rendre la symétrie parfaite en supposant l'omission d'un vers dans la tirade d'Hémon, après le v. 690. Ce type, assez simple, où les adversaires s'affrontent à armes égales aussi bien dans le débat oratoire que dans la stichomythie, se présente comme un diptyque dont les deux brèves interventions du coryphée seraient les charnières.

A cette structure parallèle où le second personnage utilise chaque fois le même nombre de vers que le premier quand il lui répond, créant ainsi une responsion de type antistrophique comparable à celle des chants alternés, s'oppose la structure symétrique du second exemple, représenté par la deuxième scène du premier épisode d'*Électre* (v. 328-471). Les deux sœurs, Électre et Chrysothémis, en cherchant à justifier chacune son comportement, se dressent l'une contre l'autre, notamment dans une stichomythie de 30 vers (v. 385-414). Cette stichomythie est placée exactement au centre de la scène: elle est précédée de 57 vers (v. 328-384) et suivie de 57 vers (v. 415-471). De plus, les deux premiers échanges de la première partie comptent 41 vers, la suite en rassemblant 16; les deux premiers échanges de la seconde partie comptent 16 vers, la suite 41. On peut représenter la répartition des vers de la manière suivante:

57	41	13	(Chrys.)
		28	(Él.)
	16	3	(coryphée)
		4	(Chrys.)
		2	(Él.)
		7	(Chrys.)

stichomythie de 30 vers (15 Él., 15 Chrys.)

57	16	2	(Él.)
		14	(Chrys.)
	41	33	(Él.)
		2	(coryphée)
		6	(Chrys.)

L'ensemble est organisé symétriquement de part et d'autre de la stichomythie centrale qui joue le rôle d'une mésode, soit A B A' ou A^1 A^2 B $A^{2'}$ $A^{1'}$.

A côté des structures parallèles ou symétriques, des constructions plus complexes apparaissent, dont la scène 2 du cinquième épisode d'*Ajax* offre un bon exemple. Une discussion s'élève entre Ulysse et Agamemnon au sujet de Teucros et de sa décision d'enterrer, malgré la défense d'Agamemnon, le cadavre d'Ajax. De l'entrée d'Ulysse à la sortie d'Agamemnon (v. 1318-1373) la discussion occupe 56 vers: 14 vers de dialogue entre les deux rois (v. 1318-1331), 7 pour Ulysse et 7 pour Agamemnon, répartis symétriquement (2-2-2-1 / 1-2-2-2), une tirade d'Ulysse de 14 vers (v. 1332-1345), une stichomythie de 24 vers s'achevant par 4 vers d'Agamemnon, soit 28 au total (v. 1346-1373). Dans cette scène, la répartition des vers se fait par 7 et par multiples de 7 (14, 28, 56) selon une construction linéaire fondée sur un module de base et sur ses multiples, comme le montre le tableau suivant:

28	14 (7 × 2)	dialogue entre Ulysse (7) et Agamemnon (7)
	14 (7 × 2)	tirade d'Ulysse
28	28 (7 × 4)	stichomythie Agamemnon/Ulysse (24 vers), conclue par 4 vers d'Agamemnon
56	(7 × 8):	total

Pour le type de construction, ce passage peut être rapproché de la première scène du quatrième épisode d'*Électre* (v. 1098-1231), où Oreste, qui ne s'est pas fait connaître, arrive avec Pylade et l'urne censée contenir les cendres du frère d'Électre. Le dialogue entre Oreste, le coryphée et Électre occupe 28 vers (v. 1098-1125), soit 7 × 4; la question d'Électre: « Que dis-tu, étranger? » (Τί δ' ἔστιν, ὦ ξέν') se situe au 15e vers (v. 1112), coupant le dialogue en deux parties à la fois opposées et égales, de 14 vers (7 × 2) chacune. La tirade d'Électre se lamentant sur le sort d'Oreste et sur le sien (v. 1126-1170) compte 42 trimètres, soit 7 × 6, où s'insèrent trois éléments exclamatifs numérotés comme es vers (v. 1160-1162). La fin de la scène comporte 3 vers du coryphée et 2 d'Oreste (v. 1171-1175), puis une longue stichomythie de 44 vers (v. 1176-1219) entre Électre et Oreste, qui, avec la révélation qu'Oreste est vivant et présent, s'achève en une hémistichomythie de 7 vers (v. 1220-1226); au déséquilibre des v. 1209-1210, où Oreste dit un hémistiche et Électre un vers et demi, répond celui des v. 1222-1223, où Électre dit un hémistiche et Oreste un vers et demi, ce qui rétablit l'équilibre de l'ensemble, soit 25 vers ½ pour chacun des personnages. A la fin de l'hémistichomythie se produit un changement: Électre s'adresse non plus à Oreste, mais au chœur («O femmes chéries, femmes de ma ville...», Ὦ φίλταται γυναῖκες, ὦ πολίτιδες), qui lui répond en la personne du coryphée (v. 1227-1231), de sorte que pendant 5 vers le dialogue entre le frère et la sœur s'interrompt avant de reprendre sous une forme différente, dans un chant alterné semi-lyrique. L'ensemble de la scène se présente donc de la manière suivante:

28 (7 × 4)		dialogue en deux parties (14 et 14)	
42 (7 × 6)		tirade d'Électre	
56 (7 × 8)	5	répliques du coryphée (3) et d'Oreste (2)	
	44	stichomythie	d'Électre et Oreste
	7	hémistichomythie	d'Électre et Oreste
5		répliques d'Électre (3) et du coryphée (2)	

On notera la symétrie, soulignée par des pointillés, des deux groupes de cinq vers qui encadrent l'ensemble de la stichomythie.

Dans la seconde scène du deuxième épisode d'*Œdipe Roi* (v. 297-462), Tirésias révèle à Œdipe la vérité à laquelle le roi de Thèbes se refuse à croire. La scène se divise en deux parties égales: d'une part l'introduction du coryphée (3 vers), la première tirade d'Œdipe (16 vers) et le dialogue entre Tirésias et Œdipe (64 vers), soit au total 83 vers (v. 297-

379); d'autre part, à la suite de l'affirmation catégorique de Tirésias, «Ce n'est pas Créon qui te perd, c'est toi» (v. 379), la seconde tirade d'Œdipe (24 vers), une brève intervention du coryphée (4 vers) et la réplique de Tirésias (21 vers), un nouveau dialogue entre Œdipe et Tirésias (18 vers) et la seconde tirade du devin (16 vers), soit encore au total 83 vers (v. 380-462):

83	3	introduction du coryphée
	16	première tirade d'Œdipe
	64	dialogue entre Tirésias et Œdipe
83	24	seconde tirade d'Œdipe
	4	intervention du coryphée
	21	réplique de Tirésias
	18	dialogue entre Œdipe et Tirésias
	16	seconde tirade de Tirésias

Le nombre des vers dits par Œdipe, 82, est, à une unité près, égal à la moitié de ceux qui constituent la scène.

La notion de scène, à laquelle il a été fait appel plusieurs fois au cours de cet exposé, paraît avoir été ignorée d'Aristote, qui, dans sa *Poétique* (12, 1452 b 20-21) définit l'épisode comme «une partie entière de la tragédie» (μέρος ὅλον τραγῳδίας) qui se trouve placée entre «des chants entiers du chœur». Il ne mentionne pas de subdivisions de cette partie qualifiée d'entière, mais les faits de symétrie, de parallélisme et de construction modulaire relevés dans des scènes entières montrent que, pour Sophocle, la notion existe bien. Peut-on alors étendre ces observations à un épisode entier, voire à plusieurs épisodes d'une même tragédie? Nous allons chercher à répondre à cette question en examinant d'abord la structure d'*Électre*.

La seconde scène (v. 328-471) du premier épisode de cette tragédie présente une structure symétrique qui vient d'être décrite (*supra*, pp. 44-45): deux parties égales de 57 vers encadrent une stichomythie de 30 vers, soit au total 144 vers

(57 + 30 + 57). Le second épisode (v. 516-822) se divise en trois scènes. Dans la première, Clytemnestre et Électre s'affrontent, la mère adressant des remontrances à sa fille et cherchant à justifier sa conduite passée, Électre discutant les arguments de sa mère et finissant par l'insulter: le total des vers est aussi de 144 (v. 516-659). L'arrivée du précepteur, venu annoncer la prétendue mort d'Oreste et en raconter toutes les circonstances, marque le début de la seconde scène, qui compte une nouvelle fois 144 vers (v. 660-803). La scène s'achève avec la sortie du précepteur et de Clytemnestre; restée seule, Électre clame son désespoir dans un monologue de 19 vers (v. 804-822) qui, à la manière d'une épode, constitue la scène finale de l'épisode. L'égalité du nombre des vers des deux premières scènes (144 et 144) et la reprise du total des vers de la scène immédiatement précédente (144) ont peu de chances d'être l'effet du hasard, surtout si l'on tient compte de la structure symétrique de cette dernière scène (57 [16 + 41] - 30 - 57 [41 + 16]).

L'étude détaillée de la première scène du deuxième épisode confirme cette impression. Elle comporte trois tirades: deux de Clytemnestre (v. 516-551 et 634-659), avec 36 et 26 vers, une d'Électre (v. 558-609), avec 52 vers [4], soit au total 114 vers (36 + 26 + 52). La suture entre la première tirade de Clytemnestre et la réplique d'Électre est assurée par 6 vers de dialogue (v. 552-557); entre cette réplique et la seconde tirade de Clytemnestre (v. 610-633), le nombre des vers dialogués est doublé, soit 12, et ils sont suivis de 12 vers en distichomythie; le total des vers dialogués de tout genre est donc de 30 (6 + 12 + 12). On retrouve ainsi, avec une distribution différente, les totaux de 114 et de 30 que l'on

[4] R. P. Winnington-Ingram (*Sophocles. An Interpretation* (Cambridge 1980), 220 n. 13) fait justement remarquer: «Opposed speeches in Euripides tend to be of approximately equal length. It may be worth noticing that, while Clytemnestra is given 36 lines, Electra is given 52, but the *rational* portion of her speech ends at 594 (37 lines)!»

avait dans la scène finale de l'épisode précédent. Si l'on prend garde à l'unique intervention du coryphée (v. 610-611) qui suit la réplique d'Électre à Clytemnestre, on distinguera dans la scène deux volets inégaux : 96 vers d'une part (v. 516-611), 48 de l'autre (v. 612-659), soit un rapport de 2 à 1, qui est aussi celui de la tirade d'Électre (52 vers) à la seconde tirade de Clytemnestre (26 vers) [5].

La scène suivante (v. 660-803), qui commence avec l'arrivée du précepteur, compte elle aussi 144 vers, répartis de la manière suivante : le récit de la prétendue mort d'Oreste, qui occupe une tirade de 84 vers (v. 680-763), est encadré de deux parties dialoguées dont la première (v. 660-679), où le précepteur annonce la mort d'Oreste au 14e vers, compte 20 vers, et dont la seconde (v. 764-803), qui fait connaître les réactions du coryphée, de Clytemnestre et d'Électre, en compte 40 (avec une tirade de 15 vers pour Clytemnestre). Le rapport entre les deux parties d'encadrement est de 1 à 2, inverse de celui qui reliait les deux volets de la scène précédente. Le total des vers dits par le précepteur est de 96 (84 + 12), nombre dans un rapport de 2 à 1 avec les 48 vers dits par les autres personnages (Clytemnestre : 36 ; Électre : 8 ; coryphée : 4). On notera l'importance des multiples de 12 dans le détail de la scène :

tirade du précepteur	84 = 12 × 7
autres vers dits par le précepteur (9 + 3)	12 = 12 × 1
(d'où total des vers dits par le précepteur	96 = 12 × 8)
vers dits par Clytemnestre	36 = 12 × 3
vers dits par Électre et le coryphée (8 + 4)	12 = 12 × 1
(d'où total des vers dits par les autres personnages	48 = 12 × 4)

[5] Si — et ce sera l'unique exception à la règle que je me suis imposée — on tient compte non plus des seuls éléments formels, mais du contenu et du mouvement de la scène, on observera que la seconde tirade de Clytemnestre est une prière, en relation avec le sacrifice dont elle parle au v. 630, dans la distichomythie ; du coup, la scène se divise en deux parties dont la première (v. 516-629) compte 114 vers et la seconde (v. 630-659) 30 vers.

Le troisième épisode d'*Électre* est fait d'une scène unique de 187 trimètres (v. 871-1057) : Chrysothémis vient annoncer à Électre le retour de leur frère, Électre la détrompe et lui propose d'agir avec elle pour tuer Égisthe ; au terme d'une vive discussion, les deux sœurs se séparent. La scène comporte trois tirades, deux de Chrysothémis (v. 892-919 et 992-1014, soit 28 et 23 vers) et une d'Électre (v. 947-989, soit 43 vers), et divers éléments de stichomythie et de distichomythie dont le plus long (v. 1023-1049) se trouve placé vers la fin de l'épisode. Si l'on déduit du total des vers la tirade d'Électre, la plus longue, on obtient 144 (187 – 43). Le même nombre 43 est celui des vers qui suivent immédiatement la seconde tirade de Chrysothémis, au moment où le coryphée s'adresse à Électre, et s'étendent jusqu'à la fin de l'épisode (v. 1015-1057). Le nombre 43 revient enfin dans le total des vers dits par Électre dans le dialogue. Dans l'épisode entier, l'équilibre entre tirades et dialogue est parfait pour Électre (43 vers de part et d'autre), approché à une unité près (en raison du total impair, 187) pour l'ensemble des personnages (tirades : 94 [28 + 23 + 43] ; dialogue : 93).

La première scène (v. 1098-1231) du quatrième épisode a déjà été analysée (voir *supra*, pp. 45-46) ; il suffit de rappeler le rôle qu'y jouent les nombres multiples de 7 : 14, 28, 42 et 56 [6]. Après le duo lyrique d'Électre et Oreste (v. 1232-1287), le dialogue reprend (v. 1288-1325) entre le frère et la sœur qui mettent au point leur plan de vengeance en deux tirades de 13 (Oreste) et 21 vers (Électre), suivies de 4 vers dialogués, soit au total 38 vers. Une nouvelle scène commence lorsque le précepteur sort du palais (v. 1326-1383) : tirade du précepteur (13 vers comme pour Oreste à la scène précédente), qui invite les jeunes gens à la prudence (v. 1326-1338), et bref dialogue

[6] Sur le rôle des multiples de 7, voir aussi la première scène du troisième épisode d'*Antigone* (*supra*, pp. 43-44) et la deuxième scène du cinquième épisode d'*Ajax* (*supra* p. 45).

(v. 1339-1345) avec Oreste (7 vers); puis dialogue de 8 vers entre Électre et Oreste à propos de l'identité du précepteur (v. 1346-1353), suivi d'une tirade de 10 vers où Électre exprime sa joie et sa reconnaissance (v. 1354-1363), soit au total 18 vers; enfin deux courtes tirades du précepteur (8 vers), qui rappelle que le moment d'agir est venu, d'Oreste (4 vers), qui invite Pylade à pénétrer dans le palais (v. 1364-1375), et prière d'Électre à Apollon (v. 1376-1383), soit 12 (8 + 4) et 8 vers. La scène est donc faite de 58 vers au total (20 + 18 + 12 + 8) dans une structure qui présente des symétries internes (20-18-20 et, pour le dernier total de 20, 8-4-8) et externe (38 [de la scène précédente]-20-38), l'addition des deux scènes aboutissant à 96 vers (12 × 8). Le nombre des vers dits par Électre dans la seconde des deux scènes est de 22, dans un rapport de 2 à 1 avec ceux que dit Oreste, 11.

L'épisode final compte, après un *commos*, 66 trimètres répartis entre les deux scènes par lesquelles s'achève la tragédie (v. 1442-1507). Le bref dialogue entre Égisthe et Électre (v. 1442-1465) est fait de trois éléments de 8 vers, une stichomythie occupant la place centrale: 8 [6 + 2] — 8 (stichomythie) — 8 [6 + 2]; Égisthe récite 16 vers, Électre 8, dans un rapport de 2 à 1 qui est aussi celui du dialogue à la stichomythie. Dans la dernière scène (v. 1466-1507), qui se passe en présence du cadavre de Clytemnestre, la tirade d'Électre pressant Oreste de tuer Égisthe est placée au centre: comptant 7 vers ½, elle est précédée de 17 vers ½ de dialogue entre Égisthe et Oreste, et suivie de 17 vers dits par les deux mêmes personnages, soit au total 42 vers (7 × 6); la répartition des vers entre Égisthe et Oreste est égale (17 vers ¼ pour chacun) malgré l'inégalité des répliques.

Reste le prologue de la tragédie. Il compte 85 vers dans les éditions, mais seulement 84 trimètres, car le v. 77 n'est qu'un cri d'Électre (Ἰώ μοί μοι δύστηνος) qui gémit à l'intérieur du palais. La tirade initiale du précepteur, destinée avant tout à informer le spectateur (22 vers), est suivie d'une tirade d'Oreste qui expose son plan de vengeance (54 vers); au cri d'Électre, un bref dialogue s'engage entre les deux hommes (8 vers: 2 + 2 + 4). Au total, 56 vers sont dits par Oreste, 28 par le précepteur, dans un rapport de 2 à 1 qui est déjà apparu plusieurs fois dans l'analyse des épisodes.

Le nombre des trimètres du prologue, 84, nous livre deux des clés de la structure de la tragédie. Ce nombre [7] est en effet le produit de 7 et de 12. Le premier facteur, évident dans le total des vers dits par Oreste (56 = 7 × 8) et par le précepteur (28 = 7 × 4) dans le prologue, reparaît dans la première scène du premier épisode: 77 vers (7 × 11), avec une tirade d'Électre de 56 vers (7 × 8) et un dialogue entre elle et le coryphée de 21 vers (7 × 3). Le facteur 12 apparaît dans la scène suivante et dans les deux premières scènes du deuxième épisode, qui comptent chacune 144 vers (12 × 12). Les deux scènes dont le nombre des vers n'est pas un multiple de 12, la première du premier épisode (77 vers) et la dernière du deuxième (19 vers), ont ensemble 96 vers (77 + 19 = 96 = 12 × 8), le total des vers des deux épisodes étant de 528 (77 + 144 + 144 + 144 + 19 = 528 = 12 × 44). On a vu comment, dans le troisième épisode, la triple répétition du nombre 43 était comme une invitation à reconnaître dans 187 le résultat de l'addition de 144 et de 43. Les multiples de 7 (14, 28, 42, 56) et de 12 (96) sont à la base de la structure du quatrième épisode et se retrouvent dans l'épisode final (42 [7 × 6] d'une part, 24 [12 × 2] de l'autre), dont le total des vers, 66 (6 × 11), est comme un rappel de la scène initiale du premier épisode, qui compte 77 vers (7 × 11); la somme de 66 et 77, 143 (13 × 11), est, à une unité près, égale au nombre 144 (12 × 12) déjà signalé trois fois. Le total des vers des trois derniers épisodes: 187 + 227

[7] Nombre qui est aussi celui des vers de la tirade où le précepteur raconte la prétendue mort d'Oreste (v. 680-763).

[131 + 38 + 58] + 66 [24 + 42], est de 480, encore un multiple de 12 (12 × 40). Il s'ensuit que le total des trimètres dans la pièce entière (84 + 528 +480) ne peut être qu'un multiple de 12: 1092 (12 × 91). Et 91 est lui-même un multiple de 7 (7 × 13). Ainsi les deux nombres de base de la structure de la tragédie, 7 et 12, se trouvent associés dans le décompte d'ensemble comme ils l'étaient, à titre d'annonce, dans le prologue: de 84 (7 × 12) on aboutit à 1092 (7 × 12 × 13). En d'autres termes, le total des vers des épisodes est égal à 12 fois celui du prologue: 1008 [528 + 480] = 12 × 84 = 12 × 12 × 7. Enfin, comme pour établir un lien entre les trois blocs multiples de 12, soit 84, 528 et 480, le personnage d'Électre participe à la *parodos*, ce qui est inhabituel, pour ne pas dire exceptionnel, et chante dans le *commos* qui, de façon non moins exceptionnelle, est substitué à un *stasimon* entre les deuxième et troisième épisodes, c'est-à-dire à la suture entre les blocs, multiples de 12, qui regroupent respectivement les deux premiers épisodes et les trois autres [8]. Le tableau ci-joint permet de prendre une vue d'ensemble de la répartition des trimètres dans la tragédie.

ELECTRE

Prologue (v. 1-85) *		84 trimètres	84 (12 × 7)
Premier épisode (v. 251-471)		221 trimètres	528 (12 × 44)
Scène 1 (v. 251-327)	77		
Scène 2 (v. 328-471)	144		
Deuxième épisode (v. 516-822)		307 trimètres	
Scène 1 (v. 516-659)	144		
Scène 2 (v. 660-803)	144		
Scène 3 (v. 804-822)	19		

[8] Cette division en deux parties rappelle la composition en diptyque des plus anciennes tragédies de Sophocle; voir aussi la discussion, p. 70.

Troisième épisode (v. 871-1057)		187 trimètres	
Scène unique	187		
Quatrième épisode (v. 1098-1383)		227 trimètres	
Scène 1 a (v. 1098-1231)	131 **		
[Commos (v. 1232-1287)]			
Scène 1 b (v. 1288-1325)	38		480
Scène 2 (v. 1326-1383)	58		(12 × 40)
Cinquième épisode (v. 1398-1510)		66 trimètres	
[Commos (v. 1398-1441)]			
Scène 1 (v. 1442-1465)	24		
Scène 2 (v. 1466-1507)	42		

Total: 1092 trimètres (12 × 7 × 13)

* Le vers 77 est anapestique et non iambique (cri d'Électre à l'intérieur du palais).

** Les vers 1160-1162 sont anapestiques (cris d'Électre au milieu de sa plainte).

Avant de nous interroger sur le sens de ces décomptes, sur le rôle de ces calculs, il convient d'examiner si le cas est isolé dans les tragédies de Sophocle. Et puisqu'*Électre* est une tragédie tardive, qu'on l'estime ou non postérieure à celle qu'Euripide a fait jouer sous le même titre en 413, un examen de *Philoctète*, représenté en 409, peut nous fournir d'utiles éléments de comparaison.

En raison du temps dont je dispose, je me contenterai de commenter le tableau ci-dessous qui offre, scène par scène, le décompte des trimètres iambiques de *Philoctète*, établi selon les mêmes principes que celui d'*Électre*:

PHILOCTÈTE

Prologue (v. 1-134)			134 trimètres	
Premier épisode (v. 219-675)			432 trimètres	432
«Scène» 1 (v. 219-390) *	171			(12 × 36)
Scène 1 (v. 219-390, 403-506 et 519-541)		298		
«Scène» 2 (v. 403-506)	104			
Scène 2 (v. 542-627)		86		
«Scène» 3 (v. 519-675)	157			
Scène 3 (v. 628-675)		48		
Deuxième épisode (v. 730-826) **			87 trimètres	
Deuxième épisode (v. 730-826) **			87 trimètres	
Troisième épisode (v. 865-1080)			216 trimètres	216
Scène 1 (v. 865-973)		109		(12 × 18)
Scène 2 (v. 974-1080)		107		
Quatrième épisode (v. 1218-1471)			211 trimètres	
Scène 1 (v. 1218-1262) †		45		
Scène 2 (v. 1263-1292)		30		
Scène 3 (v. 1293-1307)		15		
Scène 4 (v. 1308-1401) ††		94		
Scène 5 (v. 1418-1444)		27		

Total: 1080 trimètres (12 × 90)

* Le vers 219 est réduit à une exclamation (Ἰὼ ξένοι).

** Les vers 732, 736, 739, 751, 785, 787, 790, 796 et 804 sont des cris ou des exclamations; le vers 782 est fait de deux dochmies.

† Le vers 1251 bis, rétabli par Hermann, n'a pas été décompté.

†† Les vers 1365 a et 1365 b, supprimés par tous les éditeurs depuis Brunck, n'ont pas été décomptés.

Le premier épisode (v. 219-675) est divisé en trois parties par un chant du chœur dont la strophe (v. 391-402) et l'antistrophe qui lui répond (v. 507-518) sont séparées par une centaine de trimètres; dans chacune des parties ainsi déterminées, on dénombre respectivement 171 (v. 219-390), 104 (v. 403-506) et 157 trimètres (v. 519-675). La division est tracée nettement par le poète, mais si l'on s'en tient à la notion de scènes marquées par l'entrée ou la sortie d'un personnage, comme il a été fait pour *Électre* et comme il sera fait pour la suite de *Philoctète*, l'épisode comporte trois scènes, dont la seconde commence avec l'arrivée du marchand (v. 542) et se termine avec son départ (v. 627). La première scène (v. 219-541, moins les chants du chœur v. 391-402 et 507-518) compte 298 trimètres (171 + 104 + 23), la seconde 86 (v. 542-627) et la troisième 48 (v. 628-675). Quelle que soit la division adoptée, le total des trimètres de l'épisode est de 432 (171 + 104 + 157, ou 298 + 86 + 48). Ce nombre est un multiple de 12 (12 × 36) égal à la somme des trois scènes successives et égales que nous avons vues dans *Électre*, avec 144 vers chacune (432 = 144 × 3).

Laissant provisoirement de côté le deuxième épisode, nous observons que les deux scènes du troisième ont un nombre de trimètres presque égal: 109 pour la première (v. 865-973) et 107 pour la seconde (v. 974-1080): le total est de 216 (109 + 107), soit exactement la moitié du nombre des vers du premier épisode (216 = 432: 2 = 12 × 18). Le quatrième et dernier épisode (v. 1218-1471) est fait de cinq scènes qui comptent respectivement 45 (v. 1218-1262), 30 (v. 1263-1292) et 15 vers (v. 1293-1307) pour les trois premières, qui sont en décroissance régulière, 94 pour la quatrième (v. 1308-1401) et, séparés par un système anapestique, 27 pour la cinquième (v. 1418-1444). Le total des vers du dernier épisode est donc de 211 (45 + 30 + 15 + 94 + 27). En additionnant le prologue, avec 134 trimètres (v. 1-134), le deuxième épisode, avec

87 trimètres (v. 730-826), et le quatrième épisode, avec 211 trimètres (v. 1218-1471), on obtient le total de 432, déjà vu pour le premier épisode (432) et dont le nombre des vers du troisième épisode (216) est exactement la moitié. D'autres corrélations méritent d'être relevées: le total des vers des deuxième et quatrième épisodes, soit 87 et 211, est de 298, comme celui de la longue première scène (v. 219-541) du premier épisode; le nombre des vers du deuxième épisode (87) est, à une unité près, égal à celui de la seconde scène (86) du premier épisode; le nombre des vers du prologue, 134, est égal au total des vers des deux dernières scènes du premier épisode (86 + 48). Mais il faut s'arrêter pour en venir au résultat final: *Philoctète* compte au total 1080 trimètres (134 + 432 + 87 + 216 + 211), soit 12 × 90; pour *Électre*, le total était de 1092, soit 12 × 91.

*

* *

Les observations qui viennent de vous être présentées sont fondées sur le texte de Sophocle tel qu'il nous a été transmis par les manuscrits médiévaux — l'apport des papyrus est réduit à peu de chose pour cet auteur — et tel qu'il figure dans les éditions critiques; aucune retouche au nombre des vers du texte n'a été apportée de mon chef [9]. Ces observations, dont le nombre et la cohérence montrent qu'elles ne sont pas dues au hasard, attestent d'abord, pour *Électre* et *Philoctète*, la fidélité de la tradition médiévale. Il ne s'ensuit pas que cette fidélité soit égale pour les autres tragédies. Je me contenterai de mentionner brièvement le cas d'*Œdipe à Colone*. Cette pièce, qui a été représentée après la mort de Sophocle par les soins de son petit-fils, offre entre le

[9] Avec les éditeurs, depuis Brunck, j'ai écarté du décompte les vers 1365 a et 1365 b de *Philoctète*.

prologue et les divers épisodes des relations numériques exactes ou approchées qui témoignent d'un type de construction analogue [10]:

ŒDIPE A COLONE

Prologue (v. 1-116)		116 trimètres
Premier épisode (v. 254-509)		254 trimètres
Scène 1 (v. 254-323) *	68	
Scène 2 (v. 324-509)	186	
Deuxième épisode (v. 549-667)		119 trimètres
Scène unique		
Troisième épisode (v. 720-1043)		298 trimètres
Scène 1 (v. 720-832)	113	
Scène 2 (v. 844-875)	32	
Scène 3 (v. 891-1043)	153	
Quatrième épisode (v. 1096-1210)		115 trimètres
Scène unique		
Cinquième épisode (v. 1249-1555)		253 trimètres
Scène 1 (v. 1249-1446) **	197	
[Commos (v. 1447-1499)]		
Scène 2 (v. 1500-1555)	56	
Sixième épisode (v. 1579-1779)		91 trimètres
Scène unique (v. 1579-1669)		

* Les vers 315 et 318 ne sont que des exclamations.
** Le vers 1271 est une exclamation.

Le prologue et les deuxième et quatrième épisodes ont un nombre de trimètres presque égal, soit, dans l'ordre, 116, 119 et 115; les premier et cinquième épisodes ont le même nombre de vers à une unité près, soit 254 et 253; le troisième épisode, le plus long, compte 298 trimètres, nombre que

[10] Dans l'analyse en cinq mouvements symétriques qu'il propose de la tragédie, R. P. WINNINGTON-INGRAM (*op. cit.*, 254) constate que les mouvements sont à peu près de la même longueur, le troisième étant le plus long, et il ajoute: «This symmetrical design is handled and modified with a Sophoclean flexibility».

nous avons rencontré dans *Philoctète* pour la longue scène 1 du premier épisode et pour la somme des deuxième et quatrième épisodes; enfin, la somme des vers des deuxième (119), troisième (298) et sixième (91) épisodes est égale à 508, soit le double du premier (254) et du cinquième à une unité près (253).

Il suffirait d'un rien pour établir un équilibre exact, par exemple en ajoutant un vers, qui aurait été perdu dans la traduction manuscrite, au quatrième épisode (qui passerait de 115 à 116) et au cinquième (qui atteindrait le total de 254). La tragédie entière compterait alors, au lieu de 1246 trimètres, 1248, soit 12 × 104. Mais on voit les risques d'une telle pratique.

A en juger par les faits que nous avons relevés, les tragédies les plus récentes de Sophocle présentent une structure numérique dont le caractère ne peut pas être aléatoire. Des faits comparables apparaissent dans les tragédies plus anciennes, tels ceux qui ont été mentionnés au début de cet exposé à propos d'*Antigone*, d'*Ajax* et d'*Œdipe Roi*, mais l'ensemble de la structure n'est pas aussi net, sans qu'on puisse déterminer si la différence est due à des variations dans les principes de composition de Sophocle ou à des fautes de la tradition manuscrite. Ce sera l'objet d'une autre recherche.

D'autres questions restent en suspens, même pour des pièces comme *Électre* ou *Philoctète*, dont la structure est bien assurée. Je ne fais que les mentionner ici, en me réservant d'y revenir dans la discussion si le besoin s'en fait sentir. En voici quelques exemples: les tétramètres trochaïques, fort rares chez Sophocle il est vrai [11], sont, malgré leur caractère de stiques, exclus de la structure, qui est bâtie exclusivement sur le décompte des trimètres iambiques; dans les morceaux semi-lyriques, les trimètres iambiques alternant avec des vers

[11] Dans *Œdipe Roi*, 16 tétramètres remplacent les anapestes traditionnels à la fin de la tragédie (v. 1515-1530); *Philoctète* contient 6 tétramètres (v. 1402-1407); *Œdipe à Colone*, 4 (v. 887-890).

chantés font partie dudit morceau et ne participent pas à la structure fondée sur les seuls trimètres du dialogue parlé; l'intégration, dans cette structure, des chants du chœur (*parodos* et *stasima*), des chants alternés lyriques ou semi-lyriques, des systèmes anapestiques et des tétramètres trochaïques est un problème capital auquel je m'intéresse, mais que je me contenterai de signaler ici.

Une autre question, non moins importante, est celle de l'originalité de Sophocle: la structure numérique décelée avec certitude dans certaines de ses tragédies lui est-elle propre, ou est-elle une pratique d'usage courant chez les poètes dramatiques? Je penche pour la seconde solution [12]. Mais, que Sophocle innove ou qu'il suive une tradition littéraire antérieure, il reste que son mode de composition paraît être le suivant: une fois établi le cadre dans lequel va se développer l'action tragique, Sophocle détermine le contenu des épisodes et des scènes non seulement selon les nécessités de l'action, mais en tenant compte, pour le nombre des vers qu'il leur affectera, de calculs arithmétiques qui peuvent surprendre. Tant qu'il s'agit de parties chantées, des calculs périodologiques paraissent indispensables dans un genre où la musique et la chorégraphie jouent un rôle important, sinon décisif. Dans le dialogue serré, de type stichomythique, l'égalité des répliques, en longueur comme en nombre, est la loi de cette pratique. Mais partout ailleurs, dans le dialogue ordinaire, dans les tirades, dans les monologues, comment croire que le poète se livre à de savants exercices d'équilibre ou de symétrie qui restreignent sa liberté et brident son inspiration?

C'est là un argument auquel les hellénistes sont très sensibles. Autant ils sont prêts à reconnaître, dans tous les types de poésie lyrique, l'existence de règles impératives que le poète admet au départ (le schéma métrique de la strophe

[12] Ce que confirment, avec une prudence insuffisante à mes yeux, les travaux récents de W. BIEHL, notamment ses éditions d'*Oreste* (1975) et d'*Ion* (1979) d'Euripide.

alcaïque ou de la strophe sapphique, par exemple) ou se fixe lui-même avant de composer ou dès le début de sa composition (la première strophe ou la première triade, dans la lyrique chorale, détermine la forme de la suite de l'œuvre), autant ils répugnent à admettre l'existence de telles contraintes dans le dialogue parlé de la tragédie. A ceux qui allégueraient les règles de la tragédie classique française, avec son découpage en cinq actes et son respect des trois unités, il est aisé de répondre en montrant la souplesse de la tragédie grecque, qui n'est pas astreinte aux trois unités et dont le nombre des épisodes varie au gré du poète. Mais comment nier, au vu des observations faites au cours de cet exposé, que Sophocle respecte des règles de composition, même si elles sont étrangères à l'idée que nous nous faisons aujourd'hui de la manière d'écrire une tragédie?

Il faut rappeler, à ce propos, que les premières observations sur la composition symétrique de certaines parties du récitatif tragique ont été faites au milieu du siècle dernier par Prien, Ritschl et Weil. La systématisation qu'ont voulu en faire quelques philologues dans le dernier quart du XIXe siècle semble avoir dévalorisé les premiers résultats obtenus. Il suffit de se reporter à la structure d'*Ajax* «in der supponierten älteren Fassung» que J. J. Oeri décrit à la fin (p. 44) de son étude sur *Die Sophokleische Responsion*, parue à Bâle en 1903, pour comprendre les réticences de la plupart de ses contemporains. La tragédie est divisée en huit parties disposées en deux volets où elles se répondent deux à deux: les parties I et II sont égales respectivement aux parties VII et VIII; de même, les parties III et IV sont égales aux parties V et VI. Ces relations à la fois parallèles et symétriques pourraient être représentées de la manière suivante:

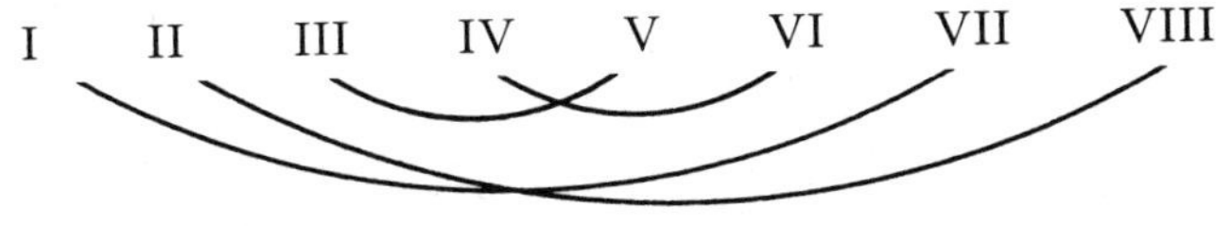

Le résultat est séduisant, mais pour l'obtenir il a fallu :

a) ne pas décompter les vers 333, 336, 339, 737, 974, 1062 qui ne sont pas des trimètres iambiques [13];

b) reconnaître comme inauthentiques les vers 327, 554 b, 571, 812, 839 à 842;

c) admettre une lacune d'un vers à l'intérieur du vers 1305;

d) considérer comme des remaniements — c'est-à-dire des additions postérieures du poète — les passages 263-281 (soit 19 vers), 480-484, 1266-1271, 1291-1294.

Les hellénistes du temps d'Oeri, et on les comprend, ont été effrayés de ces corrections violentes, qui leur ont paru trop souvent faites pour rétablir des équilibres défaillants ou créer des équilibres inexistants.

Aussi, pour éviter de prêter à mon tour le flanc à des critiques justifiées, j'ai adopté dans cet exposé une démarche qui me paraissait prudente, peut-être à l'excès. J'ai parié, en quelque sorte, sur la fidélité de la tradition manuscrite alors que je savais d'expérience combien les vicissitudes de la transmission du texte peuvent entraîner de fautes [14]. Il me semble n'avoir pas cédé à ce démon qui, de tentation en tentation, attire le philologue dans l'enfer des reconstitutions. C'est pourquoi je pense que les observations que je vous ai présentées, notamment les correspondances et les enchaînements dans le nombre des vers, témoignent d'une volonté délibérée du poète et ne sont pas l'effet du hasard. Sophocle détermine par ce moyen la structure à l'intérieur de laquelle il composera son œuvre.

Un tel mode de composition, qui implique un cadre préalable comme ces édifices modernes dont l'ossature est

[13] Il s'agit là de cris ou d'exclamations qui doivent être écartés du décompte des trimètres, comme cela a été fait dans nos propres relevés.

[14] Il suffit de renvoyer, à titre d'exemple, au chant alterné final d'*Électre*, mentionné à la p. 41-42, n. 2.

érigée jusqu'au sommet avant qu'on ne commence à mettre en place la façade et les autres murs, peut nous paraître surprenant, ou même irréaliste. Et cela d'autant plus que les analyses présentées ne portent que sur des éléments formels : division en épisodes et en scènes, distinction des tirades et du dialogue, traitement particulier des stichomythies, attribution des vers à tel ou tel personnage ; tout ce qui relève du contenu a été écarté délibérément, par crainte d'un possible subjectivisme et afin que la démonstration reste fondée sur des faits objectifs, aisément constatables et ne donnant pas prise à la critique. Mais alors ne risque-t-on pas de vider la tragédie de son contenu dramatique et de tuer tout ce qui est de nature poétique? En fait, il n'est pas question de privilégier la structure ; il faut seulement reconnaître son existence et, lorsqu'elle est aussi bien conservée que dans *Électre* ou *Philoctète*, l'admettre telle quelle, ce qui n'est pas sans conséquence pour l'établissement du texte. Et pour ce qui est d'une opposition fondamentale entre l'inspiration poétique la plus haute — celle d'un Hölderlin dans les derniers hymnes, celle d'un Rilke dans les *Élégies de Duino* — et des calculs mathématiques antérieurs à la composition, je voudrais citer ce qu'en dit un poète parlant d'une de ses œuvres, Paul Valéry. Son poème *Le cimetière marin* venait d'être expliqué en Sorbonne — ce qui, à l'époque, ne se produisait pas du vivant de l'auteur. En guise de préface à l'« Essai d'explication » que Gustave Cohen avait tiré de son cours, Valéry livra quelques confidences [15] dont je reproduis un passage : « Si l'on s'inquiète... de ce que j'ai « voulu dire » dans tel poème, je réponds que je n'ai pas *voulu dire*, mais *voulu faire*, et que ce fut l'intention de *faire* qui a *voulu* ce que j'ai *dit*...

[15] Editées dans *Variété III* (Paris 1936), 57-74 ; le passage cité ici est aux pp. 68-69.

Quant au «Cimetière Marin», cette intention ne fut d'abord qu'une figure rythmique vide, ou remplie de syllabes vaines, qui me vint obséder quelque temps. J'observai que cette figure était décasyllabique, et je me fis quelques réflexions sur ce type fort peu employé dans la poésie moderne; il me semblait pauvre et monotone. Il était peu de chose auprès de l'alexandrin, que trois ou quatre générations de grands artistes ont prodigieusement élaboré. Le démon de la généralisation suggérait de tenter de porter ce *Dix* à la puissance du *Douze*. Il me proposa une certaine strophe de six vers et l'idée d'une composition fondée sur le nombre de ces strophes.»

Cette confidence réclame une glose pour qui n'est pas familier avec la poésie française. L'alexandrin est un vers de douze syllabes. Une strophe de six décasyllabes compte soixante syllabes, soit l'équivalent de cinq alexandrins (6 × 10 = 5 × 12). Enfin, *Le cimetière marin* est un poème de vingt-quatre strophes, soit, à raison de six vers chacune, cent quarante-quatre vers (12 × 12), et nous rejoignons là, par un cheminement différent mais non pas tout autre, les scènes de 144 vers d'*Électre* et les totaux à base 12 d'*Électre* (12 × 91) et de *Philoctète* (12 × 90); les cent quarante-quatre décasyllabes du poème français sont en quelque sorte la monnaie de cent vingt alexandrins, et nous avons, une fois de plus, le «*Dix* à la puissance du *Douze*». On pourrait gloser aussi sur l'opposition établie entre le *dire* et le *faire* en rappelant l'étymologie si claire du mot ποιητής en grec, et comparer la «figure rythmique vide, ou remplie de syllabes vaines» qui vient obséder le poète à ce premier vers de la première des *Élégies de Duino* qui fut donné à Rilke un jour de tempête, au bord de l'Adriatique, et mit fin à une longue période de stérilité artistique.

Il ne faudrait pas déduire de ce rapprochement entre Valéry et Sophocle, établi à vingt-quatre siècles de distance, qu'il existe deux types de poésie, l'un où l'inspiration spontanée ferait fi de toute règle et l'autre où le poète calculerait à l'avance le cadre qu'il va remplir en le respectant. La «figure rythmique vide» de Valéry est antérieure à ses calculs. Et Rilke est aussi l'auteur des *Sonnets à Orphée*; or le sonnet est un poème à forme fixe qui compte toujours 14 vers.

Avec ces dernières remarques, j'espère avoir rassuré ceux d'entre vous que pourrait choquer ou scandaliser l'idée d'un Sophocle composant ses tragédies selon une structure numérique, que les limites en soient tracées à l'avance ou déterminées progressivement au cours de la composition, par approximations successives. Que l'on croie ou non à l'existence de contraintes que le poète s'impose au préalable ou qui viennent s'imposer à lui, il reste — et sur ce point nous serons tous d'accord — que son art n'en souffre pas, comme le montrent, dans leur variété, les autres exposés de ces XXIXes Entretiens.

DISCUSSION

Mme de Romilly: Je voudrais remercier M. Irigoin des résultats étonnants qu'il vient de nous communiquer. Certains sont extraordinairement frappants. Évidemment, l'on peut s'interroger sur la possibilité pour l'auditeur de saisir des harmonies et des équilibres aussi subtils. Mais j'aimerais rappeler que M. Irigoin avait fait à notre Académie des Inscriptions une communication relative à l'*Hélène* d'Euripide. Il y montrait des rapports aussi savants entre les diverses parties de cette tragédie et M. H. I. Marrou avait répondu à une question comme celle que je viens de poser en rappelant qu'en musique, et chez Bach en particulier, il y a des constructions tout aussi précises et complexes, que l'auditeur ne peut évidemment pas saisir; mais il saisit une impression générale d'ordre. Il pourrait en être de même dans des cas comme ceux qui nous occupent. De toute façon, même si l'on n'est pas convaincu par toutes les analyses, certaines suffisent à montrer qu'il s'agit d'un art mesuré, structuré, équilibré, qui se situe à l'opposé des interprétations 'primitivistes' trop souvent acceptées dans les évocations modernes du théâtre grec: la religion, la passion, l'angoisse peuvent s'exprimer selon le plus savant de tous les ordres. Et il est frappant que cela se révèle au niveau des parties parlées et à l'échelle de grands ensembles.

M. Knox: L'exposé de M. Irigoin nous fera beaucoup réfléchir. Il révèle, dans les dialogues parlés de la tragédie sophocléenne, des structures qu'on peut qualifier, sans exagérer, de mathématiques. Pour les équivalences et correspondances quantitatives qu'il nous a montrées à l'intérieur d'une scène — dans le deuxième épisode de l'*Œdipe Roi* par exemple, ou dans la première scène du troisième épisode de l'*Antigone*, je suis convaincu de l'exactitude et de l'importance des rapports découverts par M. Irigoin. Pour les rapports structuraux entre deux, ou même trois épisodes, rapports qui certainement échappaient à l'assistance — le fait, par exemple, que l'*Électre* est bâtie selon une formule 91 × 12, que le total de vers parlés dans le troisième épisode du *Philoctète* est exactement la moitié du total du quatrième — je m'avoue embarrassé.

Dans le premier cas — la symétrie à l'intérieur de la scène, reposant sur deux tirades de même longueur — l'assistance, comme le poète, était dans un monde connu: celui des discours exactement égaux, réglés par la clepsydre, dans les procès qui se déroulaient devant les héliastes. Mais les autres correspondances complexes, cachées, ne sont pas apparentes; il est dès lors difficile de comprendre en vue de quels effets le poète s'y serait astreint. Pourriez-vous nous expliquer, M. Irigoin, comment vous concevez l'intention du poète, son but, pour ainsi dire, dans la création des correspondances les plus arcanes et complexes?

M. Winnington-Ingram: Would it not be wise, as a control, to test the plays of Aeschylus and Euripides to see if similar numerical phenomena are to be found there? If so, they might be regarded as a traditional technique; if not, the question arises why Sophocles alone of the tragedians employs it.

M. Irigoin: Assurément, M. Winnington-Ingram a raison de me conseiller d'examiner si des faits numériques similaires se rencontrent ou non chez Eschyle et chez Euripide. En parlant d'une éventuelle originalité de Sophocle dans ce domaine, j'ai laissé entendre qu'on avait affaire, selon moi, à une pratique d'usage courant chez les poètes dramatiques. Mais, découvrant ces faits à l'occasion de nos Entretiens sur Sophocle, je n'ai pas eu le temps d'analyser de la même manière les œuvres des autres tragiques. Il conviendrait en outre de s'assurer, pour chaque tragédie, de l'état de conservation du texte. Mon propos, pour le moment, était de vous soumettre mes observations, de connaître vos premières réactions, d'accueillir d'éventuelles suggestions ou critiques.

En réponse à M. Knox, je dirai que diverses possibilités d'interprétation s'offrent à nous: volonté délibérée du poète, qui établit à l'avance un cadre précis, à remplir ultérieurement; détermination progressive des éléments au cours de la composition, avec des approximations nécessaires et des retouches finales pour assurer l'équilibre de la construction; on peut songer à d'autres explications encore; mais il y en a une — une seule — que j'exclus: celle qui consiste à attribuer au hasard les résultats des dénombrements que je vous ai soumis.

M. Seidensticker: Es scheint mir (darin stimme ich mit B. Knox überein), dass die numerische Analyse vor allem für die Einzelszene von Bedeutung sein kann, indem sie uns z.B. die symmetrische Ausgewogenheit eines Agons oder einer Streitstichomythie und damit die strukturelle Basis des dramatischen Rhythmus der Szene vor Augen stellt. Unsicher scheint mir dagegen der interpretatorische Gewinn des Versuchs, mehrere Szenen oder ganze Stücke auf zugrunde liegende konstante Zahlenverhältnisse zu untersuchen, eben weil dabei der dramatische Rhythmus unberücksichtigt bleibt. Zwei Szenen mit gleicher Verszahl oder Verszahlen, die sich auf dieselben Grundzahlen (z.B. 7 oder 12) zurückführen lassen, können doch total verschieden sein in ihrem dramatischen Rhythmus und in ihrem thematischen Gewicht, d.h. dem Rezipienten keineswegs das Gefühl emotionaler und thematischer Symmetrie vermitteln, das die zugrunde liegenden Zahlenverhältnisse suggerieren könnten.

Hinzu kommt, dass die wachsende Freiheit, mit der Sophokles in seinem Spätwerk die Bauformen der griechischen Tragödie handhabt, in einem schwer zu erklärenden Widerspruch zu den von Ihnen vorgelegten verblüffenden Zahlen zu stehen scheint.

Mme de Romilly: Mais on peut admettre que le rythme intérieur et la régularité extérieure se superposent, coexistent.

M. Irigoin: Par ses remarques, M. Seidensticker met bien en relief la difficulté que j'ai moi-même rencontrée en préparant mon exposé. A l'intérieur d'une scène, l'helléniste est tout prêt à reconnaître des faits de symétrie ou d'équilibre, d'autant plus que certains, dans le cas des stichomythies par exemple, sont créés de façon automatique. En pareil cas, il ne peut que constater un accord entre la base structurelle et le rythme dramatique.

Mais lorsque des faits de ce genre apparaissent dans deux scènes du même épisode, dans deux épisodes, voire dans la tragédie entière, comment ne pas éprouver une inquiétude, qu'elle soit spontanée ou réfléchie?

Lorsque, pour *Électre*, j'ai constaté que des dénombrements non significatifs en apparence se regroupaient en de plus grands ensembles qui, numériquement, semblaient significatifs, j'ai eu le sentiment que c'était trop beau pour être vrai: ne risquais-je pas d'être le jouet du hasard? Un peu plus tard, l'examen de *Philoctète*, confirmant les observations faites sur *Électre*, m'a un peu rassuré.

Aujourd'hui, la situation me paraît être la suivante. Ou bien on dénie toute signification aux résultats du dénombrement des vers, et pour M. Seidensticker c'est au nom du désaccord entre le rythme dramatique de scènes qui comptent le même nombre de vers, pour d'autres c'est en raison de l'impossibilité, pour les spectateurs, d'enregistrer ces effets lorsqu'ils se produisent à distance ou sous forme de récapitulations. Ou bien, observant que les nombres ont été obtenus à partir de divisions formelles aisément vérifiables et sans que, dans un souci d'objectivité, il ait été tenu compte de leur valeur et de leur contenu dramatique, on est amené à s'interroger sur l'existence d'un fait supplémentaire, d'interprétation peut-être difficile, mais qu'il faudra bien, d'une façon ou d'une autre, intégrer au commentaire et donc à l'idée d'ensemble que nous nous faisons d'une tragédie de Sophocle.

Que ce fait se manifeste dans les dernières de nos tragédies, où le poète assouplit les formes traditionnelles, n'est pas une objection en soi. C'est d'abord une constatation qu'il restera à expliquer.

M. Winnington-Ingram:

a) Is the audience likely to have been sensitive to these correspondences, to all or to some of them; and if so, in a precise way (which seems highly unlikely) or in an approximative or sub-conscious way (in which case exact numerical correspondence will not matter)?

b) One should distinguish:

(i) structures demanded by the dramatic rhythm, which might involve such correspondences, but are as likely—or more likely—to run against them;

(ii) the general love of symmetry and balance characteristic of much Greek art, visual and verbal;

(iii) the numerically based correspondences (sometimes operating at a considerable distance) which are the subject of M. Irigoin's paper.

M. Irigoin: Il me paraît bien présomptueux, pour ne pas dire impossible, de me mettre à la place des spectateurs d'Athènes pour déterminer comment ils percevaient correspondances et équilibres numériques. Je ferai donc une entorse au principe d'objectivité formelle que j'ai adopté dans ma recherche, en vous renvoyant, à propos d'*Électre*, aux deux phases que M. Winnington-Ingram reconnaît dans l'évolution de l'héroïne et à leur correspondance avec la division de la tragédie en deux parties, que j'ai proposée pour des motifs d'équilibre numérique (voir *supra*, pp. 53-54): les spectateurs pouvaient être sensibles à la coïncidence de l'évolution dramatique avec les éléments de la construction formelle. Mais le problème fondamental reste pour moi, avant tout, de savoir si ces faits d'ordre numérique sont des réalités dont il faut tenir compte. Les distinctions proposées par M. Winnington-Ingram sont certainement valables. Il a bien vu l'importance que j'accordais aux faits de la troisième catégorie. Mais je crois avoir déjà répondu assez longuement à M. Seidensticker sur ce dernier point.

Mme de Romilly: La musique a été évoquée tout à l'heure: je précise que c'était seulement pour ce qui concerne les auditeurs et la possibilité pour eux de percevoir des équilibres d'ensemble sans connaître les secrets qui étaient en cause. Quoi qu'il en soit, la structure des parties chantées prouve assez que l'inspiration la plus riche et la plus souple peut se combiner avec une rigueur formelle très stricte — et même dans des ensembles étendus, comme le début de l'*Agamemnon* par exemple. D'ailleurs la mémoire des Grecs d'alors était beaucoup plus grande et mieux exercée que la nôtre: sinon, comment expliquer les échos à distance dans une pièce, les allusions souvent éloignées, les parodies? Il n'est donc pas impossible qu'ils aient été sensibles (l'auteur comme le public, cette fois) à des équilibres formels beaucoup plus étendus que ce à quoi nous sommes sensibles. Je crois que les avertissements méthodologiques sont précieux, que l'enquête doit absolument être étendue à Eschyle et à Euripide, que les résultats peuvent être nuancés, et le rapport avec le sens examiné ; mais quelque chose nous a été montré qui peut, une fois ainsi nuancé et complété, revêtir une grande importance.

M. Reverdin : Ne nous égarons pas. Le spectateur d'une tragédie n'a ni le temps ni les moyens d'en analyser les structures, de compter les vers, de repérer le schéma métrique des strophes. Il la saisit, si l'on peut dire, globalement ; il éprouve des sentiments de sympathie ou d'antipathie pour les personnages ; il craint ou il espère ; il s'indigne ou il approuve.

Les Anciens déjà, et les archéologues modernes après eux, ont scruté le Parthénon : ils y ont repéré des rapports numériques ; ils ont montré à quels effets tend l'*entasis* des colonnes, la ligne légèrement bombée des gradins, l'agencement des métopes et des triglyphes d'angle. Tout cela, nous le savons ; mais quand nous nous trouvons devant le Parthénon, que ce soit pour la première ou pour la centième fois, c'est le monument dans son ensemble que nous saisissons d'un regard global ; l'harmonie qui s'en dégage nous frappe, mais nous ne nous demandons pas de quoi elle est faite : nous l'accueillons avec joie. C'est a posteriori seulement que nous nous interrogeons, que nous analysons, que nous reconnaissons la présence dans le monument de structures numériques très subtiles.

Il en va de même quand nous pénétrons dans le théâtre de l'Asclepieion d'Epidaure. Il nous faut compter les gradins pour découvrir les correspondances numériques que l'architecte y a inscrites. Or notre premier souci n'est pas de procéder à ce décompte : nous nous laissons simplement séduire par l'harmonie du monument, par sa grandeur et par son charme.

Le spectateur d'une représentation tragique n'a pas le temps d'analyser ; encore une fois : il accueille globalement la pièce au fur et à mesure qu'elle déroule devant lui ses épisodes et ses parties lyriques.

M. Irigoin : La comparaison proposée par M. Reverdin est fort suggestive. L'impression de beauté que l'on ressent devant un monument en raison de son équilibre, de son harmonie, de la pureté de ses lignes, est pour la plupart des gens une appréhension globale : on ne cherche pas à restituer dans le détail les calculs de l'architecte, mais on perçoit comme un tout les effets qu'il a voulus.

Dans ces conditions, si Sophocle veut que son œuvre donne à l'auditoire une impression générale d'harmonie et d'équilibre, le plus simple et le plus sûr pour lui n'est-il pas de calculer avec exactitude les éléments destinés à s'équilibrer et à s'harmoniser entre eux, plutôt que de se contenter de mesures approximatives en estimant que le spectateur ne verra pas de différence?

M. Taplin: Clearly the details of formal analysis into 'episode' and 'scene' are crucial for your thesis, and I think there are problems. I have in mind, above all, the way that in his later plays Sophocles breaks down the sequence of episode-stasimon-episode by using various kinds of lyric dialogue (or *kommos*) in the structural transitions, where earlier we find strophic choral odes. This is in keeping with the tendency, already observed, towards a greater freedom and fluidity of technique in his later work.

I would like to draw attention to a question of this sort arising from your analyses of the formal structure of *Ph.* and *OC*:

a) You treat the lyric at *Ph.* 827-64 as dividing the 2nd from the 3rd episode. Yet it is not a purely choral lyric (see Neoptolemus' hexameters at 839-42); and there are no departures or arrivals, but instead, Philoctetes' sinking into unconsciousness and his revival. This may be regarded as separating two episodes, but it is clearly much less marked than a traditional stasimon.

b) The lyric at *OC* 1447-99, on the other hand, is treated by you as a *kommos* within the fifth act, dividing two scenes. It is true that it includes three sets of iambic trimeters spoken by Oedipus and Antigone (in the pattern 2-1-2), but it is preceded by the departure of Polynices at 1446 and followed by the return of Theseus at 1500. Surely this lyric has a more strongly divisive function within the structure than *Ph.* 827-64.

M. Irigoin: Pour distinguer les épisodes et les scènes, j'ai jugé préférable — dans le souci d'objectivité qui a été le mien au cours de ma recherche — de reprendre telle quelle la répartition que Kl. Aichele a présentée dans le recueil de W. Jens (ed.), *Die Bauformen der griechischen Tragödie* (München

1971), 50-51, puisque la division qu'il propose est indépendante de tout présupposé numérique.

Il est certain que, dans les tragédies les plus récentes de Sophocle, des chants alternés jouent le rôle de séparation entre les épisodes, rôle qui est normalement dévolu aux *stasima*. S'il n'y a pas, au sens strict, sortie et entrée d'un acteur de part et d'autre du chant dialogué de *Philoctète* mentionné par M. Taplin, il reste que, en s'endormant et en se réveillant, Philoctète effectue l'équivalent d'une sortie et d'une entrée: son sommeil est une absence.

Dans *Œdipe à Colone*, la présence de deux personnages sur la scène, Œdipe et Antigone, entre le départ de Polynice et l'entrée de Thésée, et la poursuite du dialogue entre le père et la fille pendant que le chœur chante, me paraissent exclure que le *commos* marque ici la séparation entre deux actes: la continuité est évidente!

M. Taplin: Unfortunately I have found Aichele's analyses far from satisfactory, and the application of a less mechanical analysis of the type proposed in my *Stagecraft of Aeschylus* (Oxford 1977), 49-60 (cf. 247) leads to many divergences. Above all the more fluid construction of later Sophocles calls for a less rigid schema. In *Philoctetes* there is only one purely choral ode of the traditional type (676 ff.); in *OC* note the rapid lyric dialogue between two acts at 510 ff.

M. Irigoin: Je viens de m'expliquer sur le choix du relevé d'Aichele qui d'ailleurs, pour Sophocle, ne me paraît pas mauvais. Pour le reste, il est certain que Sophocle, dans ses dernières tragédies, adopte des formes plus simples, qui s'écartent de la rigidité du schéma traditionnel. Mais on n'oubliera pas que, si *Philoctète* ne compte qu'un chant purement choral, *Œdipe à Colone* en comporte quatre, c'est-à-dire autant qu'*Œdipe Roi*.

M. Knox: Dans *Œdipe à Colone*, vous comptez 253 trimètres dans le cinquième épisode, chiffre qui correspond aux 254 du premier; en plus ce chiffre 254 est exactement la moitié du total produit par l'addition des trimètres des épisodes deux, trois et quatre, c'est-à-dire 508. Mais il me semble que vous avez négligé les quinze trimètres qui se trouvent insérés, à intervalles, dans le *commos* du cinquième épisode (vv. 1447-1499).

M. Irigoin: Ces quinze trimètres se présentent en trois groupes identiques de cinq vers, distribués régulièrement. Le premier et le dernier sont dits par Œdipe, celui du milieu, par Antigone (à l'intérieur d'un chant alterné). Ces groupes jouent un rôle d'épirrhême après chacune des strophes chantées par le chœur, à l'exception de la dernière. Les trimètres sont donc partie intégrante d'un morceau semi-lyrique. Or, je l'ai dit (*supra*, p. 60), «les trimètres iambiques alternant avec des vers chantés font partie dudit morceau et ne participent donc pas à la structure fondée sur les seuls trimètres du dialogue parlé». Je n'ai pas prétendu que ces trimètres fussent chantés et vous avez eu raison d'insister sur le fait qu'ils ne se distinguent pas, par leur forme, des trimètres du dialogue.

J'aimerais toutefois revenir sur votre question. Le grand problème, à mes yeux, est celui de l'intégration, dans la structure que j'ai cherché à restituer, de tous les éléments qui n'appartiennent pas au dialogue parlé en trimètres; chants du chœur, chants alternés lyriques ou semi-lyriques, systèmes anapestiques et vers d'un emploi rare, comme le tétramètre trochaïque et l'hexamètre dactylique. La tragédie est faite de tous ces éléments disparates. Il ne suffit pas de restituer la structure des parties parlées, il faut rendre compte de la construction dans son ensemble. Comme je l'ai dit en passant dans mon exposé, c'est un problème capital, et il nous reste à le résoudre.

M. Steiner: Trois remarques s'imposent.

a) Il faut se méfier des analyses 'logistiques', voire mathématiques, que certains poètes, tels Poe et son admirateur Paul Valéry, fournissent de la genèse de leurs poèmes *après coup*. Ces analyses tendent à la fabulation mandarine et même au franc canular.

b) Les analogies entre les aspects mathématiques-numériques de l'architecture et de la musique d'une part, celles d'un texte parlé ou écrit de l'autre, ne doivent être invoquées qu'avec une extrême prudence. Les paramètres géométriques et algébriques d'un bâtiment se laissent, jusqu'à un certain point, rigoureusement démontrer. La musique (classique, du moins) se construit à partir de matrices formelles qui permettent une 'paraphrase', une analyse numérique. La phénoménologie langagière ne permet que très rarement pareille anatomie.

Prennent un caractère plus ou moins strictement dénombrable les palindromes, acrostiches, anagrammes, poèmes miroirs, etc., c'est-à-dire les exercices de virtuosité ludique tels que les pratique, par exemple, le baroque. Mais c'est une règle quasi générale que la construction formellement dénombrable d'un texte est en proportion inverse de sa signification substantielle. C'est le trivial qui se laisse strictement formaliser.

c) Il me semble très possible que la méthodologie que nous propose cette conférence soit pertinente pour des textes brefs, tels qu'un poème lyrique, un sonnet, une stichomythie. Je ne pense pas que de tels schémas d'énumération précise s'appliquent à une masse critique textuelle de l'ordre de grandeur d'une pièce ou d'un roman. Nous ne savons presque rien des rythmes psychosomatiques qui engendrent (?) en nos cultures certaines récurrences, certaines harmonies et pulsions structurelles profondes. Il est difficile de penser qu'il s'agisse là d'une 'volonté délibérée' du poète, notamment à l'échelle d'une pièce sophocléenne.

M. Irigoin: Je remercie M. Steiner de me mettre en garde contre les analyses proposées, après coup, par certains poètes. L'exemple de Valéry a été cité à titre de comparaison et non comme un élément de démonstration.

En revanche, je ne suis pas prêt à le suivre quand il oppose fondamentalement langage et musique, car la poésie participe de l'un et de l'autre: elle reste langage, mais par son rythme elle est aussi musique (sans compter qu'en grec l'accent de hauteur crée l'amorce d'une ligne mélodique).

La troisième remarque de M. Steiner va dans le sens des réticences qui ont été exprimées par plusieurs participants, mais elle s'inspire de motifs différents. Ces derniers doutaient de la possibilité, pour les spectateurs, de percevoir des correspondances à distance et des équilibres dans des ensembles aussi grands qu'un épisode ou une tragédie entière. M. Steiner, lui, refuse toute signification aux correspondances numériques parce qu'elles portent sur ce qu'il appelle une «masse critique textuelle»: la longueur d'une tragédie est telle que des phénomènes inattendus peuvent s'y produire, qu'ils soient dus à des récurrences inconscientes de la part de l'auteur ou à des particularités inexplicables qui apparaissent dans les séries de grands nombres, par exemple pour la répartition des nombres premiers. Les critiques de M. Steiner sont donc d'un ordre tout différent des premières. Comme celles-ci, elles devront être prises en considération dans l'interprétation d'ensemble des faits que je vous ai présentés; mais les convergences que j'ai déjà relevées entre plusieurs tragédies ne m'incitent pas à penser que ces phénomènes soient d'ordre aléatoire.

III

George Steiner

VARIATIONS SUR CRÉON

La fascination, la pression qu'exerçent sur la poétique, sur la théorie politique, sur les débats philosophiques en Occident le mythe d'Antigone et la pièce de Sophocle, sont inséparables de la présence de Créon. Antigone, pour sa part, est absente d'une majeure partie de la pièce. Après sa sortie vers la nuit, le drame appartient à Créon. Refléchissant à la construction apparemment 'scindée' du texte sophocléen, nombreux sont les commentateurs qui proposent comme plus adéquat le titre de 'Antigone et Créon'. Dans les variantes sur les thèmes et motifs du mythe après Sophocle, le rôle de Créon a fait l'objet d'autant de controverses et de reprises que celui d'Antigone. L'intimité du conflit a noué et défini réciproquement leurs identités.

Les origines de Créon, les fonctions formelles et structurelles du personnage à l'intérieur du cycle thébain sont d'une extrême obscurité. Il se pourrait que le noyau en remontât aux rivalités politiques et militaires qui opposèrent Sparte et Thèbes. Créon serait un condottiere lacédémonien victorieux qui avait pris le pouvoir dans Cadmée, mais qui, de ce fait même, serait resté un *outsider* en quête de légitimité. Une scolie des *Phéniciennes* d'Euripide nous fait connaître Créon en qualité d'obscur prédécesseur du lumineux Œdipe.

Ce Créon-ci aurait sacrifié son propre fils à la Sphinx dévorante, sans pouvoir, pour autant, débarrasser ses sujets des exigences meurtrières du monstre. Mais même aux sources opaques du mythe, certaines analogies structurelles persistantes entre Créon et Œdipe se font sentir. Les rixes qui éclatent entre Œdipe d'une part, Créon et Tirésias de l'autre, préfigurent exactement celles qui dressent l'un contre l'autre Créon et Tirésias. Les deux rois se retournent rageusement contre leur fils. Tous deux sombrent dans la ruine et l'autodestruction du fait d'une irrationalité impérieuse.

Les incertitudes, cependant, les indices d'un redoublement structurel qui se rattachent au personnage de Créon, ne proviennent pas seulement de l'obscurité de l'arrière-fond mythique ou de notre perte des épopées dites thébaines.

Nombreuses sont les représentations de Créon dans les tragédies grecques et dans les fragments de tragédies. Il n'est pas possible de réconcilier sur tous les points les diverses conceptions de sa personne. Le Créon tel qu'il est connu d'Eschyle dans *Les Sept contre Thèbes* n'est parent ni de Laios ni d'Œdipe. Le Créon d'*Œdipe Roi*, où son rôle est empreint d'innocence et de noblesse, n'est ni celui d'*Antigone* ni celui d'*Œdipe à Colone*. Dans ce que nous savons de l'*Antigone* d'Euripide, Créon, sous l'influence du *deus ex machina*, pardonne à Hémon et à Antigone et reconnaît leur enfant comme son héritier légitime [1]. Dans *Les Phéniciennes*, la pièce qui est, avec *La Thébaïde* de Stace, à l'origine de la plupart des Créons postérieurs au bas moyen âge, le personnage devient complexe, quasiment au point d'atteindre une contradiction interne à la fois fonctionnelle et psychologique.

Créon est, ici, oncle paternel d'Etéocle. Il se tient aux côtés du jeune prince en qualité de stratège et de conseiller. C'est lui qui propose la défense des sept portes par sept preux. Etéocle sent peser sur lui l'imminente fatalité. S'il disparaît,

[1] Cf. T. B. L. Webster, *The Tragedies of Euripides* (London 1967), 181-4.

c'est à Créon que doit revenir la couronne. Ce sera à Créon de protéger sa sœur Jocaste et d'assurer l'union d'Hémon et d'Antigone. Quant au vieil Œdipe, furieux derrière les murs du palais, «il se pourrait que ses malédictions nous détruisent tous». Puis vient un motif capital, et qui pourrait indiquer la volonté d'Euripide de 'corriger' le modèle sophocléen: c'est Etéocle qui ordonne à Créon d'interdire l'inhumation de Polynice. Si Polynice périt au combat, puisse-t-il ne jamais trouver de sépulture en terre thébaine. «Et serait-ce un ami, que souffre la mort quiconque voudrait l'enterrer» (*Phoen.* 777) — commandement dans lequel le mot φίλων est chargé de résonances sophocléennes.

D'atroces ironies guettent le Créon d'Euripide. Il a fait appel à Tirésias pour lui demander comment sauver la cité en péril. Nous savons ce qui en résultera. C'est le fils de Créon, Ménécée, 'le jeune étalon' qui doit être sacrifié pour rendre Arès propice, pour compenser le massacre des guerriers surgis des dents du Dragon lors de la fondation de Thèbes par le lointain Cadmos, de ces guerriers 'aux casques d'or' (y aurait-il ici, je me demande, ainsi que dans la désignation de Ménécée comme 'étalon', bête sacrée à Arès, un sourd vestige des origines spartiates de la maison de Créon?). La riposte de Créon à cette atroce exigence est profondément humaine et paternelle. «Que nul homme ne me rende glorieux (εὐλογείτω) en tuant mes enfants" (*Phoen.* 967). Ce seul vers d'Euripide concentre une entière répudiation des valeurs morales et psychologiques qu'incarne le personnage de Créon dans l'*Antigone* de Sophocle. Le Créon d'Euripide va plus loin: il est prêt à mourir pour son fils, il est en premier lieu père, il n'est qu'en second lieu homme d'Etat héroïque. C'est pour devancer le sacrifice de son père que Ménécée se jette du haut des murailles.

Le mélodrame bat son plein. Etéocle et Polynice s'entretuent dans leur folie homicide. Sorti du palais, Œdipe, ombre démente du passé, prononce avec Antigone le long *threnos*, la lamentation sur l'extinction de la Maison de Laios. Le rôle de Créon est presque sacerdotal : « Je ne parle ni par insolence, ni par hostilité » (*Phoen.* 1592-1593). Tirésias a proclamé sans ambages que la ville malheureuse ne saurait retourner au salut tant que demeure dans son enceinte le vieillard souillé par le destin. A cet endroit, notre texte est défectueux. Mais il existe indubitablement un contraste entre le ton, le registre de sensibilité du dialogue entre Antigone et Créon chez Euripide d'une part, et chez Sophocle de l'autre. Dans les *Phéniciennes*, une lassitude immense l'emporte. Créon se plie à la demande humble et désespérée d'Antigone : elle ne fera que laver les dépouilles de son frère, elle ne lui donnera qu'un baiser d'adieu. Elle menace de tuer Hémon si le mariage lui est imposé. La riposte de Créon est contenue dans l'un des vers les plus équilibrés, les plus harmonieusement serrés de la pièce. Créon de dire que les impulsions altières d'Antigone ne sont pas exemptes de folie, d'obsession destructrice (μωρία : 1680). Ayant dit cela, Créon ordonne calmement à Antigone de quitter Thèbes.

L'épilogue est marqué de lacunes et de lectures incertaines. Le vers 1744 ne nous permet pas de voir clair quant aux manœuvres des gardes après la sortie de Créon. Mais il semblerait qu'Antigone ait pu enlever le corps de Polynice pour l'enterrer en dehors des ὅρια du territoire civique. Cette solution — dont nous trouvons des analogies souvent étudiées dans le droit attique ainsi que dans *Les Lois* de Platon — serait symptomatique du traitement nuancé du mythe chez Euripide. C'est à cette nuance que correspond le statut complexe de Créon.

Nous ne savons que fort peu de choses de l'*Antigone* d'Astydamas, qui remporta un premier prix en 342-41 av. J.-C. [2]. A en juger d'après le précis qu'en donne Hygin,

[2] Cf. G. Xanthakis-Karamanos, *Studies in Fourth-Century Tragedy* (Athens 1980), 48-53.

Créon agit en tyran. Ayant découvert le mariage clandestin d'Hémon et d'Antigone, le despote commande à Hémon de tuer sa femme. Son fils lui obéit puis se suicide. Mais la version qu'Hygin nous fournit de ce drame n'est pas certaine: l'intervention d'Héraclès, telle qu'elle ressort des fragments, suggère au contraire un dénouement heureux (suggestion qui pourrait se rattacher aux indices fournis par certains mythographes sur une parenté, du moins titulaire, entre le divin Héraclès et la lignée de Créon).

C'est l'adaptation de Sophocle faite au IIe siècle av. J.-C. par Lucius Accius qui semble avoir instruit Virgile du thème du conflit entre Antigone et Créon. Ce sera, en revanche, chez Euripide que le Bas-Empire, qu'Alexandrie et que Byzance puiseront leurs connaissances de Créon. En partant de Sénèque, les variantes épiques et oratoires sur 'la matière de Thèbes' telles que nous les trouvons dans le *Roman de Thèbes* du XIIe siècle, dans la *Théséide* de Boccace et ses deux célèbres imitations anglaises, le *Knight's Tale* de Chaucer et le *Story of Thebes* de Lydgate, contiennent des échos lointains, souvent presque imperceptibles, de Sophocle, et se fondent directement sur *Les Phéniciennes* et l'usage de ce texte chez Stace. L'enjeu est important: c'est précisément l'ambiguïté du personnage de Créon tel qu'il est dépeint par Euripide et par Stace, c'est précisément la dialectique qui oppose la prouesse guerrière et l'intelligence politique d'un côté, l'ambition meurtrière, l'aveuglement et le destin suicidaire de l'autre, qui donna à l'imagination des poètes, aux arguments des philosophes, une fructueuse liberté.

Chez Stace, Créon, affolé par la mort cruelle de son fils, provoque le duel fratricide d'Etéocle et de Polynice. Dans *La Thébaïde* de Racine (1664), Créon devient soupirant d'Antigone, voyant en cette union la seule possibilité d'assurer pour son régime des fondements légitimes. C'est à la faveur de son républicanisme stoïque qu'Alfieri, dans son *Antigone* (1777), fait de Créon le type même du tyran, de l'absolutiste à outrance. Chez Alfieri, il ne s'agit pas d'une apologie, pour creuse qu'elle soit, de la raison d'Etat, mais tout simplement du portrait d'un mégalomane. Mais au moment même où Alfieri campe ce Créon quasi caricatural, dans ces dernières décennies du XVIIIe siècle, commence la réhabilitation du frère de Jocaste, la réévaluation poétique, philosophique, psychologique de la personne, des motivations, de la conduite de Créon. C'est vers la fin des Lumières — coïncidence historique lourde de signification — que commence le retour aux complexités et aux richesses de la thématique de Créon, latentes dans l'*Antigone* de Sophocle. Déja la très célèbre représentation de la pièce dans la mise en scène de Ludwig Tieck, avec chœurs et interludes musicaux composés par Mendelssohn, à Potsdam en 1841, nous fait entrevoir un Créon de haute noblesse, placé sous la tragique contrainte des lois de la cité.

Il est évident que cette transmutation du personnage est, avant tout, l'œuvre de Hegel. Tenter une esquisse, fût-elle des plus sommaires, des lectures de l'*Antigone* de Sophocle par Hegel, lectures qui s'échelonnent de ses années scolaires au *Stift* de Tübingen jusqu'aux leçons sur la philosophie de la religion et le concept du droit étatique publiées à titre posthume, dépasserait de très loin le cadre de cette communication (elle-même extraite d'une étude en cours sur les 'Antigones' dans la poétique et la pensée occidentale). Qu'il suffise de dire que la récupération hégélienne du conflit Antigone-Créon sur les plans ontologique, métaphysique, politique, moral et jurisprudentiel constitue l'un des actes herméneutiques, l'un des exercices de recréation analytique et transformatrice les plus puissants, les plus conséquents dans l'évolution de la mentalité moderne et dans l'histoire des rencontres spirituelles *et* philologiques (j'insiste sur ce double aspect) entre la civilisation grecque antique et son héritage en Occident. S'il est un Créon après Sophocle, il est aussi un Créon après Hegel.

Je ne puis ici qu'esquisser les grandes lignes du débat.

Nombreux sont les exégètes et commentateurs qui définissent le conflit essentiel du mythe et de sa version sophocléenne comme celui qui affronterait un code archaïque et familial d'une part et ce que l'on pourrait appeler la raison d'Etat péricléenne de l'autre. C'est en vertu de cette conception que le langage de Créon, sa rigueur juridique et ses tours tactiques dans la polémique sont qualifiés de 'sophistiques' — non pas dans un sens moralement péjoratif, mais dans une perspective technique et historique. Représentant des 'lumières séculaires', Créon s'oppose au transcendantalisme archaïque et focalisé sur la mort qu'incarne Antigone. La déchéance hideuse du clan de Laios serait la démonstration même du caractère périmé et 'maniaque' des mobiles d'Antigone. Le formalisme abstrait, le caractère impersonnel du gouvernement de Créon sont la promesse d'un avenir moins chaleureux mais plus lucide, plus à la mesure de l'homme. Sans doute subsiste-t-il, dans la présentation du personnage chez Sophocle, d'importants vestiges de malaise, de critique envers ce schéma 'progressiste'. Le grand poète était, pour sa part, bien trop conscient de la part des ténèbres, de la part nocturne mais sanctifiée et nourricière de l'irrationnel dans la dynamique immédiate de la conscience des mortels. Néanmoins, nous trouvons dans son *Antigone*, tout autant que dans certains dialogues platoniciens, un examen pénétrant et non entièrement négatif de l'assise du 'sophiste' [3].

Une thèse contraire est avancée avec tout autant de conviction. Ce serait Créon qui, lui, représenterait les valeurs conservatrices. C'est lui le gardien des normes solidement établies de la vie civique, telles que nous les rencontrons dans les prescriptions contre l'ensevelissement du traître en terre

[3] Cf. W. SCHMIDT, «Probleme aus der sophokleischen Antigone», in *Philologus* 62 (1903), 6-9, et R. F. GOHEEN, *The Imagery of Sophocles' Antigone* (Princeton 1951), 92.

natale dans le livre X des *Lois* de Platon et dans ce qui semble avoir été (à en croire Thucydide et Xénophon) l'usage athénien. La provocation d'Antigone ne provient pas de source antique ou primitive. Elle reflète, bien au contraire, l'aube précaire d'idéaux humanistes, d'une éthique de la conscience privée, annonciatrice de Socrate, voire pré-chrétienne, et qui trouvera, selon Hölderlin et d'autres, son aboutissement logique chez Kant. L'appel d'Antigone aux 'lois non écrites' est un appel à l'avenir de l'histoire de la conscience, et, de ce fait même, un défi aux principes reconnus de cohérence dans la cité tels que Créon tente de les sauvegarder [4]. Le refus de Créon de se prêter au jeu libre d'une sensibilité novatrice ferait de lui 'l'anti-sophiste' par excellence et l'homme des réalités.

L'une des lectures les plus influentes a été celle de Karl Reinhardt, pour qui Créon est le type même de l'individu moralement, psychologiquement et intellectuellement borné. Créon est circonscrit, jusqu'à l'aveuglement, dans les bornes de sa profonde médiocrité [5]. Même l'étrange séquence de fatalités qui contrarie ses bonnes intentions à la fin du drame ne serait que le reflet de son incompétence foncière: il est, affirme Reinhardt, «celui qui vient toujours trop tard». Rien de plus faux, riposte un autre lecteur. Ce n'est pas Antigone, mais Créon qui porte en lui la perception aiguë du tragique: «Tel qu'il est devant nous à la fin de la pièce, extérieurement rompu, intérieurement humilié, et finalement entièrement conscient de l'étendue de ses responsabilités... c'est Créon qui fait appel à nos sympathies, et c'est lui qui est le plus proche d'une attitude compréhensive devant le monde tragique.» [6]

[4] Cf. H. Höppener, «Het begrafenisverbod in Sophokles' Antigone», in *Hermeneus* 9 (1936/37), et H. J. Mette, «Die Antigone des Sophokles», in *Hermes* 84 (1956), 131-4.

[5] Cf. Karl Reinhardt, *Sophokles* (Frankfurt 1933), 78 sqq.

[6] R. Goheen, *op. cit.*, 53. Cf. Georges Méautis, *Sophocle. Essai sur le héros tragique* (Paris 1957), 186.

Erreur, disent d'autres. A son heure finale, «le tyran en papier mâché est le plus commun, bien qu'aussi le plus malheureux, des humains» [7]. «D'une fibre vulgaire, sans aucune distinction d'esprit», Créon n'est ni un grand rhéteur dans le nouveau style rationaliste, ni le gardien de principes conservateurs, mais tout bonnement un politique de bas étage séduit par le pouvoir. Et néanmoins, dans son commentaire subtil sur la pièce de Sophocle, commentaire hanté par la pertinence du mythe aux événements du XXe siècle, Gerhard Nebel qualifie Créon de *begeistert*, de 'possédé'. Seule pareille 'possession' saurait expliquer une conviction inflexible, suicidaire, un impératif catégorique qui entraîne l'extinction de sa propre maison et de ses espoirs dynastiques. Non moins que d'autres hauts protagonistes dans certaines tragédies grecques, Créon est entre les mains implacables du δαίμων [8]. Pour certains commentateurs, cette possession par le démoniaque serait en quelque sorte métaphorique: elle serait l'inéluctable conséquence de cette *folliá logica* qui s'est emparée du nouveau régent de Thèbes [9]. D'autres perçoivent dans la conduite de Créon le reflet immédiat de cette vague de folie qui traque la famille de Laios et qui, sous les traits d'Eros, empoigne Hémon. Folie des grandeurs chez Créon, dont la raison succombe à son obsession de la présence altière et secrète d'Œdipe [10]. Créon est un personnage tragique en ce qu'il n'est pas en mesure de lutter avec cette ombre gigantesque.

La majorité des lecteurs de Sophocle et de ceux qui mettent en scène la pièce préfèrent juger Créon en termes d'équilibre et de structure dramatique. Si certains voient en

[7] R. P. Winnington-Ingram, *Sophocles. An Interpretation* (Cambridge 1980), 127.

[8] Cf. Gerhard Nebel, *Weltangst und Götterzorn. Eine Deutung der griechischen Tragödie* (Stuttgart 1951), 181.

[9] Cf. M. Untersteiner, *Sofocle* (Firenze 1955), I 131.

[10] G. F. Else, *The Madness of Antigone* (Heidelberg 1976), 101.

lui un personnage factice, fondamentalement creux [11], la plupart se penchent, au contraire, sur l'admirable dualité du schéma sophocléen. Créon *est* un contrepoids à Antigone, il *est* de dimensions commensurables. Le vrai problème, c'est de mettre en lumière le caractère authentique de cette 'parité'.

Ne sont-ils pas, au fond, profondément ressemblants? Leurs natures n'ont-elles pas précisément les mêmes «arêtes coupantes»? [12] Le traitement de la malheureuse Ismène par Antigone ne correspond-il point, et de près, à celui que subissent Hémon et Antigone elle-même de la part du tyran? L'affinité, l'intimité 'agonique' entre Antigone et son oncle résultent de l'équivalence, de la symétrie parfaite entre deux libertés existentielles. Ni l'un ni l'autre ne pourrait fléchir sans fausser essentiellement son être [13]. Chacun se déchiffre dans l'autre, et le langage que leur fait tenir Sophocle trahit constamment ce fatal miroitement. Tous deux sont des *auto-nomistes*, des êtres humains qui ont pris la loi entre leurs propres mains. Il se trouve qu'à l'échelle locale et temporelle leurs énonciations respectives de la justice sont diamétralement opposées. Mais ils sont jumeaux en ce qu'ils sont obsédés par le concept du droit [14]. D'où l'étroite concordance, l'homologie formelle et substantielle de leurs chutes successives. «Ce qui est terrible en eux *(Furchtbarkeit)* les précipite en avant. Ils tombent dans l'abîme comme des Titans [15].»

[11] Cf. H. Patzer, *Hauptperson und tragischer Held in Sophokles' « Antigone »* (Wiesbaden 1978).

[12] Cf. André Bonnard, *La tragédie et l'homme* (Neuchâtel 1951), 49.

[13] Cf. Gilberte Ronnet, *Sophocle, poète tragique* (Paris 1969), 187.

[14] Cf. M. S. Santirocco, «Justice in Sophocles' *Antigone*», in *Philosophy and Literature* IV 2 (1980), 186.

[15] E. Eberlein, «Über die verschiedenen Deutungen des tragischen Konflikts der Tragödie 'Antigone' des Sophokles», in *Gymnasium* 68 (1961), 30.

Mais c'est le génie de la pièce ou du mythe sous-jacent (Sophocle en fut-il l'inventeur?) que de faire de ces très réelles analogies les corrélatifs, les mises en action, de l'antithèse. L'équilibre dialectique et psychique entre Antigone et Créon n'est pas, comme le voudrait Hegel, celui de deux moralités équivalentes parce que partielles. C'est justement parce que les deux personnages se valent par leur puissance oratoire, par les dimensions de leur présence en scène, qu'une lecture valable de la pièce doit mettre en relief le contraste fondamental entre «la noble folie du sacrifice de soi» d'une part, «et la folie vicieuse» de l'arbitraire et de l'égoïsme aveugle de l'autre [16].

Par quels moyens Sophocle réalise-t-il cette différenciation entre deux sensibilités 'intimement contraires'? Quel est le secret d'un conflit poétique et éthique dont ni l'analyse ni la reprise variable à travers les millénaires ne sauraient épuiser le sens? «Le débat entre Créon et Antigone n'est pas seulement celui de la cité et du foyer familial, c'est le débat de l'homme et de la femme. Créon assimile son autorité politique à celle de son sexe.» [17] Le drame de Sophocle est riche d'échos du débat primordial, tel que nous le connaissons dans l'*Orestie*, sur les fonctions respectives des sexes, sur les primautés masculines et féminines dans l'engendrement et la parenté humaine. «C'est en accord avec son attachement farouche à la cité, avec sa mentalité déductive et étrangère à la réalité que Créon s'appuie fortement sur l'autorité patriarcale (639-47; cf. 635). Sa fixation au patriarcat, bien qu'illogique sur certains points (cf. 182-3), correspond à son attitude anti-féminine, anti-maternelle.» [18] En dernière analyse, il s'agit donc d'un conflit qui oppose les principes masculins et féminins dans la

[16] I. M. LINFORTH, *Antigone and Creon* (Berkeley 1961), 259.

[17] Charles SEGAL, *Tragedy and Civilization. An Interpretation of Sophocles* (Harvard 1981), 183.

[18] *Ibid.*, 184.

conduite de la vie, ce conflit étant, plus que tout autre, celui d'un paradoxal reflet et d'une antinomie irréductible. Suivant cette exégèse, le dire d'Antigone est littéralement 'utérin'; viscéral et immémorial, il surgit d'une communion sororale avec 'la terre et ses morts' (j'emploie à dessein, comme vous le verrez, la terminologie barrésienne). L'univers de Créon est celui de l'immanence masculine, d'un 'être-dans-le-monde' volontariste et braqué sur ces visées d'avenir que nous appelons la politique. Ainsi que l'envisage Charles Segal dans sa récente et fine lecture d'*Antigone*, Créon perçoit la terre sous une double perspective: la terre est à la fois terrain d'action politique et la masse inerte qui doit être labourée à la charrue (d'où la brutalité de sa riposte à Ismène au vers 569: après la mort d'Antigone, «Hémon trouvera bien d'autres champs à labourer»). Pour la fille-sœur d'Œdipe, au contraire, la terre est, comme le dirait Heidegger, «le logis de l'être», la matrice mystérieuse et le foyer toujours ardent des trépassés. Ce qui assure l'immense tension du débat sophocléen serait au-delà même de la finalité de la 'collision' (le mot est de Hegel) morale-politique-juridique, une polarité sexuelle, une scission originelle dans l'espèce humaine. Le πόλεμος pour ainsi dire 'organique' est cruellement visible dans le tableau final: Créon, à la fois nu et brisé dans sa condition d'homme, est debout, comme un tronc d'arbre foudroyé, entre les corps de sa femme et de son fils. Il est souverain absolu d'une terre morte. D'une terre sans femmes.

*
* *

Mais les figures de Créon dépassent de loin le cadre des sciences de l'Antiquité et des commentaires, toujours renouvelés, sur l'œuvre de Sophocle ou d'Euripide. Sa présence ambiguë fascine l'imagination politique bien au-delà du contexte littéraire. L'année 1948, par exemple, produisit non seulement la critique outrancière du Créon hégélien dans l'*Antigone 48* de Brecht (Créon y figure sous les traits d'un chef fasciste et d'un logicien du capitalisme décadent), mais aussi un singulier portrait de Créon, celui que nous propose le pamphlet lapidaire, mi-prose mi-vers, de Charles Maurras, *Antigone, vierge-mère de l'ordre* (publié à Genève par des fidèles du Maître alors en prison). Nous sommes ici devant un total renversement des valeurs coutumières, renversement dont les sources lointaines apparaissent dans les paradoxes polémiques des défenseurs de la monarchie absolue aux XVIIe et XVIIIe siècles. Maurras proclame ce qui fut sa vision de l'*Antigone* de Sophocle depuis sa première jeunesse. Les interprétations courantes de la pièce sont «un contresens complet». Il ne peut y avoir aucun doute que «l'anarchiste», que l'insurgé contre le droit civique et l'ordre politique de la cité n'est *pas* l'enfant d'Œdipe:

> «C'est Créon. Créon a contre lui les dieux de la Religion, les lois fondamentales de la Cité, les sentiments de la Cité vivante. C'est l'esprit même de la pièce. C'est la leçon qui en ressort: Sophocle n'a pas voulu nous peindre seulement le sursaut de l'amour fraternel ni même dans le personnage de Hémon, fiancé d'Antigone, celui de l'Amour tout court. Ce qu'il veut montrer aussi, c'est le châtiment du tyran qui a voulu s'affranchir des Lois divines et *humaines.*»

C'est donc Créon, et non pas Antigone, qui détruira Thèbes, acte de transgression d'une gravité ultime puisqu'il est la négation des devoirs de conservation et de sauvegarde inhérents à toute souveraineté légitime. En livrant un édit qui condamne l'inhumation de Polynice, Créon commet, dit Maurras, «un acte inconstitutionnel». Telle usurpation du droit, venant d'un souverain, telle «illégalité monstrueuse» nous permettent de distinguer clairement entre le rôle du despote et celui du vrai roi. Vu en profondeur, le despotisme de Créon incarne cette extension infiniment dangereuse de l'esprit anarchique au pouvoir politique. Nous devons, en conclut Maurras, réviser complètement notre lecture de

Sophocle. C'est Antigone, 'vierge-mère de l'ordre' (notez les résonances mystiques et catholiques de cette désignation), qui, elle, «incarne les lois très concordantes de l'Homme, des Dieux, de la Cité. Qui les viole et les défie toutes? Créon. L'anarchiste, c'est lui. Ce n'est que lui.»

L'affaire Dreyfus, les divisions politiques et familiales sous l'Occupation, le succès de l'*Antigone* d'Anouilh ainsi que les controverses que suscite ce texte (l'auteur est sommé de le défendre devant un tribunal d'épuration), sensibilisent le milieu intellectuel français aux arguments de Créon et à leurs implications. Une génération après Maurras, mais avec tout autant de brio casuistique, les 'nouveaux philosophes' et la 'nouvelle droite' se saisissent du personnage. Créon, déclare Bernard-Henry Lévy, n'est en rien le porte-parole d'une froide raison d'Etat. C'est lui, au contraire, qui invoque incessamment le haut patronage des dieux:

«Et la vérité c'est que ce prince est d'abord un prêtre, le seul prêtre de la pièce, investissant à soi seul tout le champ du sacré tel qu'il était concevable dans une cité comme Thèbes, à la fin du Ve siècle — non pas la 'loi' contre la 'foi', mais l'une conjointe à l'autre, dans cette 'loi-de-foi' qui est proprement la religion grecque...» [19].

Il en découle que le défi d'Antigone est un défi de l'ordre à la fois sacré et profane, qu'il est, au sens strict du terme, un sacrilège. Antigone «contrevient à cette Justice souveraine dont le texte dit qu'elle est bel et bien l'universalité d'un principe intangible et absolu. Tel est l'ordre du Cosmos grec que la faute d'Antigone est une faute métaphysique qui la met sans débat, non seulement hors la loi, mais hors l'ordre du monde.» D'où, commente Bernard-Henry Lévy, l'effacement total de la vie d'Antigone chez Sophocle et le spectacle «affreux de son propre devenir-rien». Sans les dieux de Créon, d'Ismène et du Chœur, il ne peut y avoir ni cité ni civilisation humaine. Et Lévy de nous apprendre que Sophocle «rapatrie toute conscience dans la clôture de la

[19] Bernard-Henry Lévy, *Le Testament de Dieu* (Paris 1979), 87.

socialité». Ce ne sont pas nos préjugés libéraux et séculaires qui peuvent tirer au clair la signification véridique de la pièce, car l'*Antigone* de Sophocle est «un drame qui est tout écrit du point de vue de Créon, sinon même à sa gloire».

Remarquez par quel biais cette affirmation 'scandaleuse' rejoint le paradoxe maurrassien d'un Créon anarchiste. La 'nouvelle droite' *rapatrie* Créon (le mot est chargé de tonalités conservatrices et chauvines militantes). C'est à nouveau Antigone qui est hors la loi. Mais la lecture de la pièce comme hymne à l'union du religieux et du civique, l'image de Créon comme roi sacerdotal, ne sont que le renversement exact des concepts de Maurras. L'ombre de Bossuet et de De Bonald plane sur ces deux lectures. Créon est un Bourbon oint de l'huile sainte.

L'interprétation de Maurras est préfigurée dans le roman-fleuve d'Alfred Döblin, *November 1918*. Ecrit dans les années 1937-43, ce roman dépeint l'Allemagne durant les semaines apocalyptiques de sa défaite militaire et des tentatives de révolution qui s'ensuivirent. Revenu du front, le jeune Dr Becker rejoint son enseignement dans le gymnase qu'il a quitté, combattant exalté, en 1914. La classe est en train de travailler l'*Antigone* de Sophocle. A l'exception d'un seul 'gauchiste', tous les élèves se rangent du côté de Créon. Sans aucun doute le Dr Becker, porteur de la Croix de Fer et grand blessé, sera-t-il du même bord. Mais voilà qu'il les scandalise en avançant la thèse même que nous trouverons chez Maurras. S'il y a dans la pièce un rebelle, c'est bien Créon. «C'est lui, de par sa volonté tyrannique, de par son orgueil de se trouver enfin vainqueur et roi, qui pense s'élever au-dessus des traditions sanctifiées et de vérités anciennes comme le temps.» C'est par la faute de son entendement, misérablement inadéquat, du poids moral et existentiel de la mort — entendement qui entraînera la ruine de la cité et la sienne — que Créon est un insurgé et un provocateur.

Il se pourrait que Döblin eût subi l'influence du très bel essai de Rudolf Bultmann sur le thème d'Antigone [20]. Le grand théologien insiste sur le fait que les mobiles de Créon ne sont ni «bêtes ni erronés». Créon n'est pas un hypocrite mégalomane. Sa foi est *reiner Diesseitsglaube* — 'pure immanence', 'mondanité absolue', au sens pascalien du terme. Il perçoit pleinement le domaine des morts mais compte l'inclure dans les normes législatives du corps civique. La lutte suicidaire qui le dresse contre sa nièce engage un humanisme et une justice immanents d'une part, et les exigences des forces toujours subversives, bien que légitimes, de Hadès et d'Eros, de l'autre. Qu'il n'y ait point de méprise: si la fin de Créon est exemplaire dans son horreur, il n'y a pas pour Antigone libération ou apothéose. Pour tous deux, juge Bultmann, la puissance de la mort est également écrasante.

Le publiciste et homme politique Conor Cruise O'Brien connaît bien son Maurras, mais il apporte à ses évocations réitérées de Créon et d'Antigone l'urgente angoisse de la tourmente irlandaise. Dans une conférence très remarquée qu'il fit à Belfast en octobre 1968, O'Brien repensa l'agonie de l'Irlande du Nord dans la perspective du soulèvement d'Antigone. «L'acte de désobéissance non-violente» par lequel Antigone veut enterrer Polynice engendre concrètement une suite de violences extrêmes. Il entraîne son suicide, la tentative d'Hémon de tuer son père et son propre suicide, la mort atroce d'Eurydice, et la destruction, non seulement de la personne du souverain, mais de l'ordre établi dans Thèbes. «Un prix bien élevé», commente O'Brien, «pour une poignée de poussière sur le cadavre de Polynice». Si l'édit de Créon est impétueux et irréfléchi, le réflexe d'Antigone ne

[20] Rudolf Bultmann, «Polis und Hades in der Antigone des Sophokles», d'abord publié en 1936 dans une *Festschrift* pour Karl Barth, puis repris dans *Glauben und Verstehen* II (Tübingen 1952).

l'est pas moins. «Ce fut la libre décision d'Antigone et cette décision seule qui causèrent la tragédie. La responsabilité de Créon, plus lointaine, plus indirecte, était d'avoir mis ce potentiel de tragique entre les mains de l'enfant têtue d'Œdipe.»

Cette glose donne à penser. La distance qui sépare Créon de la culpabilité immédiate est celle-là même de l'État dont les droits et les nécessités sont investis, d'une façon quasi anonyme, dans la volonté et la personne du prince. Le péché de Créon est d'avoir enfreint cet anonymat par un geste trop personnel encore qu'abstrait. Mais «sans Antigone», poursuit O'Brien, «nous pourrions atteindre un monde plus tranquille, plus réaliste. Les Créons pourraient en venir à respecter leurs sphères d'influence réciproque si dans leurs frontières cessaient les menaces à la loi et au bon ordre que comporte l'instabilité de l'idéalisme». Et O'Brien nous demande, avant que de répudier comme opportunistes ou réactionnaires ces paroles, de songer aux Antigones implacables de Dublin, de Belfast ou des rues de Londres. Que peut Créon?

Motif d'impuissance, de fatigue qu'approfondit Donald Davie dans son poème «La Souris de Créon» [21]. Après avoir réglé le cas de «cette fille dangereuse», Créon se replie sur la timidité, sur le dégoût de soi, qui lui sont natifs. La mise à mort d'Antigone et les terreurs qui en résultèrent ont brisé ses nerfs. Peut-être aurait-il pu fléchir la volonté fanatique de cette enfant. Le souvenir du passé cruel humilie Créon. La souris qui grignote dans sa chambre n'a rien à redouter. Créon n'est plus un justicier.

Pareils sentiments de compassion n'atteignent guère le Créon que met en scène Henri Ghéon dans son *Œdipe ou le Crépuscule des Dieux*, très probablement écrit en 1938 mais monté pour la première fois en 1951. Avec Ghéon nous

[21] Cf. Donald DAVIE, «Creon's Mouse», in *Brides of Reason* (London 1955).

revenons au coloris des *Phéniciennes* et de Stace, mais rehaussé de remarquables touches à la fois catholiques et freudiennes.

Veuve aigrie, Jocaste est dans l'attente du jeune héros qui vaincra le Sphinx et entrera dans sa couche royale. Créon est un puritain ironique, dont les visées politiques et la docilité au pouvoir reflètent une perception lucide de ces fièvres paludéennes qui sévissent dans la Maison de Laios. Pour lui le Sphinx est un redoutable *gardien* de la cité et un avertissement menaçant des lubies indécentes de la trop mûre Jocaste. En son enfance, Créon a ressenti la présence de sa sœur aînée presque comme celle d'une mère. Or, il trouve maintenant intolérables les pulsations de cette sensualité automnale. Il accuse Jocaste d'avoir poussé Laios à son voyage fatal. Il fait une allusion voilée aux motifs secrets de cette manœuvre: jamais, suggère Créon, Jocaste n'a pu pardonner à Laios la naissance redoutée du 'fils perdu' et la consigne de mort qui fit exposer le nouveau-né sur l'impitoyable montagne. Maintenant, murmure Créon, elle attend un nouvel époux «assez jeune pour être son fils» (tout comme dans le traitement du mythe chez Hofmannsthal, Freud n'est pas loin).

La célèbre 'machine infernale' explose. Quand nous retrouvons Créon, il est maître de la ville épuisée par la débâcle dynastique et la guerre fratricide. C'est maintenant que ce Créon cromwellien et purificateur peut accomplir sa mission. Il est venu en ce palais pour en chasser «la pollution, le mensonge, le sacrilège...». Qu'Etéocle soit enseveli avec honneur; que Polynice soit livré en pâture aux vautours. Quand le viel Œdipe et Antigone s'opposent à ce décret, ils le font sur un ton annonciateur déjà de valeurs évangéliques. La solution de Créon est à la fois condescendante et pragmatique. Les dieux sont durs, dit-il, et les hommes aussi. La terre est dure, mais notre labeur brisera son écorce. «C'est le métier d'un roi.» Œdipe et Antigone sont libres d'emporter les corps meurtris des frères ennemis. Mais qu'ils les ensevelissent loin de Thèbes. Ainsi la malédiction qui pèse sur cette race ne sera plus un danger pour la ville.

« C'est le métier d'un roi. » Il est difficile de penser qu'Anouilh n'a pas connu cette formule laconique de Ghéon. Car c'est bien ce petit mot *métier* qui est le pivot de l'apologie de Créon dans l'*Antigone* d'Anouilh — texte trop répandu pour que je doive m'y arrêter en détail. Je ne voudrais souligner qu'un point, trop souvent émoussé. Chez Anouilh, Créon est *vainqueur*, et ce fut là, bien sûr, la raison pour laquelle la censure allemande, après mûre réflexion, donna en 1943-44 son *imprimatur* à la pièce. Il apprend à Antigone qu'il n'y a aucun moyen de distinguer entre les corps d'Etéocle et de Polynice, tous deux réduits 'en bouillie'. La jeune 'pétroleuse' s'effondre. Peut-être eût-il mieux valu mourir « même pour une cause aussi absurde ». « Moi, je croyais. » Le verbe est dorénavant au passé. Antigone s'apprête à retourner dans sa chambre. La dialectique sournoise de Créon a miné les fondements existentiels et moraux de son geste. Les indications scéniques sont sans ambiguïté : Antigone se meut « comme une somnambule », les ressorts de son être sont brisés.

Sa décision, prise quelques instants plus tard, de relancer le défi à Créon et de le forcer à la tuer, n'a absolument rien à voir avec les données éthiques ou politiques du conflit telles que nous les présentent le mythe et le drame sophocléen. Anouilh fait basculer Créon, au moment même de sa victoire dialectique et psychologique. C'est la bonhomie bourgeoise de 'l'oncle Créon' qui révolte 'la petite Antigone', la garce noiraude, et la renvoie à la fatalité du geste gratuit et absurde. Mais elle ne réfute pas, elle ne tente même plus de réfuter les arguments de Créon.

Une remarque s'impose encore. Dans Sophocle, ainsi qu'à travers la plus grande partie des variantes du mythe, Créon est condamné à une hideuse solitude. A la fin de l'action, il est un lépreux, isolé des vivants et des morts. Tel n'est pas le cas dans l'*Antigone* d'Anouilh. La touche finale est notoire ; elle provient, je pense, d'une trouvaille précisément équivalente de *La Reine morte* de Montherlant, dont l'illustre première eut lieu, elle aussi, sous l'Occupation : c'est l'entrée du jeune page. Créon taquine doucement l'enfant. C'est folie, lui dit-il, de vouloir grandir. Il ne faudrait jamais devenir adulte. Et l'homme dont le Chœur vient justement de proclamer l'exclusion de l'humanité quitte la scène son bras appuyé sur l'épaule d'un jeune et loyal enfant. Ce tableau ne rompt pas seulement la réelle solitude de Créon, il suggère de façon plus générale un retour à la vie.

L'envoi de cet exposé si sommaire de quelques « variantes sur Créon » pourrait être le propos désenchanté émis par Dürrenmatt dans son essai *Problèmes du théâtre*, de 1955. Aujourd'hui « ce sont les secrétaires de Créon qui s'occupent de l'affaire d'Antigone ». Le trajet est long depuis Sophocle. Nous échouons dans une Thèbes de Kafka.

DISCUSSION

M. Winnington-Ingram: The remark of mine which M. Steiner kindly quoted was (as he is well aware) part of an argument (which I would still maintain) to the effect that Sophocles has, in many ways, treated the tragedy of Creon as an 'Aeschylean' tragedy (comparable to that of Xerxes), whereas it is Antigone who is the 'typical' Sophoclean hero, with a tragedy which is far more complex and subtle.

M. Seidensticker: Ich habe eine Frage zu dem von Ihnen konstatierten Unterschied der Gestaltung Kreons in der *Antigone* und in den *Phoinissen*. Es ist öfter betont worden (und eine Aufführung der Texten bestätigt m.E. diesen Eindruck), dass Kreon, der sich eben noch so leidenschaftlich um die Rettung des Sohnes bemüht hat, ihn gleich nach dem Tode des Menoikeus vergessen zu haben scheint. Verwandelt sich im Augenblick der Übernahme der Macht der euripideische 'Vater' doch wieder in dem sophokleischen 'Politiker'?

M. Knox: Encore une critique de Sophocle dans les *Phéniciennes* d'Euripide: la permission donnée par Créon à Antigone d'ensevelir le corps de Polynice hors du territoire thébain: Sophocle, en effet, avait mis dans la bouche de Créon un décret qui dépassait de loin la peine infligée aux traîtres à Athènes, c'est-à-dire un simple refus de sépulture sur le sol natal. Ici, comme dans le cas de l'*Oreste*, où l'on demande au fils d'Agamemnon pourquoi il n'a pas cité sa mère devant l'Aréopage au lieu de la tuer, Euripide propose la solution 'rationnelle' et contemporaine du problème tragique.

M. Taplin: A new papyrus fragment was published in 1980 (*POxy.* 3317) which seems to be from Euripides' *Antigone*. If it has been rightly interpreted by P. J. Parsons (in his article in *London Review of Books* for

21 Aug.-3 Sept. 1980), then we have in Euripides' play a middle-aged Antigone who yields to authority, and expresses the sentiment that ἡ εὐγένεια ... ὀξύθυμος is foolish. This would surely have to be a reaction against the Sophoclean version.

Mme de Romilly: Ce fragment pourrait n'exprimer qu'un des aspects du personnage: Iphigénie, avant de consentir à être sacrifiée, déclare aussi que n'importe quelle vie est préférable à la mort. Les personnages d'Euripide varient au cours d'une pièce: cela limite la portée des fragments.

Autre chose: je m'interroge sur le caractère exceptionnel que peut avoir la différence entre les données sur Créon dans le mythe ancien. Les auteurs gardent une grande liberté. Et l'on a des variantes, même généalogiques (Sarpédon, Ulysse).

M. Steiner: One does not need to be in any way an orthodox lévi-straussian to feel that the radical differences between the kingship status of Creon in Aeschylus' *Septem* and in *Antigone* are of importance.

M. Irigoin: A propos du *Roman de Thèbes* et de la *Théséide* de Boccace, vous avez parlé d'une connaissance directe des *Phéniciennes*. Compte tenu de ce que nous savons de la transmission du texte d'Euripide, il ne paraît pas possible que la connaissance de cette tragédie ait pu être directe au temps où le *Roman de Thèbes* a été composé; pour Boccace, les recherches d'Agostino Pertusi ont montré à quel niveau se situe le degré de probabilité, qui n'est pas nul.

Faire appel, même à titre d'hypothèse, aux traductions arabes pour expliquer, chez Chaucer, *Antigone's sad song*, me semble une solution condamnée d'avance par tout ce que nous savons du travail des traducteurs arabes des IXe et Xe siècles. Qu'ils aient disposé de textes grecs originaux ou de versions syriaques, ils se sont occupés des traités techniques, au sens le plus large — de la philosophie à la médecine, des mathématiques à la rhétorique et à la critique — mais non des œuvres littéraires, *a fortiori* des œuvre poétiques comme la tragédie.

M. Taplin: I should have thought that it was linguistically possible for "Antigone and her sad song", to mean "Antigone and the sad story (poem) about her".

M. Radt: Vielleicht ist das Problem auch anders zu lösen. Das Wort τραγῳδία hat ja bekanntlich im späteren Griechisch die Bedeutung 'Lied' bekommen, und wird daher in Spätantike und Mittelalter mit *cantus* übersetzt. Wenn Chaucer eine so späte Quelle benutzt hat, kann hinter seinem 'song' einfach die Bezeichnung des ganzen sophokleischen Stückes stecken.

Mme de Romilly: Pourquoi ne pas envisager aussi les traditions indirectes par la voie du latin, à travers des œuvres mineures, des imitations, des manuels qui ne sont pas venus jusqu'à nous? Les échos à distance des grands textes sont plus nombreux qu'on ne le croirait, et on ne peut pas toujours les dépister.

M. Irigoin: Parmi les régions où s'établissent des contacts et des échanges entre civilisations différentes, il faudrait mentionner l'Italie du Sud et la Sicile, contrées où le grec n'a pas cessé d'être parlé et où les traducteurs ont pu travailler directement sur les originaux grecs, y compris, à partir du début du XIIIe siècle, les œuvres de Sophocle et d'Euripide.

M. Steiner: There is, to be sure, no evidence whatever of any transmission of citations from a Greek tragedian via Islam. I am simply suggesting that there is a real need in comparative literature, as a discipline, for a better knowledge of the crucial encounters between the medieval latinities and vulgate on the one hand and Islamic texts on the other.

M. Knox: M. Steiner nous a révélé une telle richesse de témoignages de l'importance de l'*Antigone* de Sophocle à travers les siècles qu'on ne sait par où commencer, tant on a de questions à poser. Mais, en attendant le livre qu'il nous promet, je lui demande un renseignement sur quelque chose qui m'intéresse beaucoup: le cas Anouilh. Existe-t-il une documentation sur cette affaire et sur la façon dont elle a été traitée par le comité d'épuration?

M. Steiner: Manfred Flügge's exhaustive monograph on Anouilh's *Antigone* and cultural policies during the Occupation contains all the available material.

M. Seidensticker: Ihre Erwähnung des Churer Antigone-Modells erinnerte mich an die pointierte Formulierung Brechts im Vorwort: «philologische Interessen konnten nicht bedient werden». Daran würde ich gerne eine grundsätzliche methodische Frage anschliessen. K. von Fritz hat sich bei seinen Untersuchungen der Wirkungsgeschichte griechischer Tragödien von der Auffassung leiten lassen, dass die poetisch-theatralische Rezeption interessante (den Philologen verborgen gebliebene) Aspekte, Probleme, Schönheiten des 'Originals' erschliessen könne. Teilen Sie diese Auffassung und in welchem Umfang gilt sie für die so unterschiedlichen Kreon-Bilder, die Sie vorgestellt haben?

Mme de Romilly: Ces interprétations semblent s'être attachées à tel ou tel détail et avoir brodé, rêvé à partir de là. Sophocle a offert des images symboliques qui ont ainsi continué à vivre et à changer; mais il semble bien que sa force vienne en partie du fait qu'il n'a donné, lui, ni explications ni commentaires, ni théories (psychologiques, politiques ou philosophiques). Il a, grâce à cela, laissé des images à interpréter, qui ont encore toute l'ambiguïté et l'attrait du vécu.

M. Knox: C'est un des grands mérites de la présentation de la tradition postérieure d'*Antigone* par M. Steiner, qu'elle nous renvoie à chaque instant au texte original. Pour cette 'contradiction' que Kierkegaard a signalée, le fait que le mot μούνην, employé par Antigone dans son dernier discours (v. 941), n'est pas la vérité, puisqu'Ismène existe toujours — je trouve qu'après tout, ce n'est pas une contradiction. Car Ismène s'est montrée traîtresse à la famille, Antigone l'a formellement répudiée, puis elle a refusé l'offre que lui a faite Ismène de partager sa mort.

«Toi», dit-elle, «tu as choisi la vie, moi la mort». Il est dès lors naturel qu'elle se considère comme la seule survivante de la famille, au moment où elle se prépare à se joindre aux siens dans l'Hadès.

M. Radt: Ist es möglich, dass Antigone annimmt, Ismene sei bereits zum Tode gebracht? Aus Kreons Worten am Ende des zweiten Epeisodions (V. 578 ff.) musste sie ja schliessen, dass sie beide hingerichtet werden würden — dass Kreon das Todesurteil inzwischen auf Antigone beschränkt hat (V. 771), weiss sie nicht: sie ist nach V. 581 zusammen mit Ismene in den Palast gebracht worden, wo man die beiden Schwestern vermutlich getrennt voneinander bewacht und Ismene nach V. 781 freigelassen hat. Wenn Antigone dann allein, ohne Ismene, herausgeführt wird (V. 802 ff.), nimmt sie begreiflicherweise an, dass das Urteil an Ismene bereits vollstreckt ist.

M. Knox: M. Steiner a constaté que la contradiction découverte par Kierkegaard est bien une contradiction fondamentale: Antigone, qui défend le principe de consanguinité comme objet suprême de la loyauté, ne peut en effet 'répudier' Ismène. Mais Antigone a déjà, dans les fameux vers 905-907, qui ont déplu à Goethe, abandonné non seulement le principe de consanguinité, mais aussi le devoir envers les dieux de la mort. Dans ses derniers moments, Antigone se rend compte que sa motivation, au fond, est purement personnelle, voire irrationnelle.

Ces vers sont contestés: beaucoup de savants, non des moindres — parmi eux Jebb —, les condamnent. Mais il y a un obstacle rédhibitoire à cette solution: l'autorité d'Aristote qui cite précisément ces vers-là dans sa *Rhétorique*. Il les tenait évidemment pour authentiques; on a même le sentiment qu'ils étaient célèbres. Si vous récusez ces vers, vous avez contre vous l'autorité d'un grand philosophe et d'un grand savant plus proche que vous d'une vingtaine de siècles du texte original; il savait le grec mieux qu'aucun de nous, il avait étudié l'histoire de la tragédie, il avait écrit sur la tragédie même le livre le plus important de toute la tradition critique; il était de surcroît très sensible aux nuances du style — la *Rhétorique* en est la preuve —; il était certainement capable de signaler une contradiction fondamentale de caractère dramatique: ne l'a-t-il pas fait pour *Iphigénie en Aulide* d'Euripide? Tous les arguments contre l'authenticité de ce passage, qu'ils se fondent sur une contradiction des caractères ou sur la condamnation du style, se heurtent à l'autorité d'Aristote.

Mme de Romilly: La phrase ne peut-elle avoir une valeur symbolique? On sent Antigone dans sa solitude, sans penser au sort d'Ismène, sans se demander si celle-ci a été tuée, ni ce qu'en pense Antigone.

M. Steiner: It is my working hypothesis that the successive interpretations of Sophocles' *Antigone*, even where they are metamorphic re-creations, relate themselves to actual *données* in this inexhaustible and enigmatic drama. When Hegel insists on the *moral* distinctions to be made between Eteocles and Polyneices, he can cite Creon's account of Polyneices' barbaric, blasphemous designs on the city—an account which Sophocles never repudiates. When Kierkegaard insists on the total biological-existential singularity of Antigone, he can cite Antigone's own notorious description of herself as the *only* living child of Oedipus. The contradiction here is neither accidental nor explainable in virtue of some 'realistic' error, e.g. Antigone thinks that Ismene is dead. No, there is a radical dramatic-moral paradox in the fact that Antigone, who dies because familial bonds outweigh good and evil should *now* deny the existence of Ismene.

M. Seidensticker: Sehen Sie eine Gefahr darin, dass eine moderne Metamorphose des Stoffs zwar durch einzelne Verse des sophokleischen Stücks angeregt sein kann, an der Intention des Sophokles aber völlig vorbeigeht ? Ein Beispiel: Anouilhs Version und Käte Hamburgers Versuch den unbedingten Todeswillen der Antigone Anouilhs in den sophokleischen Text hineinzulesen. Für Sophokles' Antigone aber ist Polyneikes gerade kein Vorwand.

M. Steiner: Any serious hermeneutic theory and method, since Schleiermacher at least, repudiates the simplistic concept of "Sophocles' true intention" or our capacity ever to recapture or demonstrate such an intention. There are linguistic-historical-contextual *constraints* on what a fifth-century Attic tragedian *may* have meant. But even these are very difficult to determine confidently. We need only listen to the endless debates by philologists and critics since 1821 about the authenticity or interpolation of lines 905-20 to realise how easy it is to proclaim *post hoc* possibilities or impossibilities.

Above all, let us remember that every great stage-production, operatic version, literary variant, philosophic *reprise* (Hegel, Heidegger, Kojève) is a legitimate part of that collaborative hermeneutic process which extends from strictest philology, epigraphy, textual criticism on the one hand, to free *imitatio*, parody, pastiche, transmutation on the other. What must be done is to make productive the great middle ground between A. E. Housman's remark that a true scholar has no business having any opinion on the merits of the text which he is editing, and Brecht's contemptuous dismissal of philology at the outset of *Antigone 48*. We are all in the same (leaky) boat.

Mme de Romilly: Ne peut-on admettre au moins qu'il y a un certain nombre d'effets voulus et d'intentions perceptibles? Des formules frappantes, des traits d'insistance stylistique, des retouches à la légende sont des données de fait. Il ne s'agit pas là de mérites, mais d'indices.

M. Taplin: Am I right in thinking that this methodology tends to a breaking down of any distinction or barrier between the artist, who may do wonders with 'creative misinterpretation', and the scholar for whom misinterpretation has always been thought illegitimate? Thus a dramatist or a novelist may, for example, create a Creon who is diabolical, the embodiment of evil: this may be very powerful, it may, as has been so well shown, send us back to Sophocles with new eyes, and no one can say it is 'wrong'. But if a scholar writes of Creon "No other character in Greek tragedy... has this consistent cold unfeelingness. Iago or the Doctor in *Woyzeck* are the only parallels that I can think of" (B. Vickers, *Towards Greek Tragedy* (London 1973), 535), then we want to be able to say that he is 'wrong' (or 'right').

Would you agree that the sort of hermeneutic you speak of entails the rejection of such distinctions?

M. Winnington-Ingram: Criticism must begin with an attempt to grasp the 'meaning' of the author. This is the more important, and the more possible, in proportion to the intellectual control exercised by the author and imposed by him upon the structure of his work. Such a control is evident to a high degree in the Greek tragedians, not least in Sophocles. But of course, if criticism begins with this, it needs not necessarily end there.

Mme de Romilly: Cela semble surtout difficile dans le cas de Sophocle. On l'a vu déjà hier matin. Il y a dans son théâtre moins de certitude théologique que chez Eschyle, et moins de commentaires raisonnés que dans Euripide. Peut-être cela vouait-il son œuvre à susciter tant de désaccords et de curiosités chez les philologues, et tant de richesse chez les penseurs et poètes qui ont suivi. Nous en avons eu aujourd'hui un exemple remarquable avec l'exposé si riche de M. Steiner. Et l'extraordinaire aventure qu'il nous a décrite pourrait bien, si ce que je viens de dire est exact, nous amener à saisir un des traits distinctifs de Sophocle lui-même.

IV

Bernd Seidensticker

DIE WAHL DES TODES BEI SOPHOKLES

> To be, or not to be: that is the question:
> Whether 'tis nobler in the mind to suffer
> The slings and arrows of outrageous fortune,
> Or to take arms against a sea of troubles,
> And by opposing end them. ...
>
> *Hamlet* III, 1

I

«Irgendwann im Laufe der Evolution muss der Mensch entdeckt haben, dass er nicht nur Tiere und Mitmenschen, sondern auch sich selbst töten kann. Die Annahme ist erlaubt, dass von da an das Leben für ihn nie wieder so wie vorher war [1].» Soweit wir zurückblicken können in die

* Die in Anm. 4 (zum Selbstmord), 6 (zum Selbstmord in der Antike) und 11 (zu Sophokles) genannten Arbeiten werden im folgenden nur mit Namen und Seite (bzw. Namen, Kurztitel und Seite) zitiert.

[1] E. Stengel, *Selbstmord und Selbstmordversuch* (Frankfurt 1969), 2. Im deutschen Sprachraum wird seit geraumer Zeit mit sprachlichen, logischen und ideologischen Argumenten eine lebhafte Diskussion darüber geführt, ob der Begriff Selbstmord nicht durch einen anderen ersetzt werden könne oder gar müsse (vgl. dazu H. Aigner, *Der Selbstmord im Mythos* (s. nächste Anm.), 6-8). Die wichtigsten Vorschläge lauten: Selbsttötung, Selbstzerstörung, Selbstvernichtung, Freitod sowie Suizid. Trotz der durchaus berechtigten Einwände, die sich gegen 'Selbstmord' erheben lassen, ist es m.E. nicht sinnvoll, den im allgemeinen Sprachgeb-

Geschichte des menschlichen Geistes, finden wir bildliche und schriftliche Zeugnisse für den Selbstmord [2]. Die homerischen Epen kennen bereits verschiedene Selbstmordformen und -ursachen [3], und sowohl Achilleus als auch Odysseus sind in Augenblicken tiefster Verzweiflung — im Schmerz über den Tod des Patroklos bzw. in dem Gefühl, Ithaka niemals mehr wiederzusehen — dem Selbstmord nahe. Beide töten sich nicht. Den impulsiven Achilleus hält ein Freund zurück; den vielduldenden Odysseus bewahrt sein kühler Verstand. Dennoch dokumentiert sich in der Tatsache, dass sowohl *Ilias* als auch *Odyssee* ihren Helden in der Krise mit der Hamletfrage konfrontieren, bereits am Anfang der abendländischen Literatur, eindringlich die fundamentale Bedeutung des Selbstmords für das menschliche Leben.

Die Faszination und Beunruhigung, die jeder Selbstmord bei denen, die ihn sehen oder von ihm hören, auslöst, hat seit Homer Dichter und Philosophen, Gesetzgeber und Theologen immer wieder zur Auseinandersetzung mit dem Problem der Selbsttötung veranlasst, bis sich im 19. Jahrhundert sogar eine eigene Wissenschaft entwickelte. Nach der bahnbrechenden Studie von Emile Durkheim (1897) ist die

---

rauch fest verwurzelten Begriff durch ein 'richtigeres' Kunstwort zu ersetzen. Ich spreche daher im folgenden weiter von Selbstmord, habe jedoch durch die Formulierung des Themas als 'Wahl des Todes' auf den entscheidenden moralisch-heroischen Aspekt der Selbsttötung bei Sophokles schon im Titel meines Beitrages hinweisen wollen.

[2] H. Aigner, *Der Selbstmord im Mythos. Betrachtungen über die Einstellung der Griechen zum Phänomen Suizid von der Homerischen Zeit bis in das ausgehende 5. Jahrhundert v.Chr.* (Graz 1980; unpubl. Habil.-Schrift, die mir H. Aigner freundlicherweise zur Verfügung stellte), 14 ff.; 27 ff.

[3] *Od.* XI 277 ff. (Epikaste); X 49 ff. (Odysseus); XI 197 ff.; XV 356 ff. (Antikleia; allerdings unsicher, ob bereits bei Homer Selbstmord gemeint ist; cf. Hygin. *Fab.* 243, 1; Eustath. *ad* Hom. *Od.* XI 202); *Il.* XVIII 33 f. (Achilleus); III 173 (Helena). Todeswünsche auch *Od.* I 59; X 497 f. (Odysseus); XX 61 ff. (Penelope); XV 353 f. (Laertes).

Suizidologie zu einem überaus fruchtbaren Arbeitsfeld für Soziologen und Politologen, Mediziner, Psychologen und Psychotherapeuten geworden, deren Ergebnisse auch für den Philologen interessant und hilfreich sein können [4]. Auf der anderen Seite beweist die lange Reihe moderner Theorien zu Ursachen und Intentionen, die auf der Basis eines fast unübersehbaren statistischen Materials entworfen worden sind, wie weit wir trotz der enormen Erweiterung unserer Kenntnisse davon entfernt sind, den Selbstmord letztlich zu verstehen, und lässt Alvarez' Feststellung verständlich erscheinen: «Je zahlreicher die wissenschaftlichen Untersuchungen waren, die ich las, desto stärker festigte sich in mir die Überzeugung, ich könne nichts Besseres tun, als den Selbstmord aus der Perspektive der Literatur zu betrachten... [5]» Das soll im Folgenden geschehen [6].

[4] Die Literatur ist inzwischen so umfangreich, dass sie für den Nichtfachmann unübersehbar ist; zur Einführung: A. BAYET, *Le suicide et la morale* (Paris 1922); G. R. FEDDEN, *Suicide* (London/Toronto 1938); CH. ZWINGMANN (ed.), *Selbstvernichtung* (Frankfurt 1965); E. STENGEL, *Selbstmord und Selbstmordversuch* (Frankfurt 1969); G. SIEGMUND, *Sein oder Nichtsein* (Trier ²1970); S. PERLIN (ed.), *A Handbook for the Study of Suicide* (Oxford 1975); E. RINGEL, *Das Leben wegwerfen? Reflexionen über den Selbstmord* (Wien 1978); am meisten profitiert habe ich von J. BAECHLER, *Les suicides* (Paris 1975); interessant für die Untersuchung des Selbstmords in der Literatur: A. ALVAREZ. *Der grausame Gott. Eine Studie über den Selbstmord* (Hamburg 1974).

[5] ALVAREZ, 11.

[6] Literatur zum Selbstmord in der Antike bzw. bei Sophokles: K. A. GEIGER, *Der Selbstmord im klassischen Altertum* (Augsburg 1888); R. HIRZEL, *Der Selbstmord*, Libelli 189 (Darmstadt 1966; repr. aus *ARW* 11 (1908), 75-104, 243-84, 417-76); W. B. STANFORD, *Sophocles. Ajax* (London 1963), Appendix E, 289-290; C. JAMES, «Whether 'tis nobler. Some Thoughts on the Fate of Sophocles' Ajax and Euripides' Heracles, with Special Reference to the Question of Suicide», in *Pegasus* 12 (1969), 10-20; A. G. KATSOURIS, Τὸ μοτίβο τῆς αὐτοκτονίας στὸ ἀρχαῖο δρᾶμα, in *Dodone* 4 (1975), 203-34, und (engl. Fssg.) «The Suicide Motif in Ancient Drama», in *Dioniso* 47 (1976), 5-36 (vorwiegend deskriptiv); J. de ROMILLY, «Le refus du suicide dans l'Héraclès d'Euripide», in *Archaiognosia* 1 (1980), 1-9; H. AIGNER, *Der Selbstmord im Mythos* (s.o. S. 106 Anm. 2); dazu kommt noch die schöne Studie von Jean STAROBINSKI, «L'épée d'Ajax», in *Trois Fureurs* (Paris 1974), 11-71, auf die mich Herr Steiner während der Entretiens aufmerksam machte.

Meine Überlegungen gliedern sich dabei in einen ersten systematisch-topologischen Teil, in dem versucht wird, typische Elemente der Gestaltung des Selbstmords in der sophokleischen Tragödie zusammenzustellen, und einen zweiten Teil, in dessen Mittelpunkt die detaillierte Interpretation eines besonders interessanten Falles steht: des Aias.

II

Während sich in den erhaltenen Tragödien des Aischylos [7] zwar wiederholt Selbstmordwünsche und -ängste, -drohungen und -versuche finden, aber kein einziger Selbstmord, töten sich gleich sechs Gestalten des Sophokles selbst: Aias, Deianeira, Antigone, Haimon und Eurydike sowie Iokaste [8]. Nimmt man Elektras Todeswunsch, Philoktets Selbstmordwünsche und -drohungen und die Todessehnsucht des greisen Oidipus im Hain von Kolonos hinzu, so ist keine der sophokleischen Tragödien ohne Beziehung zum Thema Selbstmord [9].

Dieser Unterschied zwischen den beiden Tragikern muss natürlich nicht bedeuten, dass Aischylos sich für den Selbstmord nicht interessiert hätte — seine Gestaltung des *Aias*-Stoffes ist uns leider nicht erhalten —, wohl aber, dass

[7] Aischylos: *Ag.* 874-876; (*Cho.* 916); *Eum.* 746; *Supp.* 455 ff.; 788 ff.; *Prom.* (582 ff.); 747 ff.; Fr. 289 Mette; 296 (?) M. *(Aias)*; 399 M. *(Philoktet)*; 474 M., V. 778-81 *(Dikt.)*; 679 M.

[8] Die Verbrennung des Herakles auf dem Oeta rechne ich im Gegensatz zu Stanford und Aigner nicht zu den Selbstmorden. Der Tod des Herakles — als tragischer, nicht als physischer Akt — ist vielmehr Mord (bzw. fahrlässige Tötung), nicht Selbstmord.

[9] *El.* 378 ff.; 1165 ff. (συνθανεῖν); *Ph.* 747 ff.; 797 ff.; 999 ff.; 1203 ff.; 1348 f.; *OC* 101 ff.; vgl. weiter den Todeswunsch Kreons (*Ant.* 1329 ff.; dazu F 953 Radt), sowie F *178; F 698; F 952 Radt; dazu kommen aus den verlorenen Stücken: wahrscheinlich Phaidra (W. S. BARRETT (ed.), *Euripides. Hippolytos* (Oxford 1964), 12) und vielleicht Pelopia (S. RADT (ed.), *TrGF* IV, S. 239 f.).

Sophokles in besonderem Masse fasziniert war von dem Problem und seinen dramatischen und poetischen Möglichkeiten. Diese These würde noch erheblich gestärkt, wenn sich beweisen liesse, dass einige seiner Selbstmorde erst von ihm selbst in die mythische Tradition eingeführt worden sind. In nicht weniger als vier der sechs Fälle liegt die Vermutung zumindestens nahe [10].

Die statistischen Möglichkeiten, wie sie die Suizidologie so liebt, sind bei Sophokles schnell erschöpft: Vier seiner Selbstmörder sind Frauen: eine davon jung (Antigone), drei in den mittleren Jahren; zwei sind Männer, einer davon jung (Haimon), einer in den besten Mannesjahren; zwei Männer und zwei Frauen töten sich mit dem Schwert, zwei Frauen erhängen sich. Zu lernen ist daraus ebensoviel wie aus den meisten Selbstmordstatistiken, nämlich nichts.

Wichtig ist dagegen, da es sich um poetische Selbstmorde handelt, die Untersuchung der künstlerischen Gestaltung und der dramatischen und thematischen Bedeutung des Ereignisses im Rahmen des jeweiligen Textes [11]. Die Analyse der sophokleischen Selbstmorde offenbart eine Reihe interessanter Gemeinsamkeiten.

1. Fünf der sechs Selbstmorde werden, wie erwartet, von einem *Boten* berichtet [12], der über das hinterszenische Geschehen informiert. Nur im *Aias* hat Sophokles sich aus naheliegenden Gründen über die Theaterkonvention hin-

[10] Deianeira, Antigone, Haimon, Eurydike.

[11] Aus dem ständig wachsenden Strom der Sophokles-Literatur seien die folgenden Arbeiten herausgehoben, die meine eigenen Überlegungen zum Thema bzw. zu Sophokles am stärksten beeinflusst und gefördert haben: G. M. Kirkwood, *A Study of Sophoclean Drama* (Ithaca 1958); H. D. F. Kitto, *Greek Tragedy* (London ³1961); id., *Form and Meaning in Drama* (London 1956; paperback 1960); B. M. W. Knox, *The Heroic Temper* (Berkeley/Los Angeles 1964); id., «The Ajax of Sophocles», in *HSCP* 65 (1961), 1-37; K. Reinhardt, *Sophokles* (Frankfurt ³1947); R. P. Winnington-Ingram, *Sophocles. An Interpretation* (Cambridge 1980).

[12] *Tr.* 871 ff. (Deianeira); *Ant.* 1155 ff. (Antigone und Haimon); 1278 ff. (Eurydike); *OT* 1223 ff. (Iokaste).

weggesetzt und die Tat selbst, die im *Aias* des Aischylos noch berichtet worden war, auf die Bühne gebracht [13].

Die Boten sind, wie üblich, Angehörige des Hausgesindes (Diener, bzw. in den *Trachinierinnen* die Amme der Heldin), die sich, wie ebenfalls üblich, als Augenzeugen ausweisen.

2. Die *Ausführlichkeit*, mit der die eigentliche Tat berichtet wird, reicht von den drei Versen, in denen Antigones Selbstmord konstatiert wird (1220-22), über die komprimierten, aber eindrücklichen Beschreibungen der Selbstmorde Haimons (1231-39), Eurydikes (1301-5) und Iokastes (*OT* 1241-50; 1263-67) bis zu dem langen Bericht der Amme vom Tode Deianeiras (*Tr.* 899-946). Dass die Ausführlichkeit des Berichts eine Funktion des dramatischen Stellenwerts des Ereignisses ist, liegt auf der Hand:

Antigones Selbstmord ist vor allem bedeutungsvoll als Auslöser für Haimons Selbstmord, dessen Tod wiederum Eurydikes Selbstmord zur Folge hat. Alle drei Selbstmorde des Stücks gewinnen ihre Bedeutung aus ihrer Funktion für die Tragödie des Kreon, aus dessen Perspektive (Antigone, Haimon) bzw. für den (Eurydike) sie berichtet werden. Sie sind Folgen seiner Entscheidungen, für die er nun bezahlen muss. Antigones Tod bedeutet Kreon nichts. Seine detaillierte Beschreibung würde also nur vom Wesentlichen ablenken. Anders Eurydike und Haimon: Frau und Sohn. Haimons Tod ist dabei der schwerste Schlag. Sein Selbstmord ist deshalb von Sophokles am ausführlichsten und wirkungsvollsten gezeichnet; seinen Selbstmord muss Kreon sogar selbst mitansehen.

Katastrophe und Exodos des *Oidipus Tyrannos* werden beherrscht von der Blendung des Oidipus und nicht etwa

[13] Cf. J. C. KAMERBEEK, *The Plays of Sophocles. Commentaries. Part I: The Ajax* (Leiden ²1963), *ad loc.*; O. TAPLIN, *Greek Tragedy in Action* (London 1974), 86; AIGNER, 72-74.

vom Selbstmord Iokastes, der, sobald Oidipus in den Palast stürzt, ganz auf ihn und sein Schicksal bezogen ist (1251 ff.). Er vertieft die tragische Schuld des Oidipus und steigert zugleich die Furchtbarkeit seiner Situation, indem er einen Ausweg zeigt, der Oidipus nicht offensteht [14].

In den *Trachinierinnen* gewinnt der Selbstmord der Heldin ein erheblich grösseres Eigengewicht als im *Oidipus Tyrannos* oder gar in der *Antigone*, doch auch hier reicht seine Wirkung kaum über den Bericht der Amme hinaus. Die erste Hälfte des Stücks thematisiert nicht den Selbstmord Deianeiras, sondern die Tragödie einer alternden Frau, die in ihrer verzehrenden Liebe aus Angst zerstört, was sie sich bewahren will. Der Selbstmord ist Höhepunkt und Abschluss der Deianeira-Tragödie — deswegen wird er ausführlich berichtet —; doch dann beherrscht nur noch Herakles die Bühne.

Im *Aias* schliesslich bestimmt der Selbstmord des Helden von Tekmessas angsterfüllter Prophezeiung: καὶ δῆλός ἐστιν ὥς τι δρασείων κακόν (326) bis zu Aias' Sprung in sein Schwert (865) das dramatische Geschehen, ohne etwa auf diesen zentralen Teil des Dramas beschränkt zu sein. Denn auch nach dem Selbstmord beherrscht der Leichnam des gewaltigen Toten das Stück noch über die Szenen, in denen er gefunden und beklagt wird, hinaus bis zum Ende; und bereits Prolog und Parodos sind überschattet von der Ahnung, dass der grosse Aias die Schande seiner Wahnsinnstat und die Demütigung durch Athene nicht wird ertragen können, sobald er aus der Umnachtung erwacht [15].

3. In mindestens drei der fünf berichteten Selbstmorde haben die Boten die eigentliche Tat nicht gesehen [16].

[14] Cf. *OT* 1367 ff.

[15] Zu Aias als der das ganze Stück dominierenden Gestalt cf. KNOX, «The Ajax...», 1 f.

[16] *Ant.* 1220-1222 (Antigone); *Tr.* 929 ff. (Deianeira); *OT* 1251 (Iokaste).

Sophokles lässt seine Helden *einsam* sterben. Das ist natürlich. Selbstmord ist einsam. Zugleich aber ist es auch bedeutsam für die sophokleische Tragik. Die vielbeschworene existentielle Einsamkeit des sophokleischen Helden, seine äussere und innere Isolation, findet in der Einsamkeit des Todes ihren letzten symbolischen Ausdruck [17]. Antigones' Grab liegt einsam, fern der Stadt (773 f.); sie, die nach eigenem Gesetz lebt, wie der Chor sagt, stirbt allein und einsam (821 f.; 887), ohne Freunde (919). Iokaste stürzt ins Schlafgemach und verriegelt die Tür hinter sich (1244; 1261 f.) [18]; Deianeira verbirgt sich, wo niemand sie sehen kann (903) und ist später allein im Schlafgemach [19]; Aias schliesslich stirbt einsam am Meer; hier erzwingt die ungewöhnliche dramatische Technik, den Selbstmord des Helden zu zeigen, nicht zu berichten, einen weiteren Bruch der Konvention: den Auszug des Chores aus der Orchestra vor dem Ende des Stücks.

Nur bei Haimon und Eurydike hat Sophokles aus guten Gründen auf die Einsamkeit (im Augenblick des Todes) verzichtet. Im Falle Haimons war ihm der direkte Angriff des Sohnes auf den Vater als symbolischer Ausdruck dafür, wie Kreons Taten auf ihn zurückschlagen, offenbar wichtiger; im Falle Eurydikes betont der Text zwar nicht, legt es aber nahe, dass sie im Augenblick ihres Todes nicht allein ist. Da ihr Selbstmord wie der Haimons auch Elemente der Rache enthält, ist hier die Anwesenheit von Zeugen, die ihre Verfluchung Kreons hören, durchaus sinnvoll.

4. Der *Schauplatz* des Selbstmords, in der Realität meist nicht mehr als der Ort der Tat, gewinnt bei Sophokles symbolische

[17] REINHARDT, *Sophokles*, 10; KNOX, *Heroic Temper*, 32 ff.

[18] Cf. KAMERBEEK, *ad* 1244, 5 und 1261, 2.

[19] Sie wird zwar von der Amme beobachtet, aber sie weiss es nicht (914 f.); und als die Amme sieht, was ihre Herrin vorhat, eilt sie davon, um Haimon zu holen. Bei ihrer Rückkehr ist Deianeira bereits tot.

Bedeutung: Iokaste erhängt sich im Schlafgemach, wo sie dem Laios den Mörder und sich selbst den Gatten gebar; Deianeira ersticht sich auf dem Bett des Herakles, dem Mittelpunkt ihres Lebens; Eurydike tötet sich am Altar [20], dem Zentrum des Hauses und der Familie, die Kreon mit dem Tode des zweiten Sohnes endgültig vernichtet hat; Aias, der Mann von der Insel Salamis, verlässt das Lager und geht ans Meer, um sich in der Einsamkeit zu reinigen, die Symbol für seine innere Isolation ist. Haimon und Antigone sterben im Felsengrab. Die Frage, warum Kreon seine Entscheidung, Antigone steinigen zu lassen, ändert und sie lebendig begraben lässt, hat viele Antworten [21]. Sicher ist, dass kein Ort für den Tod Antigones, die 'für ein Grab' stirbt, 'passender' sein könnte, als ein Grab, und dass erst diese Form der Bestrafung die perverse Verkehrung der sittlichen Ordnung durch Kreon vollständig macht, der den Göttern der Unterwelt einen Toten verweigert und einen Lebenden aufdrängt (1068 ff.).

5. Erweist sich der Schauplatz in allen Fällen als symbolisch bedeutungsvoll, so erscheint die *Selbstmordmethode* auf den ersten Blick eher konventionell. Bezeugt sind für die griechische Tragödie fast ausschliesslich Schwert und Strick; daneben in Einzelfällen auch Gift und Sprung ins Meer, ins Feuer oder von einem Felsen [22]. Für Männer ist das Schwert üblich [23]; bei Frauen überwiegt der Strick. Die Verfügbarkeit der Mittel spielt eben zu allen Zeiten eine wichtige Rolle.

[20] Soviel ist trotz der Textverderbnis in 1301 deutlich; cf. *schol. ad loc.* und KAMERBEEK, *ad loc.*

[21] KITTO, *Form and Meaning,* 166; KNOX, *Heroic Temper*, 72 f.

[22] Gift: Stheneboia (Eur.); Meer: Ino (Eur.); Feuer: Io (Aeschyl. *Prom.* 582), Euadne (Eur. *Supp.* 980 ff.), Laodameia (Eur. *Protesilaus*); Felsen: Io (Aeschyl. *Prom.* 748 ff.), Philoktet (Soph. *Ph.* 999 ff.); Hunger (-drohung): Orestes (Eur. *IT* 973 ff.), Iphis (Eur. *Supp.* 1104 ff.).

[23] Cf. aber die Ausnahmen: Aeschyl. *Eum.* 746 (Orestes: Strick); Neophron F 3 *TrGF* I Snell (Jason: Strick).

Dass allerdings in Griechenland, wie gelegentlich behauptet wird, der Strick die selbstverständliche 'anständige' Selbstmordmethode für Frauen gewesen ist, erscheint mir auf der Basis unseres doch recht kärglichen Materials nicht so sicher, dass sich hieraus die in jüngster Zeit erstaunlich intensiv diskutierte Frage [24], warum Deianeira (wie übrigens auch Eurydike) zum Schwert und nicht zum Strick greift, zwangsläufig jedem Betrachter aufdrängen musste. Es gibt auch Anhaltspunkte dafür, dass bereits die Griechen, wie Goethe, das Erhängen als 'unedle Todesart' (und zwar auch für Frauen) empfanden [25], und Hirzel könnte recht haben, wenn er feststellt: «Wo der edle Dichter freie Hand hatte [*sc.* Deianeira und Eurydike], hat auch Sophokles der Würde seiner Personen den Tod durchs Schwert entsprechender gefunden [26].» Antigone hat im Felsengrab kein Schwert zur Verfügung; Iokaste kann wohl nur den homerischen Strick nehmen. Im Falle Deianeiras mag der Grund für das Schwert allerdings tiefer liegen, wenn auch kaum dort, wo ihn G. Devereux vermutet [27]. Die beiden Helden der Doppeltragödie stürzen sich gegenseitig ins Verderben, und sie töten sich mit den für sie und ihre Welt charakteristischen Waffen: Gewand und Schwert, die zudem symbolische Bedeutung gewinnen. Herakles verbrennt in der Liebe Deianeiras, Deianeira stirbt an der brutalen Männlichkeit des Herakles. Da Deianeira den Selbstmord auch als Selbstbestrafung versteht, ist der Tod durch das Schwert für sie zudem gleichsam der Vollzug der Strafe durch Herakles selbst. Winnington-Ingrams Hinweis darauf, dass die Form des

[24] D. Wender, «The Will of the Beast. Sexual Imagery in the Trachiniae», in *Ramus* 3 (1974), 1-17; G. Devereux, *Tragédie et poésie grecques* (Paris 1975; trad. franç.), ch. 5; Winnington-Ingram, *Sophocles*, 81 Anm. 28.

[25] Cf. das Material bei Hirzel, 44 Anm. 4.

[26] Hirzel, *ibid.*

[27] G. Devereux (*Tragédie et poésie grecques*, ch. 5) sieht den Grund in der latenten Homosexualität des Sophokles.

Selbstmords «sexually suggestive» sei, ist nach Freud evident; ob sie von Sophokles so gemeint war, muss offen bleiben.

Symbolische Bedeutung gewinnt das Werkzeug der Tat schliesslich auch im *Aias*. Hier ist das von der Wahnsinnstat blutige Schwert Symbol der befleckten Ehre des Helden; der Sprung in das Schwert soll Schwert und Ehre reinigen [28].

6. Ausser beim Selbstmord der Antigone betont Sophokles, dass die Tat in starker *emotionaler Erregung* geschieht. Iokaste stürzt «in wildem Schmerz» (1073 f.) von der Bühne, eilt in äusserster Erregung (1241) durch die Halle zum Schlafgemach und reisst die Tür hinter sich zu (1244); Eurydike ist nach dem Bericht plötzlich verschwunden (1244 f.), aber der Bote fürchtet zu Recht, dass sich hinter ihrem schweigenden Abgang tiefe Erregung verbirgt (1253 ff.); und sie stirbt mit einem Fluch auf den Lippen (1305). Haimon stürmt in heftiger Erregung (766) davon, und das nächste, was wir von ihm hören, sind seine schrillen Schreie, die aus dem Grabe dringen (1206) und der Jammer an der Leiche Antigones (1224); dann stürzt er sich mit «wilden Augen» auf den Vater, spuckt ihm ins Gesicht und tötet, als sein Schwert ihn verfehlt, sich in rasendem Zorn (χολωθείς) selbst (1231 ff.). Deianeiras Erschütterung äussert sich weniger expressiv. Das passt durchaus zu dem Bild, das wir seit dem Prolog von ihr gewonnen haben [29]. Wie Eurydike geht sie nach dem vernichtenden Bericht und der Verfluchung durch den Sohn

[28] Zur symbolischen Bedeutung des Schwerts KIRKWOOD, 222 f.; KITTO, *Form and Meaning*, 193 ff.; sowie zuletzt ausführlich D. COHEN, «The Imagery of Sophocles: A Study of Ajax's Suicide», in *G&R* 25 (1978), 24-36, der das Schwert vor allem als Symbol für «the dark side of Ajax's nature» betrachtet (dort auch weitere Literatur).

[29] Zu Deianeira vgl. besonders: E. R. SCHWINGE, *Die Stellung der Trachinierinnen im Werk des Sophokles,* Hypomnemata 1 (Göttingen 1962), 56 ff.; M. MCCALL, «The *Trachiniae*: Structure, Focus, and Heracles», in *AJPh* 93 (1972), 142-63; Ch. SEGAL, «Sophocles' *Trachiniae*: Myth, Poetry, and Heroic Values», in *YClS* 25 (1977), 99-158 (bes. 119-30); WINNINGTON-INGRAM, *Sophocles,* 75-81.

schweigend ab (813 f.). Ihre Bewegungen im Haus sind nicht wild und entschlossen; sie verkriecht sich (903), fällt jammernd am Altar nieder (904), nimmt einzelne Gegenstände in die Hand (905 f.), irrt ziellos umher (907) und klagt dem Gesinde ihr Leid (908 f.); erst dann, plötzlich, eilt sie in das Schlafgemach und beginnt mit den Vorbereitungen für den Selbstmord (915 ff.). Aias schliesslich macht sich scheinbar ruhig auf zum Strand und bewahrt auch im Augenblick des Selbstmords die unheimliche Ruhe des zum Tode Entschlossenen; und doch spüren wir auch im Todesmonolog, ja sogar in der Trugrede unter der ruhigen Oberfläche die wilde Kraft seines Hasses, den er sich bis in den Tod bewahrt [30].

Es ist wichtig festzuhalten, dass, auch wenn in allen Fällen die emotionale Erregung des Täters betont wird, allenfalls der Selbstmord Haimons als Affekttat bezeichnet werden kann. Das passt übrigens durchaus zu modernen Forschungsergebnissen. Kurzschluss-Selbstmorde sind vor allem bei Kindern und Heranwachsenden festzustellen.

7. *Letzte Worte* des Abschieds, der Klage, aber auch der Anklage finden sich in fünf von sechs Fällen. Antigone stirbt ohne jeden Zeugen; Haimons Erregung äussert sich zwar im Augenblick seines Selbstmords nicht in Worten, sondern in einer ausdrucksvollen Geste: er spuckt dem Vater schweigend ins Gesicht und greift ihn mit dem Schwert an; doch zuvor, an der Leiche Antigones, beklagt er Antigone, die Tat des Vaters und sich selbst (1224 f.). Deianeiras Abschiedsworte gelten dem Bett des Herakles (920-22); Eurydike beklagt den Verlust der Söhne und verflucht Kreon, der sie ihr genommen hat (1302-5); Iokaste beschwört die verhängnisvolle Ehe mit Laios und das Bett, das sie mit ihm und Oidipus geteilt hat (1245-50); Aias, dessen langer Monolog eine Sonderstellung unter den Abschiedsworten einnimmt,

[30] KNOX, «The Ajax...», 13-18; WINNINGTON-INGRAM, *Sophocles,* 48 ff.

ruft Götter und Erinyen um Hilfe an, verflucht seine Feinde, gedenkt seiner Eltern und verabschiedet sich vom Licht und von der Welt (815-865).

Diese Zusammenstellung zeigt auf den ersten Blick, dass Abschiedsworte für den Tragödieninterpreten das sind, was für den Suizidologen Abschiedsbriefe und letzte Tagebuchnotizen sein können: sie geben direkte und indirekte Hinweise auf die Tatmotive. Im Leben mögen letzte Worte vielfach Irrelevantes, ja Irreführendes enthalten; in der Tragödie, zumal in der sophokleischen Tragödie mit ihrer rigorosen Beschränkung auf das Bedeutsame [31] gewiss nicht. Das bedeutet andererseits aber nicht, dass letzte Worte die Selbstmorde vollständig erklären. Wie für den Selbstmordforscher gilt auch für den Tragödieninterpreten, dass neben den im Augenblick des Selbstmords (oder vorher) vom Täter ausgesprochenen Motive weitere (angedeutete, unausgesprochene, unbewusste) Ursachen eine wichtige Rolle spielen können [32].

Lassen sich die bisher zusammengestellten Elemente der Gestaltung des Selbstmords in den Tragödien des Sophokles bei allen Unterschieden im Detail doch zu *Topoi* zusammenordnen, so zählt bei der Analyse der Motive und Ursachen eigentlich nur der individuelle Fall und seine unverwechselbare komplexe Kausalität, die den Interpreten vor erheblich schwierigere Aufgaben stellt. Baechler konstatiert zurecht: «Il est extraordinairement difficile, pour ne pas dire impossible, de rendre compte d'un seul cas de suicide de manière exhaustive. Il faudrait pouvoir retracer minutieusement les moindres détails de l'évolution d'un homme et montrer comment elle l'a conduit à percevoir un problème existentiel de telle sorte que la réponse devait être la mort [33].»

[31] Kirkwood, 63 ff.; Kitto, *Form and Meaning,* 199 ff.

[32] Zur Differenzierung von Motiv und Ursache, cf. Zwingmann (ed.), p. xiv.

[33] Baechler, 87.

Glücklicherweise stellt sich das Problem bei der Untersuchung poetischer Selbstmorde nicht oder doch nicht in gleicher Schärfe. Hier lautet die Frage ja nicht: «Warum bringt Brutus sich um?», sondern: «Warum bringt sich Brutus bei Shakespeare um?». Anders als im unüberschaubar komplexen Leben, wo wir nie alles über die Hintergründe der Tat wissen können, haben wir es hier mit einem zwar komplexen aber überschaubaren Text zu tun, der die Frage nach den Gründen vollständig beantworten kann, jedenfalls, wenn der Fragesteller allen Hinweisen nachgeht, seien sie direkt oder indirekt. Das kann in diesem Rahmen natürlich nicht für alle Selbstmorde bei Sophokles geschehen. Ich beschränke mich auf den Aias; möchte aber vorher versuchen, auch für den Aspekt der Motive und Ursachen die Gemeinsamkeiten aller Fälle und ihrer künstlerischen Gestaltung zusammenzustellen.

8. *Äussere Ursache*, d.h. der Anlass, der die Tat auslöst, ist in fünf der sechs Fälle ein Erlebnis, dessen elementare Wucht so evident ist, dass der Selbstmordentschluss des Helden dem Betrachter, wenn nicht zwangsläufig, so doch gewiss natürlich erscheinen muss: Inzest (Iokaste), Tod eines geliebten Wesens, und zwar des Mannes (Deianeira), des Sohnes (Eurydike), der Verlobten (Haimon), bzw. Bestattung bei lebendigem Leibe (Antigone). Lediglich im *Aias* handelt es sich um ein Ereignis, das die tragische Qualität des Unabänderlichen erst durch den Charakter des Helden gewinnt.

9. Sophokles beschränkt sich aber keineswegs darauf, den Anlass und seine Wirkung nur zu berichten. Er zeigt vielmehr, auch in den Fällen, in denen der Selbstmord nicht im Zentrum steht, wie der Held die Wahrheit begreift (z.B. Iokaste), die ihn vernichtende Nachricht erfährt (z.B. Eurydike) oder doch seine Reaktion darauf (z.B. Antigone). In jedem Stück gibt es eine Szene, die u.a. diese Funktion der *emotionalen Vorbereitung des Selbstmords* hat.

So muss Eurydike den quälenden Bericht vom Tode des Sohnes ertragen (1180 ff.); so muss Deianeira die lange Beschreibung vom Untergang des Herakles, mit all ihren grausigen Details, über sich ergehen lassen (734 ff.); so muss Iokaste, selber bereits (seit 1016) vernichtet, auch noch mitanhören, wie Oidipus sich bei der Befragung des Boten aus Korinth Schritt für Schritt der tödlichen Wahrheit nähert (1017 ff.) [34]. Alle drei Szenen wirken wie eine psychische Folter, die das Opfer zwangsläufig unmittelbar in den Selbstmord treibt: Eurydike und Deianeira gehen schweigend ab in den Tod; Iokaste macht noch einen verzweifelten Versuch, wenigstens Oidipus zu retten, dann stürzt sie davon.

Auch in den übrigen drei Fällen gibt es Szenen, die bei allen äusseren Unterschieden funktional durchaus vergleichbar sind. Im Fall Haimons ist es die erbitterte Auseinandersetzung mit dem mächtigen Vater (632 ff.), die die emotionalen Voraussetzungen für die Affekttat im Grabe schafft und verständlich macht; im Falle Antigones konfrontiert Sophokles zwar die Heldin nicht vor unseren Augen mit der vernichtenden Nachricht, zeigt aber bei ihrem Abgang in den Tod die seelischen Qualen, die die unerwartete Änderung des Urteils ausgelöst hat (806 ff.); und im *Aias* schliesslich lässt der Dichter Tekmessa zunächst die Wirkung der Wahrheit, die Aias, aus dem Wahnsinn erwachend, allmählich begreift, ausführlich beschreiben (201 f.; 271 ff.) und führt sie uns anschliessend noch einmal direkt vor Augen (346 ff.).

In mehreren Fällen hat Sophokles die genannten Szenen, in denen die emotionale Basis für den Selbstmord entwickelt wird, mit einem letzten Höhepunkt versehen. So muss Iokaste bei ihrem verzweifelten Versuch, wenigstens Oidi-

[34] Kithairon (1026), die Füsse (1031-36), ein Hirt (1040), ein Hirt des Laios (1042-44).

pus gegen die vernichtende Wahrheit zu schützen (1056 ff.), erleben, wie er sie spöttisch abfertigt (1062 f.) und schliesslich ganz ignoriert (1068 f.). «Here is a sense of her being driven off to her death by him», stellt Cameron zu Recht fest [35]. Das gilt in noch stärkerem Masse für Deianeira, die im Anschluss an den furchtbaren Botenbericht auch noch von der hemmungslosen Verfluchung ihres Sohnes getroffen wird (807 ff.), und für Haimon, dem Kreon am Ende des Streits in seiner Wut damit droht, Antigone auf der Stelle vor seinen Augen hinrichten zu lassen, und damit gleichsam 'den letzten Tritt' versetzt (760 ff.).

In den anderen Fällen hat Sophokles von dieser wirkungsvollen dramatischen Technik keinen Gebrauch gemacht. Wenigstens einen Ansatz dazu kann man aber in der Prologszene des *Aias* erkennen. Das grausame Spiel, das Athene mit dem Helden spielt, dient nicht nur der Dokumentation seines Wahnsinns, sondern ist, wie sich später zeigt, zugleich 'the last turn of the screw' für Aias' Entscheidung zum Selbstmord.

10. Bevor ich zur Interpretation des *Aias* übergehe, seien abschliessend die *Motive* der anderen fünf Selbstmörder des Sophokles, die in der vorangegangenen topologisch orientierten Analyse des Materials bereits mehrfach angeklungen sind, kurz zusammengestellt und, soweit das möglich ist, kategorisiert [36].

[35] A. Cameron, *The Identity of Oedipus the King. Five Essays on the Oedipus Tyrannus* (New York 1968).

[36] Baechler, dessen Kategorisierung ich weitgehend folge, unterscheidet vier Typen von Intentionen (129 ff.): 1. escapiste (sous-types: fuite, deuil, châtiment); 2. agressif (sous-types: vengeance, crime, chantage, appel); 3. oblatif (sous-types: sacrifice, passage); 4. ludique (sous-types: ordalie, jeu).

Die beliebte Unterscheidung in Kurzschluss- und Bilanz-Suizid ist zu grob; bei Sophokles sind die Selbstmorde von Aias und Deianeira eindeutige Bilanz-Selbstmorde; im Falle Haimons kann man von Kurzschluss-Selbstmord sprechen; die anderen stehen dazwischen.

Baechler hat im Anschluss an A. Schütz [37] darauf aufmerksam gemacht, dass die Frage nach dem «warum» einer Handlung auf zweierlei Weise beantwortet werden kann: nämlich entweder mit «weil» (d.h. mit Kausalsätzen) oder mit «um zu» (d.h. mit Finalsätzen): [38]
X tötet sich, weil er unheilbar krank ist, bzw.
X tötet sich, um sich selbst oder seiner Familie die Leiden der unheilbaren Krankheit zu ersparen.
In dem einen Fall richtet sich der Blick auf die Ursache, im anderen auf die Ziele, die das Individuum mit dem Selbstmord verfolgt. Die hieraus abgeleitete Unterscheidung zwischen *Ätiologie* (étiologie) und *Bedeutung* (sens) von Selbstmorden erscheint mir auch für die Untersuchung poetischer Selbstmorde, wo *Ursachen* und *Intentionen* allerdings weit vollständiger und direkter miteinander verbunden sind als in der Realität, als sinnvoll.

Im Falle Iokastes sind Motiv und Intention eindeutig. Der Inzest zerstört die Vergangenheit und erlaubt keine Zukunft. Hier handelt es sich eindeutig um einen 'Fluchtselbstmord' [39]. Eurydike tötet sich, weil sie den Verlust Haimons, so kurz nach dem Verlust des anderen Sohnes nicht ertragen kann [40]. Aus der Verfluchung Kreons (1304-5) kann man ausserdem schliessen, dass die Tatsache, dass der eigene Mann und Vater den Selbstmord Haimons verursacht hat, zusätzlich schwer auf ihr lastet; ein Weiterleben ohne den Sohn, aber mit dem 'Mörder' ist unmöglich. Durch ihren

[37] A. Schütz, *Der sinnhafte Aufbau der sozialen Welt*, Suhrkamp, stw 92 (1974).

[38] Baechler, 118-21.

[39] Anders nur C. M. Bowra, *Sophoclean Tragedy* (Oxford 1944), 209, der 1245-1250 als «confession before death» und den Selbstmord als «her attempt to make peace with her real husband and with the gods» missversteht.

[40] 1301-1305 (993-995); in 1303 ist, wenn der überlieferte Text überhaupt geändert werden muss (cf. Kamerbeek, *ad loc.*), κενὸν (Seyffert) λέχος dem κλεινὸν λάχος (Bothe, Dawe) m.E. vorzuziehen (cf. G. Müller, *Sophokles. Antigone* (Heidelberg 1967), 270).

Fluch wird Kreon ihren Erinyen überantwortet [41]. Hier verbinden sich also 'Flucht-' [42] und 'Racheselbstmord' [43].

Die drei anderen Fälle sind noch komplexer. Deianeira ersticht sich, weil sie ohne Herakles nicht leben kann, aber auch, weil sie sich schuldig fühlt an seinem Tod [44], und schliesslich auch, weil sie durch ihre Tat nicht nur den Mann und ihre Ehre [45], sondern auch noch den Sohn verloren zu haben glaubt; erst damit wird der Sinnverlust total [46]. Dieser Selbstmord gehört folglich unter die beiden Kategorien, 'Flucht' und 'Selbstbestrafung'. Haimon tötet sich aus Schmerz über den Verlust der geliebten [47] Antigone; zugleich aber auch im Sturm der Gefühle nach dem wilden Angriff auf seinen Vater. In der Wendung αὑτῷ χολωθείς (1235), mit der der Bote die Tat erklärt, sind der Hass auf Kreon, der ihm die Verlobte getötet (und zugleich wohl auch sein Vaterbild, ja sein ganzes Weltbild zerstört hat [48]), sowie die Wut darüber, ihn nicht getroffen zu haben [49], unlöslich verbunden mit der Reue über den versuchten Vatermord [50].

[41] 1305 (cf. *OT* 1275).

[42] Für Baechler fiele Eurydikes Selbstmord in die Kategorie «deuil»; zur Unterscheidung von Flucht- und Schmerz-Selbstmorden, die beide der Gruppe der «suicides escapistes» zugehören, cf. BAECHLER, 129, 132/150, 153.

[43] S.u. S. 139-140 zum *Aias*.

[44] 663 ff.; 706 ff. Zur Frage von Deianeiras Schuld zuletzt WINNINGTON-INGRAM, *Sophocles*, 78 f.

[45] 719-722.

[46] Zu Deianeiras totaler Fixierung auf Haus und Familie cf. E. R. SCHWINGE, *op. cit.* (oben S. 115 Anm. 29), 56 ff.

[47] K. v. FRITZ, «Haimons Liebe zu Antigone», in *Antike und moderne Tragödie* (Berlin 1962), 227-40 (repr. aus *Philologus* 89, 1934, 19-34), vertritt die Auffassung, dass «aus den Motiven Haimons... eine persönliche Leidenschaft von Anfang bis zu Ende fernzuhalten» sei; dagegen zurecht WINNINGTON-INGRAM, *Sophocles*, 92 ff. (cf. unten S. 123-4 Anm. 54).

[48] 1177; 1225; G. RONNET, *Sophocle, poète tragique* (Paris 1969), 84 (153).

[49] So WINNINGTON-INGRAM, *Sophocles*, 94 Anm. 12.

[50] R. C. JEBB (ed.), *Sophocles. The Plays and Fragments. Part VII: The Ajax* (Cambridge 1896), *ad loc.*; G. H. GELLIE, *Sophocles. A Reading* (Melbourne 1972), 51;

Für Freudianer ist der Selbstmord Haimons natürlich ein instruktives Beispiel; sah doch Freud die entscheidende Kraft hinter dem Selbstmord in der «Einschränkung der Aggression nach aussen und der dadurch verursachten Aggression der Über-Ich gegen das Ich» [51]. Haimons Selbstmord ist also als 'Flucht-' und zugleich 'Nachfolge-Selbstmord' zu verstehen (die Griechen sprechen von ἐπαποθανεῖν) [52], daneben aber auch als Selbstbestrafung; und vielleicht enthält er sogar ein Element der Rache [53]. Im Falle der Antigone schliesslich fehlt im Text jeder explizite Hinweis auf die Motive des Selbstmords. Der elementare Schrecken, den die Vorstellung der unerhörten Strafe (849) auslöst, ist bei ihrem Abschied nicht zu überhören (806 ff.). Doch Antigone tötet sich gewiss nicht nur, weil sie den Gedanken nicht ertragen kann, lebendig begraben zu sein: die Antigone des Sophokles, die stolze Tochter des Oidipus, wie wir sie seit dem Prolog kennen, kann sich von Kreon nicht vorschreiben lassen, wann und wie sie sterben muss. Ihr Freitod ist auch ein entschlossener Akt der Selbstbehauptung und der Würde, und schliesslich mag die Entscheidung auch von dem seit dem Prolog immer wieder lautwerdenden Gedanken, ja dem Wunsch bestimmt sein, den geliebten Bruder und die Eltern im Hades wiederzusehen [54]. Für

---

K. J. Dover, *Greek Popular Morality in the Time of Plato and Aristotle* (Oxford 1974), 273 f.; nach Lysias, *Or.* XXXI (Κατὰ Φίλωνος δοκιμασίας) 20-23 verdient Angriff auf die Eltern Hinrichtung; zu Haimons Selbstmord vgl. weiter I. M. Linforth, *Antigone and Creon*, Univ. of Calif. Publ. in Class, Phil. 15 (1961), 183-259, 219 n.; H. Lloyd-Jones, in *Gnomon* 34 (1962), 739 f.

[51] Cf. W. de Boor, «Arbeiten über Selbstmord und Selbstbeschädigung — 1949», in Ch. Zwingmann (ed.), *op. cit.* (oben S. 107 Anm. 4), 13-22, 20.

[52] 1224 f.; 1236 ff. (!); cf. weiter 751 (Kamerbeek, *ad loc.*); zum ἐπαποθανεῖν vgl. das Material bei Hirzel, 5 Anm. 1.

[53] Cf. die wohlbekannten Selbstmordphantasien von Kindern: der Tod als einzige Möglichkeit, den Vater zu bestrafen.

[54] 73 ff.; (524 f.); 897 ff.; dieser Punkt ist jetzt von Winnington-Ingram, *Sophocles*, 128-49, stark betont worden; für ihn hat Antigone den Tod gewählt (555), d.h. den

Antigones Selbstmord findet sich bei Baechler keine handliche Kategorie [55]. Sie erweist sich auch in dieser Hinsicht noch als αὐτόνομος (821).

11. Am Ende des systematisch-topologischen Teils sei eine letzte Beobachtung ausgewertet, auch wenn die Gefahr besteht, dass dabei die Grenze zum Spekulativen überschritten wird.

Die Suizidologie legt bei der Analyse der Selbstmordursachen grosses Gewicht auf die *« Persönlichkeitsdisposition »* [56] und auf die lange, vorbereitende « Entwicklung zum Selbstmord » [57], ohne die das die Tat auslösende Ereignis nicht die vernichtende Wucht erreichen könne. Es scheint, dass Sophokles intuitiv etwas davon geahnt hat, wenn er in der Vergangenheit seiner Selbstmörder frühere traumatische Erlebnisse und allgemein bedrückende Lebensumstände betont oder doch andeutet: bei Antigone der bereits in den ersten Versen des Stücks evozierte furchtbare Tod erst der Eltern, dann der Brüder und das Gefühl, unter dem Fluch des Hauses zu stehen [58]; bei Deianeira das frühe Trauma der Werbung des Acheloos [59] und die langen Jahre der Ängste

---

Bruder bestattet, um durch eine Liebestat die verfluchte Familie im Hades zu versöhnen. Kreon verweigert ihr die ersehnte Vereinigung mit der Familie. « She is confronted with a continuance of life in a tomb, cut off alike from the living and the dead, utterly alone. For the moment she can see no further » (WINNINGTON-INGRAM, *Sophocles*, 140).

[55] In Frage kommt eine Kombination von « fuite » (la fuite est le fait d'échapper, par l'attentat à sa vie, à une situation ressentie comme insupportable par le sujet) und « passage » (le fait d'attenter à sa vie pour accéder à un état considéré par le sujet comme infiniment plus délectable) (BAECHLER, 129).

[56] ZWINGMANN (ed.), p. XIX.

[57] K. LEONHARD, « Psychologische Entwicklung zum Selbstmord », in ZWINGMANN, 133-43.

[58] 858 ff. (941); cf. G. F. ELSE, *The Madness of Antigone*, Abh. der Heidelberger Akad. der Wiss., Phil.-hist. Klasse, 1976, 1, 26 ff.

[59] Ausführlich von ihr selbst berichtet (9 ff.), dann noch einmal vom Chor (497 ff.); dazu kommt das Erlebnis mit Nessos (555 ff.); Deianeira war wiederholt Objekt männlicher sexueller Aggression.

und Sorgen um Herakles, die sie selbst gleich zu Beginn eindringlich beschwört [60]; bei Iokaste die Verstümmelung und Aussetzung ihres ersten Kindes [61]; bei Eurydike der nicht weit zurückliegende Tod des ersten Sohnes und bei Haimon schliesslich — wie auch bei Aias — der lastende Schatten eines übermächtigen Vaters [62].

III

Das früheste der erhaltenen sophokleischen Stücke ist zwar keine dramatische Studie *de suicidio*, sondern die Tragödie des Aias, eine tiefgreifende Analyse der unauflöslichen tragisch-dialektischen Verbindung von bewundernswerter heroischer Grösse und erschreckender, selbstzerstörerischer Megalomanie. Katalysator dieser Analyse und dramatisches Zentrum des Stücks ist jedoch die Entscheidung des Helden, sich selbst zu töten. Nirgends bei Sophokles, nirgends in der (erhaltenen) griechischen Tragödie, ja, kaum einmal, soweit ich sehe, in der langen abendländischen Geschichte der Gattung, steht der Selbstmord des Helden so im Mittelpunkt eines Dramas.

Sophokles präsentiert in Prolog und Parodos zunächst den *äusseren Anlass*, die Ursache des Selbstmords, entwickelt in der Parodos und im ersten Teil des ersten Epeisodions die *psychische Disposition*, in der und aus der der Selbstmordgedanke erwächst, entfaltet dann im ersten Monolog des

[60] Zum Leitmotiv Furcht cf. E. R. Schwinge, *op. cit.* (oben S. 115 Anm. 29), 56 ff.; R. M. Torrance, «Sophocles: Some Bearings», in *HSCP* 69 (1965), 269-327, 302; Winnington-Ingram, *Sophocles*, 75 ff.; Aigner, 82, spricht von einer «Art Vorbestimmtheit zum Freitod».

[61] 718 f. spricht sie selbst davon; 1031-1036 muss sie es anhören.

[62] Die Auseinandersetzung mit dem unbedingten Gehorsam, ja Unterwerfung fordernden Kreon (626 ff.) lässt etwas ahnen von dem autoritären Druck, unter dem Haimon aufgewachsen ist; zum Aias s.u. S. 138-139.

Helden und in der sogenannten Trugrede die *äusseren und inneren Motive, engeren und weiteren Zwänge*, die zum Entschluss führen, leuchtet vor der Tat mit der Rede des Sehers Kalchas noch einmal weit zurück in die Vergangenheit des Helden und legt so die alten Wurzeln des Unheils bloss, und zeigt schliesslich die Tat selbst.

Die *äussere Ursache des Selbstmords*, d.h. die Ereignisse, die die tragische Entwicklung ausgelöst haben und vorantreiben, gehören der Vorgeschichte des Stücks an und werden in den exponierenden Eingangsszenen berichtet und gezeigt. Aias hat die Niederlage beim Streit um die Waffen Achills nicht verwinden können und sich entschlossen, seine verletzte Ehre durch einen Racheakt wiederherzustellen. Der Versuch ist jedoch von Athene vereitelt worden, die ihn mit Wahnsinn geschlagen und in die Beuteherden des Heeres getrieben hat. Als die Verblendung weicht, sieht sich der «tapfere Aias, der furchtlose Kämpfer in brennenden Schlachten» als Sieger über harmlose Rinder, Schafe und Ziegen (364 ff.), schutzlos dem Hohngelächter seiner Feinde preisgegeben. Der Anblick, den Tekmessa dem Chor (und dem Zuschauer) enthüllt, als sie die Zelttür zurückschlägt (346), ist eine grausig-groteske Karikatur des heroischen Lebensideals, das Aias alles bedeutet, und lässt keinen Zweifel daran, dass sein verzweifelter Todeswunsch in Erfüllung gehen wird (356 ff.). Aias' Schicksal ist in diesem Moment bereits entschieden. Der Makel, den das Bühnenbild so eindrucksvoll symbolisiert, ist nur mit seinem Tod zu tilgen.

Neben der Exposition der äusseren Umstände, aus denen der Selbstmord erwächst, dienen die ersten Szenen des Stücks zugleich der Entfaltung der *psychischen Disposition des Aias*. Als der Sturm des Wahnsinns sich legt (257 f.) und Aias langsam und schwer zur Besinnung kommt (306), stürzt ihn die Erkenntnis seiner nächtlichen Tat in wilde seelische Qualen: λύπη πᾶς ἐλήλαται κακῇ (275). Sophokles bringt diesen Zustand geistig-seelischer Störung vor allem durch mehrfach jähe Verhaltens- und Stimmungswechsel zum Ausdruck. So beschreibt Tekmessa, wie er sich beim Anblick der hingeschlachteten Tiere gegen den Kopf schlägt und laut aufschreit (308) und dann lange Zeit stumm, die Hände in die Haare gekrallt, inmitten der Kadaver hockt (308-11). Als sie ihm auf seine Beschimpfungen und Drohungen hin berichtet, was geschehen ist, bricht er erneut in schrilles Jammergeschrei aus, wie sie es nie zuvor von ihm gehört hat (316 f.), und verfällt dann wieder in stummes Brüten. Lange Zeit liegt er zusammengebrochen, ohne zu essen und zu trinken inmitten der blutigen Kadaver (323 ff.); dann erschallt plötzlich sein Klagegeschrei ἰώ μοί μοι aus dem Zelt.

Diesem jähen Wechsel von schriller Klage und dumpfen Schweigen, von hektischer Aktivität und starrer Passivität entspricht das ständige Hin- und Herschwanken zwischen Selbstmitleid und Hasstiraden, zwischen stumpfer Resignation und heftiger Aggression [63].

Stanford ist der einzige Interpret, der sich mit dieser Frage eingehender beschäftigt hat. Er stellt zu Recht fest: «Sophocles portrays the psychological symptoms of impending suicide much as modern observers have described them [64]». Stanfords Beobachtungen typischer psychischer Symptome können allerdings erheblich erweitert und vertieft werden. Die moderne Selbstmordforschung hat der Frage der 'suizidalen Persönlichkeit' seit dem denkwürdigen Symposion der Wiener Psychoanalytischen Gesellschaft im Jahre 1910 schon deshalb immer stärkere Aufmerksamkeit

[63] Es handelt sich übrigens um die klassischen Symptome der Depression; cf. A. T. Beck, *Depression. Causes and Treatment* (Philadelphia 1967). Er nennt: 1. alterations in temperament: sadness, apathy, solitude: 2. negative ego-perception: blame and reproach directed against oneself; 3. regressive desires: to flee, to hide, to die; 4. anorexia, insomnia, loss of desire; 5. changes in one's level of activity: abatement and agitation.

[64] Stanford, 290.

geschenkt, weil Selbstmordprophylaxe und -therapie ohne Kenntnis typischer Persönlichkeitsmerkmale potentieller Selbstmörder kaum möglich sind; und Erwin Ringel, einer der bedeutendsten Suizidologen unserer Tage, hat auf Grund der von ihm (und anderen) beobachteten Übereinstimmungen in der seelischen Verfassung von Selbstmördern und potentiellen Selbstmördern ein 'präsuizidales Syndrom' konstatiert, das vor allem durch drei Elemente bestimmt ist: 1) Einengung, 2) gehemmte und so gegen die eigene Person gerichtete Aggression und 3) Selbstmordphantasien [65]. Eine Anwendung dieses vielfach bestätigten und inzwischen weithin anerkannten Modells auf den sophokleischen Aias erweist sich m.E. als durchaus fruchtbar [66].

Ringel unterscheidet mehrere einander ergänzende Aspekte der Einengung. Da ist zunächst einmal die *situative Einengung* (1), die nach seinen Worten gekennzeichnet ist «durch einen Verlust der Balance zwischen Lebensumständen und dem Gefühl der eigenen Möglichkeiten»; so «herrscht der Eindruck von allen Seiten behindert und umzingelt zu sein. ... Das Gefühl, nichts ändern zu können, wird zum Eindruck der Ausweglosigkeit, aus dem Pluralismus der Möglichkeiten wird die Einseitigkeit des Zwanges.» [67]

Das ist eine Beschreibung, die zweifellos auch auf den Zustand des sophokleischen Aias zutrifft, der infolge der in seinen Augen betrügerischen Entscheidung über die Waffen Achills das ohnehin labile psychische Gleichgewicht [68] ver-

[65] RINGEL, 45 ff.

[66] Cf. auch AIGNER, 66.

[67] RINGEL, 45 f.

[68] 1087 f.; WINNINGTON-INGRAM, *Sophocles*, 41; zur Frage des Betrugs bei der ὅπλων κρίσις: Aias 98, (100), 445 f., und Teukros, 1135-1137, behaupten Betrug der Atriden (cf. z.B. J. C. OPSTELTEN, *Sophocles and Greek Pessimism* (Amsterdam 1952), 51; G. GROSSMANN, «Das Lachen des Aias», in *MH* 25 (1968), 65-85, 85; KAMERBEEK, 6); Menelaos, 1136, und Agamemnon, 1238 ff., verweisen auf die

liert und seiner ohnmächtigen Wut in einem heimtückischen Racheakt Luft macht, dessen klägliches Scheitern ihn endgültig entehrt und ihm keinen anderen Ausweg mehr lässt als den Tod. Aias selber formuliert das Gefühl der situativen Einengung zunächst in den Versen 403 f.:

ποῖ τις οὖν φύγῃ;
ποῖ μολὼν μενῶ;

und begründet die Ausweglosigkeit gleich darauf ausführlich: der Heimweg nach Salamis (460 ff.) ist ihm ebenso verschlossen wie ein einsamer Heldentod vor den Mauern Trojas (466 ff.). Zu Hause kann er ohne die Symbole seiner Ehre dem Vater nicht unter die Augen treten; vor Troja kann er die verlorene Ehre nicht zurückerkämpfen, ohne zugleich den verhassten Atriden zu nutzen; d.h. er kann nicht gehen, und er kann auch nicht bleiben (403 f.). Reduziert auf die Enge seines Zeltes, umringt von hohnlachenden Feinden, gleichsam eingekreist von den blutigen Zeugen seiner Wahnsinnstat, fühlt er sich eingeschlossen von einer gewaltigen Woge, die hochaufgetürmt von einer mörderischen Sturmbö im Kreise um ihn herumrast:

ἴδεσθέ μ' οἷον ἄρτι κῦ-
μα φοινίας ὑπὸ ζάλης
ἀμφίδρομον κυκλεῖται.

(351-53) [69]

Ein suggestives Bild für die Ausweglosigkeit der Situation und zugleich für die ungeheure Dynamik der äusseren und inneren Zwänge (Ringel spricht in diesem Zusammenhang von «dynamischer Einengung» [70]), die zum Selbstmord-

Entscheidung eines Richterkollegiums; richtig (d.h. es bleibt offen) Kirkwood, 72; K. v. Fritz, «Haimons Liebe zu Antigone» (s.o. S. 122 Anm. 47), 248; Winnington-Ingram, *Sophocles*, 41. Odysseus' Worte (1340 f.), wenn nicht überhaupt nur aus der Situation heraus zu verstehen, beweisen nur, dass es ein Fehlurteil war, nicht, dass es sich um Betrug handelte.

[69] Zu dieser Auffassung des Textes cf. Kamerbeek, *ad loc.*

[70] Ringel, 48-53, bes. 52-53.

wunsch führen, der in der Tat gleich darauf zum ersten Mal aus Aias herausbricht:

ἀλλά με συνδάϊξον. (361)

Besonders erhellend für das Verständnis des sophokleischen Aias ist zweitens der Aspekt der *präsuizidalen Einengung*, die Ringel als «Einengung der zwischenmenschlichen Beziehungen» bezeichnet. «Man kann sie sich», so Ringel, «als totale Isolierung ... aber auch als Entwertung vorhandener Beziehungen ... vorstellen [71]». Soziale Isoliertheit gilt der modernen Forschung als der «am weitesten verbreitete Einzelfaktor unter den Ursachen von Selbstmordhandlungen» [72].

Aias' äussere und innere Isolation ist vollständig. Schon nach der ὅπλων κρίσις hat er sich aus der Gemeinschaft der Kämpfenden zurückgezogen und nach den Worten des Chores lange Zeit wie erstarrt im Zelt gehockt (193 ff.) [73]. Das groteske Gemetzel unter den Herden hat Aias zum Gespött des ganzen Heeres gemacht, und da er sich an dem gemeinsamen Beutebesitz vergangen hat, hat er auch die letzten Sympathien eingebüsst [74]. Μισεῖ δέ μ' Ἑλλήνων στρατός lautet sein eigenes Urteil (458), das im Verlaufe des Stücks mehrfach bestätigt wird [75], und im Kreise der Grossen zeigt allein Kalchas Mitgefühl mit Teukros und Sorge um Aias (749 ff.).

Aias ist zwar umgeben von treuen Freunden und von Tekmessa. «But it becomes clear», stellt Winnington-Ingram

[71] Ringel, 53 f.

[72] E. Stengel, «Forschungsergebnisse über das Selbstmordproblem», in Zwingmann, 123-130, 125.

[73] Die Entscheidung liegt einige Zeit zurück (193 ff.; 925 ff.); wie lange, bleibt unklar.

[74] E. Schlesinger, «Erhaltung im Untergang. Sophokles' Aias als 'pathetische' Tragödie», in *Poetica* 3 (1970), 359-87, 372.

[75] 148 ff.; 196 ff.; 719 ff.

zu Recht fest, «that Ajax has hardly more contact with his immediate than with his remoter environment» [76]. Szene für Szene offenbart sich immer deutlicher, dass er, gefangen in dem brennenden Gefühl der Schande und in seinem selbstzerstörerischen Hass, unfähig ist zur Kommunikation. Das ist im Anschluss an Reinhardt [77] so oft konstatiert und so sorgfältig analysiert worden, dass ich mich kurz fassen kann. Aias, dem es, wie Sophokles andeutet [78], schon immer schwergefallen ist, auf andere zu hören, hat diese Fähigkeit nun gänzlich eingebüsst [79]. Aias' eigenen Äusserungen, seien sie Ausdruck seiner seelischen Qualen, Begründung seiner Entscheidung zum Selbstmord oder Abschied von der Welt, sind auch dort, wo er nicht allein ist, ja selbst da, wo sie scheinbar dialogisch sind, immer zutiefst monologisch, ich-bezogen [80].

Es ist wiederholt betont worden, dass die existentielle Vereinsamung des Aias auf dem evozierten Hintergrund der Homilie besonders deutlich in Erscheinung tritt [81]. Bei Homer finden Hektor und Andromache im Augenblick des vom Tode überschatteten Abschieds am Skäischen Tor für einen kostbaren Moment in der gemeinsamen Liebe zu Astyanax zueinander [82]; bei Sophokles schafft auch das Kind

[76] Winnington-Ingram, *Sophocles*, 24.

[77] Reinhardt, *Sophokles*, 10; 21 ff.

[78] Cf. Menelaos' Worte 1069 f.; 1087 f.

[79] Knox, *Heroic Temper*, 18; «The Ajax...», 13 mit Anm. 78.

[80] Sophokles hat dafür die schöne Wendung: φρενὸς οἰοβώτας (615 f.) geprägt; vgl. P. Valéry (zit. nach Ringel, 55): «Für den Selbstmörder bedeutet jeder andere nur Abwesenheit».

[81] Reinhardt, *Sophokles*, 29 f.; W. Schadewaldt, «Hektor und Andromache», in *Die Antike* 11 (1935), jetzt in *Von Homers Welt und Werk* (Stuttgart ³1959), 207-33, 229-32; G. Perrotta, *Sofocle* (Messina 1935), 144-47; E. Schlesinger, in *Poetica* 3 (1970), 374; Winnington-Ingram, *Sophocles*, 16.

[82] W. Schadewaldt, *ibid.*; B. Seidensticker, *Palintonos Harmonia. Studien zu komischen Elementen in der griechischen Tragödie*, Hypomnemata 72 (Göttingen 1982), 34; 50-53.

keine emotionale Verbindung mehr zwischen Aias und Tekmessa [83].

Die «Einengung der *zwischenmenschlichen* Beziehungen» ist in der Tat total, und auch im Göttlichen kann (und will) Aias, der göttliche Hilfe in der Vergangenheit im Vertrauen auf die eigene Kraft hybride ignoriert hat (762 ff.) und sich von Athene grausam in die Irre geführt und verhöhnt sieht (89 ff.; 401-403; 450-453), im Augenblick der suizidalen Krise keinen Halt finden [84].

Der megalomanische Einzelgänger, sozial isoliert, zutiefst beziehungslos und einsam, auch im Kreise derer, die ihn lieben, und von den Göttern verlassen: ist das wirklich nicht mehr als die typische existentielle Einsamkeit und soziale Isolation, die seit Reinhardt als das entscheidende Signum des sophokleischen Helden gilt? [85] Ich möchte diese Frage, die kürzlich auch von Winnington-Ingram gestellt worden ist [86], mit einem klaren Nein beantworten. Bei aller Ähnlichkeit ist Aias doch anders als Oidipus und Elektra, Antigone und Deianeira. Ein Blick auf einen letzten Aspekt «präsuizidaler Einengung», den ich in Erweiterung des Ringelschen Modells als *Einengung der Gefühlswelt und des Wertsystems* bezeichnen möchte, kann das verdeutlichen.

Ringel spricht lediglich von der «*Einengung der Wertwelt*» [87] und versteht darunter in erster Linie die Verringerung des Selbstwertgefühls (a) und eine «mangelnde Beziehung zu Werten» (b).

Reduzierung oder Verlust des Selbstwertgefühls (a), das der modernen Selbstmordforschung ganz allgemein als

[83] Nur ein Ansatz dazu in V. 559.

[84] 398-400; 589 f.; cf. Winnington-Ingram, *Sophocles*, 18.

[85] Reinhardt, *Sophokles*, 10.

[86] Winnington-Ingram, *Sophocles*, 15 ff.

[87] Ringel, 56 ff. (Einengung der Gefühle erscheint bei ihm unter «situativer Einengung»).

zentraler Faktor des suizidalen Syndroms gilt, ist im *Aias* nur in Ansätzen zu beobachten, z.B. in Aias' Überzeugung, dem berühmten Vater nicht mehr unter die Augen treten zu können (434 ff.; 462 ff.), oder wenn er gegen Ende des Kommos ausruft, dass er nicht mehr wert (ἄξιος) sei, Hilfe bei den Göttern oder bei den Menschen zu suchen (398-400). Es ist bezeichnend, dass beide Äusserungen als Begründung des Todeswunsches dienen [88]. Insgesamt jedoch ist Aias eher durch ein extrem hohes Selbstwertgefühl gekennzeichnet, und gewiss begeht er, wie wir noch sehen werden, nicht Selbstmord, weil er es verloren hat, sondern weil er es nur durch den Tod uneingeschränkt bewahren zu können glaubt.

Als «mangelnde Beziehung zu Werten» (b) lässt sich die von Winnington-Ingram beobachtete Tatsache auffassen, dass er in der Fixierung auf sein persönliches Prestige taub ist für Tekmessas mahnende Beschwörung von Werten, die eigentlich zu dem von ihm erstrebten Heldenideal gehören; Winnington-Ingram nennt: «respect for aged parents, pity for the weak, and above all the claims of gratitude for services done [89].»

Wichtiger jedoch als Aias' «mangelnde Beziehung zu Werten» scheint mir die ihr zugrundeliegende «Einengung seiner Gefühlswelt» zu sein. Aias fühlt sich vom Hass der ganzen Welt verfolgt.

καὶ νῦν τί χρὴ δρᾶν; ὅστις ἐμφανῶς θεοῖς
ἐχθαίρομαι, μισεῖ δέ μ' Ἑλλήνων στρατός,
ἔχθει δὲ Τροία πᾶσα καὶ πεδία τάδε.

(457-59)

Doch dieses Gefühl ist nicht zuletzt geboren aus seinem eigenen verzehrenden Hass, der an Verfolgungswahn erin-

[88] Vgl. auch 361 und 364 ff.

[89] WINNINGTON-INGRAM, *Sophocles*, 19 (29); vgl. bereits KIRKWOOD, 105 f.

nernde Züge trägt. Dieser manische Hass trifft nicht nur die eigentlichen Gegner, Odysseus und die Atriden, sondern schliesst am Ende das ganze Heer ein (843 f.), er trifft 'Schuldige' und 'Unschuldige' in gleicher Weise, und er richtet sich sogar gegen Hektor und sein Schwert [90]. Hass beherrscht Aias von seinen ersten Klagen bis zum Selbstmord; wo er nicht offen zu Tage tritt (z.B. in der Trugrede), ist seine zerstörerische Kraft unter der ruhigen Oberfläche spürbar [91]. Hass macht ihn hart gegen die Gefühle anderer und lässt ihm selbst nur wenig Raum für andere Gefühle.

Diese Einengung der Gefühls- und Wertwelt ist es vor allem, durch die sich Aias von anderen sophokleischen Helden unterscheidet.

Das Grossartige an der sophokleischen Gestaltung dieser Einengung ist, dass es ihm gelingt, nicht nur das Gefühl der Ausweglosigkeit, sondern auch das Gefühl zu vermitteln, dass es sich um einen wirklichen Prozess der Einengung handelt, d.h. um einen Verlust von Möglichkeiten unter dem Druck mächtiger äusserer und innerer Zwänge: Aias kann sich Tekmessa nicht mehr wirklich zuwenden, aber Sophokles deutet doch an, dass es einmal anders war [92]; Aias bewahrt sich seinen wilden Hass auch im Augenblick der Selbstvernichtung, aber er fühlt doch auch, wie sehr sein Tod die Mutter treffen wird [93]; er scheidet aus einer dunklen und verhassten Welt, aber seine Abschiedsworte an das Licht, an Salamis und Athen, an Quellen, Flüsse und die weite Ebene vor Troja offenbaren, wie tief er in dieser Welt verwurzelt ist [94].

[90] 661 ff.; 817 f.; (1024 ff.); WINNINGTON-INGRAM, *Sophocles*, 19; 44.

[91] Zu der Literatur, s.o. S. 116 Anm. 30; vgl. weiter KIRKWOOD, 161; K. v. FRITZ, «Haimons Liebe zu Antigone» (s.o. S. 122 Anm. 47), 245 f.

[92] 211 f. (491, 493); 559 (Reaktion auf 520-24); 808; cf. KIRKWOOD, 104 f.; WINNINGTON-INGRAM, *Sophocles*, 30 f.

[93] 567 ff.; 845 ff.

[94] 412 ff.; 854 ff. (vgl. auch *Ant.* 806 ff.); REINHARDT, *Sophokles*, 36 f.

Es ist keine Frage, dass Sophokles durch diese Gestaltung seinem problematischsten Helden den Grad emotionaler Anteilnahme sichert, ohne den er nur als erschreckend und nicht auch als gross erscheinen würde.

Auf die beiden anderen Elemente des präsuizidalen Syndroms, die Ringel anführt, brauche ich nur hinzuweisen.

«Gehemmte und so gegen die eigene Person gerichtete Aggression» ist im Falle des Aias so evident, dass sich eine detaillierte Analyse erübrigt [95]; «Selbstmordphantasien», d.h. Selbstmordgedanken und -wünsche, -beschwörungen und -ankündigungen finden sich bei Sophokles von Aias' Anruf der Todesfinsternis als dem strahlenden Licht (394 f.) bis zu den verschlüsselten Ankündigungen der Tat in der Trugrede [96].

Bei der folgenden Untersuchung der *Motive* des Aias kann ich mich etwas kürzer fassen, da manches bereits in der ausführlichen Analyse des präsuizidalen Syndroms angesprochen oder doch angedeutet worden ist. Über den entscheidenden Grund für den Selbstmord sind sich alle Interpreten einig. Der grosse Aias, der grösste Held nach Achilleus, betrogen, wie er meint, um den ihm zustehenden Ehrenpreis und dem Gelächter des ganzen Heeres wehrlos preisgegeben, geht, so Goethe, zugrunde «an dem Dämon verletzten Ehrgefühls» [97]. Aias selbst bringt am Ende des ersten Monologs, in dem er seinen Entschluss ausführlich begründet, das zentrale Motiv auf die knappe heroische Formel: ἀλλ' ἢ καλῶς ζῆν ἢ καλῶς τεθνηκέναι / τὸν εὐγενῆ χρή (479-480). «Military virtue is everything to him, this gone he is at an end [98].»

[95] Cf. u. S. 137-138 ff.

[96] Cf. bereits 361; 387 ff.; 654 ff.; zur Doppeldeutigkeit der Trugrede besonders M. Sicherl, «Die Tragik des Aias», in *Hermes* 98 (1970), 14-37, 22-28.

[97] E. Grumach, *Goethe und die Antike* (Berlin 1949), 263.

[98] Kirkwood, 47.

In der sogenannten Trugrede (646 ff.) wird der Sinnverlust noch radikaler erfahren. In dieser Hinsicht ist das Zentrum der Tragödie [99] — Trug oder nicht, Monolog oder nicht [100] — vor allem eine zweite tiefere Begründung für den Selbstmord. Selbstmordforscher weisen darauf hin, dass es in jedem Selbstmörder zu einem letzten Kampf zwischen selbsterhaltenden und selbstzerstörenden Kräften kommt [101]. Hierin liegt die tiefe psychologische Wahrheit der Trugrede. Sophokles deutet diese emotionale Disposition, aus der die Trugrede erwächst, in den ersten Worten an (646-53). Tekmessas leidenschaftlicher Appell, die Erinnerung an Vater und Mutter und der Anblick des kleinen Sohnes, den er beim Abschied in den Armen gehalten hat, haben den scheinbar völlig unzugänglichen Aias doch erreicht. Sie haben nicht zu einer inneren Wandlung geführt [102], aber die Welt hat noch einmal Anspruch auf ihn erhoben und Aias zu einer letzten Auseinandersetzung gezwungen. So radikalisiert sich im Augenblick des Abgangs in den Tod die Frage nach der Möglichkeit weiterzuleben.

[99] Die Trugrede steht seit F. G. Welcker, «Über den Aias des Sophokles», in *RhM* 3 (1829), 43-92; 229-264 (*Kleine Schriften* II, Bonn, 1845, 264-340), 229 ff., im Mittelpunkt der Aias-Interpretation; zu der umfangreichen Literatur vgl. H. Friis Johansen, «Sophocles 1939-1959», in *Lustrum* 7 (1962), 177 f.; I. Errandonea, «Les quatre monologues d'Ajax et leur signification dramatique», in *LEC* 26 (1958), 21-40, jetzt in *Sophokles*, hrsg. von H. Diller, WdF 95 (Darmstadt 1967), 268-94; M. Sicherl, *art. cit.* (s.o. S. 135 Anm. 96), 16 ff.; D. A. Hester, «The Heroic Distemper. A Study in the Ajax of Sophocles», in *Prometheus* 5 (1979), 241-55 (bes. 247-52).

[100] Knox, «The Ajax...», 12-14; dagegen Winnington-Ingram, *Sophocles*, 47 f.

[101] Z.B. Ringel, 14; durchaus typisch ist übrigens auch, dass der Selbstmordentschluss mehr oder minder deutlich angekündigt wird und dass die Umwelt diese Ankündigungen nicht versteht oder missversteht (cf. Chor: 693 ff.; 911 ff.; Tekmessa: 807 f.).

[102] So z.B. Jebb, pp. xxxii ff.; Stanford, pp. xxvi; xxxiv f.; Appendix D; C. M. Bowra, *Sophoclean Tragedy*, 39 ff.; weitere Literatur und treffende Kritik bei M. Sicherl, *art. cit.* (s.o. S. 135 Anm. 96), 17 ff.; vgl. aber jetzt wieder E. Schlesinger, *art. cit.* (s.o. S. 130 Anm. 74), 375; und O. Taplin, *op. cit.* (s.o. S. 110 Anm. 13), 129 f.

Jetzt genügt eine Begründung allein aus der gegenwärtigen unerträglichen Situation nicht mehr. Jetzt lautet die Frage nicht mehr: «Wie halte ich dies aus?», sondern «Halte ich es denn überhaupt aus?». Die Antwort lautet auch jetzt: nein. Aias beschwört noch einmal die Welt, doch nur, das hat Reinhardt gezeigt, «um in ihr das Fremde, Gegenteilige zu sehen, woran er nur teilhaben könnte, wenn er nicht mehr Aias wäre» [103]. Aias wird nicht wie Deianeira und Iokaste, Haimon und Eurydike durch ein von aussen hereinbrechendes Verhängnis vernichtet; er wird nicht von Athene zugrunde gerichtet, die ja in der nächtlichen Wahnsinnsszene nur steigert, was in ihm angelegt ist [104]; und er tötet sich schliesslich auch nicht, weil es die einzige Möglichkeit ist, dem schimpflichen Tod durch Steinigung zu entgehen [105]. Aias stirbt an sich selbst. Aias geht unter, weil er in die Welt, so wie sie ist bzw. so wie er sie sieht und empfindet, nicht hineinpasst. Sein monomanisches Streben nach Ehre, sein rasender Stolz, seine Unfähigkeit, Zurücksetzungen zu ertragen und der daraus erwachsende aggressive Hass treiben ihn in den Tod. Der Hass auf die Atriden stürzt ihn ins Verderben. Der Hass auf die Atriden verbietet ihm einen anderen ehrenvollen Tod als den Selbstmord (466 ff.).

Die menschliche Aggression spielt vor allem in der psychoanalytischen Selbstmordtheorie seit Freud, Adler und Stekel eine dominierende Rolle. Sie sieht — im Anschluss an Freud — die Wurzel des Selbstmords in der Einschränkung der Aggression nach aussen und der dadurch verursachten Aggression gegen die eigene Person, und Stekel behauptete gar, niemand nehme sich das Leben, der nicht zuvor einen anderen habe töten wollen oder zumindest einem anderen

103 Reinhardt, *Sophokles*, 32 f.

104 Kirkwood, 102 f.; Knox, «The Ajax...», 5; Stanford, pp. LIII f.

105 Knox, «The Ajax...», 28, verweist auf 254 und 408 f.; das Motiv tritt aber hinter Aias' freiem Entschluss ganz zurück.

den Tod gewünscht habe [106]. Diese psychoanalytischen Thesen sind in ihrem radikalen Anspruch auf allgemeine Gültigkeit gewiss längst aufgegeben; der Zusammenhang zwischen Fremd-Aggression und Selbst-Aggression ist aber unbestritten und für den sophokleischen Aias durchaus aufschlussreich. Aias richtet die in langem Brüten aufgestaute Aggression zunächst nach aussen, und erst, als dieser Weg endgültig verstellt ist, nach innen und erscheint so (wie Haimon) geradezu als Musterbeispiel für die psychoanalytische Theorie; Stekel selbst hätte kein besseres Beispiel für die oben zitierte Behauptung anführen können als Aias' wilden Aufschrei:

ὦ Ζεῦ προγόνων προπάτωρ
πῶς ἂν τὸν αἱμυλώτατον
ἐχθρὸν ἄλημα, τούς τε δισσ-
άρχας ὀλέσσας βασιλῆς,
τέλος θάνοιμι καὐτός;

(387-91)

Noch bei einer weiteren Begründung des Aias für seinen Selbstmord drängen sich dem heutigen Leser Theorien der modernen Psychologie auf. Aias kann die Vorstellung nicht ertragen (οὐκ... τλητόν), dem berühmten Vater ins Gesicht zu sehen (460 ff.). Später entwirft Teukros ein Bild des alten Telamon, das Aias' tiefes Schamgefühl nachträglich psychologisch noch verständlicher macht (1008 ff.). Der Schatten des Trojaveteranen lastet offenbar schwer auf den Söhnen. Stanford, der, soweit ich sehe, als einziger die Bedeutung der Telamon-Gestalt angemessen gewürdigt hat, vermutet gewiss nicht ohne Grund, «that Ajax's supreme sensitivity to defeat was partly due to the standard set by his father» [107].

[106] W. Stekel, zitiert nach W. de Boor, *art. cit.* (s.o. S. 123 Anm. 51), 20.

[107] Stanford, pp. lvii-lix. Sind wir auf diesem Hintergrund vielleicht berechtigt, in Aias' letztem Auftrag, sein Sohn müsse hart zugeritten werden, damit er so hart werde wie der Vater (548 f.), eine Spiegelung seiner eigenen Erziehung zu sehen?

Man muss kein Psychoanalytiker sein, um die Bedeutung des Vater-Sohn-Verhältnisses im *Aias* (wie in der *Antigone*) zu spüren: auch Telamon ist ein Faktor für den Selbstmord des Aias.

Die *Intentionen* der Tat, denen ich mich nun zuwende, ergeben sich zwangsläufig aus den analysierten Selbstmordursachen. Aias selbst bestimmt das Ziel seines Selbstmordes als Bewahrung oder auch Wiedergewinnung seiner Ehre. Er will dem Vater beweisen, dass er nicht feige ist (470-72), und er will den Makel auf seiner Ehre tilgen (473 ff.). Dabei ist wichtig festzuhalten, dass Aias die Wahnsinnstat nicht etwa als 'Schuld' empfindet, sondern nur als 'Befleckung' [108] . Daraus folgt m.E. zwingend, dass der Selbstmord nicht als Selbstbestrafung oder als Versuch, sich mit Athene zu versöhnen, missverstanden werden darf [109]. Der Selbstmord ist auch kein Akt der σωφροσύνη, die Aias mögliche Art und Weise, sich in die Welt einzufügen und sich mit ihr zu versöhnen, wie Sicherl formuliert [110]. Aias versöhnt sich nicht mit der Welt, er verlässt sie; er ehrt nicht die Götter, er weicht ihnen [111]. In dieser Hinsicht gehört sein Selbstmord in die Kategorie der Fluchtselbstmorde. Aias will das Hohngelächter seiner Feinde nicht mehr hören [112], Athenes Zorn entkommen, die Welt, die er nicht akzeptieren kann, hinter sich lassen.

Daneben aber trägt der Selbstmord des Aias auch deutlich die Züge des zu allen Zeiten und in vielen Kulturen weitverbreiteten Racheselbstmords, der auch den Griechen

[108] Vgl. K. v. FRITZ, «Haimons Liebe zu Antigone», 251; KAMERBEEK, 10; STANFORD, p. XXXI f.; KNOX, «The Ajax...», 5 mit Anm. 27.

[109] So JEBB, p. XXXIV; p. XXXVIII (dagegen KAMERBEEK, 7) und zuletzt M. SICHERL, *art. cit.* (s.o. S. 135 Anm. 96), 35 f.

[110] M. SICHERL, *ibid.* (29, 30 und öfter).

[111] 656 (589 f.).

[112] 367; 382; 454 (955 ff.; 961 ff.; 988 f.; 1042 f.); dazu G. GROSSMANN, «Das Lachen des Aias» (s.o. S. 128 Anm. 68), 81-83.

nicht unbekannt war [113]. Moores Formulierung, dass Aias sich töte, «to embarrass the Atridae» [114] findet zwar keine Basis im Text; und auch der uns allen aus Kindertagen vertraute Gedanke: «sollen sie doch sehen, wie sie ohne mich fertig werden», klingt allenfalls leise an [115]. Unüberhörbar dagegen ist Aias' Anrufung der Erinyen unmittelbar vor dem Selbstmord, die er als Zeugen der Tat (ἀεὶ ὁρῶσαι), als Helferinnen (ἀρωγοί) und als Rächerinnen (ταχεῖαι ποίνιμοί τε) beschwört, seinen Tod an den Atriden, ja, am ganzen Heer zu rächen (835-44). Angesichts dieser mächtigen Verse ist Kamerbeeks Kritik an der These Delcourts, es handele sich im *Aias* um einen Racheselbstmord, nicht angebracht [116]. Aias tötet sich nicht nur, um seine Ehre zu bewahren, sondern auch, wie Knox treffend feststellt, «to perpetuate his hatred» [117]. Die Erinyen sollen ihn an den Atriden, ja, am ganzen Heer rächen. Das ist die primitive magische Vorstellung, dass das vergossene Blut — auch das des Selbstmörders — die Rachegeister auf die Schuldigen hetzt.

Zugleich jedoch ist die Behauptung des Hasses wie die Behauptung seiner Ehre auch ein Stück Selbstbehauptung, und in dieser Selbstbehauptung liegt zweifellos das Geheimnis der überwältigenden Wirkung des Selbstmörders Aias — trotz aller seiner Defekte.

Aias' Grösse (und seine Schwäche) liegen in seinem brennenden Stolz und in der kompromisslosen Megalomanie, mit der er sich selbst und seine Ideale verwirklichen will. Daran muss er zugrundegehen, zugleich aber beweist er auf seinem Weg in den selbstgewählten Tod die Grösse, deren Verwirklichung ihm das Leben versagt.

113 M. Delcourt, «Le suicide par vengeance dans la Grèce ancienne», in *RHR* 119 (1939), 154-71.

114 J. Moore, «The dissembling-speech of Ajax», in *YClS* 25 (1977), 47-66, 59.

115 466 ff.; 961 ff.

116 Kamerbeek, 12: «It is possible that in the original myth this motif [*sc.* Rache] was central, but in the tragedy of Sophocles this is certainly not the case.»

117 Knox, «The Ajax...», 28.

In der Einleitung zu dem Sammelband *Selbstvernichtung* (pp. XVIII f.) nennt Zwingmann als mögliche Selbstmordziele u.a.: «Die physische Selbstzerstörung dient der Wiederherstellung eines psychischen oder moralischen Verlustes (z.B. der Ehre) oder eines vermeintlichen Verlustes. Der Suicidant möchte vor seinen Mitmenschen oder auch vor seinem Gott 'sauber' dastehen; seine Handlung ist hier mit dem Unsterblichkeitsmythos eng verknüpft und enthält nicht selten ambivalente Komponenten, d.h. grandiose Selbsteinschätzung einerseits und ein Gefühl der Wertlosigkeit andererseits. Nicht selten ist der Suicid auch der Ausdruck eines Doppelmotivs, indem er sozusagen die 'Bezahlung' für vergangene Verfehlungen oder vermeintliche Verfehlungen und Sünden, gleichzeitig aber ein 'Heimzahlung' (Rache an den Angehörigen, der Menschheit oder dem Leben selbst) für angetanes Unrecht oder ein Unrecht, das dem Suicidanten so erscheint, darstellt.»

Es ist erstaunlich, in welchem Masse die hier zusammengefassten Ergebnisse der modernen Suizidologie auf den sophokleischen Aias zutreffen [118], und der Interpret mag sich am Schluss seiner Überlegungen zum Selbstmord bei Sophokles an die bewundernden Worte erinnern, die Freud an Arthur Schnitzler schrieb: «Ich habe mich oft verwundert gefragt, woher Sie diese oder jene geheime Kenntnis nehmen konnten, die ich mir durch mühselige Erforschung des Objektes erworben, und endlich kam ich dazu, den Dichter zu beneiden, den ich sonst bewundert. ... So habe ich den Eindruck gewonnen, dass Sie durch Intuition — eigentlich aber infolge feiner Selbstwahrnehmung — all das wissen, was ich in mühseliger Arbeit an anderen Menschen aufgedeckt habe [119].»

[118] Als 'Bezahlung von Vergehen' fasst Aias seinen Selbstmord allerdings nicht auf.

[119] S. FREUD, *Briefe 1873-1939*, ausgew. und hrsg. von E. L. FREUD (Frankfurt 1960); die beiden Sätze stammen aus zwei verschiedenen Briefen von Freud an Schnitzler (8.5.1906 und 14.5.1922).

IV

F 952 Radt lautet:

> ὅστις γὰρ ἐν κακοῖσιν ἱμείρει βίου
> ἢ δειλός ἐστιν ἢ δυσάλγητος φρένας.

Bei Sophokles lässt sich — das ist seit Hirzel [120] zu Recht immer wieder betont worden — weder direkte noch indirekte moralische [121] Kritik am Selbstmord feststellen. Die Tat löst Entsetzen aus und Jammer; der Täter gilt als elend, unglücklich, unselig (ἄθλιος, τάλας) [122]. Wird der Selbstmord bzw. Selbstmordwunsch wie im *Aias* oder in den *Trachinierinnen* einmal als Folge von geistiger Verwirrung [123] oder als Krankheit [124] aufgefasst oder als «allzu rasche Tat» [125] bezeichnet, so besteht kein Zweifel, dass diese Bewertungen der Tat nicht die Ansicht des Dichters aussprechen. Die genannten Reaktionen sind nicht mehr als die hilflosen Versuche der Beteiligten, sich die Tat, deren eigentliche Ursachen sie nicht begreifen, zu erklären. Es sind die zeitlosen Antworten Aussenstehender auf das verstörende Ereignis des Selbstmords.

Sophokles' eigenes Urteil lautet ganz anders: Selbstmord ist nicht Folge von Wahnsinn und Krankheit; er ist auch keine impulsive Fehlhandlung. Er ist vielmehr, bei allen äusseren und inneren Zwängen, aus denen er erwächst,

[120] Hirzel, 21.

[121] Ansätze zu religiösen Bedenken vielleicht *Aj.* 362, bzw. *Tr.* 888 (?); vgl. James (s.o. S. 107 Anm. 6), 14 f. (die auf *Hipp.* 814 und *HF* 1212-1213 verweist).

[122] *Aj.* 902, 925 (τάλας); 905 (δύσμορος); 1170 (δύστηνος); *Tr.* 877 (τάλαινα); 909 (δύστηνος); *Ant.* 1234 (δύσμορος); 1241 (δείλαιος); 1283 (δύστηνος); 1300 (ἀθλία); *OT* 1236 (δυστάλαινα); 1240 (ἀθλία); 1267 (τλήμων).

[123] *Aj.* 609 ff. (dazu Winnington-Ingram, *Sophocles*, 33-42; dort auch weitere Literatur).

[124] *Tr.* 882 (*Aj.* 609 ff.).

[125] *Aj.* 982 f.; vgl. auch *Ant.* 1250 (ἁμαρτάνειν).

letztlich 'Wahl des Todes', ein freier Akt der Selbstbehauptung und der Selbstachtung. Für alle Selbstmorde bei Sophokles gilt in hohem Masse, was Baechler [126] als den tiefen Sinn jedes Selbstmordes und als Wurzel der Faszination und der Beunruhigung, die er auslöst, bezeichnet: sie sind bei allen Unterschieden der Umstände, Temperamente und Ziele immer auch Proklamation des menschlichen Rechts auf Freiheit, Glück und Würde. Im Falle des Aias und der Antigone erscheint der Selbstmord zudem als Signum heroischer Kompromisslosigkeit und Grösse.

Als der euripideische Herakles sich nach seiner Wahnsinnstat töten will, hält ihn Theseus mit den tadelnden Worten zurück:

εἴρηκας ἐπιτυχόντος ἀνθρώπου λόγους. (1248)

Selbstmord als der leichte Ausweg des gewöhnlichen Mannes, als ein Beweis der Feigheit (1348), wie gleich darauf Herakles selber konstatiert. Das sieht in der Tat, wie J. de Romilly kürzlich vermutet hat, wie eine Antwort des Euripides auf den sophokleischen Aias aus: Selbstmord nicht als Behauptung und Bestätigung heroischer Grösse, sondern als Brandmal des Alltäglichen und als Zeichen der Schwäche [127].

Ganz abgesehen von der Frage, ob die Position, die Theseus und Herakles vertreten, wirklich für den ganzen Euripides gilt, wie J. de Romilly wohl zu Unrecht meint [128], und unabhängig von der Frage, ob es sich wirklich um eine radikal neue Position handelt oder ob sich ein Ansatz für diese Konzeption des Heroischen nicht vielleicht schon in dem homerischen Odysseus (oder auch in Achilleus)

[126] Baechler, 113-117.

[127] Ein Vergleich der beiden Stücke (Soph. *Aj.* und Eur. *HF*) unter diesem Aspekt vor J. de Romilly bereits bei C. James (s.o. S. 107 Anm. 6).

[128] De Romilly, 8; die uneinheitliche Haltung des Euripides zum Selbstmord muss einer eigenen Untersuchung vorbehalten bleiben.

zeigt [129]: am Ende des 5. Jahrhunderts stehen sich in den heroischen Gestalten des sophokleischen Aias und des euripideischen Herakles die beiden Positionen gegenüber, die die Diskussion um die moralische Berechtigung des Selbstmords bis auf den heutigen Tag bestimmen.

[129] S.o. S. 106.

DISCUSSION

M. Winnington-Ingram: In the first part of the *Ajax*, the emphasis falls on the restoration of τιμή, cf. especially 439 f. The perspective of the *Trugrede* is wider, involving the whole relationship of Ajax, his 'heroic' ideal to the real world in which he must live, if live at all. As to the first phase, there have been—and perhaps still are—social codes which prescribe suicide as a means for the retrieval of honour, it may be the sole means. [? Harakiri]. Was this notion Greek? In the heroic period? In the fifth century? It would be interesting to hear more about contemporary attitudes towards suicide.

M. Seidensticker: Ich glaube nicht, dass sich die Frage nach der Existenz eines 'social code', der bei Verlust der Ehre den Selbstmord zwingend vorschrieb, auf der Basis unseres kärglichen Materials mit Sicherheit beantworten lässt. Die wenigen Selbstmordfälle (Epikaste, Aias, vielleicht Antikleia), bzw. Selbstmordwünsche (Achilleus, Odysseus), von denen das Epos spricht, lassen davon allerdings ebenso wenig ahnen, wie die wenigen sicheren historischen Fälle aus dem 5. Jhdt. Auch in den Fällen, in denen man den Selbstmord als Reaktion auf den Verlust der τιμή oder als Bewahrung der τιμή verstehen kann — ich denke z.B. an Paches (Plut. *Nic.* 6,1) und an Themistokles (bei Ar. *Eq.* 80 ff.) ist von einem 'code' durch den der Selbstmörder sich zur Tat verpflichtet oder gezwungen sieht, nicht die Rede. Auf jeden Fall aber, denke ich, wüssten wir davon, wenn es so etwas wie den japanischen Harakiri-Code gegeben hätte.

Mme de Romilly: Je voudrais à cet égard dire un mot pour tenter de justifier ce que j'ai écrit sur Euripide. D'abord, il faut préciser qu'il ne s'agit pas du seul vers de l'*Héraclès* qui a été cité: les rapports avec l'*Ajax* sont multiples et se marquent dans toute la scène. D'autre part, la condamnation du suicide est très insistante. Euripide emploie le mot de 'lâcheté' que Sophocle, ailleurs, applique au fait de prolonger sa vie. Ceci, évidemment, ne vaut que pour l'*Héraclès*. Mais, pour ne citer qu'un exemple, le suicide d'Evadnè dans les *Suppliantes* est, avec celui d'Ajax, le seul suicide présenté sous les yeux des spectateurs. Or, il paraît un acte déraisonnable, et Euripide attire l'attention sur la souffrance qu'il cause (les plaintes du père qui n'apparaît que pour cela). On n'a aucune pièce où le suicide soit présenté sous un jour favorable. Il est toujours difficile de dire, avec Euripide, qu'il n'a pas varié; cela va de soi. Mais la note morale est cependant, en gros, différente.

M. Seidensticker: Ich stimme Ihnen durchaus darin zu, dass die Beziehungen zwischen dem *Aias* des Sophokles und dem Ende des euripideischen *Herakles* vielfältig sind und den von Ihnen in der zitierten Arbeit gezogenen Schluss rechtfertigen, dass Euripides hier dem Sophokles 'antwortet'. Anderseits scheint es mir — und nur gegen diese Ihre These richtete sich meine Kritik — , dass von einer durchgehenden Verurteilung des Selbstmords bei Euripides nicht gesprochen werden kann; in dieser Hinsicht scheint mir der *Herakles* sogar eher die Ausnahme zu sein. Was die von Ihnen angeführte Euadne betrifft, so wird ihre Tat von niemandem kritisiert; sie selbst betrachtet sie als einen Beweis ihrer ἀρετή (*Supp.* 1063) und als heroischen Akt, der ihr Ruhm bringen soll und wird (1015; 1059 ff.). Dass sich der Blick nach der Tat auf die Leiden richtet, die der Selbstmord auslöst, gilt auch für die Selbstmorde in der *Antigone* und ganz besonders für den *Aias* (Tekmessa, Chor, Teukros) und kann m.E. nicht als Ausdruck einer Verurteilung der Tat verstanden werden.

Auch bei Euripides erscheint der Selbstmord

1. immer wieder als der zu erwartende, richtige, ehrenvolle Ausweg aus einer unerträglichen Situation. So beurteilt, um nur ein Beispiel zu nennen, Phaidra ihren Wunsch sich zu töten als ehrenvoll (329; 716-18), und der Chor sagt, dass ihr die Tat φήμα εὔδοξος (772 f.) einbringen werde (vgl. bereits Aphrodite im Prolog, 47).

2. erscheint die Überwindung des Selbstmords z.B. im *Orestes*, keineswegs als Stärke, sondern eher als Schwäche. Wenn sich die Entschlossenheit Orests und Elektras, sich ehrenvoll selber zu töten, unter dem Zuspruch des Pylades allzu schnell in die Bereitschaft verwandelt, notfalls auch schändlich weiterzuleben, so gewinnen wir nicht den Eindruck heroischer Stärke wie bei Herakles.

Eine Untersuchung des Selbstmords bei Euripides, für die hier nicht der Platz ist, würde ein ausserordentlich buntes Bild ergeben.

M. Knox: Do we have very much evidence for the fifth-century attitude to suicide—apart from tragedy? No one, as far as I know, objects to suicide *per se* in the plays: arguments against it are, as far as I can remember, personal, like Tecmessa's to Ajax. I would be interested to hear some discussion of the way suicide was regarded in non-tragic texts.

M. Seidensticker: Das nicht-dramatische Material für eine Untersuchung der Einstellung zum Selbstmord im 5. Jhdt. ist ausserordentlich gering und stammt zudem zum grössten Teil aus viel späteren Quellen. Es enthält, soweit ich mich erinnern kann, kaum Wertungen der Tat, jedenfalls keinerlei Verurteilung. Dasselbe gilt auch für die wenigen Stellen, an denen in der aristophaneischen Komödie vom Selbstmord die Rede ist (*Ra.* 117 ff.; *Eq.* 80 ff.; *Vesp.* 303 ff.; 522 f.; *Nu.* 775 ff.; 868 ff.; 1448 ff.). In der Tragödie werden kritische Töne gelegentlich laut; einige Beispiele habe ich am Ende meines Vortrages genannt; dazu kommen bei Euripides noch zwei Fälle von religiösen Bedenken (*Hipp.* 814 und *HF* 1212-1213 wird der Selbstmord als ἀνόσιον bezeichnet). Hier mag es sich um einen Reflex pythagoreischer und orphischer Vorschriften handeln, über die Sokrates im *Phaidon* spricht (61 c ff.). Über die Verbreitung und Bedeutung solcher Kritik können wir allerdings nur spekulieren. Das Gespräch im *Phaidon* macht eher den Eindruck, als sei sie recht unbekannt. Erst bei Platon also (zum *Phaidon* kommt noch *Lg.* 873 c-d) und dann bei Aristoteles (*EN* V 15, 1138 a 4-28) finden wir explizite und begründete Verurteilungen des Selbstmords; doch ein Blick auf den platonischen Katalog der Ursachen, die einen Selbstmord rechtfertigen (*Lg.* 873 c), zeigt, dass keiner der sechs sophokleischen Selbstmorde im Staat der *Gesetze* kritisiert oder gar bestraft worden wäre.

M. Radt: Sie sagten ziemlich am Anfang, dem Oedipus im *König Oedipus* stehe der Weg des Selbstmordes nicht offen. Verstehe ich Sie richtig, wenn ich annehme, dass Sie damit meinten, Sophokles habe hier einfach nicht von dem ihm vorgegebenen Mythos abweichen können, der

Oedipus weiterleben liess? In der Situation, in der Oedipus sich nach der Entdeckung des wahren Sachverhalts befindet, wäre es doch das Nächstliegende gewesen, dass er sich das Leben nimmt. Dass er es nicht tut, ist offenbar eine Folge des Respekts, den Sophokles vor dem traditionellen Mythos hatte.

M. Seidensticker: Was Sie sagen, leuchtet mir durchaus ein. Andererseits schafft ein grosser Dichter wie Sophokles dort, wo er sich dem *äusseren* Zwang des Stoffs unterworfen sieht, doch auch immer seine eigene *innere* Motivation. Ich hatte bei meiner Formulierung die Stelle im Auge, als Oidipus dem Chor, dessen Kritik an der Blendung übrigens implizit genau die Frage stellt, warum Oidipus sich nicht getötet hat, antwortet, dass er die Vorstellung nicht ertragen könne, eines Tages seinen Vater und seine Mutter anblicken zu müssen (*OT* 1371-74). Meine Auffassung ist, dass dieser Gedanke, der sich auf die Zukunft bezieht, auch für die Vergangenheit erklärt, warum Oidipus der 'leichte Weg' des Selbstmords nicht offensteht.

Ausserdem, denke ich, stellt sich die Frage dem Betrachter des Stücks wohl kaum. Zu gut vorbereitet (vor allem durch die Metaphorik des Stücks), zu überwältigend und zu 'passend' ist diese Form der tragischen Katastrophe für den «Rätsellöser mit den strahlenden Augen», wie André Gide ihn genannt hat.

M. Knox: The possibility that Oedipus might commit suicide is suggested, it seems to me, by the words with which he greets the revelation of the truth ὦ φῶς τελευταῖόν σε προσβλέψαιμι νῦν (1183), which could just as easily be a wish for death as a reference to blinding. The messenger tells us he asked for a sword (1255)—was it so that he could kill himself? If not, why *did* he ask for a sword?

M. Seidensticker: Ja, ich halte es nicht für ausgeschlossen, dass Sophokles die Möglichkeit eines Selbstmords angedeutet hat, vielleicht um die Wirkung der Blendung zu steigern. Der Ruf nach einem Schwert in 1255 ist m.E. ambivalent. Oidipus kann an sich selber denken, aber auch daran, Iokaste zu töten — oder sich selbst und Iokaste. Muss er sich darüber in diesem furchtbaren Augenblick überhaupt im Klaren sein?

M. Steiner: One general point: we know so little about Greek views on the precise condition of different orders of men and women after death, that it is difficult to arrive at a view of the status of suicide. The very different Roman emphasis may have behind it the necrologies and 'fascination with the posthumous' of Etruscan culture.

The particular point is this: if, as Reinhardt says, Creon is "the man who always comes too late", Antigone is the young woman who 'always come too early'. Her suicide, which Sophocles makes so difficult to reconstruct, may be the final motif in a structure of impetuous and impatient haste. She can never wait, even a moment. Comparisons with the tomb-suicides and *Romeo and Juliet* are instructive.

M. Seidensticker: Ja, ich denke, auch diese Erklärung für den schnellen Selbstmord passt durchaus zu dem Bild, das wir uns seit dem Prolog von Antigone gemacht haben. Wichtig scheint mir aber, dass ihre Ungeduld und Heftigkeit, auch wenn sie den Zeitpunkt des Selbstmords erklären helfen, die Tat nicht zu einem sogenannten Kurzschluss- oder Affekt-Selbstmord machen. Er bleibt 'Wahl des Todes', ein Akt der Selbstbehauptung, der Freiheit und der Würde.

M. Taplin: But one aspect of death persists throughout tragedy: the underworld, Hades, which is dark. This is, of course, Homeric (see J. Griffin, *Homer on Life and Death* (Oxford 1980), *passim*, esp. 161-2).

One always comes back to the so-called *Trugrede*: what does it add to our understanding of Ajax's suicide? It is not enough to say (as implied by the quotation of Reinhardt) that it shows the world which Ajax *rejects*, since he applies his insights to himself. When he says at the start that Time changes even περισκελεῖς φρένες (649), he must be refering to himself; and this is confirmed by what follows: κἀγὼ γάρ...

M. Seidensticker: Ich teile durchaus ihre Auffassung, dass Aias in den ersten Versen der Trugrede auch von sich selber spricht. In dieser Hinsicht sind die Verse 846 ff. kein *Trug*, auch wenn sie falsch verstanden werden können, und von Tekmessa und vom Chor falsch verstanden werden. Der Appell Tekmessas, die Erinnerung an die Eltern und der Anblick des kleinen Sohnes haben den scheinbar so unzugänglichen Aias doch erreicht und ihn zu einer neuen, tieferen Auseinandersetzung mit seiner Entscheidung zum Selbstmord gezwungen. Aber spätestens wenn Aias ἐθηλύνθην sagt (651)—darin stimme ich B. Knox schöner Interpretation der Rede völlig zu—ist klar, dass Aias im Grunde unverändert ist. Es jammert ihn, Tekmessa und das Kind zu verlassen, aber er muss es dennoch tun. Eine solche Auffassung der ersten Verse der Rede steht nicht im Widerspruch zu den von mir zitierten Sätzen Reinhardts.

M. Knox: The ambiguity of στόμα—the edge of the sword or of the tongue—reinforces the impression that Ajax has not changed: it strengthes the suggestion of the unacceptability of continuing to live contained in the word ἐθηλύνθην. Ajax has been affected to some extent by Tecmessa's plea: at least he has not killed himself in the tent—as the audience must have expected after his closing speech in the previous *episodion*—he will go elsewhere. He feels pity for Tecmessa—but he has weakened only verbally στόμα—he will soften his tone towards her (as he does when, finally, he turns and speaks to her at the end of the monologue—e.g. 684 ff. with 585-595).

Mme de Romilly: Une remarque en passant: tout en reconnaissant la rage et les malédictions d'Ajax, il me semble que Kamerbeek n'a pas tort de nuancer un peu l'interprétation de Marie Delcourt.

M. Seidensticker: Kamerbeeks Ansicht, die Racheintention sei für den sophokleischen Aias ohne Bedeutung (*ad* 835: «this may have been the significance of the original myth, *it is not Sophocles' meaning*») scheint mir angesichts von Umfang, Inhalt und Intensität der Verse 835-44 unzutreffend. Gewiss ist Rache keineswegs die einzige oder wichtigste Intention des Aias. Das aber heisst bei der komplexen Kausalität von Selbstmorden (auch der sophokleischen) nicht, dass diese Intention unbedeutend ist.

M. Winnington-Ingram: Ajax does not commit suicide *in order that* his enemies may be pursued by the Erinyes but, in doing so, prays that they will avenge him.

M. Irigoin: En faisant sortir le chœur au v. 814, procédé exceptionnel dans la tragédie grecque et qui se justifierait ici par un changement de lieu, Sophocle n'a-t-il pas voulu souligner, d'une manière évidente pour les spectateurs, la solitude de son héros devant la mort volontaire? Ajax est seul, *absolument* seul, quand il se tue devant le public.

M. Taplin: There is a handful of other places where the chorus goes off during the play (I enumerate them all in *The Stagecraft of Aeschylus* (Oxford 1977), 375-6); but in none of the others, I think, is it the purpose of the device to create an isolation like that of Ajax. Contrast *Eumenides* where, on the contrary, the point is that the Erinyes are only just behind Orestes.

M. Seidensticker: Ja, die ungewöhnliche dramatische Technik hat im *Aias* zweifellos die Funktion, die totale Isolation und Einsamkeit des Helden, der nicht in die Welt passt, zu unterstreichen.

M. Knox: There seems to me to be a technical problem in the staging of 813 ff. The chorus goes off in two different directions (this seems to be dictated by their entry as *hemichoria* at 865): they go along the *parodoi* (or *eisodoi*, to follow Oliver's preferred terminology). But Ajax must come in for his last speech and his suicide, along one of the *eisodoi* at 815; he cannot come out of the *skene* door—that is the tents, which he left to go to the shore. Which means you have the chorus filing out along the *eisodoi*, and only when they have disappeared can Ajax start his walk to stage center—the stage will be empty for a considerable period.

M. Taplin: The problem of staging raised by M. Knox is not easily solved. It is clear from Tecmessa's words at 805-6 (and from 874-8) that the chorus splits and that half departs by each *eisodos*. Is there then a complete hiatus before Ajax enters from one side, or does he enter from the *skene*, even though he must have gone off to one side at 692? Whatever the answer, he surely planted the sword in the ground himself. The red-figure lekythos recently published by Karl Schefold (*Antike Kunst* 15 [1976], 71 ff.), whether or not influenced by Sophocles' play (and I doubt that it was), confirms the iconographic tradition of this scene.

I think that in the second part of the play the *skene* represents a thicket, and that Tecmessa comes out of it at 891 ff.; but that does not remove the problem of the entry of Ajax at 815.

M. Seidensticker: Würde die von Herrn Knox konstatierte notwendige längere Pause zwischen dem Auszug des Chores und dem Wiederauftritt des Aias, ein Moment absoluten Schweigens — noch verlängert durch das schweigende Eingraben des Schwerts — nicht eine wunderbare Vorbereitung für die Selbstmordszene sein? Die Frage, wie der Selbstmord inszeniert wurde (bzw. werden kann) ist nicht einfach zu beantworten. Gelten muss aber m.E., und zwar auch dann, wenn die Darstellung auf der neuen Lekythos nicht von Sophokles inspiriert ist, dass Aias mit dem Schwert auftritt, es einpflanzt und seinen Monolog dicht bei dem Schwert spricht, sowie ferner, dass Schwert und Selbstmord wenigstens partiell (im Hintergrund oder an der Seite der Bühne) zu sehen sind.

M. Irigoin: Pour l'interprétation des tirades d'Ajax, ne devrait-on pas tenir compte de rapprochements que paraît suggérer le nombre des vers qu'elles comportent?

Aux 51 vers de la première tirade (430-480) correpondent les 51 vers de la tirade finale (815-865); au dernier vers de la première: « Je t'ai dit tout ce que j'avais à dire» (πάντ' ἀκήκοας λόγον), répond le dernier vers de l'autre: «Désormais, c'est à ceux d'en-bas, dans l'Hadès, que je parlerai» (τὰ δ'ἄλλ' ἐν Ἅιδου τοῖς κάτω μυθήσομαι).

Les 47 vers du fameux monologue (646-692) sont, à distance, précédés d'une tirade de 47 vers dite par Tecmesse (284-330) et suivis d'une tirade de 47 vers de Teucros (992-1039) [le vers 1002 est réduit à un cri: οἴμοι]. Ces trois tirades comportent, au premier vers, une forme de l'adjectif ἅπας: 284 ἅπαν (initiale du vers), 646 ἅπανθ' (initiale du vers), 992 ἁπάντων (premier hémistiche).

Les indications que Sophocle donne ainsi aux spectateurs ne doivent pas être négligées par les commentateurs.

M. Seidensticker: Vielen Dank für den Hinweis; die numerischen Parallelen sind in der Tat erneut verblüffend. Ich muss aber gestehen, dass ich keine Antwort auf die Frage weiss, wie sie interpretatorisch auszuwerten sind.

Mme de Romilly: Les vers 317 et suivants de l'*Ajax*, évoquant les gémissements d'Ajax, ont prêté à des erreurs d'interprétation. Qu'il me soit permis de rappeler le silence avec lequel les héroïnes de Sophocle se retirent pour aller mourir: Sophocle ne manque jamais d'attirer l'attention sur ces silences: c'est à nouveau la sobriété, l'absence de commentaires, mais aussi, à nouveau, le relief dramatique ainsi atteint.

M. Seidensticker: Die Verse 317 ff. (bzw. 305 ff.) bieten m.E. keine Parallele zu den so bedeutungschweren schweigenden Abgängen Deianeiras und Eurydikes (und Iokastes), die in der Tat den bevorstehenden Selbstmord dramatisch vorbereiten, ja symbolisch vorwegnehmen. Im Falle des Aias charakterisiert Sophokles die psychische Disposition, aus der die Entscheidung zum Selbstmord, der noch fern ist, erwächst, gerade durch den mehrfachen Wechsel von dumpfem Schweigen und lauten Jammergeschrei (308-311-317 [früher 321 f.] 325-333).

V

Oliver Taplin

SOPHOCLES IN HIS THEATRE

I shall conclude with some big questions about the end of *OT*: I start with a small one about the beginning of the play. In Sophocles' original production was Oedipus presented as lame; was he "majestic but for his tell-tale limp"? [1] The question gambols in the wake of Jean-Pierre Vernant's new and characteristically brilliant essay on "Lameness, Tyranny, Incest in Legend and History" [2]. I maintain, though not confidently, that Sophocles' Oedipus did *not* limp, because such a peculiar stage device would call for some comment, and yet the text nowhere alludes to any abnormality of gait (nor does *OC*). In his dialogue with old Corinthian (1031 ff.) the pinning of his feet as a baby is referred to as an ἀρχαῖον κακόν and δεινόν γ' ὄνειδος, and as the origin of his name; but neither here nor anywhere else is there any allusion to a persisting disability. This is not the mere musing it might seem at first sight. If Oedipus were to limp this would be, right from the start, a flaw betokening the imperfection of his lot and his eventual downfall. This flaw would undermine

[1] F. Fergusson, *The Idea of a Theater* (Princeton 1949), 19; quoted with approval by B. Knox, *Oedipus at Thebes* (Yale 1957), 263 n. 68, and in a stage-direction in his new collaboration with R. Fagles (New York 1982), 139.

[2] *Arethusa* 15 (1982), 19 ff. (published as I was making my final draft).

the paradigmatic extremity of Oedipus' tragedy, the complete reversal of life-lot which has been well brought out by Vernant himself [3]. I shall return to this at the end; my point for now is that issues such as that of Oedipus' limp, which face any director (whether or not he feels any compunction about respecting Sophocles' own conception) cannot and should not be shirked by the scholar and literary critic (whether or not the man of the theatre takes any notice of him). In fact the barrier between the academy and the theatre is slowly breaking down, and scholars are now asking some of the questions that confront any conscientious director or actor.

I have heard this kind of approach to literary interpretation through the dramatist's use of his theatre attacked because it attempts to limit, or close, the possible readings of the play. Some modern literary studies set polysemy and multivalence against definitive accounts, and advocate the openness of autonomous reading rather than the dictates of authorial intention. In keeping with this tendency Charles Segal has recently tried to save both presentations of Oedipus—both limping and apparently flawless—in the early scenes of *OT*: "In the paradoxes of this play the two possibilities are not mutually exclusive and may in fact be mutually necessary" [4]. The fact remains that in Sophocles' own production Oedipus either did or did not limp. We may not be in a position to decide with confidence, but the call for a decision will not go away. The critic, if he is determined to maintain the unrestricted creativity of the reader, must turn his back on at least one restriction, Sophocles' own realization in his own theatre.

[3] *Tragedy and Myth in Ancient Greece* (Paris 1972; English transl., Brighton 1981), chapter 5; first published in *Echanges et communications. Mélanges offerts à Claude Lévi-Strauss* (Paris 1970), II 1253 ff.

[4] On p. 139 n. 25 of his excellent study of visual symbolism in Sophocles, in *CW* 74 (1980/81), 125-142.

I shall try to show how Sophocles carefully gives significance to his stage space and to the movements within it, how he charts a kind of theatrical geography [5]. I would single out this sense of stage direction, along with his use of stage-objects (the chief subject of Segal's essay), as Sophocles' specialities in theatrical technique. In our intimate enclosed theatres it is not usual to create a strong sense of locality. It may be because of the interior stage-space that most plays are set in a place that lacks definition. (In fact some of the best local scenes are created by a demarcation within the area of the stage, such as the hovel on the heath near Dover, or the chalk circle at Nuka.) Within his huge acting space in the open air in the light of day and set in the surrounding physical landscape, Sophocles could fashion a more definite locality. The grove of the Eumenides and the bronze threshold at Colonus come first to mind; but I hope to show that this is the culmination of a persistent concern with the theatre as a representation of men moving or staying still within the physical terrain of the world.

The Greek stage is, in a sense, a place where three roads meet. Rather as Greek tragedy captures a crucial 'now' within the past and future on either side [6], so the *orchestra* is a fateful place where the drama gravitates from all others, a place where journeys converge and culminate. This concentration of time and place is not some mere dramaturgical rule. To either side are the two *eisodoi*. These are roads [7]. The actor cannot step in or out of sight in a couple of paces as in most indoor theatres. These roads may lead to the city, or may lead away, abroad; they can be the beginning and end of

[5] It was with mixed feelings that I found similar metaphors used of the theatre of Racine by Roland BARTHES, in *Sur Racine* (Paris 1960), 15 ff.

[6] Cf. J. de ROMILLY, *Time in Greek Tragedy* (Ithaca 1968), chapter 1.

[7] Cf. N. C. HOURMOUZIADES, *Production and Imagination in Euripides* (Athens 1965), 77. For the term *eisodos* rather than *parodos* see my *Stagecraft of Aeschylus* (Oxford 1977), 449.

momentous journeys. A particular significance may be established for them within each play. By contrast the third way, the door of the *skene*, usually leads into a house or palace, and is, so to speak, a 'cul-de-sac'—as in all Greek houses, there is no back door. The house is fixed, introverted, enclosed: the *eisodoi* lead outside, beyond, towards openness and change.

*
* *

Oedipus' limp is unlikely but not ruled out. Can we say with more confidence from which side of the scene Polynices arrived at *OC* 1254? I have no answer to the historical question of whether he entered by the right or left, east or west *eisodos* [8]; but that is a more restricted and restrictive challenge than to map Polynices' movements in relation to the overall geography of the play. In suppliant plays part of the pattern of expectations is that one direction leads abroad, while the other leads to the protecting city—it is more important to recognise this division than to know which was right and which left. The suppliant arrives or has arrived from one direction, the pursuer follows from there, the side of danger: the rescuer, usually the friendly king, comes from the other direction, that of safety [9].

In *OC* these bearings are firmly and straightforwardly established. In one direction lies Athens and Colonus: from there comes any hope of protection—the Colonean, the chorus, above all Theseus. The other direction, which Oedipus and Antigone come from at the very beginning,

[8] I discuss this question briefly, but with full bibliography, in *Stagecraft of Aeschylus*, 450-1. The most significant recent discussions are Hourmouziades (*op. cit.* in p. 157 n. 7), 128-36 and K. Joerden, in *Die Bauformen der griechischen Tragödie*, ed. W. Jens (München 1971), 369 ff.

[9] Cf. *Stagecraft*, 239; 451, on Aeschyl. *Supp.*

leads abroad, especially to Thebes: thence come pursuit and danger. Ismene prepares for the threat, and Creon embodies it (see 396 ff.; 455 ff.; cf. 653 ff.). She does not, however, prepare for Polynices also; we do not suspect another approach until Theseus at 1156 ff. breaks the news that a man is nearby. He is a suppliant,

προσπεσόντα πως
βωμῶι καθῆσθαι τῶι Ποσειδῶνος, παρ' ὧι
θύων ἔκυρον ἡνίχ' ὡρμώμην ἐγώ.

(Polynices himself recalls his supplication to Poseidon at 1285-8.) Theseus here specifically reminds us how he rushed to the rescue at 887, leaving his rituals incomplete:

τίς ποθ' ἡ βοή; τί τοὔργον; ἐκ τίνος φόβου ποτὲ
βουθυτοῦντά μ' ἀμφὶ βωμὸν ἔσχετ' ἐναλίωι θεῶι
τοῦδ' ἐπιστάτηι Κολωνοῦ;

This hasty arrival will have been from the direction of Athens, the direction in which Theseus will have departed at 667—the opposite, that is, to that which Creon has come from, and by which Antigone has been dragged off, and by which Creon threatens to haul Oedipus. Only this opposition will reflect the dramatic shape of the action. So Sophocles makes it clear that Polynices enters at 1249 ff. from the 'Athens side' of the theatre [10].

This is, I suggest, a telling (as well as neglected) difference between Polynices and Creon. They duplicate the rôle of the pursuer, they both come to Colonus to fetch off Oedipus to help them at Thebes [11]. But once the parallel is

[10] Cf. A. D. Fitton-Brown, *Greek Tragedies as First Performances* (Leicester 1970), 13; K. Joerden, in *op. cit.* (p. 158 n. 8), 387; 395 (in contradiction of his table on p. 380); *contra* R. C. Jebb, *Sophocles. The Plays and Fragments. Part II. The Oedipus Coloneus* (Cambridge 1928), p. 199: "on the spectators' left", for him the direction abroad; also B. Knox - R. Fagles, *op. cit.* (p. 155 n. 1), 342.

[11] Cf. the good discussion by P. Burian, in *Phoenix* 28 (1974), 408 ff., esp. 422-4.

established the contrasts press in. They are particularly concentrated on the two arrivals, both marked by Antigone's reporting the approach to her blind father in a dialogue with antilabe (720-23 and 1249-53). Creon marches on boldly with the support of henchmen (οὐκ ἄνευ πομπῶν), and sets about softening the chorus: Polynices is alone and in tears (ἀνδρῶν γε μοῦνος... etc.), and he is at a loss to do anything except rebuke himself for his own negligence. As preparation for Creon there are the warnings of Ismene and the fears of Oedipus—he is man of violence: Polynices is a suppliant, Theseus has spoken for him, even more, Antigone has made a moving plea that Oedipus should speak to her brother, and, by implication, should be kind to him (1181-1203)[12]. Possibly he is costumed as a suppliant rather than as a soldier?[13] Add to all this that Creon arrives from the side of danger, while Polynices comes from the side of security. It is a small touch but carefully signalled and confirmed, comparable with Sophocles' insistence against tradition on the primogeniture of Polynices (Ismene at 374-5, as well as Polynices himself at 1292-6 and 1422-3).

The opposition of symbolic topography which opens these two scenes gives extra point to the way they end. After being exposed as an unscrupulous manipulator of lies and force, Creon is escorted off by Theseus and a guard of Athenians to recover the daughters. Polynices, on the other hand, tries no lies or threats and uses no force, yet he is even more terribly cursed. Oedipus repeatedly tells him to go to

[12] On forgiving in Greek tragedy see J. de ROMILLY, *La douceur dans la pensée grecque* (Paris 1979), 77 ff., esp. 84.

[13] Admittedly he talks more than enough of his military support in 1301-25, but I am inclined to believe that there has been a large interpolation in that passage, even possibly all of 1308-25: see M. D. REEVE's case against 1313-22 in *GRBS* 11 (1970), 291-2. (I was glad to see this taken seriously by M. L. WEST, in *Gnomon* 53 (1981), 527 n. 19.)

his doom (ἔρρε 1383; στεῖχε... ἰὼν 1393; cf. the chorus at 1398 ἴϑ' ὡς τάχος πάλιν). Polynices does not defy or deprecate his father's curse. He laments the way he has to go: it is a journey whose destination is the grave—οἷον ἄρ' ὁδοῦ τέλος... (1400). Antigone begs him not to go, and he argues with her (1432-5):

καὶ μή μ' ἐπίσχῃς γ' · ἀλλ' ἐμοὶ μὲν ἥδ' ὁδὸς
ἔσται μέλουσα δύσποτμός τε καὶ κακὴ
πρὸς τοῦδε πατρὸς τῶν τε τοῦδ' Ἐρινύων ·
σφῷ δ' εὐοδοίη Ζεύς, τάδ' εἰ τελεῖτέ μοι. [14]

So he departs to Thebes, to death, by the road opposite to that he entered by. Charles Segal has remarked that "the road is the single most dominant spatial metaphor of the play" [15]. While Prodicus' parable of the choice of Heracles is the most celebrated example of the image, the archetype of the rough and smooth roads of life goes back to Hesiod, and Theognis, facing a dilemma, pictures himself as one standing at a cross roads [15a]. As so often, the theatre is able to produce a powerful fusion of the metaphorical and the literal.

I cannot attempt here a proper account of the significance of Polynices within the play. It will be clear, however, that I do not regard his treatment as merely the punishment of another villain in the same class as Creon. It is not enough to point to Polynices' crimes and to Oedipus' Δίκη: Polynices

[14] I follow R. D. Dawe's Teubner text unless otherwise remarked. Here I readily follow his athetesis of 1436 (first Dindorf).

[15] Ch. Segal, *Tragedy and Civilization. An Interpretation of Sophocles* (Cambridge, Mass. 1981), 368; see also P. E. Easterling, in *PCPhS* N.S. 13 (1967), 11-12. For a good collection of material on the image in early Greek literature as a whole see O. Becker, *Das Bild des Weges und verwandte Vorstellungen im frühgriechischen Denken*, Hermes Einzelschr. 4 (Berlin 1937).

[15a] Prodicus Fr. 2 Diels-Kranz (*Vorsokr.* II 84 B 2), *ap.* Xen. *Mem.* II 1, 21 ff.; Hes. *Op.* 287-292 (see M. L. West, *ad loc.*); Theognis 911 ff. ἐν τριόδωι δ' ἕστηκα· δύ' εἰσὶ τὸ πρόσϑεν ὁδοί μοι· / φροντίζω τούτων ἥντιν' ἴω προτέρην...

honestly admits his faults and appeals to Αἰδώς [16]. We welcome the exposure and humiliation of Creon, but surely our response to the destruction of Polynices is not meant to be similar. Nor am I happy with the explanation that Oedipus has by this stage ceased to be human, that he is already before death demonic. At least I think Knox goes too far when he writes "he both foresees and determines the future" [17]. For Oedipus still has a 'blind spot'. He is much concerned for the future well-being of his daughters; almost his last act in this life is to entrust them to Theseus, enjoining him τελεῖν δ' ὅσ' ἂν / μέλλῃς φρονῶν εὖ ξυμφέροντ' αὐταῖς ἀεί (1634-5). Clearly he does not foresee that Antigone is soon to come to an untimely end, alone, unmarried, unwept. Yet the play foresees this, and firmly though deftly insists on it. Bowra's claim that "at the end of *Oedipus at Colonus* no unresolved discords remain" is surely deluded [18]. Polynices, before he goes, pleads that, if he is killed and his sisters come home to Thebes, they should bury his corpse and give it due honours, and so win praise (1405-13, cf. 1435). At the very end (1769 ff.) Antigone asks Theseus for an escort to help her and Ismene go to Thebes and try to prevent the bloodshed. Theseus, as asked by Oedipus, agrees to do anything within his power that is πρόσφορα. The allusion is inescapable: Antigone will not prevent the bloodshed, the brothers must die, and she must die for caring for Polynices' body. Oedipus did not see that in cursing Polynices he was also dooming

16 Cf. P. Burian, *art. cit.* (p. 159 n. 11), 424. P. E. Easterling, *art. cit.* (p. 161 n. 15), 6-10 shows the justice of Oedipus' appeal to Δίκη, but does not convince me that his son's appeal to Αἰδώς is outweighed.

17 *The Heroic Temper* (Berkeley 1964), 160; cf. 148: "Now he does know surely, sees clearly; the gods give Oedipus back his eyes, but they are the eyes of superhuman vision."

18 *Sophoclean Tragedy* (Oxford 1944), 349; my gloomier view is similar to that of R. P. Winnington-Ingram, *Sophocles. An Interpretation* (Cambridge 1980), 248 ff., esp. 274 f.

Antigone. The final stage-movement of the play is Antigone's departure by the *eisodos* which goes in the direction of Thebes, an ironic outcome to Polynices' prayer σφῷ δ' εὐοδοίη Ζεύς—an unresolved discord.

*

* *

OC is not, I maintain, the only tragedy of Sophocles whose ending is equivocal, disturbingly divergent from a more straightforward resolution. The final stage-direction aggravates rather than relieves a tragic doubt. I shall look briefly at *Electra* and *Philoctetes* before going on to consider the earlier *Oedipus* play at greater length.

A choice of two obvious endings seems to confront us as *Electra* progresses; and most modern criticism has, in effect, been divided between the interpretations which each would imply. The 'traditional' view concludes with Orestes and Electra justly reclaiming their ancestral palace where they will live comfortably for the rest of their days. The 'ironic', and more pessimistic, view, which has become dominant in recent years, predicts that trouble will start moments after the end of the play—remorse, Erinyes, exile and all the rest [19]. Exile, at least, should be ruled out. By ending the play with the entry of Orestes into the palace (the *skene*) Sophocles is positively diverging from Aeschylus, whose play ends memorably with the flight of Orestes away from Argos pursued by Furies. Euripides' *Electra* is even more different (and while leaving the problem of priority open, I would not object if my observations on the endings were taken to weigh

[19] Full bibliography for both views in CH. SEGAL, *Tragedy and Civilization*, 461 notes 2 and 3. There has since appeared a defence of the 'traditional' view of more than traditional sophistication by T. A. SZLEZÁK, in *MH* 38 (1981), 1-21.

in favour of putting Sophocles last). Euripides' play ends with the departure of both Orestes and Electra into separate exile. Orestes has not even reached the ancestral palace; his return from exile is, in effect, turned back at the borders of the land (see line 96). On the other hand the highly unconventional way that Sophocles stops his play abruptly half way through the standard sequence of the killing is, by itself, warning against over-confidence in the future. Of the many worrying points brought to bear by Winnington-Ingram, Segal and others—some more cogent than others—it is particularly Aegisthus' notorious question, just before being taken inside, which hangs over the ending without a reassuring answer (1497-8):

ἦ πᾶσ' ἀνάγκη τήνδε τὴν στέγην ἰδεῖν
τά τ' ὄντα καὶ μέλλοντα Πελοπιδῶν κακά;

The stage topography seems purposefully to reject exile; but the future of Orestes and Electra *within* this ancestral palace does not look bright either.

It is a commonplace that *Philoctetes* has a double ending, one before and the other after the epiphany of Heracles. I have argued that there is a third, earlier, ending when Philoctetes has been deserted and goes into his cave to await death (1217) [20]. I used to regard each succeeding conclusion as more satisfactory than the one before; but consideration of Sophocles' endings in his theatre has provoked second thoughts.

The *skene* represents Philoctetes' cave, the ἄοικον... οἴκησιν (534), where he has eked out his solitary life for so many years. One of the two *eisodoi* is used, if at all, only for Philoctetes' first entry at 219; it leads to the interior of

[20] *GRBS* 12 (1971), 35-43. Structurally speaking we seem to have had a final lyric dialogue lament ending with an exit; only with retrospect does it emerge as an act-dividing lyric dialogue.

Lemnos, his private terrain, which he so vividly evokes (esp. 936 ff.; 1146 ff.) [21]. The other *eisodos*, by contrast, is used and about to be used throughout the play. It goes to the shore and Neoptolemus' ship; its destination does not end there, however, since the ship's voyage divides between the possibilities of Troy and of home in Greece [22]. The significance of this path to the ship changes repeatedly throughout the play, depending on whether the intended journey leads to Troy or Greece, and whether Philoctetes is about to go deceived or knowing, by force or choice.

When Philoctetes finds that he has been deceived he turns back to his cave (952 ff.; cf. 1081 ff.):

ὦ σχῆμα πέτρας δίπυλον, αὖθις αὖ πάλιν
εἴσειμι πρὸς σὲ ψιλός, οὐκ ἔχων τροφήν...

And when he finally goes inside at 1217, there is a certain grim rightness to this ending. The last χρηστός (see line 437) is left in his desert landscape to achieve a kind of ironic symbiosis with the wild creatures who had nourished him. We are bound, however, to feel much happier about the ending which is imminent at line 1402 ff., since Neoptolemus has been restored to friendship and honesty, and has discovered his own φύσις (see esp. 1310-3). The instinctive sympathy between the two men has now grown into a bond such that they will stand together against the dishonesty and cowardice of the rest of the world. As they begin to take the path to

[21] I have come to doubt the entry from the cave advocated by A. M. DALE, *Collected Papers* (Cambridge 1969), 127-8, partly because the association of man and terrain is enhanced by using this *eisodos* on just this one occasion. οὐκ ἔξεδρος, ἀλλ' ἔντοπος ἀνήρ in 211 must mean "the man is not far off, but near" (Jebb). Cf. D. B. ROBINSON, in *CQ* 19 (1969), 34-9.

[22] There is some comparison with the way that one *eisodos* in *Antigone* goes out of the city into the plain, and there divides to two places which are important for the play: (i) where the corpse of Polynices lies (see esp. 249 ff.; 407 ff.; 1196 ff.), (ii) the tomb-like rock chamber which is Antigone's place of punishment (see esp. 773 ff.; 1204 ff.).

Greece we must desire and endorse this outcome [23]. But Heracles blocks it: he has come to tell them the will of Zeus, κατερητύσων θ' ὁδὸν ἣν στέλληι (1416). They will finally depart by that same *eisodos*, but it will lead to Troy, to cure and glory and reintegration into society. We are, I suggest, bound to compare this journey with the two we have seen earlier, the first with Philoctetes staying on Lemnos by himself for ever, the other leading to a noble stand with Neoptolemus against a society not worth reintegration. I am now persuaded that, having set up the comparison, Sophocles encourages our doubts about his final ending by including lines 1440-41, the call for piety at the sack of Troy [24]. Addressed to almost anyone but Neoptolemus, the sentiment might have been a mere cliché. His deeds at the sack of Troy were so notorious that even this small warning suddenly grows into an insistent black cloud on the horizon that had seemed set fair. Once again Sophocles refuses the road of unsullied redemption; again he subtly yet devastatingly flaws our untragic hopes for happiness and integrity.

*

* *

The basic stage-map of *OT*, finally, is simple and conventional. The *skene* represents the royal palace, one *eisodos* leads to the city of Thebes, the other leads abroad. From the city direction come and go the priest and suppliants, the chorus, Teiresias and Creon (after his first

[23] Alexis Minotis told me that at the Greek National Theatre production at Dodona in 1981 (where he directed and played *Philoctetes*) there was enthusiastic applause by the audience who thought the play had ended, before they were interrupted by Heracles; when the applause was resumed at the end it was less enthusiastic.

[24] See esp. R. P. Winnington-Ingram, *op. cit.* (p. 162 n. 18), 297-303. P. E. Easterling, in *Illinois Class. Studies* 3 (1978), 34-39 and Ch. Segal, *op. cit.* (p. 161 n. 15), 355-61 still find the actual ending ultimately more satisfying ("we surely must feel that going to Malis is a second best. . .", Easterling p. 37).

entry). It appears that Oedipus himself does not use that *eisodos*, but makes all his appearances from the palace, as does Jocasta of course. For most of the play everyone, including Oedipus, believes that he originally came to that house from outside. It turns out that he is the true-born heir, yet that discovery brings no joy (cf. Teiresias at 452-4). Teiresias, riddling with imagery of a sea voyage, warns that the navigation of Oedipus' life has not been as fortunate as it seems (420-23):

> βοῆς δὲ τῆς σῆς ποῖος οὐκ ἔσται λιμήν,
> ποῖος Κιθαιρὼν οὐχὶ σύμφωνος τάχα,
> ὅταν καταίσθηι τὸν ὑμέναιον, ὃν δόμοις
> ἄνορμον εἰσέπλευσας εὐπλοίας τυχών; [25]

For it transpires that this is the house where he was born, and indeed conceived, in the ancestral θάλαμος. It is there, to the νυμφικὰ λέχη, that Jocasta goes to kill herself (1241 ff.), and there that Oedipus finds her and puts out his eyes (1260 ff.). Not all the waters of Istros and Phasis could wash this palace clean (see 1223-31).

The third direction gathers associations in a more complex way, for Sophocles pieces together, beyond it, a sort of chart of Oedipus' past. The three characters who come from that *eisodos* are Creon, returning from Delphi, the old man from Corinth, and the old shepherd from Mount Cithaeron [26]. These are three of the four landmarks which (as though viewed from the top of Parnassus) are linked by the route of Oedipus' life-journey.

[25] The language is strained, but Dawe's lacuna after 422 seems provoked by an insistence that the seer should speak plainly.

[26] K. Joerden, in *op. cit.* (p. 158 n. 8), 386-7 seems to neglect 758-64 and other passages in having the old shepherd come from the side of the city. Also I can see no basis for his division of the *eisodoi* into a side of truth and a side of falsehood. This seems to be a temporal rather than spatial division: in the past delusion came from all three directions, now truth comes from all three.

The fourth landmark is the first to be mapped in the course of the play. In the dialogue between Oedipus and Jocasta at 729 ff. we learn about the junction of the three roads in Phocis. Before long (774 ff.) this is plotted on a journey which led from Corinth to Delphi and from Delphi to Thebes. We have heard often how Oedipus arrived in Thebes [27]: now we realise that he came to face the Sphinx fresh from his encounter in Phocis. Oedipus' voyage continues to be reconstructed in reverse. Next comes the revelation that the Corinthian had taken the baby Oedipus from Mount Cithaeron, and given him to Polybus at Corinth (1025 ff.). He had him from another shepherd on the mountain (1038 ff.); and there the track stops for the brief choral song at 1086 ff. It is not long before Oedipus is pressing the old servant on the question of where *he* got the baby from—τίνος πολιτῶν τῶνδε κἀκ ποίας στέγης; (1164). The person who best knows the last link is inside the very palace before which they are standing: ἡ δ' ἔσω / κάλλιστ' ἂν εἴποι σὴ γυνὴ τάδ' ὡς ἔχει (1171-2). The journey has come full circle.

Oedipus does not use that *eisodos* during the entire play, yet we are made to reconstruct the two fateful occasions in the past when he moved along it. First, carried away by the servant, when he was less than three days old (717-8); then returning, years later, fresh from his triumph over the Sphinx—the bridegroom on his hymeneal procession. The journey starts and ends in the same θάλαμος, in the same harbour:

ἰὼ κλεινὸν Οἰδίπου κάρα
ὧι μέγας λιμὴν αὑτὸς ἤρκεσεν
παιδὶ καὶ πατρὶ
θαλαμηπόλωι πεσεῖν. (1207-10)

[27] First and especially at lines 35-6; cf. also 258 ff.; 396.

Sophocles' play embodies physically Vernant's analysis of the whole shape of the myth: "the story of Oedipus is that of his return to his place of origin" [28].

This carefully plotted circuit underlies Oedipus' powerful speech at 1369-1415. Now that he knows the truth there could be no pleasure or point in seeing his parents, his children, the city of Thebes or the citizens (1369-90). He tells over the sequence which has brought this about.

First, ἰὼ Κιθαιρών, τί μ' ἐδέχου... (1391-3)
then ὦ Πόλυβε καὶ Κόρινθε καὶ τὰ πάτρια
λόγωι παλαιὰ δώμαθ'... (1394-7)
then ὦ τρεῖς κέλευθοι καὶ κεκρυμμένη νάπη,
δρυμός τε καὶ στενωπὸς ἐν τριπλαῖς ὁδοῖς...
(1398-1401)

and so to Thebes (δεῦρ' ἰὼν 1402), and to the last of Oedipus' apostrophes of past landmarks ὦ γάμοι γάμοι... (1403 ff.) [29]. When this track leads him ineluctably to deeds too monstrous to name, Oedipus pleads for release, for a way out of the circle of his life (1410-12)

ὅπως τάχιστα, πρὸς θεῶν, ἔξω μέ που
ἐκρίψατ', ἢ φονεύσατ', ἢ θαλάσσιον
καλύψατ', ἔνθα μήποτ' εἰσόψεσθ' ἔτι.

This brings us to the last exploitation of the *eisodos* which leads abroad: the way that it is *not* used at the end of the play [30]. I do not need to detail all the passages which prepare

[28] *Art. cit.* (p. 155 n. 2), 23. Cf. also R. LATTIMORE, *The Poetry of Greek Tragedy* (Baltimore 1958), 100; J. HAY, *Oedipus Tyrannus. Lame Knowledge and the Homosporic Womb* (Washington D.C. 1979), 93-101.

[29] On the interpretation of 1403-8 see C. W. MACLEOD, in *CQ* 32 (1982), 232-3, now reprinted in his *Collected Essays* (Oxford 1983), 45-6.

[30] I made a beginning on this topic in my *Stagecraft* (*op. cit.* in p. 157 n. 7), 184 (a discussion of 'false endings') and in *Greek Tragedy in Action* (London/Berkeley 1978), 45-46. Since then I have had the benefit of reading a draft of an article on the end of *OT* by Dr. Malcolm Davies, now published in *Hermes* 110 (1982), 268-77. Among those few others who have seen that there is a point worth discussing I would single out H. D. F. KITTO, *Poiesis. Structure and Thought* (Berkeley 1966), 200-242, esp. 214-6, and B. SEIDENSTICKER, in *Hermes* 100 (1972), 260.

us for the play to end with Oedipus' departure from Thebes into exile—there are over twenty, some slight, many prominent. They include a prophesy by Tiresias (417-9, though note the indefinite ποτε):

καὶ σ' ἀμφιπλὴξ μητρός τε καὶ τοῦ σοῦ πατρὸς
ἐλᾶι ποτ' ἐκ γῆς τῆσδε δεινόπους ἀρά,
βλέποντα νῦν μὲν ὄρθ', ἔπειτα δὲ σκότον.

And he adds the detail ξένην ἔπι / σκήπτρωι προδεικνὺς γαῖαν ἐμπορεύσεται (455-6). Once he knows the truth, Oedipus' desire to leave his ancestral home and to be cast out into the wild is violent and almost obsessive. The messenger warns of it even before the blind Oedipus is seen (1290-1):

ὡς ἐκ χθονὸς ῥίψων ἑαυτόν, οὐδ' ἔτι
μενῶν δόμοις ἀραῖος ὡς ἠράσατο.

Oedipus sings of exile (1340-44)

ἀπάγετ' ἐκτόπιον ὅτι τάχιστά με,
ἀπάγετ', ὦ φίλοι, τὸν μέγ' ὀλέθριον...

and then he speaks of it in the great rhesis summarised above (1381-2, 1410-11 quoted). When Creon arrives Oedipus' first request to him is (1436-7):

ῥίψον με γῆς ἐκ τῆσδ' ὅσον τάχισθ', ὅπου
θνητῶν φανοῦμαι μηδενὸς προσήγορος.

And he reiterates his pressing requirement at greater length in 1449-58, where he specifies Cithaeron—οὑμὸς Κιθαιρὼν οὗτος (1452)—as the place he will go to die.

These passages must be the foundation of what has probably been the single most potent idea, or deep structure, in recent interpretations of *OT*, the ritual of the φαρμακός, the scapegoat [31]. This is constantly assumed, and never denied, in Vernant's influential essay, and he presumably endorses the observation, which he says others had already made, that "at

[31] For an account of this ritual see W. BURKERT, *Griechische Religion...* (Stuttgart 1977), 139-42.

the end of the tragedy, Oedipus is hounded from Thebes just as the *homo piacularis* is expelled. . ." [32]. Yet it is not in fact Sophocles' *Oedipus* which ends like this, it is Seneca's. The comparison with Seneca is revealing since he spells out the kind of ending which Sophocles has led us to expect—magnificent, cathartic, off into the wild taking with him the sins of the world—*mortifera mecum vitia terrarum extraho* [33]. Those who have looked closely at Sophocles' ending are agreed that that is not the way it is. We might wish that the wording of the trochaic dialogue at 1515-23 were clearer, but there can be little doubt, even without the preliminary covering of the same ground at 1422-45, that, when at 1521 Oedipus says ἄπαγέ νύν μ' ἐντεῦθεν ἤδη and Creon confirms this, στεῖχέ νυν. . ., Oedipus goes into the palace to await a Delphic decision [34]. We are left free to think that sooner or later he will go into exile, if that is what the god grants (see 1438-9; 1518), that he will sooner or later (ποτε) fulfill Teiresias' prophesy. But not

[32] J.-P. Vernant, *op. cit.* (p. 156 n. 3), *passim*; the quotation is from p. 100 of the English translation. Two other influential expositions of the scapegoat Oedipus are the first chapter of F. Fergusson, *op. cit.* (p. 155 n. 1) and R. Girard, *Violence and the Sacred* (Paris 1972; English transl. Baltimore 1977), esp. chapter 3.

[33] Line 1052 to the end: *quicumque fessi corpore et morbo graves*
semanima trahens pectora, en fugio exeo;
relevate colla. mitior caeli status
post terga sequitur: quisquis exilem iacens
animam retentat, vividos haustus levis
concipiat. ite, ferte depositis opem;
mortifera mecum vitia terrarum extraho.
violenta Fata et horridus Morbi tremor,
Maciesque et atra Pestis et rabidus Dolor,
mecum ite, mecum. ducibus his uti libet.

[34] In order to avoid this conclusion W. M. Calder III, in *CPh* 57 (1962), 219 ff. has to stretch the words unconvincingly; for example he glosses τοῦ θεοῦ μ' αἰτεῖς δόσιν in 1518 as "CR (*still sympathetic but with a slight tone of surprise*): You are asking me for what the god has already granted you". D. A. Hester, in *PCPhS* 23 (1977), 45-46 has recently revived the theory that lines 1515 *ad fin.* replace Sophocles' original ending which was similar to that in Seneca. This easy way out disregards the preliminary dialogue at 1422-45.

yet. Twice in *OC* at 433-44 and 765-71 Oedipus recalls, at some length and with some bitterness, how when at first he had longed for exile it had not been granted; and how when he had eventually grown reconciled to staying at home and his θυμός had subsided (see 438; 768), then—χρόνιον 441—then he was cast out [35]. This possible future does not diminish the grim burden of the end of *OT* as it is.

In terms of stage geography Creon refuses to let Oedipus escape down the *eisodos* that leads abroad, away, elsewhere: instead he commands him to go back inside the *skene*, the 'cul-de-sac', by himself without even his daughters—back into his ancestral palace, the place where he was conceived and wedded, where he put out his eyes. The easy ending, which would be a kind of second start for Oedipus, is refused. As Colin Macleod put it "he has to go on being humiliated and guilt-ridden where he belongs" [36].

I would therefore reverse Charles Segal's pronouncement that "Oedipus begins and ends as a man without a house" [37]. At the beginning of *OT* he seems to be without an established house, but in truth he has one and is already living in it (cf. Teiresias at 452-3 ἐγγενὴς / φανήσεται Θηβαῖος). At the end he must live on in that house. He longs to leave it, to dwell in the wild mountains, but he is not allowed to. The point is, I think, that exile would be some sort of release, to be a scapegoat would be a kind of redemption; Sophocles insists that Oedipus' paradigmatic reversal of fortune should be

[35] While these passages might be seen as a conscious link between the two plays, it is not as close as is claimed by B. SEIDENSTICKER, *art. cit.* (p. 169 n. 30), 261.

[36] Personal communication quoted in full in my book (*op. cit.* in p. 169 n. 30), 46.

[37] Ch. SEGAL, *op. cit.* (p. 161 n. 15), 224. Throughout his chapter Segal seems to me to be trying to have it both ways: to retain the scapegoat pattern (which looms large throughout the book and is applied to *Aj.*, *Ant.* and *OC* as well as *OT*), and yet not to deny the fact that the play does not end with the cathartic departure. This does not face the way that Sophocles invokes the scapegoat solution in order to *reject* it.

complete, without mitigation. Even worse than the homeless lot of the man who in Achilles' account draws only from the jar of evils (Hom. *Il.* XXIV 531-3), it is even more realistic and painful to live on in the same house with the past [38].

The scapegoat pattern is not the only way that modern interpretations of *OT* have found redeeming gains in the final scenes. One thinks, above all, of the final chapter of Knox's *Oedipus at Thebes* which concludes [38a] "Sophocles' tragedy presents us with a terrible affirmation of man's subordinate position in the universe, and at the same time with a heroic vision of man's victory in defeat". In most accounts there is a strong compensating undertow near the end, such as "But surely the *Oedipus Rex* is also a play about human greatness" or "Yet in the very excess of his suffering lies man's claim to dignity. Powerless and broken, a blind beggar hounded out of the city, he assumes a new grandeur", or "Yet what ultimately emerges from the *OT* is not a sense of total chaos and despair but a quality of heroism in the power of self-knowledge" [39]. But there is no power. Oedipus is free with imperatives, but they are not obeyed. His last words are μηδαμῶς ταύτας γ' ἕληι μου, and Creon overrules him with

πάντα μὴ βούλου κρατεῖν·
καὶ γὰρ ἁκράτησας οὔ σοι τῶι βίωι ξυνέσπετο. (1522-3) [40]

[38] I think that Jeannette KING misses this point about *OT* (and also about Creon at the end of *Ant.*) in chapter 2 of her generally admirable *Tragedy in the Victorian Novel* (Cambridge 1978). She writes (p. 47): "On the one hand there is the traditional tragic ending—the hero's death—and on the other the modern 'unfinished' ending—life goes on". I am not sure that any of Sophocles' surviving tragedies has her 'traditional' ending.

[38a] B. KNOX, *op. cit.* (p. 155 n. 1), 196.

[39] The quotations are from E. R. DODDS, *The Ancient Concept of Progress* (Oxford 1973), 76 (first published in 1966); G. STEINER, *The Death of Tragedy* (London 1961), 9 f.; Ch. SEGAL, *op. cit.* (p. 161 n. 15), 247.

[40] I am taking it that lines 1524-30 are not by Sophocles, while leaving it open whether they replace some choral lines; see R. D. DAWE, *Studies on the Text of Sophocles* I (Leiden 1973), 266-73.

And if Oedipus needs to be told this, how much has he gained in self-knowledge? [41]

Oedipus does not depart in the direction he so desperately wishes to take; he does not keep his daughters with him; the things he used to have κράτος over have not stayed with him. We, the audience, share Oedipus' disappointment and duress: we long for the resurgence, the grand gesture, the cathartic departure. Sophocles denies them by changing the direction of a few paces. He uses his theatre to stop *us* from finding a way out of his tragedy.

[41] The main purpose of M. Davies' article (see p. 169 n. 30) is to raise this question. He phrases his answer epigrammatically: "To put it positively, his character is so strong that it has remained intact amid the rubble of his outer state. To put it negatively, he has learned nothing". I should like to thank Professor John Gould and Mr. R. B. Rutherford for their good advice.

DISCUSSION

M. Knox: On that limp, I now rather regret that I was led astray by Francis Fergusson's attractive phrase, because that limp has now become part of the Levi-Straussian incest-autochthony stew. Not that I ever thought of him as trailing his leg like Laurence Olivier in Richard III: a slight hint of lameness was all I thought of. It was based of course on the exchange between Oedipus and the herdsman at 1031-35 but I would like to renounce it now.

M. Taplin: I wonder if the point of ἄλγος in 1031 might be that a male child would not normally be exposed unless it had some physical weakness or deformity? Line 1033 suggests to me the reluctant acknowledgment of something long concealed, rather than an allusion to an obvious limp.

M. Radt: But ἄλγος would be a very strange word to denote a physical defect.

M. Knox: I am impressed by your treatment of the entrances in *OC*: as you present them, they reinforce the themes of the play eloquently. But I wonder about the Polynices entrance. Theseus comes back from the 'Theban' side, after his rescue of the daughters. He knows that there is a suppliant sitting at the altar of Poseidon (so he has been told, λόγος 1150, φασιν 1156). How has he been told? The altar of Poseidon, at which he was sacrificing when he was interrupted by the cries of the Chorus lies, according to you, in the other direction, towards Athens and so it is from that direction that Polynices enters, not from the same direction as Creon. So some messengers must have gone to tell Theseus, on his way back from the pursuit, about Polynices at the altar. But why does the altar have to be in the direction of Athens? We are told that Poseidon is the tutelary deity of Colonos (54). Theseus comes from Athens (549) and leaves Oedipus at 667 to go and offer sacrifice to Poseidon. Why does he have to go back in the direction of Athens? Why not in the direction of Thebes? In that case he would have seen Polynices on his way back from the pursuit. One more point. Polynices is sent on his way by the chorus νῦν τ' ἴθ' ὡς τάχος πάλιν—*back* to Thebes (1398).

M. Seidensticker: Ist es denkbar, dass der Altar Poseidons (1158) uns einen Hinweis auf die Richtung gibt, aus der Polyneikes kommt? Muss dieser Altar nicht auf der Seite von Kolonos und Athen liegen? Auf jeden Fall scheint es mir *dramatisch* wirkungsvoller, wenn der Hiketes Polyneikes nicht von der gleichen Seite kommt, wie der Aggressor Kreon, sondern von der 'Seite der Sicherheit', auftritt und nach dem Fluch des Vaters, auf der 'Seite der Gefahr', d.h. in Richtung Theben, wo er seinen Tod finden wird, abgeht.

M. Winnington-Ingram: Polynices enters from the altar of Poseidon, i.e. from Colonos. I find it difficult to suppose that Colonos was envisaged as lying on both sides of the stage-area, though doubtless it was close at hand. Is it too hard to suppose that a message had come to Theseus behind the stage, as it were? (Of course, if we knew that the Chorus entered by *one eisodos* only, this would virtually settle the question.)

M. Taplin: I can see that there is a danger of circularity in the argument from 'dramatic sense', none the less I do not think that Bernard Knox's arguments outweigh those in favour of having Polynices enter from the 'Athens side'. πάλιν in 1398 need not be pressed literally: he should go away again. Bernard Knox himself points to the clear indications in 1150 and 1156 that Theseus has only heare about the stranger at the altar of Poseidon and has not seen him: this militates, if anything, in favour of an entry by Polynices from the opposite side from Theseus at 1096.

M. Winnington-Ingram: In *Electra*, Electra ends up, with Orestes, inside the house. I feel that Sophocles wished neither to exclude the subsequent pursuit of Orestes (which would go against the legend), nor positively to imply it (which would raise issues and rouse emotions that he did not wish to develop). Remember that Erinyes have been at work in the house for a long time. One will still be there: Electra (cf. 185-192)!

M. Taplin: Good point. Cassandra at Aeschyl. *Ag.* 1188 ff. sees the κῶμος of the Erinyes ἐν δόμοις. . . δύσπεμπτος ἔξω. Those who maintain that the legend did not dictate the exile of Orestes point, of course, to the *Odyssey*.

M. Winnington-Ingram: As for the entry of Philoctetes, the main argument for the view that he enters from the cave is not that a sudden appearance (with the famous bow) would be dramatically effective (though this it would be), but that, if he entered by an *eisodos*, he would be seen for some little time by the audience, though *not*, apparently, by the Chorus, who use words of sound, but not of sight (201-19). This for me is conclusive.

M. Taplin: If, as I prefer, Philoctetes was to make his entry along the *eisodos*, it would be a long painful stage-movement. I imagine that he would first come into sight at about line 210; and I do not see why the chorus should not be supposed to have seen him. It is admittedly strange dramatic technique for them to comment so exclusively on the sound he makes.

M. Knox: On the ambiguous end of *Philoctetes*, I too am convinced by Winnington-Ingram's demonstration that the reference to εὐσέβεια at Troy casts a shadow over the future. I have always felt that it was a disturbing ending and pointed out in *The Heroic Temper* that the nostalgia in Philoctetes' final address to the island suggests his dismay at the prospects of the future.

M. Steiner: My own bias is to emphasize the absolute character of certain tragedies. But is Oliver Taplin not placing *too* much weight on the single detail of blind Oedipus' return to the palace? The play has been rich in indications that the carrier of pollution must be removed from the city. Oedipus himself alludes to an as yet unknown future. He will await the oracle in the palace. This does not really constitute the Sartrian 'zero-ending' suggested by Taplin. Moreover, though it seems unlikely that this play could have been related to others in a trilogy, the point is not absolutely certain. Finally, even *if* the re-entrance into the palace shows Oedipus to be stripped of all power, it most certainly does not rob him of his paradoxical magnificence.

M. Winnington-Ingram: The situation is somewhat similar to that at the end of *Electra*, the main difference being that the exile is specifically fore-shadowed (which the pursuit of Orestes is not). Sophocles, however, wished to concentrate upon the individual destiny of the hero as at the point the action has reached. Apart from the two great unwitting crimes, the past is vaguely handled, and the future (including the cursing of the sons) is left in "the lap of the gods". Oedipus is left not only shut in with his memories by his blindness, but shut in within the house.

M. Knox: I think you go much too far in your presentation of the dark aspects of the final scene in *Oedipus Tyrannos*. Certainly Oedipus has been deprived of power, as Creon tells him: the fact that he had to tell him speaks volumes for his unconquerable spirit. And he dominates the last scene with three long speeches. The other character, Creon, does nothing after his first attempt to get Oedipus off stage (1424 ff.), but react to the blind polluted hero. And there is one passage in which he looks forward to the future 1455 ff. He knows that his destiny must be some δεινὸν κακόν otherwise he would not have been saved from death: nothing else can touch him, no disease or anything else. He is reserved for something κακόν but it will also be δεινόν—strange, terrifying, something to be wondered at—nothing, in any case, ordinary.

Mme de Romilly: Je crois qu'il ne faut pas considérer seulement le *sort* du héros (même au futur), mais l'impression morale qui se dégage pour le spectateur. Celle-ci tient vraiment à l'œuvre, à la façon dont elle oriente les sympathies, dont elle entoure le héros, dont elle explique sa conduite. L'écrasement de fait n'est pas tout: il laisse la place à un «and yet...»!

M. Seidensticker: Wenn ich Sie richtig verstanden habe, Herr Taplin, sind Sie der Auffassung, die ich durchaus teile, dass die Schlüsse von *Elektra, Philoktet* und *Oedipus in Kolonos* dramatisch offen und emotional ambivalent sind? Warum wollen Sie im Falle des *Oedipus Tyrannos* auf diese Komplexität verzichten?

M. Taplin: Yes, I concede that my argument is too extreme, and is inconsistent with my case that other Sophoclean endings are not black and white. And we must at least pity Oedipus. I hope that, none the less, there was value in putting the extreme position, and in emphasising the way that the final stage-direction purposefully contradicts the preparation for immediate expulsion. But I am swayed by the considerations raised and particularly by lines 1455-7. There is, so to speak, a chink of light, a suggestion of future release; but the ending is still very dark. I think I am influenced by the fate of Creon at the end of *Antigone*. He is denied the release of death, and at the end of the play is shut in his palace with the corpses of his wife and son. He must live with this own disaster.

M. Winnington-Ingram: On Mr. Steiner's point about connected trilogies: trilogies may have been an option for tragedians after Aeschylus, but there is virtually no evidence that it was taken up by Sophocles. The three Theban plays, as we all know, were not a trilogy.

M. Radt: Our only testimony for a connected Sophoclean trilogy is the inscription mentioning Sophocles' Τηλέφεια (DID B 5,8, in *TrGF* I p. 39). What the *Suda* has about Sophocles having given up writing tetralogies (T 2,5 f., in *TrGF* IV p. 41) cannot be built upon because of the corruption of an essential word.

Mme de Romilly: La disparition des trilogies s'accorde bien avec l'augmentation de la longueur des pièces, du nombre des acteurs, des péripéties de l'action. La pièce, avec de tels moyens, peut se suffire à elle-même.

M. Taplin: I have worked on the usual assumption that Sophocles did not compose connected trilogies; and I do not think the fourth-century inscription from Aexone tells much against this. Our total dearth of Sophoclean *didaskaliai* means that we do not know the titles of any trio of plays which he produced in the same year.

M. Knox: I would like to add a few words to Oliver Taplin's remarks on the *pharmakos* theory which is so fashionable these days—Fergusson, Girard and Vernant have all evoked it in different ways. It is true that the play is full of references to pollution and to the expulsion of the man who is its cause. But this is the normal terminology of the law courts which dealt with cases of φόνος—as we know from the orators. The ritual of the expulsion of the φαρμακός is something quite different and it is also a subject on which there is much less information than might be supposed from some of the interpretations in which it is invoked. The evidence for the active killing of a scapegoat figure, for example, is almost non-existent: what we have accounts of, or rather references to, are symbolic expulsions—beatings with plants and similar phenomena. The usual highly charged account of the expulsion and killing of the scapegoat is attributed to Hipponax but the fragments of Hipponax contain no such sensational details as the choice of the ugliest man, the killing of the *pharmakos* and the burning of the body: these all come from the accompanying text of that quite untrustworthy character Tzetzes.

M. Taplin: The fascination of the scapegoat for modern critics may be in part *interpolatio Christiana*, or rather *interpolatio Judaica*.

M. Radt: I have just a little question. I wondered why you had the shepherd come from Kithairon. At the time of Oedipus' birth, he used of course to drive his flock to pasture on Mount Kithairon. But now he is a very old man, whom I always imagine as spending his old age in a farmstead, far away from Thebes of course (cf. 760 ff.), but not in the mountains.

Mme de Romilly: J'avais dirigé autrefois un travail sur la montagne dans la tragédie grecque. Ce travail n'a pas été publié mais il était très suggestif (l'idée m'en était venue à la suite du livre de R. Lattimore, *The Poetry of Greek Tragedy*). On y voyait que la montagne était une sorte de lieu symbolique, s'opposant à la cité. On fuit la cité en allant εἰς ὄρος. La montagne comporte d'ailleurs deux degrés: en haut, sur l'Olympe, très loin, les dieux. Plus près, la nature sauvage, Dionysos, Pan, etc... Ceci expliquerait que l'on pense spontanément au Cithéron, où un berger est d'ailleurs à sa place.

M. Taplin: It is true that it is not specified that he has come from Mount Citheron; but he has been sent at his own request ἀγρούς . . . κἀπὶ ποιμνίων νομάς (761).

There is a memorable 'pan' of the Greek landscape in the superb simile at *Iliad* XII 277-86. The snow falls on the mountain peaks (κορυφάς) and the foothills (πρώονας ἄκρους) and the grasslands (πεδία) and the arable fields (ἔργα), and finally on shore and sea.

(I quite agree, by the way, about the excellence of Lattimore's neglected book.)

M. Steiner: Taplin's stress on the triadic geography of the tragic scene evokes the cardinal motif of the *triodoi* and the *trivium/trivia* in *Oedipus the King, Oedipus at Colonus* and the *Oedipus* of Seneca. Whereas Hercules' choice between *two* roads is characteristic of the binary typology of choices between virtue and vice, light and dark, life and death etc., a *triadic* configuration, as we find it in the Oedipus myths and on the Greek stage, points to what is structurally, topologically and existentially *undecidable*. It almost defines the recursively ambiguous, perplexing and formally indefinite ending of certain great tragic conflicts and their representations. Hecate of the *trivia*, the burial of suicides at the junction of three-roads, intimate some almost archetypal association between *triodoi* and the tragic. The very fact that the 'third road' is the one which leads backward, is key to the Oedipus myth. As Vernant says, this is a myth of fatal homecoming.

M. Irigoin: Une τρίοδος est ce que nous appelons en français une «patte d'oie», c'est-à-dire un endroit où la route se divise en deux (σχιστή, v. 733), comme un Y avec ses deux branches. Le voyageur se trouve alors placé devant une alternative — prendre l'une ou l'autre des deux voies qui s'offrent à lui — mais non pas devant un triple choix, car la troisième solution, qui consisterait à faire demi-tour, le ramènerait à son point de départ. Remontant en quelque sorte le temps, annulant le parcours déjà fait, il aboutirait à une «remise à zéro».

M. Radt: I think we should make a clear distinction here. The τρίοδος in Prodikos' myth and Theognis is a symbol for the choice between t w o things: there is no third possibility, since the third road is the one along which one has been coming, i.e. one's life up to the moment of choice, and this cannot be turned back. The meeting of three roads in the theatre, on the other hand, to which Mr. Taplin has drawn our attention, does indeed give three possibilities.

Mme de Romilly: Je me demande en fait si la notion des 'trois routes' a une si grande importance symbolique pour l'ensemble de la pièce. Il n'y a aucune insistance chez Sophocle, et il semble s'agir surtout d'un endroit à la fois dangereux pour une rencontre et aisé à repérer pour la géographie. Le choix de l'endroit peut impliquer une ombre, sans pour autant engager tout le sens.

M. Seidensticker: Herrn Steiners Hinweis auf die Unlösbarkeit 'triadischer Konfiguration' erinnert mich daran, dass Oedipus, als er am Ende des *Oedipus in Kolonos*, am Ende seines langen tragischen Lebensweges erneut an einen Dreiweg kommt (1592), haltmacht und sich niedersetzt. Es sind die Götter, die mit Donner (1606) und auf direktem Anruf (1627) für ihn entscheiden; und vielleicht kann man auch sagen, dass im *Philoktet* erst göttliche Intervention (Herakles) das 'triadische Problem' (Troja, Lemnos, Heimkehr) löst, das alle menschlichen Versuche nicht haben lösen können.

M. Knox: I would just like to point out that the three roads are of no particular importance in the Oedipus story except as a means of identification and recognition: Oedipus does not have to choose between two roads—he knows where he is going—away from Corinth, as he says—and he could have got into a fight over right of way just as well on one road as at the meeting-place of three (or rather the bifurcation of one).

M. Taplin: I think some extremely interesting points have been made. In *OT*, Oedipus' return into the palace is a turning back down the road he has come along, back to his origins, but it is a route imposed on him, not of his choice. We must, of course, beware of any oversimple superimposition of the three ways in and out of the *orchestra* upon the choices, so often insoluble, of tragedy.

Of the three possibilities in *Philoctetes*, for instance, one lies inside the *skene*, both the others along one of the two *eisodoi*.

It would make a lot of sense if in *OC* the way by which Oedipus goes to his death (1555) were to be into the *skene*, representing the grove, rather than by either *eisodos*. The gods would then lead Oedipus by the third road. The problem is, as Bernard Knox has pointed out to me, that the messenger tells of familiar landmarks while earlier in the play it appears that the grove is inviolate, ἄβατον (37, 39, 167 etc.). The problems of Greek tragedy seem often to be insoluble on several levels!

VI

Stefan Radt

SOPHOKLES IN SEINEN FRAGMENTEN

Was die Fragmente zu unserem Sophoklesbild beitragen kann selber auch nur fragmentarisch sein. Zu den grossen Fragen der Sophoklesinterpretation — Aufbau und Handlungsführung der Dramen, Gestaltung der Personen, Funktion des Chors u. dgl. — haben die Fragmente nichts zu bieten. Aber gewisse Teilaspekte von Sophokles' Kunst kennen wir nur aus den Fragmenten, und auf diese Aspekte möchte ich mich vor allem konzentrieren: an erster Stelle die Stoffe, die Sophokles für seine Stücke gewählt hat (I-II); ferner Sophokles als Satyrspieldichter (III); und schliesslich eine ganze Reihe kleinerer Nova, die wir in den Fragmenten finden (IV). Ausserdem möchte ich kurz auf einige Parallelen zu bereits aus den erhaltenen Stücken bekannten Elementen hinweisen (V), und zum Abschluss auf ein paar besonders schöne und bemerkenswerte Fragmente eingehen (VI).

I

Um festzustellen welche Stoffe Sophokles für seine Dramen gewählt hat, brauchen wir natürlich erst einmal eine möglichst vollständige Liste der Titel seiner Stücke.

Nun besitzen wir für die Zahl der sophokleischen Dramen zwei verschiedene Angaben. Nach der *Vita* (T 1, 76 f.) [1], die sich auf Aristophanes von Byzanz beruft, gab es von Sophokles 130 Dramen (ἔχει δὲ δράματα ... ρλ΄), von denen 17 für unecht erklärt wurden; die *Suda* dagegen (T 2, 9) behauptet, Sophokles habe 123 Stücke aufgeführt (ἐδίδαξε), fügt aber hinzu, dass Manche eine viel höhere Zahl angeben. August Böckh und Theodor Bergk wollten beide Zeugnisse miteinander in Einklang bringen: Böckh, indem er die 123 der *Suda* in 113 änderte (was nach der *Vita* die Zahl der echten Stücke gewesen wäre), Bergk, indem er in der *Vita* die 17 — die Zahl der unechten Stücke — durch 7 ersetzte. Natürlich ist es keineswegs ausgeschlossen, dass solche Änderungen das Richtige treffen (die von Bergk konjizierte 7 hat sich inzwischen sogar in einer Handschrift gefunden — allerdings, nach dem Zeugnis Rudolf Schoells, als Korrektur einer ursprünglich geschriebenen 17: sie ist also auch dort vielleicht nur Konjektur...). Aber das Korrigieren von Zahlen bleibt ja, wenn man über keine weiteren Daten verfügt, eine reine Spielerei. Und vielleicht ist überhaupt gar kein Fehler unserer Überlieferung im Spiel: der Widerspruch könnte sich auch daraus erklären, dass die *Vita* alle bekannten Stücke zählt (ἔχει), die *Suda* dagegen nur die zur Aufführung gekommenen (ἐδίδαξε), d.h. die in den Didaskalien genannten. Wie dem auch sei: auf Grund dieser beiden Zeugnisse können wir nicht genau sagen, wieviel Stücke Sophokles geschrieben hat.

Bei diesem Stand der Dinge liegt es nahe, einfach die uns überlieferten Titel sophokleischer Dramen zu zählen. Aber so einfach ist das nicht! Erstens werden manche überlieferten Titel mit mehr oder weniger Recht bezweifelt; ausserdem wird des öfteren vermutet, dass zwei (manchmal sogar drei) verschiedene Titel Bezeichnungen für ein und dasselbe Stück

[1] Alle Zitate (und einige Abkürzungen) nach meiner Ausgabe *Tragicorum Graecorum Fragmenta* (*TrGF*) Vol. IV (Göttingen 1977).

gewesen seien; und schliesslich hat man aus unseren Quellen auch noch Titel sophokleischer Stücke erschlossen. Diese drei Faktoren haben dazu geführt, dass wir über die Zahl der Titel sophokleischer Dramen die verschiedensten Angaben finden: bei Pearson (I pp. XVIII ff.) z.B. sind es 132 bzw. (nach Abzug aller zweifelhaften) 112, bei W. Schmid (*Geschichte der griechischen Literatur* I 2 [München 1934], 325) 114 (mit der unverständlichen Anmerkung [325 [6]] «Identifizieren können wir noch 112 Stücke»), bei A. v. Blumenthal (in *RE* III A 1, *s.v.* Sophokles, 1079, 45 ff.) 130 [2].

Will man hier etwas mehr Exaktheit und Klarheit schaffen, dann muss man an erster Stelle natürlich alle Titel weglassen die auf Konjektur beruhen. Damit scheiden nicht nur Ἄδμητος, Αἴγισθος, Ἄλκηστις, Βάκχαι, Ἴβηρες, Ἰνώ, Ἰοκάστη, Ναϊάδες, Νεανίσκοι, Νεοπτόλεμος, Οἰνεύς, Οἰνώνη, Πτωχεία und Ὠρείθυια aus [3], sondern auch Εὐρύπυλος, ein von Aristoteles erwähnter Titel, dessen Zuweisung an Sophokles nicht mehr ist als eine Konjektur, die durch *POxy.* 1175 + 2081 (b) zwar wahrscheinlich, aber keineswegs sicher geworden ist, was oft vergessen wird (vgl. *TrGF* IV p. 195).

Zweitens müssen von den überlieferten Titeln all diejenigen ausser Betracht bleiben, die mehr oder weniger verdächtig sind. Das sind auf jeden Fall Ἀλείτης, Ἰάμβη, Ἱπποδάμεια, Κασάνδρα [4], Κρῆτες, Κῶμος, Μήδεια, Ξοανηφόροι,

[2] Dass die Zahl genau zu der Angabe der *Vita* stimmt, ist sicher kein Zufall!

[3] Nicht dagegen Οἰκλῆς. Dieser Titel ist zwar eine Konjektur — überliefert ist Ἰοκλῆς; aber dieser Ἰοκλῆς ist zweimal ausdrücklich für Sophokles bezeugt (F 468-469) und lässt sich nicht als Korruption eines sonst bekannten sophokleischen Titels interpretieren, um so weniger als die Verschreibung Ἰοκλῆς für Οἰκλῆς auch sonst begegnet (z.B. Aeschyl. *Sept.* 609; Eur. *Supp.* 925).

[4] F 897, wo — wie die von mir seinerzeit leider übersehene Ausgabe von L. Di Gregorio (*Scholia vetera in Hesiodi Theogoniam*, Milano 1975) zeigt — alle Handschriften ἐν Κασάνδρᾳ bieten. Da unmittelbar nach Sophokles Lykophrons Vers *Alex.* 6 zitiert wird, in dem es von Kassandra heisst δαφνηφάγων φοίβαζεν ἐκ λαιμῶν ὄπα, liegt der Verdacht nahe, dass hier in unserer Überlieferung etwas schief gegangen ist.

Οἰλεύς, Πάνδαρος, Πελίας, Προμηθεύς und Τάλως. Dass man übrigens nicht zu schnell an überlieferten Titeln zweifeln soll, haben neuere Funde gezeigt: Μοῦσαι (bezweifelt von Casaubonus und Brunck) wird bestätigt durch CAT B 1, 25 (*TrGF* I p. 57), Ἰξίων und Πρίαμος (beide bezweifelt von Welcker) durch DID A 4 b 6 ff. (*TrGF* I p. 31) bzw. Phot. *Lex.* (cod. Zavord.) *s.v.* ἀφήλικες, Τυνδάρεως (bezweifelt von Welcker und Anderen) und Φρύγες (bezweifelt von Bergk und Wecklein) durch Phot. *Lex.* (cod. Berol.) 89, 20 bzw. 151, 7. Es ist also methodisch falsch, ganz selten zitierte Titel einzig auf Grund dieser Seltenheit zu verdächtigen, wie dies z.B. noch Schmid (*GGL* I 2, 451) bei dem *Theseus* tut.

Drittens muss man sich davor hüten, überlieferte Titel allzu schnell miteinander gleich zu setzen. Natürlich kommt es nachweislich vor, dass griechische Dramen statt nach ihrem Titel nach einer darin auftretenden Person zitiert werden (siehe Pearson, I p. XIX), und so ist es z.B. höchst wahrscheinlich, dass, wenn Erotian aus Sophokles' *Pelias* die Worte λευκὸν αὐτὴν ὧδ' ἐπαίδευσεν γάλα zitiert (F 648), die offenbar auf Tyro zu beziehen sind, er die erste oder zweite *Tyro* meint, und dass die von Stobaios aus Sophokles' *Hippodameia* zitierten Verse (F 472) aus seinem *Oinomaos* stammen (in welchem Stück, wie wir durch F 474 wissen, Hippodameia eine der *dramatis personae* war). Aber ausser der Einmaligkeit des Zitats gibt es keinen einzigen Grund, den von einem späten Rhetor zitierten *Kerberos* mit dem *Herakles* zu identifizieren (was Pearson [I p. XIX] als eine objektive Tatsache präsentiert), und es ist auch keineswegs «difficult to avoid the conclusion that *Ion* was an alternative title for the *Creusa*..., and *Clytaemnestra* either for the *Iphigenia* or the *Aegisthus*» [5]. Ebenso willkürlich ist z.B. die seit Welcker

[5] A. C. PEARSON (ed.), *The Fragments of Sophocles* I (Cambridge 1917), p. XIX (wo «alternative title» übrigens ein irreführender Ausdruck ist: es handelt sich hier ja nicht um einen 'offiziellen' zweiten Titel, wie bei Ἀτρεὺς ἢ Μυκηναῖαι u. dgl.

allgemeine Identifizierung der *Eriphyle* mit den *Epigonoi* (die Nauck zwar nicht mitgemacht hat aber doch wahrscheinlich fand) sowie die von Toup vorgeschlagene und ebenfalls allgemein übernommene Gleichsetzung des *Herakles* mit den Ἐπὶ Ταινάρῳ σάτυροι (eine Gleichsetzung, die Nauck dazu verführt hat, sogar einen neuen Titel Ἡρακλῆς ἐπὶ Ταινάρῳ σατυρικός zu konjizieren, den Pearson [I 167 f.] mit Recht abgelehnt hat, aber Schmid z.B. als etwas fest Gegebenes hantiert [*GGL* I 2, 83; 325 [8]; 451; 464 [12]]). Ja, gegen die Gleichung *Eriphyle* = *Epigonoi* spricht sogar eine Tatsache, über die die Verteidiger dieser Gleichung sich, wie mir scheint, oft zu leichtfertig hinwegsetzen (vgl. Pearson I 132 [1]; Schmid, *GGL* I 2, 437 [7]), die Tatsache nämlich, dass für den römischen Dichter Accius ausser einer Tragödie *Epigoni* — die, wie man aus Cic. *De opt. gen. or.* 18 schliessen darf, eine Nachbildung des gleichnamigen sophokleischen Stückes war (siehe *TrGF* IV p. 184) — auch eine *Eriphyla* bezeugt ist: wenn die sophokleische *Eriphyle* mit seinen *Epigonoi* identisch wäre, müsste man dieselbe Identität auch bei Accius annehmen [6].

Dieselbe Zurückhaltung sollte man auch bei der Annahme von Doppeltiteln beobachten. Überliefert sind uns für Sophokles nur vier Doppeltitel: Ἀτρεὺς ἢ Μυκηναῖαι, Μάντεις ἢ Πολύϊδος, Ναυσικάα ἢ Πλύντριαι, Πανδώρα ἢ Σφυροκόποι. Nur für diese vier Dramen ist also ein Doppeltitel

[siehe weiter unten], sondern, wie Pearson auch selber ausdrücklich sagt, um «the results of lapse of memory, carelessness of citation, or confusion by a copyist»). Wenn Pearson dann fortfährt: «but hesitation is pardonable before we accept the identification of the *Theseus* with the *Phaedra*» etc. (Sperrung St. R.), so illustriert das aufs schönste den grundlegenden Unterschied seiner Haltung mit der hier empfohlenen: für Pearson ist «hesitation» offenbar etwas was man in diesen Fragen möglichst vermeiden soll, für mich dagegen eine unentbehrliche Vorbedingung für eine reinliche Trennung von Überlieferung und Konjektur.

[6] Was O. Ribbeck, *Die römische Tragödie im Zeitalter der Republik* (Leipzig 1875), 487 ff., der Welckers Gleichsetzung übernahm, denn auch konsequent getan hat.

gesichert: die von Toup vermutete Identität des Ἀχαιῶν σύλλογος mit den Σύνδειπνοι — mag sie auch noch so wahrscheinlich sein (siehe *TrGF* IV pp. 163 und 425) — muss aus dem Spiele bleiben, ganz zu schweigen von Bruncks Annahme eines Dramas Νίπτρα ἢ Ὀδυσσεὺς ἀκανθοπλήξ (siehe *TrGF* IV p. 373); und auch die drei überlieferten Helena-Titel — Ἑλένης ἀπαίτησις, Ἑλένης ἁρπαγή, Ἑλένης γάμος — wird man, wenn man feststellen will, was uns überliefert ist, wohl oder übel als drei verschiedene Stücke zählen müssen.

Wenn man nach diesen Prinzipien verfährt, ergibt sich dass uns die Titel von 115 verlorenen Stücken sicher überliefert sind (siehe Anhang I). Zusammen mit den 7 erhaltenen Tragödien macht das 122 — also eine Zahl die kaum von der der *Suda* abweicht. Leider können wir trotzdem nicht sicher sein, dass wir damit fast alle Titel von Sophokles' Stücken kennen, denn es ist natürlich gut möglich, dass diese Liste von 122 Titeln noch Alternativ-Titel oder Personennamen statt Titel enthält. Aber dass wir in dieser Liste den weitaus grössten Teil der sophokleischen Titel vor uns haben, darf man doch wohl mit einer gewissen Zuversicht annehmen.

Wenn dem aber so ist, fällt es auf, dass in unseren Quellen nur 13 Stücke ausdrücklich als Satyrspiele bezeichnet werden [7], während wir doch mindestens etwa die doppelte Zahl

[7] Ἄμυκος, Ἀμφιάρεως, Διονυσίσκος, Ἐπὶ Ταινάρῳ, Ἡρακλεΐσκος, Ἡρακλῆς, Ἰχνευταί, Κηδαλίων, Κρίσις, Κωφοί, Μῶμος, Σαλμωνεύς, Ὕβρις. Auch hier hat die Vermengung von Überliefertem mit Konjekturalem zu den verschiedensten Angaben geführt: PEARSON (I p. XXI) nennt als «universally admitted or strictly proved to be satyric» 16 Stücke (in seiner Liste fehlen Ἐπὶ Ταινάρῳ und Ἡρακλεΐσκος, und sind Ἀχιλλέως ἐρασταί, Ἑλένης γάμος, Ἔρις, Πανδώρα und Τήλεφος hinzugefügt) und SCHMID (*GGL* I 2, 325) behauptet «Titel von Satyrspielen können wir mit Sicherheit noch 15 nachweisen» (es folgt Pearsons Liste ohne Τήλεφος und mit dem Zusatz ἐπὶ Ταινάρῳ zu Ἡρακλῆς [Naucks Konjektur, siehe oben]); v. BLUMENTHAL (*RE, s.v.* Sophokles, 1079, 55 ff.) zählt 16 sichere Satyrspiele (er lässt Ἡρακλῆς weg und fügt Ἄδμητος,

erwarten. Pearson (I p. XVI; vgl. p. XXII) wollte das mit der Annahme erklären, dass schon die alexandrinische Bibliothek nicht mehr alle sophokleischen Satyrspiele besessen habe, und berief sich dafür auf eine Bemerkung Elmsleys in seinem *Medea*-Kommentar. Elmsley hat dort [8] anlässlich der Mitteilung in der Hypothesis zur *Medea*, das zugehörige Satyrspiel *Theristai* sei nicht erhalten, darauf hingewiesen, dass die *Vita* des Euripides (Ed. Schwartz (ed.), *Scholia in Euripidem* I [Berlin 1887]), p. 4, 8 ff.) angibt, von den 92 euripideischen Dramen seien 70 Tragödien und 8 Satyrspiele erhalten, und daraus mit Recht geschlossen, dass die bereits für die Alexandriner verlorenen euripideischen Stücke hauptsächlich Satyrspiele waren. *So far so good.* Aber etwas Entsprechendes nahm Elmsley nun auch für Aischylos an, wofür er sich stützte auf die Mitteilung in dessen *Vita* (§13; *Aeschyli Tragoediae*, ed. U. de Wilamowitz-Moellendorff [Berlin 1914], p. 5, 8 ff. = *Aeschyli septem quae supersunt tragoedias* ed. D. Page [Oxford 1972], p. 333, 2 ff.) ἐβίω δὲ ἔτη ξγ', ἐν οἷς ἐποίησε δράματα ο' καὶ ἐπὶ τούτοις σατυρικὰ ἀμφὶ τὰ ε'.

'Αχιλλέως ἐρασταί, 'Ελένης γάμος und Τήλεφος hinzu); sogar P. Guggisberg (*Das Satyrspiel* [Diss. Zürich 1947), 99), der bestrebt ist, Bezeugtes von Mutmasslichem zu trennen, behauptet «Als Satyrspiele sind urkundlich direkt zwölf... gesichert» (er setzt 'Ηρακλῆς gleich mit 'Επὶ Ταινάρῳ); D. F. Sutton, in seiner «Handlist of Satyr Plays» gibt unter der Überschrift 'Demonstrably Satyric' eine Liste von 20 Titeln, in der 'Επὶ Ταινάρῳ fehlt und 8 konjekturale Satyrspiele — Ἄδμητος, 'Αχιλλέως ἐρασταί, Δαίδαλος, 'Ελένης γάμος, 'Ιάμβη, Ἴναχος, Πανδώρα, Σύνδειπνοι — erscheinen (*HSCP* 78, 1974, 140); in *The Greek Satyr Play* desselben Verfassers (Beitr. zur Klass. Philol. 90, Meisenheim am Glan 1980) finden wir (S. 36) als "known Sophoclean satyr plays" 15 Stücke aufgezählt (denen man noch den versehentlich ausgefallenen *Salmoneus* [vgl. S. 56] hinzufügen muss): die äusserst hypothetischen Fälle Ἄδμητος, Δαίδαλος, 'Ιάμβη und Σύνδειπνοι bilden hier, zusammen mit F 730 a-g, eine besondere Gruppe, die "with a reasonable degree of certainty" als satyrisch betrachtet werden könne; V. Steffen schliesslich hat in seine *Satyrographorum Graecorum reliquiae* (Poznań 1935) nicht weniger als 28 sophokleische Titel aufgenommen, und in seinen *Satyrographorum Graecorum fragmenta* (1952) sind es immer noch 24.

[8] *Euripidis Medea* (Oxonii 1818), 71 (= ^{2}Lipsiae 1822, 56).

Das ist aber ein äusserst verdächtiger Text: mit Recht haben hier Viele Anstoss genommen an der globalen Angabe ἀμφὶ τὰ (wofür übrigens einige Handschriften die Variante ἀμφίβολα bieten, in der sich möglicherweise ein Element des ursprünglichen Wortlauts erhalten hat). Andere halten die Zahl 5 für korrupt (so z.B. Page), und Wilamowitz stellt resigniert fest «corruptela insanabilis». Auf einen solchen Text kann man nicht bauen, und Elmsleys Annahme, dass von Aischylos in der alexandrinischen Bibliothek nur noch 5 Satyrspiele vorhanden waren, verliert damit ihre Grundlage. Dieser Annahme widerspricht übrigens auch die Tatsache, dass der Κατάλογος τῶν Αἰσχύλου δραμάτων (p. 7 f. Wil. = 335 Page) — der doch ohne Zweifel auf alexandrinische Gelehrsamkeit, wahrscheinlich auf die *Pinakes* des Kallimachos, zurückgeht — mindestens 10 Satyrspiele enthält [9]. Und noch ein weiterer Einwand kommt hinzu: dass Stücke verloren gegangen seien, wird uns nur für Euripides berichtet — in unseren Testimonien über Aischylos und Sophokles hören wir nichts dergleichen. Dann ist es aber methodisch geboten erst einmal davon auszugehen, dass die alexandrinischen Gelehrten sämtliche aischyleischen und sophokleischen Dramen besassen, und nicht, wie Elmsley bei Aischylos und Pearson bei Sophokles, von vornherein mit einem voralexandrinischen Verlust von Stücken zu rechnen.

Die Diskrepanz zwischen der Gesamtzahl der uns überlieferten sophokleischen Titel und der Zahl der ausdrücklich als Satyrspiel bezeichneten Stücke lässt sich auch ganz einfach und natürlich ohne eine solche Hypothese erklären, nämlich mit der Annahme, dass bei vielen uns überlieferten Titeln die Bezeichnung 'Satyrspiel' weggeblieben ist, genau wie bei den *Diktyulkoi* und *Isthmiastai* des Aischylos, die in

[9] Ἀμυμώνη, Δικτυουλκοί , Θεωροὶ ἢ Ἰσθμιασταί, Κερκυών, Κίρκη σατυρική, Κήρυκες, Λέων, Λυκοῦργος, Πρωτεύς, Σφίγξ.

unseren Quellen niemals als Satyrspiele bezeichnet werden und deren Satyrspielcharakter erst die Papyri erwiesen haben. Und auch sonst wird der Zusatz σατυρικός (-ή) oder σάτυροι in unseren Quellen sehr oft weggelassen, am auffallendsten in dem aischyleischen Κατάλογος, wo von den 10 sicheren Satyrspielen (siehe die letzte Fussnote) nur eines — *Kirke* — als solches bezeichnet ist; dass die *Amymone* des Aischylos ein Satyrspiel war, wissen wir nur durch die berühmte Didaskalie *POxy.* 2256 fr. 3 (= DID C 6), 3 (die eine alte Vermutung von Aloys Hirt bestätigt hat): die übrigen Zeugen (Aeschyl. Fr. 13-15 N ^{2}) nennen das Stück nur 'Αμυμώνη *tout court*; von den 5 Zeugen, die wir für den sophokleischen *Momos* besitzen, fügt nur einer (F 424) zu dem Titel das Wort σατυρικός hinzu, bei dem *Kedalion* tut das nur einer (F 326) von 6 Zeugen, usw. usw.

Wenn man dies alles bedenkt, kann meiner Ansicht nach kein Zweifel daran sein, dass man die fehlenden Satyrspiele des Sophokles (und des Aischylos) in erster Linie unter den uns überlieferten Titeln suchen muss. Dass hat man natürlich auch schon längst getan, aber immer nur gleichsam instinktiv. Es schien mir nicht überflüssig, die Berechtigung dieser Praxis einmal prinzipiell zu begründen, zumal sich daraus eine wichtige methodische Konsequenz ergibt: wenn nämlich eine begründete Vermutung besteht, dass ein überlieferter sophokleischer (oder aischyleischer) Titel ein Satyrspiel war, dann wird diese Vermutung durch die hier vorgelegten allgemeinen Erwägungen erheblich verstärkt (jedenfalls mehr als wenn man mit Pearson [bzw. Elmsley] annimmt, dass eine ganze Reihe von Satyrspielen gar nicht unter den überlieferten Titeln vorkomme). Auf diese Art wird es fast sicher, dass 'Αχιλλέως ἐρασταί und Πανδώρα Satyrspiele waren, und für den *Inachos* in hohem Grade wahrscheinlich [10].

[10] Vgl. O. Taplin, *The Stagecraft of Aeschylus* (Oxford 1977), 431 ^{3}; B. Seidensticker, in G. A. Seeck (Hrsg.), *Das griechische Drama* (Darmstadt 1979), 218.

Weitere nicht unwahrscheinliche Kandidaten, die man aus dem Titel, den Angaben über den Inhalt, oder dem Ton einzelner Fragmente erschlossen hat, sind Ἑλένης γάμος, Καμικοί, Κέρβερος, Ποιμένες, Σίσυφος, Σύνδειπνοι, Ὑδροφόροι, Φινεύς. Aber auch hinter anderen, uns eventuell ganz tragisch anmutenden, Titeln können Satyrspiele stecken! Wer wäre z.B. ohne das ausdrückliche Zeugnis unserer Quellen je auf den Gedanken gekommen, in dem *Amphiareos* und dem *Herakles* des Sophokles oder in dem aischyleischen *Lykurgos* Satyrspiele zu vermuten?

II

Mit der Feststellung, welche sophokleischen Titel als sicher überliefert zu betrachten sind, und der Widerlegung der Hypothese, dass ein beträchtlicher Teil der sophokleischen Satyrspiele den alexandrinischen Philologen unbekannt gewesen sei, haben wir eine einigermassen feste Grundlage gewonnen, um uns ein Bild davon zu machen, welche Stoffe Sophokles für seine Dramen benutzt hat.

Die 122 sicher überlieferten Titel lassen sich in folgende Gruppen einteilen:

1. Trojanischer Sagenkreis: sicher Αἴας, Αἴας Λοκρός, Αἰχμαλωτίδες, Ἀλέξανδρος, Ἀντηνορίδαι, Ἀχαιῶν σύλλογος, Ἀχιλλέως ἐρασταί, Ἑλένης ἀπαίτησις, Ἑλένης ἁρπαγή, Ἑλένης γάμος, Ἠλέκτρα, Ἰφιγένεια, Κρίσις, Λάκαιναι, Λαοκόων, Μέμνων, Ναύπλιος πυρκαεύς, Ναυσικάα, Νίπτρα, Ὀδυσσεὺς ἀκανθοπλήξ, Ὀδυσσεὺς μαινόμενος, Παλαμήδης, Ποιμένες, Πολυξένη, Πρίαμος, Σίνων, Σύνδειπνοι, Τρώϊλος, Φαίακες, Φιλοκτήτης, Φιλοκτήτης ὁ ἐν Τροίᾳ, Φρύγες (32 Stücke); vermutlich Αἰθίοπες, Ἀνδρομάχη, Ἔρις, Ἑρμιόνη, Εὐρύαλος, Εὐρυσάκης, Κλυταιμήστρα, Μῶμος, Ναύπλιος καταπλέων [11], Πηλεύς, Σκύριοι, Τεῦκρος, Χρύσης (13 Stücke) [12].

[11] Dieses Stück könnte eventuell auch zu den *Telephos*-Dramen (Gruppe 9) gehört haben: siehe *TrGF* IV p. 354.

[12] Über den *Telephos* siehe die übernächste Fussnote.

2. Thebanischer Sagenkreis: Ἀλκμέων, Ἀμφιάρεως, Ἀντιγόνη, Ἐπίγονοι, Ἐριφύλη, Οἰδίπους Τύραννος (6).

3. Argonauten: sicher Ἄμυκος, Κολχίδες, Λημνίαι α'β', Ῥιζοτόμοι, Σκῦθαι, Φινεύς α'β' (8); vermutlich Ἀθάμας α'β' [13], Φρίξος (3).

4. Herakles: sicher Ἡρακλεΐσκος, Ἡρακλῆς, Τραχινίαι (3); vermutlich Ἀμφιτρύων, Ἐπὶ Ταινάρῳ, Ἰφικλῆς, Κέρβερος (4).

5. Tantalos, Pelops etc. (sofern nicht zu Gruppe 1 gehörend): Ἀτρεύς, Θυέστης α'β'γ', Νιόβη, Οἰνόμαος, Τάνταλος (7).

6. Attische Sagen: sicher Αἰγεύς, Θησεύς, Ἴων, Οἰδίπους ἐπὶ Κολώνῳ, Πρόκρις, Τηρεύς, Τριπτόλεμος, Φαίδρα (8); vielleicht Δόλοπες, Κρέουσα (2).

7. Sagen um Minos: Δαίδαλος, Καμικοί, Μάντεις, Μίνως (4).

8. Perseus: sicher Ἀκρίσιος, Ἀνδρομέδα, Δανάη (3); vermutlich Λαρισαῖοι (1).

9. Telephos: sicher Ἀλεάδαι, Τήλεφος [14] (2); vermutlich Μυσοί (1) [15].

10. Verschiedenes: Διονυσίσκος, Εὔμηλος, Ἠριγόνη, Θαμύρας, Ἴναχος, Ἰξίων, Ἰοβάτης, Ἱππόνους, Ἰχνευταί, Κηδαλίων, Μελέαγρος, Οἰκλῆς, Πανδώρα, Σαλμωνεύς, Σίσυφος, Τυνδάρεως, Τυρώ α'β', Φοῖνιξ (19).

11. Unklar: Κωφοί, Μοῦσαι, Τυμπανισταί, Ὕβρις, Ὑδροφόροι, Φθιώτιδες (6).

[13] Einer der beiden Ἀθάμαντες kann auch ein Dionysos-Drama gewesen sein: siehe weiter unten.

[14] Obwohl es möglich bleibt, dass dies Stück, ebenso wie die gleichnamigen Tragödien des Aischylos und des Euripides, von der Verwundung und Heilung des Telephos durch Achill handelte (und also zu Gruppe 1 gehörte), ist dies weniger wahrscheinlich geworden durch die Entdeckung, dass Sophokles eine ganze *Telepheia* geschrieben hat. Denn da zu dieser Trilogie so gut wie sicher ausser dem *Telephos* auch die *Aleaden* gehört haben, liegt es nahe anzunehmen, dass, ebenso wie die *Aleaden*, die ganze Trilogie der Vorgeschichte des Telephos gewidmet war, die ja Stoff genug zu mehreren Dramen bietet.

[15] Siehe auch oben S.

Da springt sofort der überragende Anteil des trojanischen Sagenkreises — fast 28% bzw. 37% der sicher überlieferten Titel — in die Augen. Er ist auch erheblich grösser als bei Aischylos und Euripides: von den 80 sicher überlieferten aischyleischen Titeln können wir mit Sicherheit 18 und vielleicht 21, d.h. 22% bzw. 26%, dem trojanischen Sagenkreis zuweisen [16]; für Euripides (78 sicher überlieferte Titel) lauten diese Zahlen 15 und 17 (19% bzw. 22%) [17].

Andere auffallende Unterschiede mit den beiden anderen Tragikern oder mit einem der beiden sind:

a) die geringe Rolle der Dionysos-Sage. Diesem Sagenkreis lässt sich mit Sicherheit nur ein Stück, der *Dionysiskos*, zuweisen, wozu vielleicht noch eines der beiden *Athamas*-Dramen kommt (vgl. *TrGF* IV p. 100) [18]: Aischylos dagegen hatte den Stoff für mindestens 8, vielleicht sogar für 10 seiner Dramen der Dionysos-Sage entnommen [19] (bei Euripides ist der Anteil der Dionysos-Sage ebenso gering wie bei Sophokles: ausser den *Bakchen* kommt bei ihm nur noch die *Ino* in Frage).

b) der erhebliche Anteil attischer Stoffe (Gruppe 6: 6,6% bzw. 8,2%), die bei Aischylos nur eine untergeordnete Rolle spielten (sicher nur Ἐλευσίνιοι, Πέρσαι, Ὠρείθυια; vielleicht

[16] Sicher Ἀγαμέμνων, Θρῇσσαι, Εὐμενίδες, Ἰφιγένεια, Κίρκη, Μέμνων, Μυρμιδόνες, Ὅπλων κρίσις, Ὀστολόγοι, Παλαμήδης, Πηνελόπη, Πρωτεύς, Τήλεφος, Φιλοκτήτης, Φρύγες, Χοηφόροι, Ψυχαγωγοί, Ψυχοστασία; höchstwahrscheinlich Κᾶρες, vielleicht Νηρεΐδες und Σαλαμινίαι.

[17] Sicher Ἀλέξανδρος, Ἀνδρομάχη, Ἑκάβη, Ἑλένη, Ἠλέκτρα, Ἰφιγένεια ἡ ἐν Αὐλίδι, Ἰφιγένεια ἡ ἐν Ταύροις, Κύκλωψ, Ὀρέστης, Παλαμήδης, Πρωτεσίλαος, Σκύριοι, Τήλεφος, Τρῳάδες, Φιλοκτήτης; vielleicht Ἔπειος und Φοῖνιξ.

[18] Welckers Annahme, dass die sophokleischen Ὑδροφόροι dasselbe Thema hatten wie die aischyleischen, beruht einzig und allein auf der Gleichheit des Titels; dass Dionysos in dem Stück genannt wurde (F 674), beweist natürlich nichts.

[19] Sicher Βάκχαι, Βασσάραι, Ἠδωνοί, Λυκοῦργος, Νεανίσκοι, Πενθεύς, Σεμέλη ἢ Ὑδροφόροι, Τροφοί; vielleicht Ἀθάμας und Ξάντριαι.

noch Κερκυών; daneben hatte Aischylos Attisches in die *Eumeniden* und vielleicht auch in den *Prometheus Pyrphoros* eingearbeitet). Die Tendenz setzt sich fort: bei Euripides ist der Anteil attischer Stoffe noch bedeutend grösser als bei Sophokles (sicher 10, vielleicht sogar 11 Stücke [20], d.h. 13% bzw. 14%).

Ein weiterer und, wie mir scheint, oft nicht genug beachteter Unterschied gegen Aischylos zeigt sich bei näherer Betrachtung von Sophokles' 'trojanischen' Stücken. Hier sehen wir nämlich, dass Sophokles seine Stoffe nur verhältnismässig selten aus Homer geschöpft hat. Sichere Dramatisierungen homerischer Episoden sind nur Ναυσικάα (nach dem ζ der *Odyssee*) und Νίπτρα (nach dem τ der *Odyssee*), und dazu kommen vermutlich noch die Φαίακες: das sind also höchstens (bei 32 Stücken) 9% und im Mindestfall (bei 45 Stücken) 6,7% seiner 'trojanischen' Dramen und 2,4% der sicher überlieferten Titel — für seine übrigen 'trojanischen' Stücke (24% bzw. 34% der sicher überlieferten Titel) hat Sophokles den Stoff dem epischen Kyklos entnommen. Da bietet Aischylos ein ganz anderes Bild: von seinen 18 sicher 'trojanischen' Dramen (oben S. 196) lassen sich 7 (d.h. 39%, und 8,75% der sicher überlieferten Titel) unmittelbar auf homerische Episoden zurückführen [21] (und drei weitere Dramen — Κᾶρες, Νηρεΐδες und Σίσυφος πετροκυλιστής — sind vermutlich von Homer angeregt); nur 11 seiner 'trojanischen' Dramen (14% der sicher überlieferten Titel) stammen aus dem Kyklos. Bei Euripides dagegen

[20] Sicher Αἰγεύς, Ἐρεχθεύς, Ἡρακλεῖδαι, Θησεύς, Ἱκετίδες, Ἱππόλυτος α′β′, Ἴων, Πειρίθους, Σκίρων; vielleicht Ἀλόπη.

[21] Κίρκη (*Odyssee* κ), Μυρμιδόνες (*Ilias* Π-Σ), Ὀστολόγοι (entweder Odysseus als Bettler oder, wahrscheinlicher, die Bestattung der getöteten Freier), Πηνελόπη (genauer Ihnalt unbekannt; aber Penelope ist eine ausgesprochen homerische Gestalt, und Aeschyl. Fr. 187 N² jedenfalls eine deutliche Reminiszenz an Hom. ξ 199; τ 172 ff.), Πρωτεύς (δ 351 ff.), Φρύγες (*Ilias* Ω), Ψυχαγωγοί (*Odyssee* λ).

spielt Homer als Lieferant dramatischer Stoffe eine ebenso geringe Rolle wie bei Sophokles: nur eines seiner Stücke — der *Kyklops* — geht sicher und ein anderes — der *Phoinix* — vielleicht auf Homer zurück (d.h. 1,3% bzw. 2,6% der sicher überlieferten Titel).

Was wir so an Hand der überlieferten Titel feststellen können, wirft auch ein Licht auf zwei antike Testimonien. Bei Athenaios (VII 277 e = T 136, 8 f.) sagt der Deipnosophist Zoilos, Sophokles habe soviel Freude an dem epischen Kyklos gehabt, dass er ganze Dramen in der Nachfolge des Kyklos gedichtet habe [22] (eine Bemerkung, der wir die erste, von Casaubonus unternommene, Sammlung der Sophoklesfragmente verdanken: siehe *TrGF* IV p. 9). Sieht man ab von der falschen — und wohl auch kaum beabsichtigten — Suggestion als hätten die anderen Tragiker keine Dramen aus dem Kyklos gemacht, dann steht hinter dieser Bemerkung offenbar die richtige Beobachtung einer besonderen Vorliebe des Sophokles für kyklische Stoffe (d.h. für solche aus dem trojanischen Kyklos; der thebanische spielt bei Sophokles gerade eine geringere Rolle als bei Aischylos und Euripides [23]): denn auch Euripides hat seine Stoffe zwar häufiger dem trojanischen Kyklos entnommen als Aischylos, aber doch bedeutend weniger oft als Sophokles [24].

[22] Pearsons handgreiflich falsche Wiedergabe (I p. xxiii) «to such an extent that throughout the whole of a play he would follow closely the epic narrative» ist offenbar von dem Wunsch diktiert, dies Zeugnis in Einklang zu bringen mit T 1, 80 f.: vgl. unten S. 202, Anm. 32.

[23] Bei Sophokles lassen sich 6 Stücke (5% der sicher überlieferten Titel) auf den thebanischen Kyklos zurückführen (oben Gruppe 2); bei Aischylos ebenfalls 6 (7,5%): Ἀργεῖοι, Ἐπίγονοι, Ἑπτὰ ἐπὶ Θήβας, Λάιος, Οἰδίπους, Σφίγξ; bei Euripides 7 oder 8 (9% bzw. 10%): auf jeden Fall die beiden Ἀλκμέωνες, Ἀντιγόνη, Οἰδίπους, Ὑψιπύλη, Χρύσιππος, Φοίνισσαι, vielleicht auch Κάδμος.

[24] Sicher für 14, vielleicht für 15 Stücke (nämlich die oben S. 196 aufgezählten Titel ohne die 'homerischen' Stücke Κύκλωψ und Φοῖνιξ), d.h. 18% bzw. 19% der sicher überlieferten Titel.

Das zweite Testimonium ist der Paragraph der *Vita* des Sophokles, der von seiner Homernachfolge handelt (§20 = T 1, 80 ff.). Er fängt an mit dem seltsamen Satz (Pearson, I p. XXIII[2], nennt ihn «unintelligible») τὸ πᾶν μὲν οὖν Ὁμηρικῶς ὠνόμαζε, in dem möglicherweise eine Korruptel steckt (statt ὠνόμαζε hat Bergk οἰκονομεῖ, Michaelis ᾠκονόμησε vorgeschlagen, und Lechner wollte Ὁμηρικὸς ὠνομάζετο lesen). Dieser Satz wird dann begründet mit den Worten τούς τε γὰρ μύθους φέρει κατ' ἴχνος τοῦ ποιητοῦ· καὶ τὴν Ὀδύσσειαν δὲ ἐν πολλοῖς δράμασιν ἀπογράφεται. Angesichts der soeben festgestellten Tatsache, dass nicht mehr als 2 oder 3 sophokleische Stücke von der *Odyssee* inspiriert waren, kann der zweite Teil dieses Satzes nicht bedeuten, dass Sophokles zu vielen seiner Dramen den Stoff aus der *Odyssee* genommen habe [25]. Es müssen vielmehr die vielen Anklänge an einzelne Züge, Motive, Wendungen u. dgl. der *Odyssee* gemeint sein, von denen der Verfasser der *Vita* auch gleich in dem nächsten Satz ein Beispiel gibt: παρετυμολογεῖ δὲ καθ' Ὅμηρον (τ 406 ff.) καὶ τοὔνομα τοῦ Ὀδυσσέως (F 965).

ὀρθῶς δ' Ὀδυσσεύς εἰμ' ἐπώνυμος κακῶν·
πολλοὶ γὰρ ὠδύσαντο δυσμενεῖς ἐμοί.

Darauf deutet auch die Fortsetzung ἠθοποιεῖ τε καὶ ποικίλλει καὶ τοῖς ἐπινοήμασι τεχνικῶς χρῆται Ὁμηρικὴν ἐκματτόμενος χάριν. ὅθεν εἰπεῖν † Ἰωνικόν τινα † μόνον Σοφοκλέα τυγχάνειν Ὁμήρου μαθητήν. καὶ ἄλλοι μὲν πολλοὶ μεμίμηνταί τινα τῶν πρὸ αὐτῶν ἢ τῶν καθ' αὑτούς, μόνος δὲ Σοφοκλῆς ἀφ' ἑκάστου τὸ λαμπρὸν ἀπανθίζει· καθ' ὃ καὶ μέλιττα ἐλέγετο: für den

[25] Was Pearsons Übersetzung «and in several of his plays he produces an exact copy of the *Odyssey*» (I p. XXIII) zumindest suggeriert (vgl. auch den Ersatz von πολλοῖς durch «several», der, wie es scheint, den bei dieser Deutung entstehenden Widerspruch mit den Tatsachen abschwächen soll); und wenn Welcker zu diesem Satz der *Vita* bemerkt (*Die griechischen Tragödien* 87) «Aus der Odyssee finden wir drey Tragödien genommen», so hat er ihn offenbar ebenso verstanden, und den Widerspruch zwischen πολλοῖς und 'drei' auf sich beruhen lassen...

unbekannten Kritiker, dem die *Vita* hier folgt, bestand die Homernachfolge des Sophokles offenbar in der Entlehnung von einzelnen Elementen und Kunstmitteln, durch die er seinen Stücken eine homerische χάρις verliehen hat [26]. Etwas ähnliches muss auch der Akademiker Polemon mit seinem Ausspruch gemeint haben (T 115), Homer sei ein epischer Sophokles und Sophokles ein tragischer Homer. Und wenn Eustathios, wie er das so oft tut, Sophokles φιλόμηρος oder τοῦ Ὁμήρου ζηλώτης nennt oder sonst von seiner Homernachfolge spricht, so bezieht sich das auch immer auf Einzelelemente, die er bei Sophokles nachgeahmt findet (siehe Anhang II). Eustathios ist damit ein Vorläufer der modernen Untersuchungen zur Homernachfolge des Sophokles — angefangen mit Henri Estiennes *De Sophoclea imitatione Homeri, seu de Sophoclis locis imitationem Homeri habentibus, dissertatio* [27], — die gezeigt haben, dass die Entlehnung einzelner Elemente aus Homer bei ihm auf Schritt und Tritt begegnet [28] — ein faszinierendes Thema, dessen Bearbeitung noch kaum über Stellensammlungen hinausgekommen ist:

[26] Mit der Erklärung von Sophokles' Beinamen 'Biene' aus diesem ἀπανθίζειν steht der Anonymus ganz allein: normal wird er aus Sophokles' 'Süsse' erklärt (T 2, 5; 109; 111; 112; in T 110 ist die Erklärung unverständlich).

[27] = Henrici Stephani *Annotationes in Sophoclem & Euripidem*... (1568), 86-95.

[28] Besonders bekannte Fälle in den Fragmenten sind F 965 ~ τ 406 ff. (vgl. oben; Sophokles lässt Odysseus selber die Etymologisierung seines Namens geben, die Homer dem namengebenden Grossvater in den Mund legt) und F 453-454 ~ λ 119 ff. (die Ereignisse, die bei Homer Teiresias prophezeit, sind dramatische Handlung geworden; Aischylos dagegen hatte in seinen Ψυχαγωγοί den prophezeienden Teiresias auf die Bühne gebracht, also die homerische Handlung selber dramatisiert); in die Σύνδειπνοι, deren Thema aus den *Kyprien* stammt, hat Sophokles, wie es scheint, die Episode ϑ 75 ff. eingearbeitet (siehe P. Von der Mühll, *Ausgewählte kleine Schriften* [Schweizer. Beitr. zur Altertumswiss. 12] (Basel 1976), 150 f.); meistens können wir in den Fragmenten natürlich nur blosse wörtliche Anklänge feststellen, z.B. die Formel ἄναξ ἀνδρῶν F 221, 22, den Ausdruck νὺξ ϑήλεια F 1053 (der vermutlich auf dem homerischen ϑῆλυς ἐέρση [ε 467] beruht: siehe Pearson), den Vers (F 155) γλώσσης μελίσσῃ τῷ κατερρυηκότι (der stark A 249 τοῦ καὶ ἀπὸ γλώσσης μέλιτος γλυκίων ῥέεν αὐδή erinnert [und also vielleicht ebenfalls auf Nestor bezogen war?]) u. dgl.

«De Sophocle Homeri discipulo è il lavoro che vorrei fare, ma una vita non basterebbe» war ein Stossseufzer des alten Eduard Fraenkel! [29]

Doch wir müssen noch einmal zu dem Satz der *Vita* zurückkehren, von dem wir ausgegangen sind. Was die Worte καὶ τὴν Ὀδύσσειαν δὲ ἐν πολλοῖς δράμασιν ἀπογράφεται bedeuten, ist inzwischen klar geworden. Aber was ist mit dem ersten Teil jenes Satzes — τούς τε γὰρ μύθους φέρει κατ' ἴχνος τοῦ ποιητοῦ — gemeint? Da ὁ ποιητής bei einem nacharistotelischen Autor doch nur noch den Dichter der *Ilias* und der *Odyssee* und nicht den ganzen epischen Kyklos bezeichnen kann, bedeuten auch diese Worte offenbar nicht, was sie auf den ersten Blick zu bedeuten scheinen, nämlich dass Sophokles den Stoff seiner Dramen aus Homer geschöpft habe und dabei seiner Quelle genau gefolgt sei. Vielmehr werden wir mit Welcker (*Die griechischen Tragödien*, 87) annehmen müssen, dass der Urheber dieser Bemerkung die in *Ilias* und *Odyssee* verstreuten Hinweise und Anspielungen auf andere Episoden des trojanischen Sagenkreises und auf andere Sagen überhaupt meinte [30]. Nach der Ansicht dieses Kritikers hätte Sophokles also überall, wo er bei Homer auf eine solche Anspielung stiess, den Hinweis sofort aufgenommen und die angedeutete Episode zum Gegenstand eines Dramas gemacht (nur so kann ich mir den Ausdruck κ α τ ' ἴ χ ν ο ς τοῦ ποιητοῦ erklären) [31]. Nun gibt es bei Homer tatsächlich eine ganze Reihe Anspielungen dieser Art. Welcker erinnerte z.B. an die Themen des *Meleagros*, des

[29] *Due seminari romani di Eduard Fraenkel...*, Sussidi eruditi 28 (Roma 1977), 15 (zu *Aj.* 512); vgl. auch *ibid.*, 26 (zu *Aj.* 758 ff.).

[30] Zu einer solchen Auffassung der Homernachfolge bei den Tragikern vgl. Procl. *In Plat. Remp.* I p. 171, 18 ff. Kroll οὐχ οἱ τραγῳδιοποιοὶ μόνον πολλὰ τῶν παρ' Ὁμήρῳ βραχείας μνήμης ἠξιωμένα σκηνὰς καὶ ὑποθέσεις ἐποιήσαντο τελείας.

[31] Was man sich bei Pearsons Interpretation — «His plots follow in the tracks of Homer» (I p. xxiii) — denken soll, ist mir nicht klar.

Iobates und des *Thamyras*, die respektive in I 543 ff., Z 155 ff. und B 594 ff. berührt werden; ebenso könnte man etwa die Κρίσις auf Ω 28-30, den Ὀδυσσεὺς ἀκανθοπλήξ auf λ 134-6 und die *Elektra* auf α 29 ff. zurückführen. Aber schon diese Beispiele zeigen wie gezwungen die Hypothesen sind, zu denen diese Methode führt. Ihrem Urheber lag offenbar daran, Sophokles' Abhängigkeit von Homer so gross wie möglich erscheinen zu lassen: wollte er etwa die von Anderen — mit Recht, wie wir sahen — betonte stoffliche Abhängigkeit vom epischen Kyklos nicht wahr haben? [32]

Bemerkenswert ist schliesslich noch, dass Sophokles den Stoff für seine wenigen 'homerischen' Stücke aus der *Odyssee* und nicht aus der *Ilias* geschöpft hat. Bei den 'homerischen' Dramen des Aischylos stammen die Stoffe zwar überwiegend ebenfalls aus der *Odyssee*, aber mindestens zwei Stücke, *Myrmidonen* und *Phryger*, hatten Episoden der *Ilias* zum Inhalt, und zwar ganz wesentliche Episoden dieses Epos; in den *Phrygern* hat Aischylos das letzte Buch der *Ilias* dramatisiert, und in den *Myrmidonen* überhaupt das Kernstück der *Ilias*, die Aussendung des Patroklos und seinen Tod. Auch in solcher Wahl des Stoffes zeigt sich die viel stärkere Direktheit der Homernachfolge des Aischylos [33], der in dieser Hinsicht viel eher die Bezeichnung 'tragischer Homer' verdienen würde. Die Tatsache, dass man nicht ihm sondern Sophokles diesen Namen beilegte und das Homerische gerade an Sophokles hervorhob, zeigt eben, dass man dabei nicht so sehr an die Stoffe als vielmehr an den Ton, die Farbe, die χάρις der sophokleischen Dramen dachte.

[32] Es ergibt sich also, dass die beiden Testimonien T 136, 8 f. und T 1, 80 ff. nicht nur nicht auf dasselbe hinauslaufen, wie PEARSON meint (I p. XXIII; vgl. oben S. 198), sondern vielleicht sogar die Gegenpole in einer Diskussion über Sophokles' Quellen repräsentieren.

[33] Vgl. den Unterschied in der Bearbeitung von Teiresias Prophezeiung λ 100 ff. (oben S. 200, Anm. 28).

III

Ferner verdanken wir den Fragmenten natürlich unsere Kenntnis des sophokleischen Satyrspiels. Bis zu der Veröffentlichung der *Ichneutai* (1912) wussten wir davon allerdings so gut wie nichts — nur das 1892 von Hugo Rabe aus dem *Lexicon Messanense* publizierte Fragment des *Dionysiskos* (F 171) liess etwas von Sophokles' Charme in dieser Gattung ahnen. Dann kam der Fund eines grossen Teiles der *Ichneutai*, der uns nicht nur Sophokles als Satyrspieldichter zeigte, sondern auch endlich Vergleichsmaterial zu dem euripideischen *Kyklops* bot, der bis dahin das Bild, das man sich vom Satyrspiel machte, bestimmt hatte. Die Erwartungen waren hochgespannt, vor allem natürlich bei denen, die den *Kyklops* nicht sonderlich schätzten [34], wurden aber, nach den ersten Reaktionen auf den neuen Fund zu urteilen, enttäuscht: Bemängler des *Kyklops* wie Wilamowitz enthielten sich eines Werturteils, während diejenigen die den *Kyklops* schätzten ganz offen aussprachen, dass sie Euripides' Stück besser fanden [35].

[34] Z.B. U. v. Wilamowitz-Moellendorff, in *Die griechische und lateinische Literatur und Sprache*, Die Kultur der Gegenwart I 8 (Leipzig/Berlin ^{3}1912), 85: «Das Satyrspiel hat gewiss den Dichtern, die neben der Begabung für die Tragik auch goldenen Humor und naive Lustigkeit besassen, Gelegenheit zu höchst reizvollen Werken gegeben. Unglücklicherweise haben wir nur den *Kyklopen* des Euripides, dem jene Eigenschaften abgingen»; vgl. auch *Griechische Tragödien* III^{6} (Berlin 1922), 13 ff.

[35] Am krassesten Pearson (I 229): «However interesting the discovery of the new fragments may be, they will scarcely enhance the reputation of the poet. The dramatic value of the play is insignificant, and the comic relief not greatly exhilarating. It is fair to admit that the more amusing scenes probably occurred in the latter part of the play... . But the part which is preserved is less lively and entertaining than the *Cyclops*... . Yet, although it is impossible to rate highly the importance of the play as we know it, we must beware of pronouncing a final judgment on what is actually a torso, more particularly as the recovered fragment has merits of its own which may be pleaded in mitigation of an adverse verdict». Aber auch der erste Herausgeber, A. S. Hunt, hatte offenbar Mühe, nicht zu ungünstig über die *Ichneutai* zu urteilen (*The Oxyrhynchus Papyri* IX [London 1912],

Inzwischen hat sich das Urteil eher zugunsten der *Ichneutai* gewandelt [36].

Aber lassen wir Werturteile beiseite, die ja letzten Endes weniger über das Beurteilte als über die Urteilenden aussagen. Die grosse Neuigkeit, die die *Ichneutai* brachten, war die Entdeckung des vollkommen unproblematischen, unbeschwert-heiteren, ganz naturnahen Satyrspiels, wie es vermutlich vor Euripides die Regel gewesen ist. Euripides hat ebenso wie in seinen Tragödien auch im *Kyklops* Fragen und Zweifel, die ihn und seine Zeit beschäftigten, laut werden lassen — vgl. vor allem Polyphems Lob des Materialismus (316 ff.) und Odysseus' Kritik an den Göttern (354 f.; 606 f.) — und damit das Urwüchsig-Naturhafte des alten Satyrspiels durchbrochen; und denselben Effekt hat das von Rudolf Kassel (*RhM* 98, 1955, 283 ff.) aufgezeigte ironische Spiel, das Euripides in diesem Stück mit der tragischen Würde des Odysseus und mit Reminiszenzen an seine homerische Vorlage treibt. Nichts von all solcher 'sophistication' bei

---

33 f.): «So far as the papyrus extends there is nothing so amusing as the scene in the *Cyclops* where Silenus acts as cup-bearer to Polyphemus. The imitation by the Satyrs of dogs upon the scent no doubt lent itself to fun of a rather boisterous kind, though there is throughout much less coarseness than in the drama of Euripides... . Small comic touches are also noticeable here and there... . But < ! > there is a general air of light-heartedness and good humour which in the complete piece must have been very attractive».

36 Vgl. etwa W. Schmid, *GGL* I 3, 1, 538 f.; A. Lesky, *Die tragische Dichtung der Hellenen* (Göttingen ^{3}1972), 503 («Seit wir die *Ichneutai* des Sophokles zum grössten Teil haben und uns eine Vorstellung von den *Diktyulkoi* und *Isthmiastai* des Aischylos machen können, haben wir ein Bild des attischen Satyrspiels gewonnen, hinter dem der *Kyklops* etwas zurückbleibt»); G. A. Seeck, in E. Vogt, *Griechische Literatur*, Neues Handbuch der Literaturwiss. 2 (Wiesbaden 1981), 185^{5} («der 'Kyklops' des Euripides wirkt neben den Resten, die wir von Satyrspielen des Aischylos («Netzzieher») und Sophokles («Spürhunde») besitzen, etwas blass»). Damit hat sich Th. Bergks Prophezeiung erfüllt (*Griech. Literaturgeschichte* III [Berlin 1884], 565): «Freilich wenn uns ein Satyrdrama des Aeschylus oder eines anderen älteren Tragikers erhalten wäre, dann dürfte neben dem kecken, grossartigen Humor jener Dichter der Kyklops des Euripides ziemlich matt und farblos erscheinen».

Sophokles! Die Atmosphäre, in die er uns in den *Ichneutai* versetzt, ist der eigenen Zeit und Kultur ganz und gar entrückt: es ist die reine ungebrochene Natur, voll frischer Heiterkeit und mit einem Anflug von Märchenhaftem, in der die Zuhörer sich nach den vorangegangenen Tragödien erfrischen und entspannen können. Dieselbe Atmosphäre atmen auch die seitdem gefundenen Fragmente der aischyleischen Satyrspiele *Diktyulkoi* und *Isthmiastai*, so dass die Vermutung nahe liegt, dass dies die ursprüngliche Stimmung des Satyrspiels gewesen ist und dass Euripides, ebenso wie er die Tragödie entmythisiert, das Satyrspiel gleichsam 'denaturiert' hat (wobei, was Pohlenz implizite suggeriert, Einfluss der Komödie eine Rolle gespielt haben kann [37]). Damit soll übrigens kein Werturteil ausgesprochen sein. Dass dem euripideischen Satyrspiel die unbekümmerte Heiterkeit der *Ichneutai* fehlt und sein Humor mehr 'sophisticated' ist, bedeutet noch nicht, dass der *Kyklops* ein schlechteres Drama ist. Dass er auf jeden Fall viel mehr komische Effekte enthält als die *Ichneutai*, lässt sich nicht leugnen. In dem uns erhaltenen Teil der *Ichneutai* kommt eigentlich nur ein einziger Lacheffekt vor: Silens Flucht beim Erklingen der Leiertons (F 314, 205 ff.), nachdem er kurz vorher (145 ff.) die Satyrn wegen ihrer Angst vor Geräuschen abgekanzelt und seinen eigenen Mut herausgestrichen hat. Der etwa doppelt so lange *Kyklops* dagegen bietet eine ganze Reihe grösserer Lacheffekte — Silen hat sich mit Spuren einer Schlägerei versehen um das unschuldige Opfer spielen zu können (226 ff.); Silen beschwört die Wahrheit seiner Lügengeschichte beim Leben seiner Söhne, was die Söhne

[37] M. Pohlenz, *Die griechische Tragödie* (Göttingen ^{2}1954), 236 f. Auf Einfluss der Komödie liesse sich auch das obszöne Element im *Kyklops* (169 ff.; 179 ff.) zurückführen, das keineswegs notwendig zu dem Erotischen — einem typischen Satyrspiel-Motiv (vgl. z.B. Aischylos' *Amymone* und *Diktyulkoi*, vermutlich auch Sophokles' Ἀχιλλέως ἐρασταί, und die von B. Seidensticker [oben S. 193, Anm. 10] 245 aufgezeigte Parodie dieses Motivs im *Kyklops* [582 ff.]) — gehören muss.

mit einem Gegen-Schwur beim Leben ihres Vaters erwidern (268 ff.); Silen sorgt dafür, dass er beim Betrunkenmachen des Kyklopen selber nicht zu kurz kommt (542 ff.); Polyphem schleppt Silen als Ganymed in seine Höhle (582 ff.); die Satyrn, die selber gebeten hatten bei der Blendung des Kyklopen mithelfen zu dürfen (469 ff.; vgl. 483 ff.), und eben noch von ihrem felsenfesten Mut geredet haben (596), entschuldigen sich im entscheidenden Augenblick mit lächerlichen Ausflüchten (635 ff.)[38] — und dazu noch eine Anzahl kleinerer (z.B. 186 f.; 220 f.; 266 f. [Anrede des Riesen mit Deminutiva!]; 313 ff.). Es ist klar, dass, wenn man nach der Zahl der komischen Effekte urteilt, der *Kyklops* viel besser abschneidet; lässt man dagegen die frische Natur- und Märchenstimmung mit ihrer 'befreienden Fröhlichkeit'[39] schwerer wiegen, dann wird man die *Ichneutai* bevorzugen: so erklärt sich letzten Endes, wie mir scheint, die verschiedene Wertung dieser beiden Stücke.

Ein wichtiger Unterschied mit dem *Kyklops*, den N. C. Chourmouziades (Σατυρικά, 'Αθήνα 1974, 72 ff.) mit Recht betont, zeigt sich auch in der Funktion des Chors: während die Satyrn im *Kyklops* nur den Hintergrund für die Handlung abgeben, in die sie selber nicht eingreifen (das einzige Mal wo sie in die Handlung miteinbezogen werden sollen, scheitert das an ihrer Feigheit), sind sie in den *Ichneutai* ganz wesentlich an der Handlung beteiligt — ja, in dem uns erhaltenen Teil des Stückes spielen sie geradezu die Hauptrolle. Da auch in den *Isthmiastai* des Aischylos die Satyrn als

[38] Weggelassen habe ich das etwas billige Fehldirigieren des blinden Kyklopen durch die Satyrn (680 ff.). O. Zwierlein (in *Gnomon* 39, 1967, 453 f.) sieht noch einen grossen Lacheffekt am Ende des Stückes, wo das Wort ἀμφιτρῆτος (707) plötzlich zeigt, dass Polyphems Höhle noch einen zweiten Ausgang hatte und damit die ganze Voraussetzung der vorhergehenden Handlung aufhebt; angesichts der nicht geringen Ironie, die wir ohnehin im *Kyklops* feststellen können, scheint mir das, im Gegensatz zu A. Lesky (vorletzte Fussnote), 503[372], keineswegs ausgeschlossen.

[39] W. Kranz, *Geschichte der griech. Literatur* (Leipzig 1939), 167.

Träger der Handlung fungieren, dürfen wir auch hierin das Ursprünglichere erblicken, um so mehr als ja auch in den beiden anderen dramatischen Gattungen die Funktion des Chors immer mehr reduziert worden ist. Diese aktive Teilnahme des Chors an der Handlung hat wohl mit zu der grösseren Naturnähe des frühen Satyrspiels beigetragen.

Berührungspunkte mit Aischylos finden wir auch sonst in den Resten der sophokleischen Satyrdramen. Apollons Aufruf an alle Umwohnenden am Anfang der *Ichneutai* (39 ff.) entspricht dem Hilferuf in Aischylos' *Diktyulkoi* (Fr. 464, 18 ff. Mette); die Heiterkeit, die Silens Glatze bei dem kleinen Dionysos erregt (F 171), finden wir in demselben aischyleischen Stück zurück bei dem kleinen Perseus (Fr. 474, 786 ff. Mette); und die Konfrontierung der Satyrn mit einer neuen Erfindung — in den *Ichneutai* die Leier, im *Dionysiskos* der Wein (F 172) — hat eine Parallele im dem mit grosser Wahrscheinlichkeit dem aischyleischen Satyrspiel *Prometheus* zugewiesenen Fragment (207 N^2), wo ein Satyr das ihm unbekannte Feuer küssen will. So liegt es nahe zu vermuten, dass das sophokleische Satyrspiel viel mit dem aischyleischen gemein hatte.

Über mehr als Vermutungen kommen wir hier nirgends hinaus. Ja, man kann sich fragen, ob es überhaupt erlaubt ist, auf Grund von so wenig Material Vermutungen allgemeiner Art aufzustellen. Schliesslich besitzen wir nicht mehr als höchstens die Hälfte eines der etwa 30 Satyrspiele, die Sophokles geschrieben haben muss, und die Reste, die wir von den Satyrspielen des Aischylos haben, sind zwar sehr eindrucksvoll aber an Umfang noch viel geringer. Man kann nur hoffen, dass die Papyri uns hier noch weiteres Material schenken werden. Wie gerne wüssten wir z.B. mehr von der *Krisis* des Sophokles, einer Dramatisierung des Parisurteils, in der Aphrodite sich parfümierend und im Spiegel betrachtend, Athene dagegen sich mit Öl einreibend und trainierend auftrat (F 361)!

IV

Aber auch manch anderen Aspekt von Sophokles' Kunst lernen wir ausschliesslich aus den Fragmenten kennen.

An erster Stelle ist da die in einer Inschrift des 4. Jahrhunderts v. Chr. aufgetauchte Mitteilung, dass Sophokles eine Τηλέφεια geschrieben hat (DID B 5, 8). Wenn hier der grosse Sophokles gemeint ist — und nicht, wie Snell (*TrGF* I p. 17) vermutet hat, sein Enkel (*TrGF* 62 [I p. 208]) —, dann besitzen wir damit ein ausdrückliches Zeugnis für eine sophokleische Inhaltstrilogie (bzw. -tetralogie), an deren Existenz man früher zweifeln konnte.

Dass auch Sophokles ebenso wie Euripides eine ränkeschmiedende Frauengestalt schaffen konnte, zeigt die auf uns gekommene und, wie es scheint, glaubwürdige Zusammenfassung seines *Euryalos*. In diesem Stück kam Euryalos, ein unehelicher Sohn des Odysseus, der in Epirus gezeugt und aufgewachsen war, mit einem Brief seiner Mutter nach Ithaka. Hier wird er in Odysseus' Abwesenheit von Penelope empfangen, die schon früher von dem Verhältnis, dessen Frucht Euryalos ist, gehört hat. Als Odysseus eintrifft, überredet Penelope ihn, den Fremden sofort umzubringen, da er es auf sein Leben abgesehen habe. Und so tötet Odysseus, ehe er weiss wen er vor sich hat, seinen eigenen Sohn (*TrGF* IV p. 194).

Auch hat Sophokles, ebenso wie Aischylos und Euripides, den Geist eines Verstorbenen auf die Bühne gebracht: in seiner *Polyxena* trat der Schatten des Achilleus auf (F 523).

Neu ist ferner die Unterbrechung einer Botenrede durch eine lyrische Partie im *Eurypylos* (F 210, 30 ff. — vorausgesetzt dass dies Fragment wirklich Sophokles gehört) [40].

[40] Vgl. U. v. Wilamowitz-Moellendorff, *Kleine Schriften* I 352; O. Taplin (oben S. 193, Anm. 10), 82⁴.

Ein in den erhaltenen Tragödien unbekanntes Element ist auch die offenbar ziemlich ausführliche Routebeschreibung, die Demeter im *Triptolemos* dem Titelhelden gab (vgl. *TrGF* IV p. 446) und die an Aischyleisches erinnert (abgesehen von dem bekannten Abschnitt im *Gefesselten Prometheus* [705 ff.], in dem Prometheus der Io ihren künftigen Irrweg schildert, kam so etwas auch im *Befreiten Prometheus* vor [Fr. 195-199 N²], wo Prometheus dem Herakles die Stationen auf dem Weg zu den Hesperiden beschrieb). Ausser seinem grossen Vorgänger mag auch sein Freund Herodot Sophokles zu diesem geographischen Exkurs angeregt haben.

Auf stilistischem Gebiet bringen die Fragmente uns mehrere Spezimina des in homerischer Weise breit ausgeführten Gleichnisses, das, soweit ich sehe, in den erhaltenen Stücken so nicht vorkommt [41]. Zwei besonders schöne Beispiele sind F 149, wo Sophokles die Liebe mit einem Stück Eis vergleicht, das Kinder gierig in die Hände nehmen und dann, wenn die Kälte ihnen weh tut, wieder fallen lassen möchten, aber doch weiter festhalten, und das grossartige F 659 — von Henri Weil (*REG* 3, 1890, 339) als 'la perle du recueil' bezeichnet —, in dem Tyro sich in ihrer Trauer um ihr von der Stiefmutter abgeschorenes Haar mit einer jungen Stute vergleicht, der man die Mähne abgeschnitten hat und die von wildem Schmerz ergriffen wird als sie beim Trinken im Fluss ihr Spiegelbild erblickt. Ebenso episch breit vergleicht in F 871 Menelaos den dauernden Wechsel seines Schicksals mit dem ständigen Zu- und Abnehmen des Mondes; und in F 23 haben wir offenbar den Anfang solch eines 'homerischen' Gleichnisses vor uns.

Auch sophokleische Wortspiele lernen wir, soweit ich sehe, erst durch die Fragmente kennen. Ausser den auffal-

[41] In Frage käme nur *Ant.* 586-92, ein Gleichnis das jedoch in einem Chorlied steht und dadurch viel weniger homerisch wirkt als die oben zitierten Fragmente, die sämtlich aus gesprochenen Partien stammen.

lenden Katachresen ἰσχάς für 'Anker' (F 761), Ἀναξιδώρα für Demeter (F 1010)[42] und Ἀργειφόντης für Apollon (F 1024) gehört hierzu vor allem der witzige Gebrauch von Eigennamen als Epitheta in F 887 Ζεὺς νόστον ἄγοι τὸν νικόμαχον/ καὶ παυσανίαν καὶ ἀτρείδαν[43]. Schon Aischylos (Fr. 406 N²) hatte den Hades ἁγησίλαος genannt, Simonides (*Poetae Melici Graeci*, ed. D. L. Page [Oxford 1962], Fr. 614 p. 311) und Bakchylides (13, 58) hatten Zeus das Epitheton ἀρίσταρχος gegeben, und auch bei Aristophanes finden wir Parallelen (*Eq.* 570 ὁ θυμὸς εὐθὺς ἦν ἀμυνίας; *Nub.* 1162 παῖς... λυσανίας... κακῶν). Aber Sophokles geht einen Schritt weiter, indem er solche Epitheta nicht Personen (oder, wie Ar. *Eq.* 570, dem θυμός, der die Person repräsentiert), sondern dem ganz unpersönlichen νόστος beilegt (den er vielleicht auf diese Art personifizierte?): die nächste Parallele hierzu ist Adespota F 97 λαβὼν ἀριστόνικον ἐν μάχῃ κράτος (*TrGF* II p. 44)[44].

Auch sonst bieten die Fragmente gelegentlich humorvolle Formulierungen, wie wir sie aus den erhaltenen Stücken nicht kennen, z.B. das sonst nur bei Komikern und

[42] Sophokles führt Ἀναξι- also auf ἀνάγω zurück (vgl. Ἀνησιδώρα F 826), während der Zuschauer zuerst an die Ἄνακες denken musste (Ἀναξίδωρος war sogar der Name eines Atheners aus Sophokles' Zeit!): siehe Fr. Bechtel, *Die hist. Personennamen des Griechischen...* (Halle 1917), 44.

[43] Naucks Erklärung (ἀτρείδαν 'von Furcht befreit'), die sich auf Euphorions ἀτρέα δῆμον (siehe die nächte Fussnote) stützt, scheint mir völlig befriedigend; den in meinem Apparat verzeichneten Konjekturen ist jetzt noch H. Lloyd-Jones' κατ' Ἀτρειδᾶν (in *CR* N.S. 31, 1981, 177 f.) hinzuzufügen.

[44] Die aischyleischen Beispiele θυσίαν ... οὐ δεισήνορα (*Ag.* 153) und ἀντήνορος σποδοῦ (*Ag.* 443) sind insofern anders als es sich dort nicht um normale, zeitgenössische Namen handelt; dasselbe gilt für Euphorions ἀτρέα δῆμον Ἀθηνῶν und χεῖρ' ἱπποδάμειαν (Fr. 125/126 Powell = 127 v. Groningen = 161/161 B de Cuenca) sowie für das zweimal bezeugte εἰρήνη πολύβοια (*Etym. Gen.* s.v. ἀνὰ δρύμα [= Euphor. Fr. 177 P. = 195 v. Gr.]; *PSI* 1390 C II 4 [=Euphor. Fr. 24 c 48 v. Gr. = 38 C 46 de C.]) (unsicher ist *POxy.* 2526 B fr. 2 [=Euphor. Fr. 193 e v. Gr.], 8 π]ολυνείκεος). Sophokles hat als letztes Epitheton zwar auch einen solchen Namen gebraucht, aber dessen Interpretation durch die zwei vorangehenden normalen Namen vorbereitet.

dem kaiserzeitlichen Kyniker Oinomaos belegte Wort ἡμίκακος (F 1051), den schönen Vers βλέφαρα κέκληται δ' ὡς καπηλείου θύρα (F 711) — was offenbar bedeutet 'er hält die Augen unentwegt offen'! — und das vor kurzem entdeckte F 144a φάλανθον Νέστορος κάρα, wo das Komische nicht nur in dem Kontrast zwischen der hochpoetischen Umschreibung der Person mit κάρα c. gen. und dem prosaisch-alltäglichen Adjektiv liegt, sondern auch darin, dass das in solchen Umschreibungen völlig verblasste Wort κάρα hier ganz buchstäblich genommen ist. Für die zwei erstgenannten Fragmente hat man auf Grund ihres humoristischen Tones Herkunft aus Satyrspielen vermutet; daran könnte man auch bei dem letzteren denken, was bedeuten würde, dass der Ἀχαιῶν σύλλογος ein Satyrspiel — und dann wohl auch sicher mit den Σύνδειπνοι identisch (vgl. *TrGF* IV p. 425 f.) — war.

Ein metrisches Novum für Sophokles sind schliesslich die akatalektischen iambischen Tetrameter in den *Ichneutai* (F 314, 298-328).

V

Im übrigen finden wir in den Fragmenten natürlich viel bereits Bekanntes. Ich hebe nur einiges hervor was mir bemerkenswert scheint.

1. Dramatisch- und Bühnen-Technisches.

Eine unerwartete Wendung am Ende, wie sie der *Philoktetes* bietet, hatte auf jeden Fall auch der *Athamas*, in dem der Titelheld im letzten Augenblick von Herakles (auch hier als *deus ex machina*?) gerettet wurde (*TrGF* IV p. 99 f.).

Eine ἀναγνώρισις durch σημεῖα, wie wir sie aus der *Elektra* kennen, kam in mindestens einem der beiden *Tyro*-Dramen vor, wo Tyro und ihre Söhne sich an dem Trog wiedererkannten, in dem Tyro sie ausgesetzt hatte (*TrGF* IV p. 463)[45].

Einen Wechsel der Szene, wie im *Aias* (815 ff.) und in Aischylos' *Eumeniden* und *Aitnaiai*, gab es offenbar auch — vielleicht sogar mehrmals — in den Ἀχιλλέως ἐρασταί (*TrGF* IV p. 165 f.).

Tötung von Menschen hat Sophokles wie im *Aias* auch in der *Niobe* auf die Bühne gebracht, wo man — vorausgesetzt dass F 441 a und 442 mit Recht diesem Stück zugewiesen werden — Apollon und Artemis vom Dach des Palastes auf die Niobiden schiessen sah und deren Schreie und flehentliche Bitten hörte (den Tod der Opfer selber sah man offenbar ebensowenig wie im *Aias*): siehe W. S. Barrett, bei R. Carden (ed.), *The Papyrus Fragments of Sophocles* (Berlin/New York 1974), 184 f.

Dass eine Gottheit ausser als *deus ex machina* redend auftritt — was wir in den erhaltenen Stücken nur im *Aias* finden[46] — kam auch in den *Ichneutai* (F 314, 1 ff.; 451 ff.: Apollon) und im *Inachos* vor (F 272: Hermes); und wenn man F 10 c und 441 a mit Recht Sophokles zugeschrieben hat, kommen noch zwei weitere Fälle hinzu: Athene im *Aias Lokros* und Apollon (vielleicht auch Artemis) in der *Niobe*.

[45] Wenn Menander *Epitr.* 325 ff. Sandbach die sophokleische *Tyro* vor Augen hatte — was doch höchst wahrscheinlich ist —, dann kommt das πηρίδιον γνωρισμάτων, von dem er redet, auf seine eigene Rechnung: Aristoteles unterscheidet das γνώρισμα in der *Tyro* ja gerade ausdrücklich von kleineren Erkennungszeichen wie περιδέραια. — Dass Sophokles hier von Euripides abhängig sein müsse (A. Hähnle, Γνωρίσματα [Diss. Tübingen 1929], 23; 52 ff.; übernommen von W. Schmid, *GGL* I 2, 428), ist eine jener Behauptungen, die nur dadurch möglich werden, dass man sich den Umfang dessen was von der griechischen Literatur verloren gegangen ist, nicht vergegenwärtigt.

[46] Vgl. W. Schmid, *GGL* I 2, 330⁰. Schmid hat die Beispiele aus den *Ichneutai* und dem *Inachos* nicht berücksichtigt, und kommt so zu der Behauptung (*ibid.*, 460): «Das Auftreten von Göttern ist bei ihm seltener und dezenter geworden: Athena im Aias redet unsichtbar»...

2. Stilistisches.

Bemerkenswerte Epitheta: βυρσοφώνης von Salmoneus, der Zeus' Donner imitierte, indem er mit getrockneten Häuten (βύρσαι) bespannte [47] Kessel hinter seinem Wagen her über den Boden scheppern liess (F 10 c; Zuweisung an Sophokles allerdings nicht ganz sicher), ζευξίλεως von einem König (F 133, 6), κυαμόβολος von einem — anachronistisch, wie bereits die antiken Grammatiker bemerkten — durchs Bohnenlos gewählten Richter (F 288) und σκηπτροβάμων vom Adler des Zeus (F 884).

Dass Sophokles den tragischen ὄγκος auch zu weit treiben konnte (vgl. z.B. *El.* 54 τύπωμα χαλκόπλευρον; *OT* 193-194 παλίσσυτον δράμημα νωτίσαι πάτρας ἄπουρον), illustriert der schon von Theophrast als Beispiel des Abgeschmackten zitierte Vers ἀπυνδάκωτος οὐ τραπεζοῦται κύλιξ (F 611) und die fast paratragodisch klingende Frage ἵπποισιν ἢ κύμβαισι ναυστολεῖς χθόνα; (F 127) [48]; vgl. auch die sehr preziösen Ausdrücke δρυοπαγῆ στόλον (F 702) für einen Holzpflock und ἀσπάθητον χλαῖναν (F 877) für ein als Bekleidung dienendes Fell.

Doch das sind Ausnahmen. Viel öfter können wir uns auch in den Fragmenten freuen über treffende Formulierungen — etwa F 479, 4 τερπνόν ἀργίας ἄκος von dem von Palamedes erfundenen Brettspiel, oder F 595 κερκίδος φωνή von dem Gewebe durch das die ihrer Zunge beraubte Philomela ihrer Schwester berichtet, was mit ihr geschehen ist — und gut gefundene Vergleiche wie F 35 ἀσπὶς μὲν ἡμὴ

[47] Das muss doch, wie Haslam mit Recht annimmt, die Funktion der Häute gewesen sein, nach der Apollodor uns mit seinen Worten βύρσας ... ἐξηραμμένας ἐξ ἅρματος μετὰ λεβήτων χαλκῶν σύρων (*Bibl.* I 9, 7 = I 89 Wagner) raten lässt. Zu βυρσοφώνης vgl. Eur. *Ba.* 513 βύρσης κτύπος vom Klang der Tympana.

[48] Die wohl A. E. HOUSMAN vorgeschwebt hat bei V. 10 seines köstlichen *Fragment of a Greek Tragedy* (jetzt leicht zugänglich bei K. BARTELS, *Klassische Parodien* [Zürich 1968], 16 ff.): «Sailing on horseback, or with feet for oars?»

λίγδος ὡς πυκνομματεῖ [49], F 800 Λυδία λίθος σίδηρον τηλόθεν προσηγάγου [50], F 685 ἀλλ' εἰσὶ μητρὶ παῖδες ἄγκυραι βίου, F 393 ψυχῆς ἀνοῖξαι τὴν κεκλῃμένην πύλην, F 568, wo es von der Macht des Gesanges heisst, dass sie «die schmale Landenge des Lebens instandhält» [51], oder F 947, wo Sophokles das von der τύχη regierte menschliche Leben mit dem Brettspiel vergleicht, bei dem man den Fall der Würfel hinzunehmen und sein Spiel danach zu richten hat:

στέργειν δὲ τἀκπεσόντα καὶ θέσθαι πρέπει
σοφὸν κυβευτήν, ἀλλὰ μὴ στένειν τύχην.

Das 'tricolon crescendo' (vgl. z.B. *Aj.* 896; *El.* 13; 1291) finden wir in F 210, 73 τὸν παῖδα καὶ γέροντα καὶ νεανίαν; F 774, 1 μύω τε καὶ δέδορκα κἀξανίσταμαι; F 941, 6 σπουδαῖον, ἡσυχαῖον, ἐς βίαν ἄγον; 12 ἐν θηρσίν, ἐν βροτοῖσιν, ἐν θεοῖς ἄνω; F 949, 2 νοῦς φροῦδος, ἔργ' ἀχρεῖα, φροντίδες κεναί.

Ein prächtiges Beispiel einer *praeteritio* (vgl. *Tr.* 499 ff.) bietet F 799, wo Odysseus sich dieser Figur bedient, um dem Diomedes alle Schande aus seiner und seines Vaters Vergangenheit aufzuzählen.

49 Ein durchlöcherter Schild wird mit einer Bronzegussform verglichen: siehe D. Müller, *Handwerk und Sprache*, Beitr. zur Klass. Philol. 51 (Meisenheim am Glan 1974), 166 f.

50 Zu dem «Vergleich ohne wie» siehe R. Kassel, in *RhM* 116 (1973), 110 ff.

51 λάθα Πιερίσιν στυγερὰ / κἀνήρατος · ὦ δύνασις / θνατοῖς εὐποτμοτάτα μελέων, / ἀνέχουσα βίου βραχὺν ἰσθμόν. Zu dem letzten Vers bemerkt A. C. Pearson (II pp. 207-8) «This remarkable figure, which will not bear logical analysis, has no exact parallel in Greek literature». Aber sehr hilfreich für die logische Analyse des Bildes ist Mark Aurel IV 3, 7 ἀλλὰ τὸ δοξάριόν σε περισπάσει; ἀπιδὼν εἰς τὸ τάχος τῆς πάντων λήθης καὶ τὸ χάος τοῦ ἐφ' ἑκάτερα ἀπείρου αἰῶνος (sc. μὴ περισπῶ). Hier wird die Vergessenheit der der Mensch bald anheimfällt, und damit die Nichtigkeit des Ruhmes, aus der Unendlichkeit erklärt, die zu beiden Seiten seines Lebens, d.h. vor seiner Geburt und nach seinem Tode, gähnt. Eine ähnliche Vorstellung liegt offenbar der Sophoklesstelle zu Grunde. Das Leben ist eine schmale Landenge, die von beiden Seiten durch die Flut der λήθη bedroht und nur durch die Macht des Gesanges vor solcher Überflutung bewahrt wird. Der Gesang wird ja von Generation zu Generation weitergegeben und schützt so die Menschen, die er besingt, vor der Vergessenheit — sie leben im Gesang weiter: so hält die Macht des Gesanges «den schmalen Isthmos des Lebens instand».

VI

Zum Schluss möchte ich noch kurz auf ein paar inhaltlich besonders schöne oder bemerkenswerte Fragmente hinweisen (wobei ich mir die Freiheit nehme ganz meinem persönlichen Geschmack zu folgen). Es ist bezeichnend, dass die meisten dieser Fragmente aus Stobaios stammen: seine Anthologie enthält ja die nach inhaltlichen Gesichtspunkten ausgesuchten 'Rosinen' der griechischen Literatur (und hat uns fast ein Drittel der aus verlorenen sophokleischen Dramen zitierten Verse erhalten [52]).

Ein paar solcher besonders schönen Fragmente habe ich bereits erwähnt: die 'homerischen' Gleichnisse F 149 und F 659, das Fragment über die Macht des Gesanges (F 568) und die Mahnung, sich der τύχη gegenüber wie ein guter Brettspieler zu benehmen (F 947).

Ich nenne ferner die Rhesis aus dem *Tereus* (F 583), in der eine Frau — offenbar die durch ihre Heirat mit Tereus nach Thrakien verschlagene athenische Königstochter Prokne — das Los der Frauen beklagt, die, sobald die sorglose Kindheit vorüber ist, aus dem Hause gestossen und an Wildfremde verhandelt werden, denen sie dann für den Rest ihres Lebens Loyalität schuldig sind. Herr Knox hat auf die Verwandtschaft dieses Fragments mit der bekannten Klage der euripideischen Medea (230 ff.) aufmerksam gemacht [53] und daraus mit Recht geschlossen, dass das Los der Frau eine im späten 5. Jahrhundert vieldiskutierte Frage gewesen sein muss.

Ebenfalls aus einer längeren Rede stammt das grosse Fragment 941 über die Macht der Kypris, dessen grossartiger

[52] Indirekt überliefert sind uns im Augenblick 988 ganze oder so gut wie ganze Verse und 213 Teile von Versen (ausserdem noch 346 Einwortfragmente); davon stammen, wenn man die Teilverse als halbe Verse rechnet, 334, 5 aus Stobaios (und 94 weitere aus anderen Florilegien). Die Papyri haben uns bisher 260 ganze oder so gut wie ganze Verse und 2106 oft winzige Teile von Versen beschert.

[53] *YClS* 25 (1977), 220 f. = *Word and Action* (Baltimore/London 1979), 312 f.

Schwung trotz aller textkritischen Probleme noch unverkennbar ist und das sich dem herrlichen Lied aus der *Antigone* (Ἔρως ἀνίκατε μάχαν 781 ff.) ebenbürtig an die Seite stellt. Besonders eindrucksvoll sind die entgegengesetzten Prädikate, die hier der Liebe beigelegt werden (V. 3-7):

ἔστιν μὲν Ἅιδης, ἔστι δ' ἄφθιτος βίος,
ἔστιν δὲ λύσσα μανιάς, ἔστι δ' ἵμερος
ἄκρατος, ἔστ' οἰμωγμός. ἐν κείνῃ τὸ πᾶν
σπουδαῖον, ἡσυχαῖον, ἐς βίαν ἄγον.

Nebenbei: die λύσσα in V. 4 erinnert an das berühmte Wort des alten und, wenn wir unseren Testimonien (T 74-80) glauben dürfen, in der Liebe sehr erfahrenen Sophokles, der auf die Frage, ob er noch imstande sei einer Frau beizuwohnen, geantwortet haben soll: «Still! Ich bin glücklich, dass ich dém wie einem besessenen und wüsten Herren (λυττῶντά τινα καὶ ἄγριον δεσπότην) entronnen bin» (T 80).

Sehr lieb ist mir F 636:

φεῦ φεῦ, τί τούτου χάρμα μεῖζον ἂν λάβοις,
τοῦ γῆς ἐπιψαύσαντα κᾆθ' ὑπὸ στέγῃ
πυκνῆς ἀκοῦσαι ψακάδος εὑδούσῃ φρενί;

(Verse, an die ich immer denken muss, wenn ich im Bett liegend den Regen aufs Dach tropfen höre): hier hat der Lebensgeniesser Sophokles ein charakteristisches Wohlgefühl des Menschen schön beobachtet und treffend beschrieben.

Ganz modern mutet der Ausspruch an, dass seelische Missgestimmtheit zu körperlicher Krankheit führen kann (F 663: τίκτουσι γάρ τοι καὶ νόσους δυσθυμίαι), ebenso wie F 910, wo Sophokles die Tatsache, dass der Mensch auch vor Freude weinen kann, daraus erklärt, dass Schmerz und Freude auf dieselbe Stelle der menschlichen φρένες wirken [54].

[54] Diesen Sinn fordert der Zusammenhang: das überlieferte φύει ist offenbar korrupt (H. Lloyd-Jones, in *CR* N.S. 31 (1981), 178 vermutet φέρει).

Ich schliesse mit einem Fragment, das für mich in kürzester und schönster Form die ganze Weisheit, Frömmigkeit und Harmonie dieses Dichters zusammenfasst (F 843):

τὰ μὲν διδακτὰ μανθάνω, τὰ δ᾽ εὑρετὰ
ζητῶ, τὰ δ᾽ εὐκτὰ παρὰ θεῶν ᾐτησάμην.[55]

Anhang I: Verzeichnis der sicher überlieferten Titel verlorener sophokleischer Dramen

Ἀθάμας α΄	Δανάη	Θυέστης β΄
Ἀθάμας β΄	Διονυσίσκος σατυρικός	Θυέστης γ΄
Αἴας Λοκρός	Δόλοπες	Ἴναχος
Αἰγεύς	Ἑλένης ἀπαίτησις	Ἰξίων
Αἰθίοπες	Ἑλένης ἁρπαγή	Ἰοβάτης
Αἰχμαλωτίδες	Ἑλένης γάμος	Ἱππόνους
Ἀκρίσιος	Ἐπίγονοι	Ἰφιγένεια
Ἀλεάδαι	Ἐπὶ Ταινάρῳ σάτυροι	Ἰφικλῆς
Ἀλέξανδρος	Ἔρις	Ἰχνευταὶ σάτυροι
Ἀλκμέων	Ἐριφύλη	Ἴων
Ἄμυκος σατυρικός	Ἑρμιόνη	Καμικοί
Ἀμφιάρεως σατυρικός	Εὔμηλος	Κέρβερος
Ἀμφιτρύων	Εὐρύαλος	Κηδαλίων σατυρικός
Ἀνδρομάχη	Εὐρυσάκης	Κλυταιμήστρα
Ἀνδρομέδα	Ἡρακλεΐσκος σατυρικός	Κολχίδες
Ἀντηνορίδαι	Ἡρακλῆς σατυρικός	Κρέουσα
Ἀτρεὺς ἢ Μυκηναῖαι	Ἠριγόνη	Κρίσις σατυρική
Ἀχαιῶν σύλλογος	Θαμύρας	Κωφοὶ σάτυροι
Ἀχιλλέως ἐρασταί	Θησεύς	Λάκαιναι
Δαίδαλος	Θυέστης α΄	Λαοκόων

[55] Est ist wohl kein Zufall, dass dies, bei allen offenkundigen Unterschieden, anklingt an das Wort eines dem Sophokles in Vielem kongenialen Dichters und Weisen: «Das schönste Glück des denkenden Menschen ist, das Erforschliche erforscht zu haben und das Unerforschliche ruhig zu verehren» (J. W. von GOETHE, Sophienausgabe II 11, 159, 7 ff. = *Maximen und Reflexionen* 1207 Hecker [Schriften der Goethe-Gesellschaft 21, Weimar 1907, 250]).

Λαρισαῖοι
Λημνίαι α΄
Λημνίαι β΄
Μάντεις ἢ Πολύϊδος
Μελέαγρος
Μέμνων
Μίνως
Μοῦσαι
Μυσοί
Μῶμος σατυρικός
Ναύπλιος καταπλέων
Ναύπλιος πυρκαεύς
Ναυσικάα ἢ Πλύντριαι
Νιόβη
Νίπτρα
Ὀδυσσεὺς ἀκανθοπλήξ
Ὀδυσσεὺς μαινόμενος
Οἰκλῆς
Οἰνόμαος
Παλαμήδης
Πανδώρα ἢ Σφυροκόποι
Πηλεύς
Ποιμένες
Πολυξένη
Πρίαμος
Πρόκρις
Ῥιζοτόμοι
Σαλμωνεὺς σατυρικός
Σίνων
Σίσυφος
Σκύθαι
Σκύριοι
Σύνδειπνοι
Τάνταλος
Τεῦκρος
Τήλεφος
Τηρεύς
Τριπτόλεμος
Τρωΐλος
Τυμπανισταί
Τυνδάρεως
Τυρώ α΄
Τυρώ β΄
Ὕβρις σατυρική
Ὑδροφόροι
Φαίακες
Φαίδρα
Φθιώτιδες
Φιλοκτήτης ὁ ἐν Τροίᾳ
Φινεύς α΄
Φινεύς β΄
Φοῖνιξ
Φρίξος
Φρύγες
Χρύσης

Anhang II: Die von Eustathios als Homernachahmungen bezeichneten Sophoklesstellen

Das Verzeichnis der in *TrGF* IV unter T 116 aufgeführten Stellen beruhte auf H. W. Millers Einleitung seines Artikels «Ὁ φιλόμηρος Σοφοκλῆς *and Eustathius*» (*CPh* 41, 1946, 99-102) und handschriftlichen Angaben Valckenaers. Eine Durchsicht sämtlicher von Miller gesammelten Sophokleszitate bei Eustathios ergibt nicht weniger als 37 weitere Stellen, an denen Eustathios ausdrücklich von homerischen Entlehnungen oder Nachahmungen bei Sophokles spricht. Übrigens ist Millers Sammlung keineswegs vollständig: von den Stellen die ich für T 116 dem Manuskript Valckenaers entnommen hatte, fehlt bei ihm 1293, 31; vier weitere Stellen in der folgenden Liste (676,

64 ff.; 694, 26 f.; 699, 39 f.; 1602, 6 f.), die ebenfalls bei Miller fehlen, verdanke ich — in dieser Reihenfolge — M. van der Valk (dessen Sammlung von Sophokleszitaten bei Eustathios ich zur Kontrolle einsehen durfte), T. Hedberg (*Eustathios als Attizist* [Diss. Uppsala 1935], 129), Gottfried Hermann (*Sophoclis Oedipus Rex*... [Lipsiae ^{3}1833], 178) und H. Stephanus' Abhandlung *De Sophoclea imitatione Homeri* (a.a.O. [oben S. 200], 88); fast sämtliche Parallelen, die er in dieser Abhandlung zieht, stammen aus Eustathios) [56]; eine vollständige Liste wird erst möglich sein, wenn wir einen *Index fontium* zu Eustathios besitzen (den uns hoffentlich van der Valks eiserner Fleiss schenken wird). Die Homernachahmungen bzw. -entlehnungen, die Eustathios an den bisher aufgetriebenen Stellen signalisiert, sind:

A 412 ~ *Aj.* 423 ff. (126, 39 ff.; παραφράζων); vgl. Σ 105
B 182 ~ *Aj.* 15 f. (198, 2 ff.; κἀντεῦθεν ὁ φιλόμηρος Σ. λαβὼν ἀφορμήν)
B 215 ~ *Ph.* 443 f. (205, 26 ff.; παραφράζων)
B 811 ~ *El.* 894 (351, 9; ἀκολουθῶν)
Γ 59 ~ *OT* 58 (383, 21; μίμημα); vgl. Z 333
Δ 22 ~ *El.* 159 (440, 37 f.; παρὰ τῷ φιλομήρῳ Σ.)
E 4 f. ~ *Ant.* 1146 f. (514, 45 f.; ὁ ζηλωτὴς Ὁμήρου Σ.)
E 296 ~ *Ant.* 1268; 1314 (548, 42 ff.; ἐξ Ὁμήρου λαβόντες οἱ ὕστερον, ὡς δηλοῖ καὶ Σ.)
E 367 ~ *Aj.* 845 (557, 9 f.; παραφράζων [sic cod. teste v.d. Valk: περι- ed. pr.])
E 378 ~ *Ph.* 434 (558, 34 f.; ἐνταῦθα λαβών)
E 553 ~ *OC* 1551 (581, 26 f.; ὅθεν λαβών)
E 800 ~ *Aj.* 90 (610, 8 f.; ἐντεῦθεν λαβών)
Ξ 253, Ψ 63 ~ *El.* 781 (632, 32 f.; μεταποιηθέν)
Z 205 ~ *Aj.* 847 (637, 19; ἐντεῦθεν λαβών)

[56] Einige weitere Ergänzungen zu Millers Sammlung gibt M. van der VALK (ed.), *Eustathii Commentarii ad Homeri Iliadem pertinentes*... I (Lugduni Bat. 1971), p. LXXXVII (§ 91) mit Anm. 2.

Z 333 ~ *OT* 58; *El.* 929; 1078 ff. (645, 16 f.; παρὰ τῷ φιλομήρῳ Σ.); vgl. Γ 59
Z 419 ~ *Ant.* 81 (652, 29 f.; παραφράσας)
Z 464 ~ *Ant.* 246 f. (666, 57; πρὸς μίμησιν)
H 96 ~ *Aj.* 1182 (668, 38 f.; παραφράζων); vgl. Θ 163
H 182 ~ *Aj.* 1287 (675, 34 f.; παρέφρασεν)
H 212 ~ *Tr.* 938 (676, 64 ff.; ἔοικε ... ἀρχὴν ἐντεῦθεν λαβεῖν ... ὁ τὸ στόμα πληθύνας Ὁμηρικῷ ζήλῳ)
H 479 ~ *OC* 1463 (692, 53; ἐκ τοῦ ... λαβών)
Θ 8 ~ *El.* 1059; 54 (694, 26 f.; Ὁμηρικῷ ζήλῳ)
Θ 68 ~ *Ant.* 415 f. (698, 27 f.; παραφράζων)
Θ 72 ~ *OT* 961 (699, 39 f.; ἐκ τοῦ ... λαβοῦσα ἡ τραγῳδία ἔφη); vgl. X 209
Θ 163 ~ *Aj.* 1182 (705, 7; ἐξ αὐτοῦ ... ἀντιστρόφως τῷ Ὁμηρικῷ); vgl. H 96
Θ 307, 524 ~ *OT* 159 (714, 63; παρὰ τῷ Ὁμηρικῷ ζηλωτῇ Σ.)
I 327 ~ *Aj.* 1311 f. (754, 21 f; ἐντεῦθεν μεθοδευθείς)
I 342 ~ *OT* 338 (755, 13 ff.; δέδωκε τῷ Σ. μέθοδον)
I 363 ~ *Ph.* 354; 480 (756, 18 ff.; ὁ φιλόμηρος Σ.)
I 378 ~ *Aj.* 665 (757, 14 f.; τῷ Σ. γέγονεν ἀφορμή)
I 453 ~ *Ph.* 683 (763, 1 f.; Ὁμηρικὸν ... παρὰ Σ.)
I 575 ~ *OT* 17 f. (775, 21; ὅθεν λαβών)
I 607 ff. ~ *OT passim* (777, 51; μιμησάμενος)
K 173 ~ *Aj.* 786 (796, 56 f.; παραφράζων)
K 279 f. ~ *Aj.* 34 f. (805, 26 f.; ἐξ ὧν ... λαβὼν ὁ παρὰ τῷ Σ. Ὀδυσσεὺς λέγει παραφραστικῶς)
K 394 ~ *Tr.* 94 (814, 22 f.; ὁ φιλόμηρος Σ. μεταλαβών)
Λ 6 ff. ~ *Aj.* 4 (826, 51 f.; τὴν ... Ὁμηρικὴν τῶν νηῶν στάσιν δηλοῖ καὶ Σ.)
Λ 385 ~ *Aj.* 1120 (851, 59; Ὁμηρικῷ ζήλῳ)
Λ 386 ~ *Aj.* 1122 (851, 58; παραφράζων ὁ φιλόμηρος Σ.)
M 21 ~ *Aj.* 420 (890, 21 f.; ὁ φιλόμηρος Σ.)
M 37 ~ *Aj.* Titel (891, 26 f.; μήποτε ὁ τοῦ Ὁμήρου ζηλωτὴς Σ. ἐντεῦθεν ... ἐπέγραψε); vgl. N 812

M 237 ff. ~ *OT* 707 ff. (902, 2 ff.; ὁ φιλόμηρος Σ.); vgl. β 181 f.
N 588 ~ F 1084 (948, 20; ἀκολουθῶν δηλαδὴ τῷ ποιητῇ)
N 812 ~ *Aj.* Titel (961, 24 f.; ὅθεν ἴσως καὶ Σ. λαβὼν ... ἐπέγραψε); vgl. M 37
Ξ 164 ~ *Ph.* 827 (974, 25; ἐντεῦθεν λαβών)
Ξ 253 ~ *El.* 781 (632, 32 f.; siehe oben)
O 101 ~ *OT* 914 (1007, 51 f.; ἐντεῦθεν λαβών)
O 657 f. ~ *Aj.* 1079 (1036, 12 f.; ἐντεῦθεν λαβών)
Π 492 ~ *El.* 302 (1072, 41 f.; ἐκ τοῦ ... λαβών)
Π 722 ~ *El.* 1090 ff. (1083, 17 f.; παρὰ τῷ Ὁμηρικῷ ζηλωτῇ Σ.)
P 105 ~ *OT* 1396; 1035 (1097, 23 f.; ἐντεῦθεν παραξέσας)
P 154 ~ *Aj.* 245 f. (1100, 26 f.; παρὰ τῷ φιλομήρῳ Σ.)
Σ 105 ~ *Aj.* 423 ff. (1133, 50 f.; ὠφέλησε ... ταῦτα τὸν φιλόμηρον Σ.); vgl. A 412.
Σ 318, 323 al. ~ *Aj.* 319 ff. (1140, 26; ὁ φιλόμηρος Σ.)
Σ 264 ~ *OT* 205 (1142, 21 f.; ἐντεῦθεν λαβών)
X 209 ~ *OT* 961; *OC* 1508 (1266, 39 f.; ἐκ τῶν ... λαβών); vgl. Θ 72
Ψ 63 ~ *El.* 781 (632, 32 f.: siehe oben)
Ψ 152 f. ~ *Aj.* 1173 f. (1293, 31 f.; ὁ φιλόμηρος Σ.)
Ψ 590 ~ *OT* 617 (1317, 52 f.; κατὰ τὸν φιλόμηρον Σ.)
Ω 551 ~ *El.* 137 ff. (1364, 48; μιμούμενος)
β 181 f. ~ *OT* 707 ff. (1440, 39 f.; Ὁμηρικῷ ζήλῳ); vgl. M 237 ff.
γ 152 ~ *Aj.* 363 (1461, 64; λαβὼν ἐντεῦθεν ὁ ζηλωτὴς αὐτοῦ [sc. Ὁμήρου] Σ.)
γ 371 ff. ~ *Aj.* 14 (1473, 20 ff.; ἐντεῦθεν μίμησιν λαβών)
ε 478 f. ~ *OC* 676 f. (1547, 11 f.; κατά τινα μίμησιν Ὁμηρικήν)
ϑ 378 ~ *Ph.* 392 (1602, 6 f.; ὁρμηθεὶς ἐντεῦθεν)
λ 128 ~ F 454 (1675, 52; παραφράζων)
λ 386 ~ *Ant.* 1284 (1691, 47 f.; λαβὼν ἐντεῦθεν)

Die Parallele zu I 575 (die auf einem verderbten Text beruht: vgl. *TrGF* IV p. 345) und die zu λ 128 (siehe zu F 454) hat Eustathios aus den Homerscholien, die zu Z 464, K 394 und ε 478 f. aus den Sophoklesscholien (die er kannte: siehe M. v.d. Valk [letzte Fussnote], p. LXXXVII[5]). Die übrigen stammen wohl grösstenteils von ihm selber (zu Δ 22 beruft er sich auf τινὲς ['fontem nescio' v.d. Valk]). Sie sind manchmal sehr weit hergeholt (z.B. M 37 und N 812; die richtige Erklärung des Titels Αἴας μαστιγοφόρος, die Eustathios offenbar vergessen hatte, steht sowohl in der Hypothesis als in dem Scholion zu V. 110) oder recht äusserlich (z.B. E 800; Θ 307); aber beachtenswert ist z.B. die Parallele die er zweimal (M 237 ff.; β 181 f.) mit Iokastes Verhöhnung der Orakel (*OT* 707 ff.) zieht und der Vergleich von I 607 ff. mit der tragischen Ironie im *König Ödipus*.

Im übrigen sei mit Nachdruck darauf hingewiesen, dass die obige Liste nur solche Fälle enthält, in denen Eustathios ausdrücklich sagt, dass Sophokles etwas aus Homer entlehnt oder nachgeahmt hat (die Wendungen, mit denen er das tut, sind jedesmal dazu angegeben). Daher fehlt in dieser Liste z.B. seine schöne Beobachtung, dass, während Hektor bei Homer (Z 479) betet, sein Sohn möge es seinem Vater nicht nur gleich tun, sondern ihn sogar weit übertreffen, der hochmütige sophokleische Aias in seinem Segenswunsch (*Aj.* 550 f.) das Übertreffen des Vaters weglässt: ὁ μὲν τοῦ Σοφοκλέους Αἴας ὑπέρφρων πλαττόμενος ʽγένοιο πατρὶ ὅμοιος' ἐπεύχεται τῷ υἱῷ, τὴν δὲ τοῦ ἀμείνονος αὔξησιν εἰπεῖν ὀκνεῖ, ὡς μὴ ἐγχωροῦν γενέσθαι οὕτω διὰ τὸ μεγαλεῖον τοῦ πατρός, Ἕκτωρ δὲ τὸν ἑαυτοῦ υἱὸν καὶ ἀμείνονα γενέσθαι αὐτοῦ ἐθέλει, καὶ οὐχ ἁπλῶς ἀμείνονα ἀλλὰ καὶ κατὰ πολύ (656, 45 ff.); auf die Gleichartigkeit der beiden Segenswünsche hatten bereits die Sophoklesscholien hingewiesen, aber erst H. Stephanus (*ibid.*, 93) hat, mit vollstem Recht, *Aj.* 550 f. ausdrücklich für eine Nachahmung von Z 476 ff. erklärt.

DISCUSSION

M. Seidensticker: Es würde mich interessieren zu wissen:

1) ob sich die statistischen Angaben zu Beginn Ihres Vortrages erweitern lassen um eine Feststellung, für wieviele der nicht erhaltenen Stücke des Sophokles sich a) der Stoff und b) die Handlungsstruktur (wenigstens in groben Zügen) bestimmen lassen;

2) ob es sich, auf Grund von Hinweisen in den erhaltenen Tragödien oder den Fragmenten, in Einzelfällen feststellen (oder doch begründet vermuten) lässt, dass einzelne Stücke zusammen aufgeführt worden sind? Ausgangspunkt meiner Überlegung ist die aeschyleische *Orestie*, wo man seit langen darauf hingewiesen hat, dass die überraschende Ausführlichkeit, mit der im *Agamemnon* von Menelaos Schicksal die Rede ist (*Ag.* 617 ff.) sich u.a., als Vorbereitung auf das zur *Orestie* gehörende Satyrspiel *Proteus* verstehen lässt. Könnte man vielleicht κατ' ἀναλογίαν in der Ausführlichkeit, mit der Teukros im *Aias* von dem Schicksal spricht, das ihn nach der Heimkehr erwartet, eine Vorbereitung auf den *Teukros* sehen, d.h. vermuten, dass *Aias* und *Teukros* zusammen aufgeführt worden sind?

M. Radt: Was Ihre erste Frage betrifft: a) Der Stoff lässt sich für 20 Stücke (einen Ἀθάμας, Ἀνδρομέδα, Διονυσίσκος, Ἑρμιόνη, Εὐρύαλος, Ἴναχος, Ἰχνευταί, Καμικοί, Κολχίδες, Κρίσις, Λάκαιναι, Λημνίαι, Μάντεις, Ναύπλιος πυρκαεύς, Ναυσικάα, Ὀδυσσεὺς ἀκανθοπλήξ, Ὀδυσσεὺς μαινόμενος, Οἰνόμαος, Τηρεύς, eine Τυρώ) sicher, und für 10 weitere (Ἄμυκος, Θαμύρας, Λαοκόων, Μελέαγρος, Νιόβη, Παλαμήδης, Πολυξένη, Τεῦκρος, Φαίδρα, Φιλοκτήτης ὁ ἐν Τροίᾳ) mit grosser Wahrscheinlichkeit angeben: das sind zusammen also ein gutes Viertel der 115 sicher überlieferten Titel. Für alle übrigen können wir nur Vermutungen aufstellen; sogar über den Stoff von Stücken mit so sprechenden Titeln wie Ἑλένης ἀπαίτησις, Ἑλένης ἁρπαγή und Ἑλένης γάμος sind ganz verschiedene Hypothesen möglich; b) die Handlungsstruktur dagegen lässt sich bei keinem einzigen der verlorenen Dramen bestimmen (abgesehen natürlich von den *Ichneutai*); dazu ist einfach nicht genug erhalten, und es ist schon viel wenn wir, wie beim *Inachos*, eine Reihe von Personen angeben können, die in dem Stück auftraten.

Zu Ihrer zweiten Frage: sichere Hinweise darauf, dass zwei Stücke zusammen aufgeführt worden sind, gibt es, soweit ich sehe, nicht. Aber die Zusammengehörigkeit von *Aias* und *Teukros*, die Sie auf Grund von *Aj.* 1008 ff. vermuten, scheint mir keineswegs ausgeschlossen. So könnte man auch aus *Ph.* 1423 ff. schliessen, dass der *Philoktet in Troja* zusammen mit dem *Philoktet* aufgeführt worden ist.

M. Knox: Does the inscription which mentions the *Telepheia* give any indication that it was a trilogy, as seems to be generally assumed? It seems to me a most unlikely hypothesis. If it is indeed a play by our Sophocles (and not by a fourth-century poet of the same name) it is more likely to be a single play: the inscriptions of the fourth-century which contain lists including an ἀρχαία give the title of one play only.

M. Radt: Die Inschrift sagt Σοφοκλῆς ἐδίδασκε Τηλέφειαν — es handelt sich also nicht um die Wiederaufführung eines alten Stückes (oder man müsste annehmen, dass der junge Sophokles ein Stück seines Grossvaters inszeniert hat). Und die Endung -εια kann doch auch nicht für ein einzelnes Stück gebraucht werden.

M. Knox: The objection that the ending -εια would be unsuitable for a single play can be discussed: In the *Frogs* we have πρῶτον δέ μοι τὸν ἐξ Ὀρεστείας λέγε and the response is to recite the beginning of the *Choephoroe*!

M. Radt: Ich bin sicher, dass Ὀρέστεια an der Aristophanesstelle kein Einzelstück bezeichnet. Das Suffix -εια ist doch charakteristisch für ein grosses, sich aus mehreren Teilen zusammensetzendes, literarisches Ganzes, und ich glaube daher eher, dass Aristophanes die beiden Orestes-Dramen *Choephoroi* und *Eumeniden* meint. Aber selbst wenn er nur die *Choephoroi* meinen sollte, wäre es noch bedenklich, den Titel Τηλέφεια auf ein einziges Drama zu beziehen, da Sophokles ja sicher einen *Telephos* geschrieben hat, und die doppelte Bezeichnung *Telephos* und *Telepheia* für ein und dasselbe Stück doch äusserst unwahrscheinlich wäre.

M. Taplin: The inscription was set up to honour *choregoi* and so I think Snell's suggestion that it refers to the younger Sophocles (who was successful in 387 and 375 B.C.) should not be ruled out (but see A. Pickard-Cambridge, *The Dramatic Festivals of Athens*, 2nd ed. [Oxford 1969], 55).

M. Radt: Die Möglichkeit, dass es sich um den jüngeren Sophokles handelt, lässt sich in der Tat nicht ausschliessen. Die Siege sind in dieser Inschrift offenbar chronologisch geordnet. Als Regisseure werden nacheinander genannt: Ekphantides, Kratinos, Timotheos, Sophokles. Alles hängt hier davon ab, wann der uns völlig unbekannte Timotheos gelebt hat. Wenn er ins 4. Jh. gehört, muss es sich um den jüngeren Sophokles handeln. Wenn aber z.B., wie Luppe vermutet hat, Timotheos gar kein Tragödiendichter war, sondern nur jemand der als Regisseur für Achaios auftrat, ist der ältere Sophokles ohne weiteres möglich.

M. Irigoin: A en juger par l'inventaire critique que M. Radt nous a donné des titres des pièces de Sophocle, il semble que les drames satyriques aient particulièrement souffert des vicissitudes de la tradition. Leur disparition s'est-elle produite avant les travaux des grammairiens alexandrins ou plus tard? Dans la première hypothèse, peut-on estimer que le drame satyrique est un genre littéraire qui a vieilli plus vite (ou moins bien) que la tragédie?

M. Radt: Voralexandrinischer Verlust von Satyrspielen ist uns nur für Euripides bezeugt, und ich habe versucht zu zeigen, dass es nicht nötig ist, ihn auch für Aischylos und Sophokles anzunehmen. Aber die Tatsache, dass von Euripides' Satyrspielen schon früh so viel verloren gegangen ist, lässt in der Tat, wie mir scheint, auf ein geringeres Interesse wenigstens für s e i n e Satyrspiele (im Gegensatz zu seinen Tragödien) schliessen.

M. Taplin: It is notable that when we have so many more papyrus fragments of Euripides than of the other two they include relatively little satyr drama.

M. Radt: Ja, das ist eine schöne Bestätigung für den von Elmsley erschlossenen voralexandrinischen Verlust euripideischer Satyrspiele.

M. Taplin: The change of scene in *Achilleos erastai*, alleged by the *hypothesis* to *Aitnaiai*, is not really comparable with *Eumenides* and *Ajax*, since it was a satyr play. While we do not know of any other place in satyr drama where the chorus left the stage or where there was a change of scene this would not be surprising in this less disciplined genre.

M. Radt: Sie haben vollkommen recht. Immerhin werden die *Achilleos erastai* in diesem Testimonium in einem Atem mit den *Eumeniden* und den *Aitnaiai* genannt; daraus könnte man schliessen, dass ein solcher Szenenwechsel auch im Satyrspiel nicht häufig war.

Mme de Romilly: Dans les fragments cités par M. Radt, certains proviennent de citations, d'autres de trouvailles en partie fortuites. J'imagine que la plupart des beaux effets de style et des pensées frappantes appartiennent à la première catégorie. Et je pense qu'il serait très intéressant de savoir en vue de quoi était faite la citation, ce qui permettrait de se faire une idée des diverses curiosités et de l'état des connaissances selon les époques et les genres.

M. Radt: Ja, die besonders schönen und treffenden Beispiele, die ich zitiert habe, stammen alle aus der indirekten Überlieferung, der weitaus grösste Teil aus Stobaios. Solche nach moralischen Gesichtspunkten ausgewählten Stellen, die wir neben Stobaios auch kleineren Florilegien, Plutarch und anderen Moralisten verdanken, bilden, inhaltlich gesehen, bei weitem den wichtigsten Teil der uns indirekt überlieferten Fragmente. Den anderen Teil bieten uns Grammatiker, Etymologika u. dgl., die etwas aus Sophokles zitieren (oft ist es nur ein einziges Wort!), um eine sprachliche oder stilistische Eigentümlichkeit oder ein seltenes Wort zu belegen. Das gilt übrigens alles nicht nur für Sophokles sondern für poetische Fragmente überhaupt.

M. Irigoin: Il faudrait aussi distinguer, parmi les citations, celles qui sont faites de première main et celles qui sont tirées de recueils spécialisés, dont les papyrus nous ont fourni des exemples nombreux: anthologies, florilèges, etc. Un recueil de ce genre (in R. Pack, *The Greek and Latin*

Literary Texts from Greco-Roman Egypt [Ann Arbor ²1965], n° 1571) donne des fragments de tragédies connues par la tradition médiévale. M. Radt a-t-il rencontré, en préparant son édition, des fragments de tragédies perdues conservés dans de tels recueils?

M. Radt: Nein, bisher ist, soviel ich weiss, in Florilegien auf Papyrus kein Sophoklesfragment aufgetaucht. Das einzige was sie bisher bieten ist eine Parallele zu F 201 a.

M. Taplin: I would suppose that F 887 Radt comes from a satyr play. The punning on names which would be common among the citizens in the audience seems inconceivable in tragedy.

M. Radt: Eine sehr plausibele Vermutung, der ich mich gern anschliesse!

M. Taplin: The simile in F 871 R is rather different from most epic similes in that the phases of the moon are being compared to something abstract rather than concrete.

But I am more interested in the metaphor in the first lines (... ἐν πυκνῷ θεοῦ/τρόχῳ...). The most usual metaphor for changes of Fortune in Sophocles is the scales (*Aj.* 131; *Ant.* 1158-9 etc.), but in the *parodos* of *Tr.* (122-31) we have the circular motion of the stars round the pole. The image of the *wheel* of Fortune, so ubiquitous and powerful in the Middle Ages and Renaissance (and derived, I believe, from Boethius) occurs only in this fragment, so far as I know. Am I right in thinking that this is the earliest known occurrence of the image and that it is possible that Sophocles might have invented it?

M. Radt: Zu Ihrer ersten Bemerkung: mir ging es nur um das Formale, um die homerische Breite des Gleichnisses. Dass diese sophokleischen Gleichnisse auch im übrigen den homerischen entsprechen, wollte ich nicht behaupten, und ich glaube, dass Sie da auf einen wichtigen Unterschied hingewiesen haben: die Übernahme homerischer Kunstmittel zu neuen Zwecken ist ja gerade ganz charakteristisch für Sophokles.

Was das Bild betrifft: es könnte gut sein, dass dies die älteste Stelle ist, an der wir das Bild des Glücksrades finden. Aber wir können das Fragment nicht datieren, und bei Herodot haben wir auf jeden Fall etwas Ähnliches:

Κύκλος τῶν ἀνθρωπηίων ἐστὶ πρηγμάτων, περιφερόμενος δὲ οὐκ ἐᾷ αἰεὶ τοὺς αὐτοὺς εὐτυχέειν (I 207, 2); sehr ähnlich ist auch Adespota F 700, 28 f. (= Soph. Fr. 575, 9 f. Pearson)]α γὰρ τροχοῦ δίκην [ ]. τις κυκλεῖ τύχ[η, ein Fragment das man nicht nur Sophokles, sondern auch Aischylos zugeschrieben hat! So lässt sich auch nicht sagen, ob Sophokles der Erfinder dieses Bildes ist (falsch ist auf jeden Fall G. Norwoods Behauptung, Pindar habe das Bild erfunden [*Pindar*, Berkeley/Los Angeles 1945, p. 253 n. 47], eine Behauptung die darauf beruht, dass er — dem Symbol des Rades zuliebe, unter das er die zweite *Olympie* stellen will — in *Ol.* II 35-7 eine Anspielung auf das Glücksrad sieht).

Mme de Romilly: Il semble que la roue de la Fortune soit attestée sur des monuments figurés au IVe siècle (voir D. M. Robinson, *Excavations at Olynthus* XII, pp. 236; 254; 337; etc...). Au début, il y a eu, apparemment, flottement entre Tyché et Némésis. Mais dans les textes littéraires, bien que l'on ait de nombreux passages sur les cycles, et les alternances, présidant à la prospérité humaine, ce n'est pas vraiment la roue de la Fortune, et celle-ci n'est pas normalement divinisée (pour ces 'cycles', on trouvera des références dans mon article des *Hommages à Claire Préaux*). C'est un thème essentiel chez Sophocle.

M. Taplin: We have vase-paintings inspired by Aeschylus and Euripides which can be dated to not many years after the first performance of the play in question. A notable addition to these is the painting of Aeschylus' *Sphinx* published by Erika Simon (Sitzungsb. Heidelb. Akad. d. Wiss., Philos.-hist. Kl., 1981, 5). Do you believe that we have any fifth century artistic representations inspired by Sophocles? *

* *Additional note:* Professor Reverdin has told me that he is sceptical about the connection of this painting with Aeschylus. I still think that the costumes and the mask-like features of the satyrs are evidence of an 'illustration' more than usually closely related to a drama in performance. Professor Simon has now set the painting in a larger context of satyr plays on vases in *The Eye of Greece*, ed. by D. Kurtz and B. Sparkes (Cambridge 1982), 123 ff., esp. 141-2.

M. Radt: Die langjährige Beschäftigung mit den zahllosen Hypothesen und Spekulationen über den Inhalt verlorener Dramen hat mich vielleicht zu skeptisch gemacht, aber ich glaube nicht, dass es auch nur e i n e bildliche Darstellung gibt, die sich mit Sicherheit auf ein sophokleisches Stück beziehen lässt. Der völlig überzeugende Fall des von Erika Simon veröffentlichten Vasenbildes zu Aischylos' *Sphinx* ist eine ganz grosse Ausnahme.

M. Seidensticker: Gibt es nicht eine Reihe von Vasenbildern, die man mit dem Satyrspiel *Pandora* in Verbindung gebracht hat?

M. Radt: Ja, es gibt eine Reihe von Vasen, auf denen man Gestalten mit grossen Hämmern auf einen grossen aus der Erde auftauchenden Frauenkopf schlagen sieht. Das hat man seit Welcker und Hermann oft auf Sophokles' *Pandora* bezogen, die ja als zweiten Titel Σφυροκόποι hatte und in der es sich dann um die Herstellung der Pandora durch Knechte des Hephaistos gehandelt hätte. Aber Nilsson hat dem widersprochen und diese Bilder auf die ἄνοδος der Persephone bezogen. Wenn die Beziehung auf Sophokles' *Pandora* sicher wäre, hätten wir hier tatsächlich ein sicheres Beispiel einer von Sophokles inspirierten bildlichen Darstellung.

M. Irigoin: M. Radt pourrait-il nous indiquer, même approximativement, la proportion des passages lyriques dans son édition des fragments de Sophocle? En d'autres termes, le choix des citateurs s'est-il ou non porté plus volontiers sur les parties chantées des tragédies?

A propos du F 941, dont il a cité quatre vers dans son exposé, M. Radt fait allusion aux problèmes de critique verbale posés par ce passage relatif à la puissance de Kypris. Serait-il possible d'examiner maintenant quelques-unes de ces difficultés?

M. Radt: Zu Ihrer ersten Frage: die Zitate sind nur ganz ausnahmsweise gesungenen Partien entnommen. Die längsten lyrischen Fragmente stammen aus dem *Tereus* (F 591-593), wo man sogar einmal mit Sicherheit Responsion feststellen kann (F 592,1-3 ~ 4-6; die Versuche, noch mehr Responsionen zwischen diesen Fragmenten und mit F 879 a herzustellen, haben mich nicht überzeugen können); aber das ist eine grosse Ausnahme.

Was F 941 betrifft: es lautet in meiner Ausgabe

ὦ παῖδες, ἥ τοι Κύπρις οὐ Κύπρις μόνον,
ἀλλ' ἐστὶ πολλῶν ὀνομάτων ἐπώνυμος.
ἔστιν μὲν Ἅιδης, ἔστι δ' ἄφθιτος βίος,
ἔστιν δὲ λύσσα μανιάς, ἔστι δ' ἵμερος
ἄκρατος, ἔστ' οἰμωγμός, ἐν κείνῃ τὸ πᾶν
σπουδαῖον, ἡσυχαῖον, ἐς βίαν ἄγον.
ἐντήκεται γὰρ πλευμόνων ὅσοις ἔνι
ψυχή · τίς οὐχὶ τῆσδε τῆς θεοῦ πόρος;
εἰσέρχεται μὲν ἰχθύων πλωτῷ γένει,
ἔνεστι δ' ἐν χέρσου τετρασκελεῖ γονῇ,
νωμᾷ δ' ἐν οἰωνοῖσι τοὐκείνης πτέρον.

* * *

ἐν θηρσίν, ἐν βροτοῖσιν, ἐν θεοῖς ἄνω.
τίν' οὐ παλαίουσ' ἐς τρὶς ἐκβάλλει θεῶν;
εἴ μοι θέμις — θέμις δὲ τἀληθῆ λέγειν —,
Διὸς τυραννεῖ πλευμόνων, ἄνευ δορός,
ἄνευ σιδήρου · πάντα τοι συντέμνεται
Κύπρις τὰ θνητῶν καὶ θεῶν βουλεύματα

Ich habe mich soviel wie möglich an die Überlieferung gehalten: die einzigen Konjekturen sind V. 3 βίος (βία codd.); V. 8 πόρος (βορός codd.), und die Annahme einer Lücke zwischen V. 11 und 12. Aber damit sind noch nicht alle Schwierigkeiten gelöst: das Fragment bietet noch syntaktische (V. 7/8; 11) und lexikalische (V. 13 ἐκβάλλει) Anstösse, denen man oft mit Änderungen des Textes hat abhelfen wollen. Eine eingehende Erörterung dieser Probleme scheint mir im Augenblick leider nicht möglich: dazu müssten wir ja alle den Text mit Apparat vor uns haben.

Mme de Romilly: J'ai été très intéressée par les témoignages sur le caractère 'homérique' de Sophocle. Ce caractère est très frappant, en effet. Comment expliquer que Sophocle soit plus près d'Homère qu'Eschyle?

M. Radt: Ich würde nicht sagen, dass Sophokles Homer näher steht als Aischylos. Die Homernachfolge des Aischylos war in seinen verlorenen Stücken sehr stark (er hat ja auch selber seine Dramen 'Portionen von den grossen Mahlzeiten Homers' genannt). In den *Phrygern* z.B., die schon an sich eine Dramatisierung der homerischen Λύτρα waren, hat Aischylos Hektors Leichnam auf einer grossen Waage mit Gold aufwiegen lassen: das geht zurück auf die Stelle bei Homer, wo Achill zu Hektor sagt, dass er sein Leben nicht sparen würde, οὐδ' εἴ κέν σ' αὐτὸν χρυσῷ ἐρύσασθαι ἀνώγοι/Δαρδανίδης Πρίαμος (X 351 f.). Solche direkte Umsetzung von Homerischem in dramatische Handlung ist für Sophokles nicht bezeugt (allerdings wissen wir zu wenig von seiner *Nausikaa* und seinen *Niptra*): s e i n e Homernachfolge besteht in der fortwährenden Übernahme und Adaptierung einzelner homerischer Elemente. Zusammen mit seiner gegenüber Aischylos weniger barocken Ausdrucksweise hat das offenbar dazu geführt, dass die antike Kritik ihn, and nicht Aischylos, als besonders homerisch empfunden hat.

VII

R. P. Winnington-Ingram

SOPHOCLES AND WOMEN

I have chosen this title and not "Women in Sophocles"—though whether the difference will prove to be material remains to be seen.

There is something that used to be called "the woman question". In my young days in England it was focused on the vote, on political status: there were suffragists, constitutional or militant, and the militants were known as 'suffragettes'. After the First War the vote was obtained, but the question did not go away. Women still felt, with considerable reason, that they were discriminated against, treated as 'the second sex'; and so we have the Women's Liberation Movement, or Women's Lib., a phenomenon which is almost world-wide. But what relevance, you may ask, does this have to the Greek world, to Athens in the fifth century? And is there any sense in asking whether a dramatist like Sophocles had a point of view towards women *as such* and their place in society—a point of view, that is, with any interest and significance?

You will be relieved to hear that I do not propose to discuss the position of Athenian women at length. It was strictly subordinate to the male in almost every respect, legal and social. Their lives were restricted; their place was the house, the home; their primary function to raise male heirs to the family property, but also of course to spin and weave, to cook and clean, to look after the children, with or without the help of slaves. For male society they had their husbands and male relatives, when these had time to spare for them, but most of their lives was spent in the company of other women, of children and of slaves. They were uneducated and unpolitical. That is the conventional picture and, though it needs qualification at many points [1], it has enough truth to stand, both as a broad statement of the facts and as evidence for the male attitudes which it reflects. For what we do not possess is direct evidence of how the women felt. Did they resent their lowly status? Did they—the respectable married women—envy the greater freedom which seems to have been enjoyed by the higher reaches of the demi-monde? Or did a majority of women just accept their lot, grateful for the degree of protection they enjoyed under Athenian law? No doubt reactions varied according to class, intelligence and character. We cannot say, for the woman's voice is silent: Clytemnestra and Melanippe and Medea seem to speak, but it is a man who writes their lines; and the same is true of Lysistrata and Praxagora. Which brings me to my question: is there any sense in asking whether Sophocles had a point of view towards women as such and their place in society? And my answer is yes, if the same question can be asked—and, within limits, answered—of Aeschylus and Euripides.

Euripides is easy. Euripides was *sophos*, an intellectual, avant-garde, and given to trailing his coat. He reflects 'modern' movements. Let me quote Bernard Knox [2]: "There are many signs that in the intellectual ferment of late fifth-century Athens, the problem of women's role in society

[1] Cf. J. P. Gould, in *JHS* 100 (1980), 38-59.

[2] B. M. W. Knox, in *YClS* 25 (1977), 219; 222.

and the family was, like everything else, a subject for discussion and reappraisal". Melanippe's speech [3], such of it as remains, is not very significant: women are better than men, she says (which is promising!), but the evidence she gives is their expertise in household management and various religious functions; and these are hardly controversial points. Medea is more interesting [4], because she stresses the weak position of the woman in marriage; and this appeals to her Chorus of potential feminists. Faced with Creon, on the other hand, she seeks to convince him that, clever as she is thought to be, her cleverness is nothing to be feared. But she *is* clever, and her lines—again I quote Knox—are "the complaint of a woman of great intellectual capacity who finds herself excluded from the spheres of power and action". Now this is important and directs our gaze forward to Plato and backward to Aeschylus. Plato, refusing to recognise a distinction between the sexes in point of intelligence and ability, included women along with men in the selection, education and functions of the guardian class. This was the second paradox in his famous *trikumia* and the full credit for it may belong to him. It is not unlikely, however, that such a point of view was already current in the late fifth century.

That was indeed a period of 'intellectual ferment', during which the appearance of *any* idea need not surprise us too much. What, though, of 458 B.C.? What of that sturdy old Marathon-fighter Aeschylus? Leaving on one side the doubtfully authentic *PV*, treating the *Oresteia* as a single drama, it is a remarkable fact that, out of four surviving dramas, two are concerned with the place of women in society (and I believe there are traces of this theme in a third). Why this should be I have no idea, for there is no reason to

[3] To be found conveniently in D. L. Page (ed.), *Select Papyri* III: *Literary Papyri, Poetry* (London/Cambridge, Mass. 1941), p. 112.

[4] Eur. *Med.* 230 ff.; 292 ff.

suppose that the relationship of the sexes was a burning issue in the first half of the fifth century, but it is a fact. Naturally, anyone dealing with the story of the Danaids had to treat the theme of marriage. Our trilogy is incomplete, but it does seem that marriage was treated as an honourable estate to which women must be reconciled, but in which there should be a certain mutuality of respect: marriage by capture, the rape of the bride, are replaced by the persuasive power of sexual attraction working on both parties. Turning to the *Oresteia*, though, was there any compelling reason why Aeschylus should have handled the story of the house of Atreus in terms of male domination? Yet that theme runs right through the trilogy culminating in the acquittal of Orestes on Athena's preference for the male. And who threatens male domination? It is the woman of the *androboulon kear*. There was no compelling reason why Aeschylus should have given Clytemnestra this characteristic, but he did. The poet has portrayed a dangerous woman, disruptive of society, and in the outcome the necessary male prevalence is restored. But also (if I am right) he has revealed the tragic predicament of a woman of exceptional powers in a male-dominated society. An Artemisia (should one say?): and, thanks to Herodotus VIII 93, we know what the Athenian navy thought of *her*! A Medea. A potential Guardian. For the feminist case, if one may use the term, has two aspects: there is the predicament of the average wife, there is the predicament of the gifted woman debarred an outlet for her gifts.

It is time we turned to Sophocles—a Sophocles who was writing tragedies a decade before the *Oresteia* and still writing till shortly after the death of Euripides. It is time we looked at his women, though I have little new to say and can promise no sensational conclusions. (I shall, of course, avoid the 'character-sketch' and concentrate on those points which relate, specifically, to their femininity.)

And I suppose that, at the risk of raising false hopes, I should begin with Fr. 583 Pearson. In *Tereus* a female character, presumably Procne, generalizes (like Medea) about the fate of the woman in marriage—how, after an idyllic childhood, she is thrust out from her father's home to live with boring or censorious strangers, even (as in her case) with barbarians. The fragment does admittedly have a slight Euripidean smack, but there is no good reason for denying it to Sophocles. The date of *Tereus* is uncertain, though prior to 414 B.C., and one might be inclined to place it relatively late, at a period when Sophocles occasionally shows the influence of Euripidean argumentation. There is no lack of appropriateness to the dramatic situation, but we do not have the context and cannot say whether this speech bore on the total picture of the heroine. We had better turn to extant plays.

In six plays (*Philoctetes* is all-male) there are ten female characters with speaking parts. And perhaps the first thing to say is that they are all placed firmly within the context of their femininity. There are major and minor characters; and of the latter some might be described as foils insofar as it is their main function to illuminate another personage. The most obvious cases are those of Ismene in *Antigone* and Chrysothemis in *Electra*, both of whom play the submissive feminine role by contrast with a rebellious heroine. I do not wish to enter into controversy as to their relative merits and attraction, but will simply state the view that Ismene is infinitely more interesting, subtle and attractive than the time-serving Chrysothemis. I shall come back to them briefly later on.

Of course, by using words like 'interesting' and 'subtle' I am writing a gloss on the word 'foil'. Sophocles does not use mere foils. Is Tecmessa a foil to Ajax? Perhaps: who is not? But she also stands in a significant relation to the Chorus, who are obtuse and narrow-minded as she is intelligent and sensitive. A slave who was once a princess, she is one of the most attractive characters in Sophocles; and the contrast between slave and master, between hero and concubine, is brought out most clearly in her long speech of appeal at 485 ff. (one of the most complex rhetorical structures in Sophocles). I pick out one point alone. She asks him to show *aidos* towards his parents and pity towards his child: for herself, she appeals to him in terms of their sexual relationship. The appeal is prepared, subtly, at 490 ff., where, having said that she came to join him in bed (ξυνῆλθον), two lines later she invokes the bed in which he was joined to her (συνηλλάχθης). We are thus prepared for the final eloquent and touching appeal to the memory of pleasure and the obligation which it imposes, in which she finds a touchstone of nobility. It was a relationship as lacking in symmetry as that of Deianira to Heracles, not perhaps because she was a slave, but because she was a woman. When, for that matter, she is told (586) to be *sophron*—to keep her mouth shut in fact—it is addressed not to the slave but to the woman (580). Her role, as her tragedy, is all feminine. I shall have occasion to return to her, briefly.

Jocasta enters to two quarreling males, her husband and her brother, and scolds them almost as though they were naughty children. (At this point one should perhaps say that the age-difference between husband and wife is disregarded, and it is a mistake to look for *motherly* concern. Similarly, the fact that Creon was presumably a good deal older than Oedipus is, here and in *OC*, disregarded: the suggestion is rather of three co-evals sharing the palace.) She scolds them, but it is in fact the Chorus—the political Chorus, not the un-political woman—that induces Oedipus to let Creon go. When he has gone, the Chorus say to Jocasta: why don't you take Oedipus indoors? [5] And that is where the following

[5] *OT* 678 (sung in fact, not said). An interesting glimpse into the possible functions of a wife!

scene would have been played, if staging had allowed. In it and after it, her one concern is to set her husband's fears at rest. If you will allow me to quote myself: "Jocasta is governed by her affections and will use any means, whether it is denial of Apollo or [in the following scene] prayer to Apollo, if she can calm his disturbed mind". There is nothing intellectual about her (perhaps too much advertised) scepticism, except that she argues from apparent facts quite logically and comes to a conclusion which happens to be blasphemous but is consoling to her husband. (Euripides in *Phoenissae*, by some quirk of his own, made a 'sophist' of his Jocasta, as he sometimes did of incongruous characters.) No, hers is an essentially feminine role; and when the truth comes out she commits suicide in the approved feminine way—approved, I mean, by Dr Devereux! [6] We are now approaching the three great female roles: Deianira, Antigone and Electra.

I hope I need not argue against the view that Deianira is a minor character (a foil to Heracles!): it should be enough to point out that if, in a play, there is only one person who takes a tragic decision (and pays for it), then that person cannot possibly be regarded as a minor character! In any consideration of "Sophocles and women" Deianira is a crucial—and paradoxical—case. No woman in Sophocles is more firmly set in the context of her own femininity than she is. Patient of her husband's neglect, tolerant of his amours, submissive and devoted, a mother of children, she has all the merits a wife should have by the strictest standards of fifth-century convention. And yet, out of that very devotion, by an act of *tolma* (cf. 582 f.) she causes her husband's death. But her very act of *tolma* was characteristically feminine, if widely disap-

[6] G. DEVEREUX, *Tragédie et poésie grecques* (Paris 1975), ch. V. See below on Deianira.

proved—the use of a love-charm. And it arose out of a specifically feminine situation. She acts as a woman, in a domestic context, to restore her position as a woman. There was a point beyond which her tolerance could not be stretched, and with the introduction of Iole into the household—no, into the marriage-bed—that point had been reached. She departs from her ideal, whereupon her very simplicity and inexperience ensure that through sheer incompetence she will bring about the opposite of what she intended. She commits suicide. She did not hang herself as women in tragedy often do, as Jocasta did (though not Eurydice!), but stabbed herself to death upon the marriage-bed. The central unifying theme of *Trachiniae* is the power of sex, and over the play Aphrodite presides working fatally, if in different ways, upon the man and upon the woman. Upon the man, obviously: the great male hero is defeated and destroyed through his lust for Iole. But Deianira's destruction is no mere bye-product of her husband's sexuality. Female sexuality used not to be much spoken of—or written about—in polite circles. As a Greek theme, it seemed proper to Aristophanes, the excessive demands of women being a staple of Old Comedy, gross and laughable; or else it was found, viewed pathologically, in Euripides with his notorious *pornai*, who so shocked the Aristophanic Aeschylus. No wonder scholars, "anxious" (in the words of Mrs Easterling) "to make Deianira respectable", were reluctant to admit that this middle-aged wife and mother was still in love with Heracles. Yet Sophocles has provided plenty of evidence to show that she was. "Eros rules the gods as he will", she says (443 f.), "yes, and me also". It was the threat of the *mia chlaina* (539 f.) which turned the scale; and it was on the bed of Heracles that she stabbed herself to death. To have taken the sexuality of a normal woman and made it a motive force in tragedy could be one of the most original things Sophocles ever did.

Deianira acts as a woman to retrieve a domestic situation; it is a bold act, deplorable and silly, but a feminine act (at which her innocent companions of the Chorus connive). Antigone acts—and Electra proposes to act—in a public context. Both are offending against the recognized code of womanly behaviour. These are the two great 'active' heroines; and they have sometimes been used as evidence against the prevailing view about the place of women in Athenian society. If women were indeed so passive, so secluded, could they have been shown upon the stage in such dominant roles as those of Antigone and Electra (not to mention Clytemnestra!)? This was never a very good argument, I fancy. Athenians may have known less about the Bronze Age than we do, but they did know Homer and could see traces there of a more equal relationship of the sexes, a greater freedom of coming and going. Perhaps the remarkable thing, though, is how little this is reflected in tragedy, where the male reactions and assumptions are, almost exclusively, those of the fifth century. In *Ajax*, for instance, Sophocles has deliberately recalled the scene between Hector and Andromache which shows Homeric man and woman at their best and most humane: he has recalled it to contrast the attitudes of Ajax. The main point is of course that Ajax is *not* like Hector: the fact remains that his attitude to the woman is consistent with fifth-century ideas. As for coming-and-going, the Athenian audience, if they bothered to think about it at all, were intelligent enough to realise that if, thanks to the staging, all conversation had to take place in the open air, women could not participate in it without coming out-of-doors, and for that matter, if you were to have female choruses, they must be allowed to reach the palace (or whatever) and depart without male protection. The first words of Clytemnestra to Electra are: "There you are again ranging at large" (516). Electra is palace-bound, not however just because she is a woman, but because of the things she is liable to say if she gets out! That is why she is kept shut up—and in danger of worse, while the 'sensible' Chrysothemis is discreet and lives the life of a fine lady. Let us take Electra first.

In the role of Electra there are two phases (just as there are two scenes with Chrysothemis which bring out the contrast between the two women). This is of course bound up with Sophocles' masterstroke in postponing the Recognition, the movement from phase to phase being brought about by the false report of Orestes' death. In the earlier part of the play interest is concentrated (as throughout) on the heroine, but this is a phase of words and not deeds, dominated by her obsessive devotion to the memory of her father, her obsessive longing for the return of her brother, issuing first in lamentation and then, in the scene with Clytemnestra, in rancour, provocation, and threats. She has asked the Chorus (257) what else a εὐγενὴς γυνή could do, but with her mother she shows herself the termagant, the shameless woman she knows herself to have become. Her complaints of her own plight—unwed, childless—may seem a *topos* appropriate to any virgin in distress, but they are given a sharp edge by the ever-presence of Clytemnestra raising children in the bed of Aegisthus. It is an awful picture of an awful house, brilliant even by Sophoclean standards. But it is all words, and Electra never moves out of her feminine context, though within it she shows the common characteristics of a Sophoclean hero: extremism, imperviousness to argument—and unflinching courage.

The lying tale of the Paedagogus brings about a transformation in Electra. Believing that Orestes is dead, now she will act; now she will take on the male role and display the full range of a heroism—which is never put to the test. It is hard to know how much importance should be attached to that fact. Are these *more* words? Is there an element of fantasy? There is certainly a sheer lack of realism in her great speech to Chrysothemis which might justify the term. It is interesting to observe how vengeance for the father—and εὐσέβεια as a motive—drop rather into the background [7]. All the emphasis falls upon her personal grievances and humiliation: deprivation of wealth, an old age of spinsterhood. In place of which she paints a bright picture of freedom restored, a worthy marriage achieved, universal acclaim for two sisters who will be greeted wherever they go, honoured at feasts and meetings of the people—οὕνεκ' ἀνδρείας (983), for their manly courage. Fantasy perhaps, yet we can be sure she would have made the attempt and met the fate her sister dreaded.

The lack of effective action on the part of the heroine has sometimes been seen as a defect in the play, but this is due to a failure to perceive that the essence of the tragedy is not what Electra does, but what she is, what she has become, what she has been made. She usurps—or seeks to usurp—the male role. When this was done by the Aeschylean Clytemnestra it was a danger to society; when it is done by the Sophoclean Electra it is the climax of a personal tragedy.

Of all the women in extant Sophocles only two display the common characteristics of Sophoclean 'heroes' (so well defined by Bernard Knox): Electra and Antigone—so like in some respects, so unlike in others. The two plays in which they appear may have been separated by up to thirty years, but it is hard to believe that, when Sophocles wrote *Electra* he did not have *Antigone* in mind. (Indeed the Chrysothemis in the later play, not traditional to the legend, may owe her dramatic existence to the proved utility of Ismene in the earlier.) Like and unlike. Formidable women, who refuse to accept the limitation imposed by their sex: the point is made against Electra by her sister and against Antigone by hers (61 f.), but comes out more insistently in her scenes with

[7] They do not of course drop out: cf. 955 ff.; 968 f.; 980.

Creon (484 f.; 525; cf. 740 f.), for whom it is the cardinal offence that his authority is challenged by a woman. Formidable women who insist on behaving like male heroes: obstinately determined to carry their principles to the point of self-immolation. But what are those principles? In both cases it is a matter of family, of a duty thought to be dictated by kinship. In the case of Electra it is the duty to avenge, to abet Orestes and, Orestes 'dead', to carry out the deed herself. With her decision to act she seems to take over the whole scheme of male values associated with a revenge-killing.[8] Do we not feel that, as her whole personality has been degraded by the long years of grief and rancour, so by the final change of role her essential femininity is violated? In the outcome she is not called upon to strike the blow, but her horrible παῖσον, εἰ σθένεις, διπλῆν (1415) is still to come, before the play ends with the hollow triumph of the Pelopidae.

Antigone is different. *Her* duty is to bury. Now burial rites were of course, in normal circumstances, the responsibility of men, but women as mourners were closely associated with those rites, so that we can surely say that *her* heroism, unlike Electra's, is directed towards an objective proper to a woman. Her absorption in personal relationships, her indifference to politics might be regarded as characteristically feminine. It is her defiance of authority that marks her out. To what extent this insubordination would, for a fifth-century audience, have counteracted the favourable response which humanity and decency will have prompted is a complex matter which cannot be dealt with here. Certainly, her behaviour was not that of a normal woman. But what sort of a woman was she? For one thing, she was her father's daughter (471 f.). What sort of a father? We do not know,

[8] It may not be accidental that the theme of honour is reserved for this point (973 ff.), to be picked up in the following ode (1082 ff.). It is not of course the preoccupation with honour that is significant (cf. e.g. *Ant.* 502 ff.), but the means by which it is to be won.

since *OT* had not been written and we have lost the Aeschylean Oedipus. But he was ὠμός, and she is ὠμὸν γέννημα. And indeed we can see the vein of harshness in her, not least in her dealings with Ismene. Yet she says of herself in a famous line (523) that it is her nature to join in love and not in hatred: συμφιλεῖν, not συνέχθειν. The polarity of φιλία and ἔχθρα runs throughout the play, but is complicated by ambiguities: *philoi* as kin, *philoi* as friends; friendship and enmity as a political and as a personal relationship; *philia* as affection. The dead brothers were at the same time kin and bitter enemies. Antigone carried out the burial as a duty owed to kinship, but it would be absurd to deny the tone of deep affection in which she speaks of Polynices—and later of the father, mother and brother with whom she hopes to be reunited in the world below (897 ff.) [9]. Just how remarkable a hope this was has perhaps not always been recognized. The father who cursed his sons; the mother of children incestuously bred; the brothers who killed one another. The very prototype of a divided family. Yet Antigone insists, in the teeth (one might say) of normal Greek belief, that death ends all that and in the world below the family can be reunited in love. I have suggested elsewhere [10] that it is part of the obstinate heroism of Antigone to believe—to insist on believing—that the terrible past can be abolished by her act of love. This is συμφιλεῖν indeed. What, then, of Ismene who loved Antigone so much that she wished to share her death? She would not share in her heroic act, she is left out, written off, condemned to live. She is ἐχθρά, hostile to the beloved brother and thus to Antigone (93 f.). But is this not συνέχθειν? It is—and this is where the irony of Sophocles comes in, that Antigone is still the victim of the heroic

9 The lines surely imply a community of affection, if focused upon Antigone herself. I take the brother of 899 to be Polynices, not Eteocles.

10 *Sophocles. An interpretation* (Cambridge 1980), 132 f.

polarity of friends and enemies. For an all-loving Antigone we wait for *Oedipus Coloneus.*

Of this summary survey of Sophoclean women (still incomplete) no summary is possible and from it no obvious generalisation emerges. I must confess that, until I engaged upon this paper, I did not fully realise what a wide spectrum of female characters the seven (or rather six) plays present—of female characters and situations and reactions. Women in Sophocles. But Sophocles and women? That is another matter; and as so often he retreats behind the barrier of his plays, with a *noli me tangere.* "There is my play: make of it what you will." With Aeschylus and Euripides, it is possible to discern an attitude towards women as a social phenomenon—an attitude which in Aeschylus is a fundamental concern and which in Euripides is discernible from time to time amid the scatterings of his sophistication. In Sophocles, what do we find? Social assumptions, whether expressed by men like Ajax, Creon in *Antigone*, the Colonean Oedipus, or by women like the two submissive sisters, which are broadly the male-dominated assumptions of fifth-century Athens. The only women who depart from modes of behaviour proper to the female are, with the doubtful exceptions of Deianira and Clytemnestra, Antigone and Electra. I call Deianira a doubtful exception, because her one lapse from propriety is a feminine act, Clytemnestra, because her notorious crime is (apart from its effect on Electra) left largely *exo tou dramatos*, while her subsequent outrageous behaviour takes place in the domestic setting of a palace where she lives in proper subordination to her sexual partner Aegisthus. Antigone's independence is disapproved by the Chorus, shocks Ismene and infuriates Creon, but she is not in revolt against the limitations of her sex, which she chooses to disregard in her determination to carry out a duty that her feminine instincts dictate; her very indifference to 'politics' is characteristically feminine. Electra does indeed decide to usurp the male role of violent avenger, but this is part of her personal tragedy and is not represented as a threat to society.

Perhaps, however, there is another angle from which the subject can be approached. We are in trouble, of course, with differences of vocabulary. It makes sense for us to ask if women have characteristic 'virtues'. Ask a Greek about the *arete* or *aretai* of women, and he has no difficulty in answering. *Arete* is being good at something: women are good (if they are) at household management and so on, good perhaps at doing what their husbands told them. (*Arete* is, in any case, not a useful word in the criticism of Sophocles: he uses it so seldom and in such a narrow sense.) We use 'virtue' in a wider sense. To take another word (which the classical Greeks did not use at all), we can speak of women as having a 'heroism' of their own. I have been reading an interesting paper by Mary Lefkowitz on "female heroism" [11]. First in Homer and then in Euripides, she seeks to identify, along with the active—and essentially destructive—heroism of men, a passive heroism imposed upon women by the conditions of their existence. It is not merely, however, that those conditions demand from them a courage and endurance to which Greek men might well pay tribute. It is also that the very nature of their experience gives them an insight into the working of things denied to their active 'heroic' male partners—gives to the weak what is denied to the strong, to old Priam and the Trojan women what is denied to Hector. I hope I have not distorted Ms Lefkowitz's argument. Does it work with Sophocles? Does it work with Tecmessa? Yes, in the sense that she has a *sophrosune*—an acceptance of her destiny, the capacity to make a new life—denied to a heroic

[11] Mary R. LEFKOWITZ, "L'héroïsme de la femme", in *Bulletin de l'Association Guillaume Budé* 1981, 3, 284-92. English version in *Heroines and hysterics* (London 1981), 1-11.

Ajax and calculated to evoke a sympathy which he harshly forbids. But, brightly though her intelligence and sensibility shine by contrast with a singularly obtuse Chorus, it has its limitations. It is to Antigone that we must look—not to the famous Antigone, but to that namesake who has so much better claim that it is her nature to join in love and not in hatred.

When Ismene arrives at Colonus, Oedipus proceeds to grumble away about the neglect of his sons: they are like Egyptian men who keep the home while the women go out and do the hard work. And indeed Ismene has just made, not for the first time, a hazardous journey attended by a solitary faithful male slave. Antigone has undergone every hardship, and, although she has been in the company of her natural male protector, it is she who has to look after him (γεροντaγωγεῖν, 348) and we see her doing it to the best of her ability. The normal sex-roles are indeed up to a point reversed, and yet there is nothing essentially unfeminine in the behaviour of the daughters. Ismene's part is brief and her role in the story left rather vague. Antigone is with us from beginning to end of a play which in fact ends, ironically, by foreshadowing her death. She is an important character. In what does her function consist? To tend, to guide, to inform the blind man. To advise and to persuade. The crucial case is 1181 ff. Oedipus does not expect long speeches from a girl (1115 f.) "At your age a short speech is enough". "I may be young", says Antigone, 65 lines later, "but take my advice"—and goes on to make her longest speech in the play. He takes it (it is the advice of Theseus too). He takes it in respect of granting audience to Polynices. But Antigone's words went far deeper that that: she set out the reasons why he should *not* retaliate, why he should *not* give way to his *thumos*, why in effect he should *not* behave like the *heros* he is about to become. With those scholars who hold that, being a woman, she was incapable of appreciating the true nature of divine justice, etc. etc., I am so completely out of sympathy that I prefer not to argue the case, but will merely state that the lesson she the woman tries to teach is one which he the man is not capable of understanding. She fails to persuade—fails with the Chorus, fails with her father, fails with Polynices, and, in a final attempt at reconciliation, goes to her death.

Do we go on to say that Sophocles sees in women, with their patient suffering and their insight into the cruel consequences of male heroic codes, with their pity, with their too often vain attempts to pit persuasion against violence, a mitigation of tragedy which it is their function, supremely, to provide? It would be nice to believe it, but, alas, in Sophocles things are seldom so simple. Pity and persuasion are cardinal themes in Sophocles, but they are not monopolised by women. Is there any essential difference, other than context and mode, between female persuaders like Tecmessa and the Colonean Antigone on the one hand and male persuaders like Odysseus (in *Ajax*) and Neoptolemus on the other. As for pity, there are characters who are capable of it and characters who are not. Deianira has this capacity, and so does the Colonean Antigone: but is there a significant difference between them and the Odysseus who pitied Ajax or the young Neoptolemus, not yet the savage that killed Priam at the altar, who pitied Philoctetes, sought to persuade him and, when he failed, was ready to take him home? Again, Sophocles says: "Look at the play; I have told you all you need to know".

DISCUSSION

M. Taplin: On the 'women problem' in Aeschylus: it may have been only later in the century that this become an open subject for discussion, but the argument of John Gould (*art. cit.*) can surely apply to the earlier period—that drama would present men's anxieties and 'nightmares', even those which had not been explicitly formulated.

M. Knox: This fact of the explosive potential in the situation of women finds remarkable expression in the central stasimon of the *Choephoroe* πολλὰ μὲν γᾶ τρέφει etc. (585 ff.) where the chorus recall the daughter of Thestios, who killed her son, the daughter of Nisos, who killed her father, and the women of Lemnos, who massacred their husbands.

M. Winnington-Ingram: I agree that fear, along with contempt, was a component of male reactions. I am only surprised that it should be dealt with so specifically and on such a scale (and with a degree of sympathy for the woman) by Aeschyus so early in the century.

M. Taplin: I feel that you attributed the presentation of women outside the house too much to mere dramaturgic necessity and did not do justice to the dramatic use made of this. For example, at the end of her dispute with Chrysothemis, Electra vows that she will never go back inside to female subservience ἀλλ' εἴσιθ'. οὔ σοι μὴ μεθέψομαί ποτε (1052). It is even more telling when, at the end of the prologue of *Antigone*, Ismene goes back into the house where women belong, while Antigone goes off by an *eisodos*, off into the dangerous, masculine world outside.

It is worth noting that Clytemnestra's first word of rebuke to Electra at *El.* 516 ἀνειμένη, 'given free rein', occurs also at *Ant.* 579 where Creon says (Dawe's text) ἐκ δὲ τοῦδε χρὴ / γυναῖκας εἶναι τάσδε μηδ' ἀνειμένας.

M. Winnington-Ingram: I fully accept the point.

M. Radt: Here ἀνειμένας even seems to function as a substantival opposite to γυναῖκας—if, that is, one accepts with Dawe the reading ἐκ δὲ τοῦδε: the *varia lectio* and *lectio difficilior* ἐκ δὲ τᾶσδε (which is also in the Leiden palimpsest, a fact not mentioned by Dawe) strongly favours, I think, Engelmann's ἐκδέτας δὲ (which Dain-Mazon put into the text).

Mme de Romilly: J'aimerais soulever une question qui touche à des problèmes dont je m'occupe. Si l'on considère non pas la condition féminine et la façon dont des femmes peuvent montrer des traits inhabituels d'héroïsme, mais l'évolution même de l'idéal héroïque, il est frappant de voir que, dans les œuvres conservées, Sophocle est le premier à avoir incarné l'héroïsme en des femmes. Le grec à l'origine n'avait pas de mot pour désigner une 'héroïne', et l'héroïsme était essentiellement guerrier. Puis l'idéal héroïque évolue; les héros homériques ne sont plus acceptés sans réserve par le Ve siècle; et cela se voit chez Sophocle. Mais, à ce moment-là, l'acte héroïque est confié à des êtres faibles, normalement incapables d'agir. Il relève d'un *courage moral intérieur.* Chez Euripide, il s'agira d'êtres qui n'agissent même plus, mais dont l'héroïsme consiste à accepter librement une mort presque inévitable. La place faite par Sophocle à l'héroïsme féminin marque un moment important, plus intéressant encore du point de vue des valeurs morales que du point de vue de la société.

M. Winnington-Ingram: Part of the difficulty is that 'heroism' is a modern concept. There was certainly a shift in moral values, a movement away from an uncritical admiration of traditional ἀρετή, persistent though the old values were. Both in Aeschylus and in Sophocles the tragedy springs largely from the old codes, which are shown to involve tragic consequences. Both Antigone and Electra accept and act on such a code: Electra in respect of violent retaliation, Antigone in respect of the φιλία-ἔχθρα polarity. In what way is their 'heroism' specifically feminine? Except, perhaps, that such *courage moral intérieur* was not to be expected from a woman? Courage in meeting disaster is another matter, and we see it particularly in some of the women in Euripides, but also in the Aeschylean Cassandra and in Tecmessa. This is a moral value, but not one which is primarily exemplified in the active heroines.

M. Steiner: A question and a remark:

a) Would you agree that in Sophocles' *Antigone* the status of the heroine as child/sister of Oedipus is touched on only very obliquely, and that this profound tact is essential to the economy and meaning of the play?

b) But what of the relation to Eteocles of this woman committed to φιλία? From the Renaissance on, many variants are written and felt in the light of Antigone's preference of Polynices. Master readers and dramatists have oriented their sense of Antigone's problematic and 'dark' nature around this motif (Rotrou, Racine etc. . .). Sophocles gives little guidance. Even Antigone's final reference to Eteocles is somewhat unclear. What, however, are we to feel?

M. Seidensticker: Es scheint mir, dass die von Ihnen so überzeugend herausgearbeitete tiefe Zuneigung Antigones zu Polyneikes auch das viel diskutierte Problem der Doppelbestattung erklären hilft. Das wunderbare Bild, dass Antigone an der vom Staub gereinigten Leiche des Bruders aufjammert wie eine Vogelmutter, die ihr Nest leer findet (423 ff.), stärkt nicht nur Ihre Interpretation, sondern legt auch den Schluss nahe, dass es die Liebe zu ihrem Bruder war, die Antigone noch einmal zu ihm zurückgetrieben hat (diese These ist kürzlich von G. Held in einer noch unpublizierten Dissertation (Berkeley) mit Nachdruck vertreten worden).

M. Winnington-Ingram:

a) I agree.

b) This is one of the questions which Sophocles has left in obscurity. If he has not told us how to feel, it is not for me to do so! Antigone's deep affection for Polynices, on the other hand, emerges clearly from the play. In which connection M. Seidensticker does well to call attention to the significance of *Ant.* 423 ff.

M. Irigoin: Au v. 902, νῦν δέ porte non pas sur Polynice, interpellé au vocatif malgré sa mort, mais sur τοιάδ' ἄρνυμαι: «Et aujourd'hui, voilà quelle récompense je reçois pour avoir cherché à t'ensevelir».

Ce qui me semble faire difficulté, c'est plutôt le participe présent περιστέλλουσα (v. 903), auquel R. Dawe, dans l'apparat critique de son édition, propose de substituer l'aoriste περιστείλασα. Cet aoriste, qui reprend les aoristes des vers précédents (ἔλουσα, κἀκόσμησα ... ἔδωκα), ne fait que souligner, dans une répétition, le soin qu'Antigone a pris du cadavre de Polynice. En revanche, si l'on garde le participe présent (équivalant à un indicatif imparfait *de conatu*), le cas de Polynice se trouve opposé à celui des trois autres morts (θανόντας ... ὑμᾶς) et κασίγνητον κάρα doit alors désigner Etéocle. Personnellement, je ne corrigerais pas le texte et me rallierais à cette dernière interprétation.

M. Knox: If κασίγνητον κάρα at *Ant.* 899 refers to Polynices, the rhetorical sequence is disturbed: νῦν δέ (902) seems to introduce a contrast, which is impossible if Polynices has already been referred to. The sequence is: father, mother, brother (Eteocles)—since I carried out the funeral rites for you (ὑμᾶς). But now, Polynices, trying to cover (περιστέλλουσα) your body, here are my wages. Furthermore ἔλουσα (901) cannot refer to Polynices: she could indeed claim κἀκόσμησα κἀπιτυμβίους χοὰς ἔδωκα but the washing of the corpse, an important part of the funeral ritus, she could not even attempt.

Second thoughts. According to 23-25 Eteocles was buried with all honors due to the dead by Creon but the phrase ὡς λέγουσι must mean that Antigone was not present. So it looks as if κασίγνητον κάρα must indeed refer to Polynices and not to Eteocles as the scholiast and most editors suggest.

M. Steiner: When we think of Antigone's 'special relation' to Polynices, and of the symbolism of the second burial, how costly does it become to exclude Freudian readings?

M. Taplin: In the final scene of *Seven against Thebes*, as we have it, one half of the chorus goes with Antigone to bury Polynices. It is implicitly clear that Ismene goes with the other hemichorus and the corpse of Eteocles. For myself, I have no doubt that this scene was written *after* Sophocles' *Antigone*.

In her report of Eteocles' burial at *Ant.* 23-5, Antigone's parenthesis ὡς λέγουσι clearly implies that she herself did *not* participate.

Mme de Romilly: L'insistance du vers 899 (σοί, κασίγνητον κάρα), alors qu'un mot aurait suffi, suggérerait plutôt Polynice; mais l'indication est mince et laisse place au doute.

M. Winnington-Ingram: On the matter of 897 ff. I can only state one side of the case as follows:

(i) Without indication to the contrary, κασίγνητον κάρα in this play can only refer to the brother who has been so prominent in it.

(ii) ὑμᾶς in 900 cannot include Eteocles: his burial has indeed taken place (217 ff.), but Antigone knows of it only by hearsay.

(iii) Nor can it include Polynices. In fact the only members of the family for whom Antigone had been in a position to carry out the whole operation were the father and the mother.

(iv) Eteocles is left out!

M. Taplin: I wonder if you are rather too ready to excuse Deianeira in *Trach.* for her 'feminine crime'. The way that she has kept the monstrous potion for all those years in her own dark closet is sinister.

M. Winnington-Ingram: It *is* sinister—this bomb lying in the dark all those years waiting to be detonated. But I should not regard it as an act of sinister intention.

M. Knox: Love charms were evidently something easily procurable in Athens, as we learn from the Antiphon speech Κατὰ τῆς μητρυιᾶς, a case parallel to the action of *Trachiniae*—a poison administered under the impression it was a love-potion.

M. Winnington-Ingram: Comtemporary reactions to the use of love-charms may well have been ambivalent, but Deianeira seems to have had a rather bad conscience about it. What a pity the Nurse was not there to advise her!

M. Knox: I would like to take issue with your picture of Jocasta, whose scepticism, you say, has been exaggerated. It is perfectly true that she shifts her ground to suit her purpose, which is to put Oedipus' mind at ease—she says first that the oracle came only from Apollo's priests, then that it came from the god himself, and so on. But she does this with such unscrupulous flexibility (and she is the first to dismiss the divine oracles—ὦ θεῶν μαντεύματα, ἵν' ἐστέ · 946-7), that, in spite of her prayer to Apollo (911 ff.) she is certainly the spokesman for disbelief in the central section of the play. Furthermore, she is given three lines (977 ff.) which are the most uncompromising claim that the universe is governed by blind chance to be found anywhere in fifth century literature.

M. Winnington-Ingram: I think my point that Jocasta is essentially unintellectual, being governed by her emotion towards Oedipus, will stand. I agree, however, that the issue of scepticism is important for Sophocles and accept M. Knox's criticism if I seem to underestimate it. Jocasta's transition from the apparent failure of one oracle to the sweeping generalization of 977 ff. is facile. What is far more significant, however, is that the Chorus at 863 ff., esp. 897 ff., are desperately anxious not to make such a transition—and desperately afraid that they might have to make it.

Mme de Romilly: Je voudrais présenter une suggestion et poser une question. La suggestion est relative à Chrysothémis. M. Winnington-Ingram a parlé d'une commodité dramatique, employée avec succès dans *Antigone*; je pense qu'il s'y joint une autre fonction: Sophocle, contrairement à Eschyle, aime présenter les réactions, les règles de conduite, les mobiles, auxquels obéissent les personnages. Il ne pratique pas encore l'expression de soi dans le monologue; aussi aime-t-il opposer les personnages, non seulement pour faire ressortir les contrastes, mais pour leur donner l'occasion de s'expliquer et de se justifier: Sophocle est le premier dans les tragédies conservées à avoir introduit la 'nourrice' comme confidente pour ces explications. Une sœur permet à la fois le contraste et la confidence.

La question, elle, a trait aux femmes amoureuses et au mépris de Jason, dans *Médée*, pour ces femmes toujours occupées de leur lit et de leurs amours. Il est de fait que les grandes descriptions de passion que nous avons dans la tragédie sont relatives à des femmes. Cela représente-t-il une attitude normale dans la société athénienne? Cela pourrait avoir un rapport avec l'orientation des scènes relatives à Déjanire ou Clytemnestre — scènes cependant très discrètes encore, et simplement allusives.

M. Taplin: Heracles' susceptibility to *Eros* is very important in *Trach.*; but it is true that he is not presented on stage as suffering from *Eros*, but from its consequences.

Euripides presented Perseus as falling in love at first sight in his *Andromeda* of 412 B.C. To judge by the parody in *Thesmophoriazousae* next year this was regarded as sentimental.

M. Winnington-Ingram: Certainly the use of character-contrasts is a favourite technique of Sophocles for the revelation of character and motive, as is the use of dialogue arising naturally from the situation. A pair of sisters is not, however, the only possibility. All I am suggesting is that, having used it successfully in one play, he was the more inclined to use it in another. (Sophocles never hesitated to repeat a dramatic device, but never used one twice to precisely the same effect.)

The other question is difficult to answer in general terms. No doubt it was a common (and cheap) male diatribe against women that 'they think of nothing but sex, sex, sex'! There is no description of Deianira's passion (contr. e.g. Fr. 474 Pearson), which is not a matter of the *coup de foudre* (contr. e.g. Phaedra), but an intense and long-continuing passionate physical relationship with one man, which reveals itself only through her actions and the occasional revealing word.

M. Irigoin: Les deux phases que M. Winnington-Ingram distingue et oppose dans le comportement d'Electre avant et après l'annonce de la mort d'Oreste, correspondent à la division de la tragédie en deux grands blocs — les deux premiers épisodes d'une part, les trois derniers de l'autre — que j'ai proposée (voir *supra* pp. 53-54) en tenant compte uniquement de la structure numérique de la tragédie (528 trimètres [12 × 44] et 480 trimètres [12 × 40]).

M. Taplin: The dramatic technique of having Electra outside while the murder is going on inside is unusual. It makes us feel that she is all but enacting it before our eyes.

M. Seidensticker: Mein Eindruck vom Ende der *Elektra* ist, dass Sophokles sie mit dem furchtbaren Schrei: παῖσον, εἰ σθένεις, διπλῆν (1415) gleichsam doch zur Mittäterin macht (die sie auch bei Euripides ist). Der zweite Schlag ist ihr Schlag! Die Szene ist einerseits die durchaus typische Form der Repräsentation schrecklicher hinterszenischer Ereignisse auf der Bühne, zugleich aber doch singulär in der wilden 'aktiven' Teilnahme einer Bühnenperson an der hinterszenischen Tat, auf die sonst nur reagiert wird.

M. Winnington-Ingram: On the 'second-phase' Electra, I note in particular the remarks of Seidensticker and Taplin on the final scene, with its παῖσον, εἰ σθένεις, διπλῆν on which M. Seidensticker remarks, attractively, that "the second blow is her blow". In fact she comes as near to actual participation in the murder as was possible without that physical proximity which we have in Euripides. We h e a r of that when the murderers come out. The Sophoclean technique of bringing her outside may be more subtle, since (as M. Taplin says) "she is all but enacting the murder before our eyes".

INDEX LOCORUM

A. Sophocles *

Ajax: 7, 10, 13, 15-6, 18-9, 23, 26, 33, 37, 43, 50, 59, 61, 108-9, 115, 118, 120, 122, 125-6, 128, 130-1, 133, 138-40, 142-6, 149-52, 172, 194, 212, 223-4, 226, 237, 241, 246-9.

44: 11 / 89 sqq.: 132 / 98: 128 / 100: 128 / 131: 227 / 148 sqq.: 130 / 193 sqq.: 130 / 196 sqq.: 130 / 201 sqq.: 119 / 211-212: 134 / 254: 137 / 257-258: 126 / 263-281: 62 / 271 sqq.: 119 / 275: 126 / 284: 152 / 284-330: 152 / 305 sqq.: 153 / 306: 126 / 308: 127 / 308-311: 127, 153 / 311-317: 153 / 316-317: 127 / 317 sqq.: 153 / 321-322: 153 / 323 sqq.: 127 / 325-333: 153 / 326: 111 / 327: 62 / 333: 62 / 336: 62 / 339: 62 / 346: 126 / 346 sqq.: 119 / 351-353: 129 / 356 sqq.: 126 / 361: 130, 133, 135 / 362: 142 / 364-393: 42 / 364 sqq.: 126, 133 / 367: 139 / 382: 139 / 387-391: 138 / 387 sqq.: 135 / 394-395: 135 / 394-429: 42 / 398-400: 132-3 / 401-403: 132 / 403-404: 129 / 407: 33 / 408-409: 137 / 412 sqq.: 134 / 430-480: 152 / 434 sqq.: 133 / 439-440: 145 / 445-446: 128 / 450-453: 132 / 454: 139 / 457-459: 133 / 458: 130 / 460 sqq.: 129, 138 / 462 sqq.: 133 / 466 sqq.: 129, 137, 140 / 470-472: 139 / 473 sqq.: 139 / 479-480: 135 / 480: 152 / 480-484: 62 / 485 sqq.: 238 / 490 sqq.: 238 / 491: 134 / 493: 134, 238 / 512: 201 / 520-524: 134 / 548-549: 138 / 550-551: 222 / 554 b: 62 / 559: 132, 134 / 567 sqq.: 134 / 571: 62 / 580: 238 / 585-595: 150 / 586: 238 / 589-590: 132, 139 / 609 sqq.: 142 / 615-616: 131 / 646: 152 / 646-653: 136 / 646-692: 152 / 646 sqq.: 136 / 649: 149 / 651: 150 / 654 sqq.: 135 / 656: 139 / 661 sqq.: 134 / 684 sqq.: 150 / 692: 151 / 693 sqq.: 136 / 719 sqq.: 130 / 726: 11 / 737: 62 / 749 sqq.: 130 / 758 sqq.: 201 / 762 sqq.: 132 / 805-806: 151 / 807-808: 136 / 808: 134 / 812: 62 / 813 sqq.: 151 / 814: 151 / 815: 151 / 815-865: 117, 152 / 815 sqq.: 212 / 817-818: 134 / 835: 150 / 835-844: 140, 150 / 839-842: 62 / 843-844: 134 / 844: 10-1 / 845 sqq.: 134 / 846 sqq.:

149 / 854 sqq.: 134 / 865: 111, 151-2 / 874-878: 151 / 891 sqq.: 151 / 896: 214 / 902: 142 / 905: 142 / 911 sqq.: 136 / 925: 142 / 925 sqq.: 130 / 955 sqq.: 139 / 961 sqq.: 139-140 / 974: 62 / 982-983: 142 / 988-989: 139 / 992: 152 / 992-1039: 152 / 1002: 152 / 1008 sqq.: 138, 224 / 1024 sqq.: 134 / 1042-1043: 139 / 1055: 11, 33 / 1062: 62 / 1064: 17 / 1064-1065: 12 / 1067: 12-3 / 1069-1070: 131 / 1071-1072: 11 / 1073-1076: 11 / 1081 sqq.: 11 / 1084: 11 / 1087-1088: 128, 131 / 1135-1137: 128 / 1136: 128 / 1170: 142 / 1237: 13 / 1238 sqq.: 128 / 1246-1247: 11 / 1258: 12 / 1266-1271: 62 / 1291-1294: 62 / 1305: 62 / 1318-1331: 45 / 1318-1373: 45 / 1332-1345: 45 / 1340-1341: 12, 129 / 1346-1373: 45 / 1392: 17.

Antigone: 10, 13, 15-6, 18, 23, 26, 28, 30, 32-4, 36, 41, 50, 59, 77-93, 95, 97-9, 102-4, 111, 115, 118, 120, 123, 139, 146, 149, 172-3, 179, 195, 237, 243, 246, 249-50, 252-3, 255.

8: 13 / 23-25: 253 / 27: 13 / 32: 13 / 34: 13 / 36: 13 / 44: 13 / 73 sqq.: 123 / 79: 13 / 122: 13 / 131: 13 / 141: 13 / 160: 13 / 162-163: 14 / 182-183: 87 / 189-190: 14 / 203: 13 / 209-210: 14 / 217 sqq.: 254 / 249 sqq.: 165 / 285-286: 13 / 332 sqq.: 31 / 353 sqq.: 31 / 360: 31 / 370: 30-1 / 407 sqq.: 165 / 423 sqq.: 252 / 471-472: 244 / 484-485: 244 / 502 sqq.: 244 / 523: 245 / 524-525: 123 / 525: 244 / 555: 123 / 569: 88 / 578 sqq.: 101 / 579: 250 / 581: 101 / 586-592: 209 / 626 sqq.: 125 / 631-765: 43, 66 / 632 sqq.: 119 / 635: 87 / 639-647: 87 / 639-680: 43 / 671: 26 / 683-723: 43 / 683 sqq.: 33 / 690: 44 / 740-741: 244 / 751: 123 / 760 sqq.: 120 / 766: 115 / 771: 101 / 773-774: 112 / 773 sqq.: 165 / 781: 101 / 781 sqq.: 216 / 802 sqq.: 101 / 806 sqq.: 119, 123, 134 / 821: 124 / 821-822: 112 / 843: 16 / 844-849: 16 / 846: 16 / 849: 123 / 858 sqq.: 124 / 887: 112 / 897 sqq.: 123, 245, 254 / 899: 245, 253-4 / 900: 254 / 901: 253 / 902: 252-3 / 903: 253 / 905-907: 101 / 907: 16 / 919: 112 / 941: 100, 124 / 993-995: 121 / 1015: 15-6 / 1016: 13 / 1068 sqq.: 113 / 1080 sqq.: 16 / 1083: 13 / 1155-1171: 31 / 1155 sqq.: 109 / 1158-1159: 227 / 1177: 122 / 1180 sqq.: 119 / 1196 sqq.: 165 / 1199-1200: 31 / 1204 sqq.: 165 / 1206: 115 / 1220-1222: 110-1 / 1224: 115 / 1224-1225: 116, 123 / 1225: 122 / 1231-

1239: 110 / 1231 sqq.: 115 / 1234: 142 / 1236 sqq.: 123 / 1241: 142 / 1244-1245: 115 / 1250: 142 / 1253 sqq.: 115 / 1278 sqq.: 109 / 1283: 142 / 1300: 142 / 1301: 113 / 1301-1305: 110, 121 / 1302-1305: 116 / 1303: 121 / 1305: 115, 122 / 1329 sqq.: 108.

Electra: 7, 8, 10, 28-9, 35-7, 41-2, 47, 54, 56-7, 59, 62-4, 67, 69, 70, 163-4, 176, 178, 194, 202, 211, 237, 242-4, 246-7, 256-7.

1-22: 52 / 1-85: 51, 53 / 13: 214 / 23-76: 52 / 54: 213 / 61-62: 243 / 77: 51, 54 / 86: 42 / 86-120: 42 / 88-89: 42 / 103: 42 / 103-106: 42 / 105-106: 42 / 115: 42 / 185-192: 176 / 251-327: 53 / 251-471: 53 / 257: 242 / 328-384: 44 / 328-471: 44, 47, 53 / 338: 8 / 339-340: 8 / 378 sqq.: 108 / 385-414: 44 / 415-471: 44 / 516: 241, 250 / 516-551: 48 / 516-611: 49 / 516-629: 49 / 516-659: 48, 53 / 516-822: 48, 53 / 552-557: 48 / 558-609: 48 / 590: 17 / 610-611: 49 / 610-633: 48 / 612-659: 49 / 630: 49 / 630-659: 49 / 634-659: 48 / 660-679: 49 / 660-803: 48-9, 53 / 680-763: 49, 52 / 764-803: 49 / 804-822: 48, 53 / 871-1057: 50, 54 / 892-919: 50 / 947-989: 50 / 955 sqq.: 243 / 968-969: 243 / 970: 8 / 973 sqq.: 244 / 978: 8 / 980: 243 / 982: 8 / 983: 243 / 992-1014: 50 / 1015-1057: 50 / 1023-1049: 50 / 1052: 250 / 1082 sqq.: 244 / 1098-1125: 45 / 1098-1231: 45, 50, 54 / 1098-1383: 54 / 1112: 45 / 1126-1170: 46 / 1160-1162: 46, 54 / 1165 sqq.: 108 / 1171-1175: 46 / 1176-1219: 46 / 1209-1210: 46 / 1220-1226: 46 / 1222-1223: 46 / 1227: 8 / 1227-1231: 46 / 1232-1287: 50, 54 / 1256: 8 / 1288-1325: 50, 54 / 1291: 214 / 1300: 8 / 1326-1338: 50 / 1326-1383: 50, 54 / 1339-1345: 51 / 1346-1353: 51 / 1354-1363: 51 / 1364-1375: 51 / 1376-1383: 51 / 1398-1441: 42, 54 / 1398-1510: 54 / 1413: 8 / 1415: 244, 257 / 1442-1465: 51, 54 / 1442-1507: 51 / 1466-1507: 51, 54 / 1497-1498: 164 / 1508-1510: 9.

Oedipus Coloneus: 19, 25, 28, 33, 35-6, 40-1, 57, 72-3, 78, 155, 157-8, 163, 172, 175, 178, 181-2, 195, 238, 246, 248.

1-116: 58 / 37: 183 / 39: 183 / 42: 24 / 45: 22 / 54: 175 / 92-93: 22 / 101 sqq.: 108 / 108: 24 / 167: 183 / 206: 22 / 226: 24 / 254-323: 58 / 254-509: 58 / 315: 58 / 318: 58 / 324-509: 58 / 348: 248 / 374-375: 160 / 379 sqq.: 22 / 396 sqq.: 159 / 428: 22 / 432: 22 / 433-444: 172 / 438: 172 / 440: 22 / 441: 172 / 455 sqq.: 159 / 460: 24 /

463: 24 / 510 sqq.: 73 / 525-526: 23, 34 / 539-541: 23 / 539 sqq.: 34 / 549: 175 / 549-667: 58 / 590: 24 / 592: 24 / 612-613: 24 / 619 sqq.: 25 / 627: 2 / 637: 21, 24 / 644: 23 / 646: 23 / 653 sqq.: 159 / 667: 159, 175 / 720-723: 160 / 720-832: 58 / 720-1043: 58 / 737-738: 23 / 757-760: 23 / 765-771: 172 / 768: 172 / 770: 17, 22 / 833: 24 / 844-875: 58 / 849-850: 23 / 887: 159 / 887-890: 59 / 891-1043: 58 / 919 sqq.: 26 / 1096: 176 / 1096-1210: 58 / 1115-1116: 248 / 1150: 175-6 / 1156: 21, 175-6 / 1156 sqq.: 159 / 1158: 176 / 1181-1203: 160 / 1181 sqq.: 248 / 1249-1253: 160 / 1249-1446: 58 / 1249-1555: 58 / 1249 sqq.: 159 / 1254: 158 / 1257: 17 / 1271: 58 / 1285-1288: 159 / 1292-1296: 160 / 1301-1325: 160 / 1308-1325: 160 / 1313-1322: 160 / 1333: 23 / 1342-1343: 23 / 1357: 22 / 1360 sqq.: 33 / 1383: 161 / 1393: 161 / 1398: 161, 176 / 1400: 161 / 1405-1413: 162 / 1422-1423: 160 / 1432-1435: 161 / 1435: 162 / 1436: 161 / 1446: 72 / 1447-1499: 41-2, 58, 72-4 / 1500: 72 / 1500-1555: 58 / 1508-1509: 25 / 1533-1534: 25 / 1555: 183 / 1579-1669: 58 / 1579-1779: 58 / 1592: 182 / 1606: 182 / 1626-1628: 21, 25 / 1627: 182 / 1634-1635: 162 / 1769 sqq.: 162.

Oedipus Tyrannus: 10, 16-8, 26, 30, 34, 40-1, 59, 73, 78, 110-1, 118-9, 121, 147, 155-6, 163, 166, 169-74, 177-8, 181-2, 195, 238-9, 245, 254.

35-36: 168 / 62-64: 17 / 93: 17 / 193-194: 213 / 258 sqq.: 168 / 297-379: 46 / 297-462: 46, 66 / 322: 17 / 331: 17-8 / 340: 18 / 379: 46 / 380-462: 46 / 386: 17-8 / 396: 168 / 399: 17-8 / 417-419: 170 / 420-423: 167 / 422: 167 / 443: 18 / 452-453: 172 / 452-454: 167 / 455-456: 170 / 627: 18 / 629: 18 / 678: 238 / 707 sqq.: 222 / 717-718: 168 / 718-719: 125 / 729 sqq.: 168 / 733: 181 / 758-764: 167 / 760 sqq.: 180 / 761: 180 / 774 sqq.: 168 / 863 sqq.: 255 / 897 sqq.: 255 / 911 sqq.: 255 / 946-947: 255 / 977 sqq.: 255 / 1000: 22 / 1016 sqq.: 119 / 1025 sqq.: 168 / 1026: 119 / 1031: 175 / 1031-1035: 175 / 1031-1036: 119, 125 / 1031 sqq.: 155 / 1033: 175 / 1038 sqq.: 168 / 1040: 119 / 1042-1044: 119 / 1056 sqq.: 120 / 1062-1063: 120 / 1068-1069: 120 / 1073-1074: 115 / 1086 sqq.: 168 / 1164: 168 / 1171-1172: 168 / 1183: 148 / 1207-1210: 168 / 1223-1231: 167 / 1223 sqq.: 109 / 1236: 142 / 1240: 142 / 1241: 115 / 1241-1250: 110 / 1241 sqq.: 167 / 1244: 112, 115 / 1245-1250: 116, 121 /

1251: 111 / 1251 sqq.: 111 / 1255: 148 / 1260 sqq.: 167 / 1261-1262: 112 / 1263-1267: 110 / 1267: 142 / 1275: 122 / 1290-1291: 170 / 1340-1344: 170 / 1367 sqq.: 111 / 1369-1390: 169 / 1369-1415: 169 / 1371-1374: 148 / 1378-1379: 18 / 1381-1382: 170 / 1391-1393: 169 / 1394-1397: 169 / 1398-1401: 169 / 1402: 169 / 1403-1408: 169 / 1403 sqq.: 169 / 1410-1411: 170 / 1410-1412: 169 / 1422-1445: 171 / 1424 sqq.: 178 / 1436-1437: 170 / 1438-1439: 171 / 1449-1458: 170 / 1452: 170 / 1455-1457: 179 / 1455 sqq.: 178 / 1515-1523: 171 / 1515-1530: 59, 171 / 1518: 171 / 1521: 171 / 1522-1523: 173 / 1524-1530: 173.

Philoctetes: 7, 19, 25, 28, 33, 36, 54, 56-7, 59, 63-4, 67, 69, 72-3, 163-4, 166, 177-8, 182-3, 194, 211, 237.

1-134: 55-6 / 14: 19 / 66-67: 19 / 111: 19 / 112: 19 / 119: 19 / 201-219: 177 / 210: 177 / 211: 165 / 219: 55, 164 / 219-390: 55-6 / 219-541: 56-7 / 219-675: 55-6 / 257: 17 / 387: 33 / 391-402: 56 / 403-506: 55-6 / 437: 165 / 507-518: 56 / 519-541: 55 / 519-675: 55-6 / 534: 164 / 542: 56 / 542-627: 55-6 / 600: 17 / 627: 56 / 628-675: 55-6 / 676 sqq.: 73 / 730-826: 55, 57 / 732: 55 / 736: 55 / 739: 55 / 747 sqq.: 108 / 751: 55 / 782: 55 / 785: 55 / 787: 55 / 790: 55 / 796: 55 / 797 sqq.: 108 / 804: 55 / 827-864: 72 / 839-842: 72 / 865-973: 55-6 / 865-1080: 55 / 936 sqq.: 165 / 952 sqq.: 165 / 974-1080: 55-6 / 999 sqq.: 108, 113 / 1018: 22 / 1081 sqq.: 165 / 1146 sqq.: 165 / 1203 sqq.: 108 / 1217: 164-5 / 1218-1262: 55-6 / 1218-1471: 55-7 / 1226: 33 / 1243: 33 / 1243 sqq.: 19 / 1251 bis: 55 / 1258: 19 / 1263-1292: 55-6 / 1293-1307: 55-6 / 1294: 20, 33 / 1308-1401: 55-6 / 1310-1313: 165 / 1339: 20 / 1348 sqq.: 108 / 1365 a: 55, 57 / 1365 b: 55, 57 / 1390: 17 / 1391: 17 / 1402-1407: 59 / 1402 sqq.: 165 / 1415: 20 / 1416: 166 / 1418-1444: 55-6 / 1423 sqq.: 224 / 1440-1441: 166 / 1447: 21 / 1465-1468: 21.

Trachiniae: 7, 40-1, 110-1, 114-5, 118, 120, 122, 125, 142, 195, 240, 246, 254, 256.

9 sqq.: 124 / 122-131: 227 / 240: 7 / 443-444: 240 / 497 sqq.: 124 / 499 sqq.: 214 / 539-540: 240 / 555 sqq.: 124 / 582-583: 239 / 647: 22 / 663 sqq.: 122 / 706 sqq.: 122 / 719-722: 122 / 734 sqq.: 119 / 807 sqq.: 120 / 813-814: 116 / 871 sqq.: 109 / 877: 142 / 882: 142 / 888: 142 /

899-946: 110 / 903: 112, 116 / 904: 116 / 905-906: 116 / 907: 116 / 908-909: 116 / 909: 142 / 914-915: 112 / 915 sqq.: 116 / 920-922: 116 / 929 sqq.: 111 / 971-973: 42 / 971-1003: 42 / 974-982: 42 / 981: 42 / 984-992: 42 / 991: 42.

* Loci sophoclei, quos Eustathius adseverat a Homero haustos esse, in paginis 219-221 enumerantur.

Fragmenta deperditarum fabularum (*TrGF* IV ed. St. Radt)

1) *Fragmenta certis fabulis adscripta*

F 10 c: 212-3 / F 23: 209 / F 35: 213 / F 127: 213 / F 133, 6: 213 / F 144 a: 211 / F 149: 209, 215 / F 155: 200 / F 171: 203, 207 / F 172: 207 / F *178: 108 / F 201 a: 227 / F 210, 30 sqq.: 208 / F 210, 73: 214 / F 221, 22: 200 / F 272: 212 / F 288: 213 / F 314, 1 sqq.: 212 / F 314, 39 sqq.: 207 / F 314, 145 sqq.: 205 / F 314, 205 sqq.: 205 / F 314, 298-328: 211 / F 314, 451 sqq.: 212 / F 326: 193 / F 361: 207 / F 393: 214 / F 424: 193 / F 441 a: 212 / F 442: 212 / F 453-454: 200 / F 454: 222 / F 468-469: 187 / F 472: 188 / F 474: 188, 256 / F 479, 4: 213 / F 523: 208 / F 568: 214-5 / F 583: 215, 237 / F 591-593: 229 / F 592, 1-3 et 4-6: 229 / F 595: 213 / F 611: 213 / F 636: 216 / F 648: 188 / F 659: 209, 215 / F 663: 216 / F 667: 2 / F 674: 196 / F 685: 214 / F 698: 108 / F 702: 213 / F 711: 211.

Ἀθάμας α΄: 195-6, 211, 223 / Ἀθάμας β΄: 195-6, 211, 223 / Αἴας Λοκρός: 194, 212 / Αἰγεύς: 195 / Αἰθίοπες: 194 / Αἰχμαλωτίδες: 194 / Ἀκρίσιος: 195 / Ἀλεάδαι: 195 / Ἀλέξανδρος: 194 / Ἀλκμέων: 195 / Ἄμυκος σατυρικός: 190, 195, 223 / Ἀμφιάρεως σατυρικός: 190, 194-5 / Ἀμφιτρύων: 195 / Ἀνδρομάχη: 194 / Ἀνδρομέδα: 195, 223 / Ἀντηνορίδαι: 194 / Ἀτρεὺς ἢ Μυκηναῖαι: 188-9, 195 / Ἀχαιῶν σύλλογος: 190, 194 / Ἀχιλλέως ἐρασταί: 190-1, 193-4, 205, 212, 226 / Δαίδαλος: 191, 195 / Δανάη: 195 / Διονυσίσκος σατυρικός: 190, 195-6, 223 / Δόλοπες: 195 / Ἑλένης ἀπαίτησις: 190, 194, 223 / Ἑλένης ἁρπαγή: 190, 194, 223 / Ἑλένης γάμος: 190-1, 194, 223 / Ἐπίγονοι: 189, 195 / Ἐπὶ Ταινάρῳ σάτυροι: 189-91, 195 / Ἔρις: 190, 194 / Ἐριφύλη: 189, 195 / Ἑρμιόνη: 194, 223 / Εὔμηλος: 195 / Εὐρύαλος: 194, 208, 223 / Εὐρυσάκης: 194 / Ἡρακλεΐσκος σατυρικός: 190, 195 / Ἡρακλῆς σατυρικός: 188-91, 194-5 / Ἠριγόνη: 195 / Θαμύρας: 195, 202, 223 / Θησεύς: 188-9, 195 / Θυέστης α΄: 195 / Θυέστης β΄: 195 / Θυέστης γ΄: 195 / Ἴναχος: 191, 193, 195, 212, 223-4 / Ἰξίων: 188, 195 / Ἰοβάτης: 195, 202 / Ἱππόνους: 195 / Ἰφιγένεια: 188, 194 / Ἰφικλῆς: 195 / Ἰχνευταὶ σάτυροι: 190, 195, 203-4, 206, 223-4 / Ἴων: 188, 195 / Καμικοί: 194-5, 223 / Κέρβερος: 188, 194-5 / Κηδαλίων σατυρικός: 190, 195 / Κλυταιμήστρα: 188, 194 / Κολχίδες: 195, 223 / Κρέουσα: 188, 195 / Κρίσις σατυρική: 190, 194, 202, 223 / Κωφοὶ σάτυροι: 190, 195 / Λάκαιναι: 194, 223 / Λαοκόων: 194, 223 / Λαρισαῖοι: 195 / Λημνίαι α΄: 195, 223 / Λημνίαι β΄: 195, 223 / Μάντεις ἢ Πολύϊδος: 189, 195, 223 / Μελέαγρος: 195, 201, 223 / Μέμνων: 194 / Μίνως: 195 / Μοῦσαι: 188, 195 / Μυσοί: 195 / Μῶμος σατυρικός: 190, 194 / Ναύπλιος καταπλέων: 194 / Ναύπλιος πυρκαεύς: 194, 223 / Ναυσικάα ἢ Πλύντριαι: 189, 194, 197, 223, 231 / Νιόβη: 195, 212, 223 / Νίπτρα: 190, 194, 197, 231 / Ὀδυσσεὺς ἀκανθοπλήξ: 190, 194, 202, 223 / Ὀδυσσεὺς μαινόμενος: 194, 223 / Οἰκλῆς (*sive* Ἰοκλῆς): 187, 195 / Οἰνόμαος: 188, 195, 223 / Παλαμήδης: 194, 223 / Πανδώρα ἢ Σφυροκόποι: 189-91, 193, 195, 229 / Πηλεύς: 194 / Ποιμένες: 194 / Πολυξένη: 194, 223 / Πρίαμος: 188, 194 / Πρόκρις: 195 / Ῥιζοτόμοι: 195 / Σαλμωνεὺς σατυρικός: 190-1, 195 / Σίνων: 194 / Σίσυφος: 194-5 / Σκύθαι: 195 / Σκύριοι: 194 / Σύνδειπνοι: 190-1, 194, 200, 211 / Τάνταλος: 195 / Τεῦκρος: 194, 223-4 / Τήλεφος: 190-1, 194-5, 225 / Τηλέφεια: 179, 195, 208, 224-5 / Τηρεύς: 195, 223, 237 / Τριπτόλεμος: 195, 209 / Τρωΐλος: 194 / Τυμπανισταί: 195 / Τυνδάρεως: 188, 195 / Τυρὼ α΄: 188, 195, 211-2, 223 / Τυρὼ β΄: 188, 195, 211-2, 223 / Ὕβρις σατυρική: 190, 195 / Ὑδροφόροι: 194-5 / Φαίακες: 194, 197 / Φαίδρα: 189, 195, 223 / Φθιώτιδες: 195 / Φιλοκτήτης ὁ ἐν Τροίᾳ: 194, 223-4 / Φινεύς α΄: 194-5 / Φινεύς β΄: 194-5 / Φοῖνιξ: 195 / Φρίξος: 195 / Φρύγες: 188, 194 / Χρύσης: 194.

Fr. 474 Pearson = F 474 Radt: 256 / Fr. 575, 9 sq. Pearson = *Adespota fragmenta* F 700, 28 sq., *TrGF* II: 228 / Fr. 583 Pearson = F 583 Radt: 237.

2) *Incertarum fabularum fragmenta*

F 730 a-g: 191 / F 761: 210 / F 774: 214 / F 799: 214 /

F 800: 214 / F 826: 210 / F 843: 217 / F 871: 209, 227 / F 877: 213 / F 879 a: 229 / F 884: 213 / F 887: 210, 227 / F 897: 187 / F 910: 216 / F 941: 215, 229-30 / F 941, 3-7: 216 / F 941, 4: 216 / F 941, 6: 214 / F 941, 12: 214 / F 947: 214-5 / F 949, 2: 214 / F 952: 108, 142 / F 953: 108 / F 965: 199, 200 / F 1010: 210 / F 1024: 210 / F 1051: 211 / F 1053: 200.

3) Tituli fabularum e coniectura Sophocli adscripti paginae 187 laudantur; tituli fabularum Sophocli dubie adscribendi paginis 187 et 188 laudantur.

B. Auctores Vetustiores

Accius, L., *Antigona*: 81 / *Epigoni*: 189 / *Eriphyla*: 189.

Achaeus, poeta tragicus: 225.

Aeschylus: 5-7, 40-1, 67, 70, 104, 163, 179, 191-3, 196-8, 202, 207-8, 225, 228, 230-1, 234-6, 240, 243, 246, 250-1, 255.

Ag.: 40, 70, 196 / 153: 210 / 443: 210 / 617 sqq.: 223 / 874-876: 108 / 1188 sqq.: 177 / 1410: 22.

Ch.: 9, 37, 40, 196, 224 / 302 sqq.: 9 / 585 sqq.: 250 / 824: 9 / 916: 108 / 1046: 9.

Eum.: 9, 40, 151, 157, 196-7, 212, 224, 226 / 517 sqq.: 12 / 698-699: 12 / 746: 108, 113.

Pers.: 40, 196.

Prom.: 40, 197, 235 / 582: 113 / 582 sqq.: 108 / 705 sqq.: 209 / 747 sqq.: 108 / 748 sqq.: 113.

Supp.: 6, 40, 158 / 455 sqq.: 108 / 788 sqq.: 108.

Th.: 40, 78, 98, 198, 253 / 10-19: 6 / 16: 6 / 18: 6 / 19: 6 / 609: 187.

Oresteia: 6, 87, 223-4, 235-6.

Fragmenta, Nauck²: 13-15 ('Αμυμώνη): 193 / 187 (Πηνελόπη): 197 / 195-199 (Προμηθεὺς λυόμενος): 209 / 207 (Προμ. λ.): 207 / 406: 210.

Mette: 289: 108 / 296 (?): 108 / 399: 108 464, 18 sqq. (Δικτυουλκοί): 207 / 474 (Δικτ.), 778-81: 108 / 474, 786 sqq.: 207 / 679: 108.

'Αθάμας: 196 / Αἴας: 110 / Αἰτναῖαι: 212, 226 / 'Αμυμώνη: 192-3, 205 / Fr. 13-15 N²: 193 / 'Αργεῖοι: 198 / Βάκχαι: 196 / Βασσάραι: 196 / Δικτυουλκοί: 192-3, 204-5 / Fr. 464, 18 sqq. Mette: 207 / Fr. 474, 778-81 Mette: 108 / Fr. 474, 786 sqq. Mette: 207 / 'Ελευσίνιοι: 196 / 'Επίγονοι: 198 / 'Ηδωνοί: 196 /

Θεωροί: cf. Ἰσθμιασταί / Θρῆσσαι: 196 / Ἰσθμιασταί: 192-3, 204-6 / Ἰφιγένεια: 196 / Κᾶρες: 196-7 / Κερκύων: 192, 197 / Κήρυκες: 192 / Κίρκη σατυρική: 192-3, 196-7 / Λαῖος: 198 / Λέων: 192 / Λυκοῦργος: 192, 194, 196 / Μέμνων: 196 / Μυρμιδόνες: 196-7, 202 / Νεανίσκοι: 196 / Νηρεΐδες: 196-7 / Ξάντριαι: 196 / Οἰδίπους: 198, 245 / Ὅπλων κρίσις: 196 / Ὀστολόγοι: 196-7 / Παλαμήδης: 196 / Πενθεύς: 196 / Πηνελόπη: 196-7 / Fr. 187 N²: 197 / Προμηθεύς λυόμενος: 207, 209 / Fr. 195-199 N²: 209 / Fr. 207 N²: 207 / Πρωτεύς: 192, 196-7, 223 / Σαλαμίνιαι: 196 / Σεμέλη ἢ Ὑδροφόροι: 196 / Σίσυφος πετροκυλιστής: 197 / Σφίγξ: 192, 198, 228-9 / Τήλεφος: 195-6 / Τροφοί: 196 / Ὑδροφόροι: cf. Σεμέλη / Φιλοκτήτης: 196 / Φρύγες: 196-7, 202, 231 / Ψυχαγωγοί: 196-7, 200 / Ψυχοστασία: 196 / Ὠρείθυια: 196.

Antipho, *Or.* I (Κατὰ τῆς μητρυιᾶς): 254.

Apollodorus, mythographus, *Bibl.* I 9, 7: 213.

Aristophanes: 224, 240 / *Eq.* 80 sqq.: 145, 147 / 570: 210 / 731 sqq.: 4 / 737: 4 / 1341: 4 / *Nu.* 775 sqq.: 147 / 868 sqq.: 147 / 1162: 210 / 1448 sqq.: 147 / *Ra.*: 224 / 117 sqq.: 147 / *Thesm.*: 256 / *Vesp.* 303 sqq.: 147 / 522-523: 147.

Aristophanes Byzantinus: 186.

Aristoteles: 187, 212 / *EN* V 15, 1138 a 4-28: 147 / VII 10, 1151 b 13: 2 / *Po.* 12, 1452 b 20-21: 47 / *Rh.*: 101 / III 18, 1419 a 26: 5.

Astydamas, poeta tragicus, *Antigone*: 80.

Athenaeus, VII 277 e (*TrGF* IV T 136): 198, 202.

Bacchylides, 13, 58: 210.

Boethius, Anicius Manlius Severinus: 227.

Callimachus: 192.

Cicero, M. Tullius, *De opt. gen. or.* 18: 189.

Cratinus, poeta comicus: 225.

Demosthenes: 28 / *Or.* XIX (*Amb.*) 247: 13.

Ecphantides, poeta comicus: 225.

Erotianus, grammaticus, *Vocorum Hippocraticarum collectio* π 32 Nachmanson (= Soph. F 648 Radt): 188.

Euphorio Chalcidensis: 210 / Fr. 125/126 Powell (= 127 van Groningen = 161/161 B De Cuenca): 210 / Fr. 177 Powell (= 195 v. Gron.), *ap. Etym. Gen. s.v.* ἀνὰ δρύμα:

210 / Fr. 24 c 48 van Groningen (= 38 C 46 De Cuenca), *ap. PSI* 1390 C II 4: 210 / Fr. 193 e van Groningen, *ap. POxy.* 2526 B fr. 2, 8: 210.

Eupolis, poeta comicus, Fr. 137 Kock: 21.

Euripides: 10, 34-5, 48, 67, 70, 79, 81, 88, 97-9, 104, 143, 145-7, 157, 192, 196-8, 204-5, 208, 212, 225-6, 228, 234, 236-7, 240, 246-7, 251.
Andr.: 196.
Ba.: 30, 196 / 513: 213.
Cyc.: 196, 198, 203-6 / 169 sqq.: 205 / 179 sqq.: 205 / 186 sqq.: 206 / 220-221: 206 / 226 sqq.: 205 / 266-267: 206 / 268 sqq.: 206 / 313 sqq.: 206 / 316 sqq.: 204 / 354-355: 204 / 469 sqq.: 206 / 483 sqq.: 206 / 542 sqq.: 206 / 582 sqq.: 205-6 / 596: 206 / 606-607: 204 / 635 sqq.: 206 / 680 sqq.: 206 / 707: 206.
El.: 9, 43, 54, 163-4, 196, 257 / 33: 9 / 96: 164 / 96-97: 9 / 101: 9 / 601: 9.
Hec.: 43, 196.
HF: 107, 143-6 / 1212-1213: 142, 147 / 1248: 143 / 1348: 143, 145.
Hel.: 66, 196.
Heracl.: 197.
Hippol.: 108, 197 / 47: 146 / 329: 146 / 716-718: 146 / 772-773: 146 / 814: 142, 147.
Hyps.: 198.
IA: 101, 196.
IT: 196 / 973 sqq.: 113.
Ion: 60, 197.
Med.: 43, 191, 255 / 230 sqq.: 215, 235 / 292 sqq.: 235 / 299: 2.
Or.: 60, 97, 146, 196.
Phoen.: 77-8, 80-1, 94, 97-8, 198, 239 / 777: 79 / 967: 79 / 1592-1593: 80 / 1680: 80 / 1744: 80.
Stheneboea: 113.
Supp.: 145, 197 / 925: 187 / 980 sqq.: 113 / 1015: 146 / 1059 sqq.: 146 / 1063: 146 / 1104 sqq.: 113.
Troad.: 196.
Αἰγεύς: 197 / Ἀλέξανδρος: 196 / Ἀλκμέων: 198 / Ἀλόπη: 197 / Ἀνδρόμεδα: 256 / Ἀντιγόνη: 78, 97-8, 198 / Ἔπειος: 196 / Ἐρεχθεύς: 197 / Θερισταί: 191 / Θησεύς: 197 / Ἰνώ: 113, 196 / Κάδμος: 198 / Οἰδίπους: 198 / Παλαμήδης: 196 / Πειρίθους: 197 / Πρωτεσίλαος: 113, 196 / Σκίρων: 197 / Σκύριοι: 196 / Τήλεφος: 195-6 / Φιλοκτήτης: 196 / Φοῖνιξ: 196, 198 / Χρύσιππος: 198.

Eustathius, episcopus Thessalonicensis *: 200, 218-22 / *Commentarii ad* Homeri *Od.* XI 202: 106.

* Loci eustathiani, in quibus Sophocles Homerum imitari dicitur, in paginis 218-222 enumerantur.

Herodotus: 15, 209, 227 / I 207, 2: 228 / III 81: 2 / VI 21: 36 / VIII 93: 236.
Hesiodus, *Op.* 287-292: 161 / 297: 2.
Hipponax, iambographus: 180.
Homerus *: 106, 131, 197-202, 218-222, 230-1, 241, 247.
Il.: 13, 106, 201-2 / I 249: 200 / II 594 sqq.: 202 / III 173: 106 / VI 155 sqq.: 202 / IX 543 sqq.: 202 / XII 277-286: 181 / XVI-XVIII: 197 / XVIII 33-34: 106 / XXII 351-352: 231 / XXIV: 202 / XXIV 28-30: 202 / XXIV 531-533: 173.
Od.: 106, 143, 177, 199, 201-2 / I 29 sqq.: 202 / I 59: 106 / IV 351 sqq.: 197 / V 467: 200 / VI: 197 / VIII 75 sqq.: 200 / IX 100 sqq.: 202 / X: 197 / X 49 sqq.: 106 / X 497-498: 106 / XI: 197 / XI 119 sqq.: 200 / XI 134-136: 202 / XI 197 sqq.: 106 / XI 277 sqq.: 106 / XIV 199: 197 / XV 353-354: 106 / XV 356 sqq.: 106 / XIX: 197 / XIX 172 sqq.: 197 / XIX 406 sqq.: 199, 200 / XX 61 sqq.: 106.
* Loci homerici, quos Eustathius adseverat a Sophocle imitatos esse, in paginis 218-222 enumerantur.
Hyginus: 80-1 / *Fab.* 243, 1: 106.

Isocrates, *Or.* XVI (*De bigis*) 14, 349 b-d: 22.

Lycophron, *Alex.* 6: 187.
Lysias, *Or.* XXXI 20-23: 123.

Marcus Aurelius Antoninus, imperator, IV 3, 7: 214.
Menander, *Epitr.* 325 sqq. Sandbach: 212.

Neophron, poeta tragicus, F 3, *TrGF* I pp. 93-94: 113.

Oenomaus, philosophus Cynicus: 211.

Photius, *Lex.*, Cod. Berolinensis 89, 20: 188 / 151, 7: 188 / Cod. Zavordensis, *s.v.* ἀφήλικες: 188 / *s.v.* Τυνδάρεως: 188.
Phrynichus, poeta comicus: 2.
Phrynichus, poeta tragicus: 36.
Pindarus: 228 / *Ol.* II 35-37: 228.
Plato: 235 / *Crito*: 14, 28 / 50 d: 6 / 51 b-c: 3 / 51 c: 6 / 51 e: 6 / *Leg.*: 80, 147 / IX 873 c-d: 147 / X: 84 / *Phd.* 61 c sqq.: 147 / *Smp.* 183 a: 4.
Plutarchus: 226 / *Nic.* 6, 1: 145.
Polemo, philosophus Academicus (*TrGF* IV T 115): 200.
Proclus, *In Plat. Remp.* I p. 171, 18 sqq. Kroll: 201.

Prodicus Ceus: 181 / Fr. 2 Diels-Kranz (*Vorsokr.* II 84 B 2), *ap.* Xen. *Mem.* II 1, 21 sqq.: 161.

Seneca, L. Annaeus: 81, 171 / *Oed.*: 171, 181 / 1052-1061: 171 / 1058: 171.
Simonides, Fr. 614 Page: 210.
Sophocles Aristonis, Sophoclis nepos: 208, 224-5.
Statius, P. Papinius, *Theb.*: 78, 81, 94.
Stobaeus, Ioannes: 215, 226 / III 27, 6 (= Soph. F 472 Radt): 188.

Theognis: 181 / 911 sqq.: 161.
Theophrastus: 213.
Thucydides: 15, 34-5, 84 / I 70: 4 / I 138: 3 / II 13: 27 / II 35-46: 27-8 / II 37, 3: 12 / II 40, 2: 5 / II 43: 3, 28 / II 60, 3: 29 / II 67, 4: 15 / III 82: 9 / VI 92, 4: 22.
Timotheus: 225.
Tzetzes, Ioannes: 180.

Vergilius Maro, P.: 81.

Xenophon: 84 / *Hell.* I 7, 25 sqq.: 15 / *Mem.* II 1, 21 sqq. (= Prodicus Ceus, Fr. 2 D.-K.): 161.

C. Anonyma

Adespota fragmenta, F 97 (*TrGF* II p. 44): 210 / F 700, 28-29 (= Soph. Fr. 575, 9-10 Pearson): 228.
Catalogus Aeschyli fabularum: 193 / p. 7 Wilamowitz = 335 Page: 192.
Cypria: 200.
Etymologia: 226.
Etym. Gen. s.v. ἀνὰ δρύμα (= Euphorio, Fr. 177 Powell): 210.
Florilegia: 215, 226-7.
Lexicon Messanense: 203.
Melanippes oratio, in *Select Papyri* III: *Literary Papyri, Poetry* p. 112 Page: 235.
POxy. 1175 + 2081 b: 187 / 2256 fr. 3, 3: 193 / 2526 B fr. 2, 8 (= Euphorio, Fr. 193 e van Groningen): 210 / 3317: 97.
PSI 1390 C II 4 (= Euphorio, Fr. 24 c 48 van Groningen): 210.
Roman de Thèbes: 81, 98.
Schol. ad Soph. *Aj.* 110: 222 / *ad* Soph. *Ant.* 1301: 113.
Suda, s.v. Σοφοκλῆς (T 2, *TrGF* IV pp. 40-41): 190 / T 2, 5: 200 / T 2, 5-6: 179 / T 2, 9: 186.
Vita Aeschyli 13: 191.
Vita Euripidis 4 (p. 4, 8 sqq. Schwartz): 191.
Vita Sophoclis (T 1, *TrGF* IV): 186-7 / 3 (15 sqq.): 4 / 18 (76-77): 186 / 20 (80 sqq.): 199-202.

D. Auctores Recentiores

Adler, A.: 137.
Aichele, Kl.: 72-3.
Aigner, H.: 105-8, 110, 125, 128.
Alfieri, Vittorio, Conte: 81-2.
Alvarez, A.: 107.
Anouilh, Jean: 90, 95-6, 99, 100, 102.

Baechler, J.: 107, 117, 120-2, 124, 143.
Barrett, W. S.: 108, 212.
Bartels, Kl.: 213.
Barth, K.: 92.
Barthes, R.: 157.
Bayet, A.: 107.
Bechtel, Fr.: 210.
Beck, A. T.: 127.
Becker, O.: 161.
Bergk, Th.: 186, 188, 199, 204.
Biehl, W.: 60.
Blumenthal, A. von: 187, 190.
Boccaccio, Giovanni: 81, 98.
Böckh, A.: 186.
Bonald, Louis, Vicomte de: 91.
Bonnard, A.: 86.
Boor, W. de: 123, 138.
Bossuet, Jacques Bénigne: 91.
Bothe, Fr. H.: 121.
Bowra, C. M.: 121, 136, 162.
Brecht, Bertolt: 89, 100, 103.
Brunck, R. F. Ph.: 55, 57, 188, 190.
Büchner, Georg: 103.
Bultmann, R.: 92.
Burian, P.: 159, 162.
Burkert, W.: 170.

Calder III, W. M.: 171.
Cameron, A.: 120.
Campbell, L.: 21.
Carden, R.: 212.
Casaubon, Isaac: 188, 198.
Cerri, G.: 15.
Chaucer, Geoffrey: 81, 98-9.
Chourmouziades, N. C.: cf. Hourmouziades, N. C.
Cohen, D.: 115.
Cohen, G.: 63.

Dain, A.: 42, 251.
Dale, A. M.: 165.
Davie, Donald: 93.
Davies, M.: 169, 174.
Dawe, R. D.: 42, 44, 121, 161, 167, 173, 250-1, 253.
Delcourt, M.: 140, 150.
Devereux, G.: 114, 239.
Di Gregorio, L.: 187.
Diller, H.: 136.
Dindorf, W.: 44, 161.
Dodds, E. R.: 173.
Döblin, A.: 91-2.
Dover, K. J.: 5, 123.
Dürrenmatt, Friedrich: 96.
Durkheim, E.: 106.

Easterling, P. E.: 161-2, 166, 240.
Eberlein, E.: 86.
Eckermann, J. P.: 34.
Elmsley, P.: 191-3, 226.
Else, G. F.: 85, 124.
Engelmann, R.: 251.

Erasmus Roterodamus: 35.
Errandonea, I.: 136.
Estienne, H.: 200, 219, 222.

Fagles, R.: 155, 159.
Fedden, G. R.: 107.
Fergusson, F.: 155, 171, 175, 179.
Fitton-Brown, A. D.: 159.
Flügge, M.: 100.
Fraenkel, Ed.: 201.
Freud, E. L.: 141.
Freud, Sigmund: 94, 115, 123, 137, 141.
Friis Johansen, H.: 136.
Fritz, K. von: 100, 122, 129, 134, 139.
Fustel de Coulanges, N. D.: 1.

Geiger, K. A.: 107.
Gellie, G. H.: 122.
Ghéon, Henri: 93-5.
Gide, André: 148.
Girard, R.: 171, 179.
Gnoli, G.: 15.
Goethe, Johann Wolfgang von: 1, 34-5, 101, 114, 135, 217.
Goheen, R. F.: 83-4.
Gould, J. P.: 234, 250.
Griffin, J.: 149.
Grossmann, G.: 128, 139.
Grumach, E.: 135.
Guggisberg, P.: 191.

Hähnle, A.: 212.
Hamburger, Käte: 102.
Haslam, M. W.: 213.
Hay, J.: 169.
Hedberg, T.: 219.
Hegel, Friedrich: 82, 87-8, 102-3.
Heidegger, Martin: 88, 103.
Held, G.: 252.
Hermann, G.: 55, 219, 229.
Hester, D. A.: 136, 171.
Hirt, A.: 193.
Hirzel, R.: 107, 114, 123, 142.
Hölderlin, Friedrich: 63, 84.
Höppener, H.: 84.
Hofmannstahl, Hugo von: 94.
Hourmouziades, N. C.: 157-8, 206.
Housman, A. E.: 103, 213.
Hunt, A. S.: 203.

James, C.: 107, 142-3.
Jameson, M. H.: 5.
Jebb, R. C.: 12, 21, 101, 122, 136, 139, 159, 165.
Jens, W.: 72, 158.
Joerden, K.: 158-9, 167.
Jordan, B.: 15.

Kafka, Franz: 96.
Kamerbeek, J. C.: 12, 110, 112-3, 121, 123, 128-9, 139-40, 150.
Kant, Immanuel: 84.
Kassel, R.: 204, 214.
Katsouris, A. G.: 107.
Kierkegaard, Sören: 100-2.
King, J.: 173.
Kirkwood, G. M.: 109, 115, 117, 129, 133-5, 137.
Kitto, H. D. F.: 109, 113, 115, 117, 169.
Knox, B. M. W.: 109, 111-3, 116, 131, 136-7, 139-40, 155, 159,

162, 173, 177, 215, 234-5, 243.
Kojève, A.: 103.
Kurtz, D.: 228.

Lattimore, R.: 169, 180-1.
Lechner, G. Max.: 199.
Lefkowitz, M. R.: 4, 247.
Leonhard, K.: 124.
Lesky, A.: 5, 204, 206.
Lévy, Bernard-Henry: 90.
Linforth, I. M.: 87, 123.
Lloyd-Jones, H.: 1, 123, 210, 216.
Luppe, W.: 225.
Lydgate, John: 81.

McCall, M.: 115.
Machin, A.: 40.
Macleod, C. W.: 169, 172.
Matthiessen, K.: 19, 25-6, 28-9, 36.
Maurras, Charles: 89-92.
Mazon, P.: 42, 251.
Méautis, G.: 84.
Mette, H. J.: 15, 84.
Michaelis, A.: 199.
Miller, H. W.: 218-9.
Minotis, Alexis: 166.
Montherlant, Henry de: 96.
Moore, J.: 140.
Müller, D.: 214.
Müller, G.: 16, 121.
Musgrave, W.: 21.

Nauck, A.: 189-90, 210.
Nebel, G.: 85.
Nilsson, M. P.: 229.
Norwood, G.: 228.

O'Brien, C. C.: 92-3.
Oeri, J. J.: 61-2.
Opstelten, J. C.: 128.

Pack, R.: 226.
Page, D. L.: 191-2, 234.
Parsons, P. J.: 97.
Patzer, H.: 86.
Pearson, A. C.: 187-93, 198-9, 201-3, 214.
Perlin, S.: 107.
Perrotta, G.: 131.
Pertusi, A.: 98.
Pickard-Cambridge, A.: 225.
Poe, Edgar: 74.
Pohlenz, M.: 205.
Prien, K. Fr. U.: 61.

Rabe, H.: 203.
Racine, Jean: 81, 157, 252.
Radermacher, L.: 12.
Radt, St.: 108.
Reeve, M. D.: 160.
Reinhardt, K.: 84, 109, 112, 131-2, 134, 137, 149-50.
Ribbeck, O.: 189.
Rilke, Rainer Maria: 63-5.
Ringel, E.: 107, 128-32, 135-6.
Ritschl, Fr.: 61.
Robinson, D. B.: 165.
Robinson, M. D.: 228.
Romilly, J. de: 107, 143, 157, 160.
Ronnet, G.: 86, 122.
Rotrou, Jean de: 252.

Santirocco, M. S.: 86.
Schadewaldt, W.: 131.

Schefold, K.: 151.
Schleiermacher, Friedrich: 102.
Schlesinger, E.: 130-1, 136.
Schmid, W.: 187-90, 204, 212.
Schmidt, W.: 83.
Schnitzler, Arthur: 141.
Schoell, R.: 186.
Schütz, A.: 121.
Schwartz, Ed.: 191.
Schwinge, E. R.: 115, 122, 125.
Seeck, G. A.: 193, 204.
Segal, Ch.: 7, 87-8, 115, 156-7, 161, 163-4, 166, 172-3.
Seidensticker, B.: 131, 169, 172, 193, 205.
Seyffert, M. L.: 121.
Shakespeare, William: 105, 118.
Sicherl, M.: 135-6, 139.
Siegmund, G.: 107.
Simon, E.: 228-9.
Snell, B.: 208, 225.
Sparkes, B.: 228.
Stanford, W. B.: 12, 107-8, 127, 136-9.
Starobinski, J.: 107.
Steffen, V.: 191.
Steiner, G.: 173.
Stekel, W.: 137-8.
Stengel, E.: 105, 107, 130.
Sutton, D. F.: 191.
Szlezák, T. A.: 163.

Taplin, O.: 20, 110, 136, 157-8, 164, 169, 193, 208.
Tieck, Ludwig: 82.
Torrance, R. M.: 125.
Toup, J.: 189-90.

Untersteiner, M.: 85.

Valckenaer, L. C.: 218.
Valéry, Paul: 63-5, 74-5, 131.
Valk, M. van der: 219, 222.
Vernant, J.-P.: 15, 27, 155-6, 169-71, 179, 181.
Vickers, B.: 103.
Vogt, E.: 204.
Von der Mühll, P.: 200.

Webster, T. B. L.: 78.
Wecklein, N.: 188.
Weil, H.: 61, 209.
Welcker, Fr. G.: 136, 188-9, 196, 199, 201, 229.
Wender, D.: 114.
West, M. L.: 160-1.
Wilamowitz-Moellendorff, U. v.: 191-2, 203, 208.
Winnington-Ingram, R. P.: 29, 48, 58, 85, 109, 114-6, 122-5, 128-34, 136, 142, 162, 164, 166, 245.

Xanthakis-Karamanos, G.: 80.

Zielinski, Th.: 39.
Zwierlein, C.: 206.
Zwingmann, Ch.: 107, 117, 123-4, 130, 141.

ACHEVÉ D'IMPRIMER EN OCTOBRE 1983
SUR LES PRESSES DE L'IMPRIMERIE DU
« JOURNAL DE GENÈVE », À GENÈVE, SUISSE